THE
ILLUSTRATED
DOOM
SURVIVAL
GUIDE

DON'T PANIC!

Adventures Unlimited Press

Other books of interest:

The Mystery of the Olmecs
Technology of the Gods
Pirates & the Lost Templar Fleet
Lost Continents & the Hollow Earth
Lost Cities & Ancient Mysteries of the Southwest
Lost Cities of China, Central Asia & India
Lost Ciies & Ancient Mysteries of Africa & Arablia
Lost Ciies & Ancient Mysteries of South America
Lost Ciies of Ancient Lemuria & the Pacific
Lost Ciies of North and Central America
Lost Cities of Atlantis, Ancient Europe & the Mediterranean
Atlantis & the Power System of the Gods
Vimana Aircraft of Ancient India & Atlantis
The Crystal Skulls

THE *ILLUSTRATED* DOOM SURVIVAL GUIDE

by
Matt "Doomguy"
Victor

The Illustrated Doom Survival Guide

ISBN 978-1-935487-77-7

Published by Adventures Unlimited Press
One Adventure Place
Kempton, Illinois 60946 USA

www.adventuresunlimitedpress.com
www.doomguide.com

THE
ILLUSTRATED
DOOM
SURVIVAL
GUIDE

To order more copies of this book,
or to check out our other titles go to:
www.AdventuresUnlimitedPress.com

For updates from Matt "Doomguy" Victor go to:
wwwdoomguide.com

General Survival Guidelines 1

Basic Survival Medicine... 2
Water Procurement.. 3
Food Procurement 4
Survival Use of Plants.. 5

Firecraft.. 6
Ropes and Knots 7
Shelters 8
Weapons, Tools & Equipment 9

Sustainable Gardening 10
Raising Animals 11

Desert Survival 12
Tropical Survival 13
Cold Weather Survival 14
Sea Survival... 15
Disaster Survival... 16

Projects & References 17

Weather Prediction 18
Water Crossings 19
Direction Finding 20
Stealth 21

Sources 22

CONTENTS

1 GENERAL SURVIVAL GUIDELINES

PLANNING YOUR SURVIVAL................. 1-1
THE MAN... 1-1
FOOD 1-2
WATER 1-2
SHELTER... 1-3
SURVIVAL KITS.................................... 1-3
FOOD STORAGE GUIDELINES 1-5

2 BASIC SURVIVAL MEDICINE

BASIC MAINTENANCE OF HEALTH 2-1
MEDICAL EMERGENCIES 2-3
LIFESAVING STEPS 2-4
BONE AND JOINT INJURY 2-9
BITES AND STINGS 2-10
WOUNDS 2-12
ENVIRONMENTAL INJURIES 2-15
FIELD SURGERY 2-17
FIELD DENTISTRY 2-19
PREGNANCY AND CHILDBIRTH........... 2-23

3 WATER PROCUREMENT

WATER SOURCES................................ 3-1
STILL CONSTRUCTION 3-4
WATER PURIFICATION 3-6
WATER FILTRATION DEVICES 3-6

4 FOOD PROCUREMENT

ANIMALS FOR FOOD 4-1
CRITTERS FOR FOOD........................... 4-4
TRAPS AND SNARES 4-7
KILLING DEVICES 4-15
FISHING DEVICES............................. 4-15
PREPARATION OF FISH AND GAME 4-20
FOOD DRYING 4-23

5 SURVIVAL USE OF PLANTS

EDIBILITY OF PLANTS......................... 5-1
PLANTS FOR MEDICINE....................... 5-5
MEDICINAL PLANT GUIDE 5-6
MISCELLANEOUS USES OF PLANTS 5-26

6 FIRECRAFT

SITE SELECTION AND PREPARATION 6-1
FIRE MATERIAL SELECTION 6-2
HOW TO BUILD A FIRE........................ 6-3
COOKING 6-5
HOW TO LIGHT A FIRE........................ 6-8
HELPFUL HINTS 6-12

7 ROPES AND KNOTS

SUITABLE MATERIALS 7-1
MAKING ROPE 7-2
KNOTS 7-4
LASHINGS.. 7-11
ROPE SPLICES 7-13

8 SHELTERS

SHELTER SITE SELECTION 8-1
BASIC SHELTERS................................ 8-1
THATCHING 8-8
SEMI PERMANENT SHELTERS 8-13
CAMPCRAFT 8-17
LONG TERM SHELTERS 8-21

9 WEAPONS, TOOLS & EQUIPMENT

CLUBS 9-1
EDGED WEAPONS 9-2
OTHER EXPEDIENT WEAPONS 9-4
ARCHERY EQUIPMENT 9-4
LASHING AND CORDAGE 9-6
CLOTHING AND INSULATION............... 9-6
COOKING AND EATING UTENSILS........ 9-7
TANNING ANIMAL HIDES 9-8
NATURAL GLUES............................... 9-10
BASKET WEAVING 9-11
NETTING.. 9-15
BLACK POWDER............................... 9-18
CLEANING PRODUCTS 9-22

10 SUSTAINABLE GARDENING

PLANNING A GARDEN...................... 10-1
VEGETABLE GROWING GUIDE 10-2
MEDICINE GROWING GUIDE 10-4
PROPAGATION FROM CUTTINGS 10-6
CROP ROTATION............................. 10-7
COMPANION PLANTING 10-8
COMPOSTING 10-11
SAVING SEEDS..............................10-13

11 RAISING ANIMALS

CHICKENS 11-1
TURKEYS 11-6
DUCKS AND GEESE.......................... 11-8
COMMON POULTRY ISSUES..............11-10
RABBITS..11-12

CONTENTS

12 DESERT SURVIVAL

TERRAIN 12-1
ENVIRONMENTAL FACTORS 12-2
NEED FOR WATER 12-3
HEAT CASUALTIES 12-4
PRECAUTIONS 12-4
DESERT HAZARDS 12-4

13 TROPICAL SURVIVAL

TROPICAL WEATHER 13-1
JUNGLE TYPES 13-1
TRAVEL THROUGH JUNGLE AREAS 13-3
WATER PROCUREMENT 13-3
FOOD 13-4

14 COLD WEATHER SURVIVAL

COLD REGIONS AND LOCATIONS 14-1
BASIC PRINCIPLES 14-1
MEDICAL ASPECTS 14-3
SHELTERS 14-5
FIRE 14-7
WATER 14-8
FOOD 14-9
TRAVEL... 14-9

15 SEA SURVIVAL

THE OPEN SEA 15-1
WATER PROCUREMENT 15-3
FOOD PROCUREMENT 15-4
MEDICAL PROBLEMS FACED AT SEA ... 15-5
SHARKS 15-6
DETECTING LAND 15-7

16 DISASTER SURVIVAL

THE NUCLEAR ENVIRONMENT 16-1
BIOLOGICAL ENVIRONMENTS 16-7
CHEMICAL ENVIRONMENTS 16-9
DROUGHT 16-10
FIRE 16-11
FLOOD 16-14
TSUNAMI 16-16
HURRICANE..................................... 16-16
TORNADO 16-17
LIGHTNING 16-18
EARTHQUAKE 16-19
VOLCANO.. 16-20
AVALANCHE..................................... 16-21
PLANET X 16-21

17 PROJECTS & REFERENCES

SOLAR DEHYDRATOR 17-1
ABS WATER FILTER.......................... 17-2
SOLAR STILL................................... 17-4
EVAPORATIVE COOLING 17-6
RED CABBAGE pH INDICATOR 17-8
MATHS 17-9
CONVERSION TABLES 17-14
RUNES.. 17-16

18 WEATHER PREDICTION

CLOUD FORMATIONS 18-1
BAROMETERS 18-4
GENERAL PREDICTION TIPS 18-5

19 WATER CROSSINGS

RIVERS AND STREAMS 19-1
RAPIDS... 19-1
RAFTS 19-3
OTHER WATER OBSTACLES 19-5
ROPE BRIDGES 19-6
MEASURING CROSSING DISTANCE 19-7
CALCULATING CONTAINER BUOYANCY 19-7

20 DIRECTION FINDING

USING THE SUN 20-1
USING THE MOON............................ 20-2
USING THE STARS 20-3
MAKING AN IMPROVISED COMPASS... 20-4
OTHER MEANS................................. 20-4

21 STEALTH

PERSONAL CAMOUFLAGE 21-1
METHODS OF STALKING 21-2
TRAVELLING UNDETECTED............... 21-3
TRACKING 21-5
COUNTER-TRACKING....................... 21-6

22 SOURCES

1 GENERAL SURVIVAL GUIDELINES

In the event of a worldwide catastrophe, emergency services will be stretched beyond their limit. There are simply not enough resources to look after everyone.

Do not expect rescue.

Any stockpiles the authorities may have will be depleted quickly, and more than likely will be distributed between greedy powers before you get a look in.

It is up to YOU to ensure the survival of you and your loved ones.

1.1 PLANNING YOUR SURVIVAL

In your survival strategy, do not make huge plans. Large operations are likely to be noticeable to others and there will be many who will not take steps for their own survival. Do not advertise your plans and limit your group to people you know – family and friends. Even if you don't get along with certain family members, at least you will be with people you know.

1.1.1 CHOICE OF LOCATION

Whether you have a remote property, plan to purchase one or to simply bug out at the last minute, research your location well. First choose a location that is far away from large city centres. When broad disaster strikes, people wander - even when they don't know where they are wandering to. City centres will be death traps and citizens will pour from them in large numbers. There will be a lot of starvation, desperation, confusion and fear. A stampede of scared, hungry people through your community will not do anyone any good.

A rule of thumb is to be 150 km (100 mi) from coastlines or more. Tsunamis can wash water over huge areas of land in a very short time. The power of moving water is immense and easy to underestimate, even when it is not very deep. Choose high ground, at least 20 m (60 ft) higher than the average surrounding level. Rivers can swell and floodplains will flood.

As well as being higher than the surrounding area, you should be about 200 m (600 ft) above sea level. This is the estimated rise in sea levels if the polar caps should melt.

Weather patterns as they stand today cannot be relied upon – even now the weather is changing quicker than experts can predict. Therefore you should consider the possibility of near constant downpour or drizzle in your area. Constant rainfall can liquefy soil, filling the air pockets with water and turning it into a type of quicksand. Coupled with jiggling, rumbling earthquakes, a solid bunker can sink completely into saturated soil, with you in it. The underlying ground should therefore be solid bedrock, and of course, not near a fault line.

1.1.2 TRAVELLING

When you need to travel it is best to keep a low profile. If you have a working vehicle and road travel is still possible, take the back roads. If asked, do not announce your plans or destination – say you are on a 'camping trip' or 'visiting relatives'. If you are on foot, you can follow a main road without travelling on the road itself. Keep yourself well hidden at a distance of 20-100 metres or so, depending on the cover available.

Avoid large gatherings of people. If you are well stocked with equipment and food, there will be people who feel they deserve your gear more than you do, and will not be kind about it.

1.2 THE MAN

Authorities should generally be avoided. This includes government, military and law enforcement. When panic hits, the structure and rules of society will no longer apply and you cannot assume the protectors will protect you. Members of the establishment are people too and will be just as scared and confused as everyone else, except they will probably be better armed and more trained than you. Even if you are well armed and proficient with firearms, the last thing you and your family need is a gunfight.

In the confusion and panic, military units may turn rogue, with no fear of the consequences. Remember, those in authority with a heart will most likely be AWOL looking after their families, not roaming in armed gangs. Do not approach these groups. Signalling techniques will NOT be discussed in this guide. Keep your head down.

1.2.1 SURVIVOR CAMPS

You may come across survivor camps set up by the government or military. These camps will operate under the pretence that you will work in exchange for food, shelter and medical care. Depending on your country, government and the individuals running the camp, they will range from genuine humanitarian operations to full blown slave camps.

Your possessions will be confiscated and distributed. You may not be allowed to leave and if you do manage to escape it will be by the skin of your teeth with little to no equipment. Conditions will degrade quickly as stores are depleted without incoming replacements. You cannot assume those running the camp will be fair. Such a situation can easily lead to cannibalism. Do NOT approach any official-looking camp setups. Approach ANY camp carefully.

1.3 FOOD

Do not rely on a **large** hoard of goods. Depending on your location and local government, martial law may be declared. One of the first things that will happen in such a situation is that useful civilian goods will be seized and redistributed, rendering your stockpiling efforts useless.

Neighbours may notice you buying unusually large amounts of goods ahead of time and will remember when they are starving. If you are raided by looters, packaged dry goods are easy to take and you will be left with nothing. Your 'friends' will raid you wearing balaclavas.

It is advisable to start a garden and raise small animals such as poultry and rabbits now. Such a setup is not suspicious and will keep producing when well tended. It will be far better for you than highly salted survival food anyway. It will be difficult and time consuming for thieves to harvest and it is unlikely that they will clean you out. Deploy mantraps at your own discretion.

If you are not in a position to start farming you will need to know how to live off the new landscape. Traps and snares for animals and fish are effective, quiet and relatively easy to set up. Many wild plants can be eaten but care must be taken with identification.

Do not be scared to eat small critters like bugs and worms. These are highly nutritious and even favourable in many countries. They are also abundant in most places.

1.3.1 SEEDS

Seeds should be stored in areas that are cool, dark and dry. Some seeds last longer than others but should be viable for at least three months or more. Study and practice sustainable 'seed to seed' gardening now – I can't include a complete guide in this small tome. Take special note of seed saving and storage.

Keep a varied stock of many types of seeds. You can't assume your climate will remain unchanged – in fact, you can pretty much guarantee it won't – and you may be surprised at what plants will grow. If you are having trouble cultivating certain types of plant then wait until the weather changes otherwise you may burn through your entire seed stock.

Seeds can be eaten raw but this is not advised. Commercial seeds are guaranteed to germinate via hormones and chemicals. Good for plants, not so good for humans. Some seeds are naturally poisonous and this can vary between seasons. Seeds that may be good to eat in spring may be lethal in winter. Unless you are an expert, or a gambler, DO NOT EAT SEEDS. Once they are gone you have little to zero chance of getting them back.

1.4 WATER

Water is one of the most important survival needs. You will need an endless supply of clean water for drinking, cooking and personal hygiene. VERY serious short and long term problems will arise if you are not painstakingly careful about your water supply.

1.4.1 CONTAMINATION OF TRADITIONAL WATER SOURCES

If you are near a flowing river or in an area of constant rainfall you may think you have all the water you need. However, chemical spills, acid rain, volcanic ash, changes in rainfall patterns and many other factors can affect the quality of water. Commercial water filters can remove bacteria (0.22 micron pore size) and even viruses (0.02 micron pore size) but may not remove dangerous chemicals or heavy metals. Rain and groundwater can be contaminated yet be completely clear and tasteless.

Clean water can be collected from condensation from cold surfaces, morning dew, or from plants but these methods take a long time to yield a small amount of water.

1.4.2　SEAWATER

You should never drink sea water straight under any circumstances. The body uses more water than it gains from the seawater to remove the salt. Dinking nothing but seawater can kill you in a matter of hours. You are better off drinking nothing than drinking seawater.

1.4.3　DISTILLATION

The safest and recommended solution for any water source is distillation.

Some warn that drinking distilled water over a long term can leach nutrients from your body due to the pure H^2O molecule hungry to bond with any particle it comes across. This may be true in extreme cases where your food intake is zero, but you are still better off drinking distilled water than drinking dirty water, or nothing. Something you can do is to add a small amount of seawater or salt to the water you drink. You should *almost* be able to taste the salt.

1.5　SHELTER

Even if you have a strong bunker which survives the cataclysms, it will probably not suffice for the long term unless it is built extremely strong and on stable ground. If you have the resources, a steel-reinforced concrete dome type structure (not too big) will be fairly strong.

For most, shelter will have to be rebuilt. Shelter can be built from any natural and/or scrap materials you may find. Simple tee-pee and lean-to style huts may have to do until larger structures can be constructed from wood, stone, mud-brick or anything else you can find.

The larger the structure the more time and resources will need to be dedicated towards building it so ensure the immediate needs of your group are met first.

Natural occurring shelters such as caves and hollows should be avoided if you have experienced large or small earthquakes in your area. More may be coming and even a small aftershock can entomb you in darkness.

Underground Shelters

It is not advisable to build a completely underground shelter – whether it is dug into dirt, clay, granite, or tunnelled into the side of a mountain. A quaking earth can tear a structure apart and bury you. The less you are buried the better chance of your survival. A shelter that is partially dug into the ground – for stability, and mostly above-ground is ideal.

A sloped or rounded roof will drastically reduce the risk of damage from strong winds. This can be built up cheaply from dirt. It will provide both insulation and protection from strong wind.

1.6　SURVIVAL KITS

Your survival kit may be large if you are staying put on a property, medium if you are travelling in a vehicle (or many people on foot) or a single person rucksack and whatever you can fit in your pockets. Below is a guideline only. Your kits will no doubt vary.

1.6.1　BASIC SURVIVAL KIT

This pack will weigh at *least* 15 kg until the food and water start to be depleted. Therefore the pack itself should be sturdy. It doesn't have to be fancy, just strong. Pack it so it lays flat on your back because you might be carrying it for some time. Include plastic bags and sheeting to keep the contents dry. You may be travelling in the rain indefinitely.

Your basic survival kit should include —

- This book and another small book on the wild foods in your area. Have any maps of your area you think may be necessary, but be prepared for terrain changes.

- 5 or more litres of clean water. This is not nearly enough but it is hard to carry more. Be prepared to replenish it. Note that cargo pants can hold a litre bottle in each pocket.

- As much food as you can carry. Highly compact food such as rice, flour, dehydrated vegetables, instant mash potato, porridge oats, spaghetti etc. Stock cubes are small and add nutrients and protein. Peanut butter is good to mix with rice and is excellent bait for traps. Expect to carry at least 5kg of food alone. Multivitamins should also be included.

- First aid kit, see **Basic First Aid Kit** (Page 1-5)

- Personal hygiene products including at minimum soap, toothbrush and paste.

- Water purifier or distiller kit. Spare filters if you have a purifier.
- A container of Clorox bleach (regular, not scented) for water purification. Carry an eyedropper for purifying small amounts. See **Water Purification** (Page 3-6) for quantities.
- Toilet paper. Crush the roll to save space or use the space to store small things.
- 5 cigarette lighters. These are superior to matches and will dry quickly if you get them wet. 5 will last a long time if you only use them to light campfires. It may take you quite some time before you can make fire without one.
- A few firelighters. When this runs out carry small amounts of dry kindling. Remember you don't need to use a whole firelighter for every fire your make.
- A couple of good quality knives.
- A good quality multi-tool (such as Gerber or Leatherman).
- Small hand axe.
- A hand-chainsaw will be useful for building shelters and other things.
- File and a sharpening stone. Include honing oil for the stone.
- Camping shovel.
- Stainless steel billycan and other cooking containers and utensils.
- Remember you need to clean these utensils. Containers can be cleaned by gathering small stones and/or coarse sand and swishing about with water, but save yourself the hassle and include a stainless steel scourer or dish brush. Clean utensils before they dry out.
- Fishing kit. A fishing kit can be very compact yet contain many hooks, swivels, sinkers and lures, as well as a few rolls of line. A rod and reel are not necessary.
- Plenty or cord and snare wire (enamelled winding wire also works well).
- A roll of thin galvanised wire is useful for building shelters and general binding tasks.
- 30 or more metres of rope. This is light and can be hung on the outside of your pack.
- Sewing kit. Include large needles and well as small ones and plenty of thread.
- Clothes can also be repaired by using silicone sealant (ie Silastic). Work it into the fibres.
- Firearm and ammo if it suits you.
- Small tent or tarpaulin or similar sheet of plastic to create temporary shelters from. A tarp can be more versatile than a tent, but offers little shelter unless great care is taken in construction. Even if you include a tent, a tarp should be carried as it has many uses.
- Mosquito netting.
- Sleeping bag, swag, or bedroll and blankets.
- You may want to carry some assorted heirloom seeds for when you plan to settle.
- Don't forget to pack clothes, including warm cloths and **at least** **three pairs of** **wool** **socks**. Your clothing can be rolled up with your bedding.

1.6.2 LARGER SURVIVAL KITS

When you are travelling in a vehicle or with a group of people on foot, you can take a larger selection of goods and divide the weight amongst the group.

It should contain the same basic gear as the rucksack kit, scaled up for many people. Some extra items you may include are:

- As much food and water as the group can carry. If possible tinned foods should be carried. They take up more space but require little to no water to be used in the preparation. They are also very safe from contamination and spoilage.
- Large medical kit including books and medication.
- BOOKS! Carry as many books as you can without sacrificing other needs.
- Cooking and eating utensils such as large pots and frypans.
- **Hand tools** for creating shelter, building fences, tending the garden, building other tools, repairs and general maintenance. Don't forget nails, screws, wire and other fasteners.

If you are planning to prepare an area for survival of a large group of people then the type of community you wish to create will dictate the items you need to acquire. Choose your companions wisely and remember the guidelines of keeping a low profile and not attracting attention to yourself, otherwise all your hard efforts might be in vein.

1.6.3 BASIC FIRST AID KIT

The following items should be considered when preparing a basic first aid kit —

- Elastic roll bandages. Used for sprains and pressure bandages.
- Adhesive bandages – the kind you cut to fit. Include bandaids.
- Triangular bandages – used as slings, tourniquets, to tie splints etc.
- Aspirin, paracetamol and Ibuprofen.
- Adhesive tape. This comes in handy for many things including securing splints and securing gauze pads.
- Gauze pads. Buy the larger sized pads and cut them down as needed. Gauze stops bandages from sticking to wounds.
- Alcohol swaps.
- Antacid.
- Antihistamine.
- Antiseptic ointment or spray, for reducing the risk of infection of wounds. Clean wounds first. Have a lot of this.
- Ipecac syrup in case of ingesting poisonous substances. (It makes you barf).
- Insect repellent.
- Butterfly closure strips. Used like stitches to close wounds.
- Saline. For cleaning wounds and washing eyes.
- Soap. For cleaning hands and superficial wounds after bleeding has stopped.
- Dry-wash pads or wipes.
- Disinfectant wipes.
- Diarrhoea medicine.
- Hydrocortisone cream (soothes allergic skin).
- Mirror, small and tough.
- Cotton swap.
- Tweezers, Scissors, Safety pins.
- Sterile razor blades or scalpels. (Include some way to sharpen them).
- Latex gloves. Many diseases are transmitted through body fluids.

1.7   FOOD STORAGE GUIDELINES

If you want a stockpile of food – and let's face it, you do – whether you are planning on shelter in place, loading a vehicle, or planting caches, there are some points to keep in mind —

1.7.1 BASIC NEEDS OF FOOD STORAGE

Following is the seven basic needs of food storage –

1	**Water** is extremely important. Most can survive a **maximum** of 5 to 7 days without water, and it is not a pleasant way to go. Ever had a hangover? Dying of dehydration is like having a hangover that gets progressively worse. Try to store at least a 2 week supply, which is about 25 litres (7 gal) per person, This only covers drinking water not cooking and hygiene – this is BARE **MINIMUM** <u>RATION</u> QUANTITIES. Be prepared to gather and, if necessary, purify water for your ongoing needs.
2	**Grains,** including wheat, pastas, rice, barley and oats. They contain complex carbohydrates and protein and are essential components of daily nutrition. One adult requires 70 Kg (150 lb) of wheat and 60 Kg (125 lb) of other grains per year.
3	**Beans** are a great source of protein, and a meat substitute. They can be used as is or ground into flour for breads and thickeners. One adult needs about 25 Kg (60 lb) per year.
4	**Milk** is essential for children. An adult needs about 25 litres (6.5 gal) of milk a year. This is equal to about 3.5 Kg (8 lb) of powdered milk. Children need at least 50 % more.
5	**Salt** is a preserver and can enhance the flavour of boring foods. It is also essential for the body. Store about 5 kg (10 lb) per adult.
6	**Sugar / Honey**. Store about 25 kg (60 lb) per adult. Honey lasts longer than sugar.
7	**Oil**. This is needed for cooking and a body lubricant, especially for the skin. It can be stored in liquid form (canola and olive oil store best), solid form like butter or margarine, or powdered form as shortening. Store about 10 litres (2 gal) per adult.

1.7.2 IMPORTANT NOTES

There are several mistakes that are commonly made in food storage that can have dire consequences. The following guideline will help you avoid those mistakes —

Variety

Most people don't have enough variety in their storage. It's no good to buy a ton of wheat, honey, powdered milk and salt.

Most won't survive on such a diet for several reasons —

- Many people are allergic to wheat but won't know it until eating it meal after meal.
- Wheat is too harsh for young children. They can tolerate small amounts, but not constantly.
- People get tired of eating the same thing over and over. This is called appetite fatigue.

Store plenty of other grains, such as pastas, rice, corn and oats. Also include beans and dehydrated vegetables. Don't forget about extras such as spices and sauces that you like to cook with. They don't take up much space and can make an otherwise bland meal a joy to eat. Morale is extremely important and tasty meals go along way towards this.

Don't burn through all your spices all at once, your food quality may degrade over time and you will be better off saving the flavourings for when you really need them. In other words, don't use them for making your canned meals tastier, but use them for when you have to chow down on a meal of worms, bugs and weeds.

Extended Staples

Store dehydrated or freeze-dried foods as well as canned goods. Try to add cooking oil, shortening, baking powder, soda, yeast and powdered eggs.

Vitamins

Vitamins are important, especially if you have children. Children do not store reserves of nutrients as well as adults do. A good quality multi-vitamin and vitamin C are essential.

Quick and Easy and Psychological Foods

Meals that are ready to eat with little or no preparation can be very helpful in times where you are unable, for whatever reason, to prepare your basic items. Psychological foods are things like sweets, Jell-o, pudding, chocolate, crisps, nuts etc. Not essential but great for morale.

Balance

Rather than buy a huge amount of one item at a time, buy several items in smaller amounts.

Containers

Always store your bulk foods in food storage containers. Food simply stacked in the garage is vulnerable to floods, rodents, insects and many other factors. Don't stack too high as an earthquake can topple a stack.

Don't use bin liners as these are treated with insecticides, and generally very weak. If you use plastic shopping bags, use at least 3 together and alternate the ties from top to bottom.

Use Your Storage!

Don't store food without knowing what to do with it. A stressful situation is no time to learn to deal with your supplies, or to change your diet. It is essential to become familiar with how to prepare the foods you are storing.

2 BASIC SURVIVAL MEDICINE

Illnesses and injuries can be a source of great misery if the knowledge to treat a patient is not there. A survivor may have feelings of apathy and helplessness if they cannot treat themselves or others in an extreme situation.

One person with a fair amount of basic medical knowledge can make a difference in the lives of many. Without qualified medical personnel available, it is you who must know what to do to stay alive.

2.1 BASIC MAINTENANCE OF HEALTH

To survive, you need water and food. You must also apply high personal hygiene standards.

2.1.1 WATER

Replace water as you lose it. Trying to make up a deficit may be difficult in a survival situation, and thirst is not a sign of how much water you need.

Most people cannot comfortably drink more than 1 litre of water at a time. So, even when not thirsty, drink small amounts of water at regular intervals each hour to prevent dehydration.

If you are under physical and mental stress or subject to severe conditions, increase your water intake. Drink enough liquids to maintain a urine output of at least 0.5 litres (1 pint) every 24 hours.

With a loss of water there is also a loss of electrolytes (body salts). The average diet can usually keep up with these losses but in an extreme situation or illness, additional sources need to be provided. A mixture of 1/4 teaspoon of salt to 1 litre (2 pints) of water will provide a concentration that the body tissues can absorb easily.

The following are basic guidelines for the prevention of dehydration —

- Always drink water when eating. Water is used and consumed as a part of the digestion process and can lead to dehydration.
- Acclimatize. The body performs more efficiently in general when acclimatized.
- Conserve sweat not water. Limit sweat-producing activities but drink water. Keep your shirt on if you are sweating and wear a headband. Do not let your sweat pour off you onto the ground and be wasted.
- Ration water. Until you find a suitable source, ration your water sensibly. A daily intake of 0.5 litres of a sugar-water mixture (2 teaspoons per litre) will suffice to prevent severe dehydration for at least a week, provided you keep water losses to a minimum by limiting activity and heat gain or loss.

2.1.2 FOOD

The two basic sources of food are plants and animals (including fish). In varying degrees both provide the calories, carbohydrates, fats, and proteins needed for normal daily body functions.

Calories are a measure of heat and potential energy. The average person needs 2,000 calories per day to function at a minimum level. An adequate amount of carbohydrates, fats, and proteins without an adequate caloric intake will lead to starvation and cannibalism of the body's own tissue for energy.

Plant Foods

These foods provide carbohydrates – the main source of energy. Many plants provide enough protein to keep the body at normal efficiency. Although plants may not provide a balanced diet, they will sustain you even in the arctic, where meat's heat-producing qualities are normally essential. Many plant foods such as nuts and seeds will give you enough protein and oils for normal efficiency. Roots, green vegetables, and plant food containing natural sugar will provide calories and carbohydrates that give the body natural energy.

- You can dry plants by wind, air, sun, or fire. This slows spoilage so that you can store or carry the plant food with you to use when needed.
- You can obtain plants more easily and more quietly than meat. This is extremely important when trying to maintain a low profile.

Animal Foods

Meat is more nourishing than plant food. In fact, it may even be more readily available in some places. However, to get meat, you need to know the habits of, and how to capture, the various wildlife.

To satisfy your immediate food needs, first seek the more abundant and more easily obtained wildlife, such as insects, crustaceans, molluscs, fish, and reptiles. These can satisfy your immediate hunger while you are preparing traps and snares for larger game.

2.1.3 PERSONAL HYGIENE

In any situation, cleanliness is an important factor in preventing infection and disease. It becomes even more important in a survival situation. Poor hygiene can reduce your chances of survival.

A daily shower or bath with hot water and soap is ideal, but you can stay clean without this luxury. Use a cloth and soapy water to wash yourself. Pay special attention to the feet, armpits, crotch, hands, and hair as these are prime areas for infestation and infection. If water is scarce, take an "air" bath. Remove as much of your clothing as practical and expose your body to the sun and air for at least 1 hour. Be careful not to sunburn.

If you don't have soap, use ashes or sand, or make soap from animal fat and wood ashes, if your situation allows.

To make soap

Step 1	Extract grease from animal fat by cutting the fat into small pieces and cooking them in a pot.
Step 2	Add enough water to the pot to keep the fat from sticking as it cooks.
Step 3	Cook the fat slowly, stirring frequently.
Step 4	After the fat is rendered, pour the grease into a container to harden.
Step 5	Place ashes in a container with a spout near the bottom.
Step 6	Pour water over the ashes and collect the liquid that drips out of the spout in a separate container. This liquid is the potash or lye. Another way to get the lye is to pour the slurry (the mixture of ashes and water) through a straining cloth.
Step 7	In a cooking pot, mix two parts grease to one part potash.
Step 8	Place this mixture over a fire and boil it until it thickens.

After the mixture – the soap – cools, you can use it in the semi-liquid state directly from the pot. You can also pour it into a pan, allow it to harden, and cut it into bars for later use.

If rendered properly, the fat will not retain any smell of the cooked flesh it came from. To see a more detailed treatment of soap making, see **Cleaning Products** (Page 9-22)

Keep Your Hands Clean

Germs on your hands can infect food and wounds. Wash your hands after handling any material that is likely to carry germs, after going to the toilet, after caring for the sick, and before handling any food, food utensils, or drinking water. Keep your fingernails closely trimmed and clean, and keep your fingers out of your mouth.

Keep Your Hair Clean

Your hair can become a haven for bacteria or fleas, lice, and other parasites. Keeping your hair clean, combed, and trimmed helps you avoid this danger.

Keep Your Clothing Clean

Keep your clothing and bedding as clean as possible to reduce the chance of skin infection as well as to decrease the danger of parasitic infestation. Clean your outer clothing whenever it becomes soiled. Wear clean underclothing and socks each day. If water is scarce, you can "air" clean your clothing by shaking, airing, and sunning for 2 hours. If you are using a sleeping bag, turn it inside out after each use, fluff it, and air it.

Keep Your Teeth Clean

Thoroughly clean your mouth and teeth with a toothbrush at least once each day. If you don't have a toothbrush, make a chewing stick. Find a twig about 20 cm long and 1 cm wide. Chew one end of the stick to separate the fibres. Now brush your teeth thoroughly. Another way is to wrap a clean strip of cloth around your fingers and rub your teeth with it to wipe away food particles. You can also brush your teeth with small amounts of sand, baking soda, salt, or soap.

If you have cavities, you can make temporary fillings by placing candle wax, pine tree resin, aspirin, hot pepper, tooth paste, or portions of a ginger root into the cavity. Make sure you clean the cavity by rinsing or picking the particles out of the cavity before placing a filling in the cavity. See **Field Dentistry** (Page 2-19) for more information.

Take Care of Your Feet

To prevent serious foot problems, break in your shoes before wearing them in a long term situation. Wash and massage your feet daily. Trim your toenails straight across. Wear an insole and the proper size of dry socks. Powder and check your feet daily for blisters.

If you get a small blister, do not open it. An intact blister is safe from infection. Apply a padding material around the blister to relieve pressure and reduce friction. If the blister bursts, treat it as an open wound. Clean and dress it daily and pad around it. Leave large blisters intact. To avoid having the blister burst or tear under pressure and cause a painful and open sore, do the following –

Step 1	Obtain a sewing-type needle and a clean or sterilized thread.
Step 2	Run the needle and thread through the blister after cleaning the blister.
Step 3	Detach the needle and leave both ends of the thread hanging out of the blister. The thread will absorb the liquid inside. This reduces the size of the hole and ensures that the hole does not close up.
Step 4	Pad around the blister.

Get Sufficient Rest

You need a certain amount of rest to keep going. Plan for regular rest periods of at least 10 minutes per hour during your daily activities. Learn to make yourself comfortable under less than ideal conditions. A change from mental to physical activity or vice versa can be refreshing when time or situation does not permit total relaxation.

Keep Camp Site Clean

Do not soil the ground in the camp site area with urine or feces. Dig latrines if you can. If latrines are not available, dig small "cat holes" and cover the waste. Collect drinking water upstream from the camp site. Purify all water (by distillation if possible).

2.2 MEDICAL EMERGENCIES

Some common medical problems and emergencies you may be faced with include breathing problems, severe bleeding, and shock.

Breathing Problems

Any one of the following can cause airway obstruction, resulting in stopped breathing —

- Foreign matter in mouth of throat that obstructs the opening to the trachea.
- Face or neck injuries.
- Inflammation and swelling of mouth and throat caused by inhaling smoke, flames, and irritating vapours or by an allergic reaction.
- A "kink" in the throat (caused by the neck bent forward so that the chin rests upon the chest) may block the passage of air.

When unconscious, the tongue may block the passage of air to the lungs. The muscles of the lower jaw and tongue relax as the neck drops forward, causing the lower jaw to sag and the tongue to drop back and block the passage of air. See **Open Airway and Maintain** (Page 2-4)

Severe Bleeding

Severe bleeding from any major blood vessel in the body is extremely dangerous. The loss of 1 litre of blood will produce moderate symptoms of shock. The loss of 2 litres will produce a severe state of shock that places the body in extreme danger. The loss of 3 litres is usually fatal. See **Control Bleeding** (Page 2-5).

Shock

Shock (acute stress reaction) is not a disease in itself. It is a clinical condition characterized by symptoms that arise when cardiac output is insufficient to fill the arteries with blood under enough pressure to provide an adequate blood supply to the organs and tissues. See **Prevent and Treat Shock** (Page 2-7).

2.3 LIFESAVING STEPS

Don't panic! Control your own panic and your patients. Panic does no one any good.

Perform a quick physical exam. Look for the cause of the injury and follow the basics of first aid, starting with the airway and breathing, but use your judgement. A person may die from arterial bleeding more quickly than from an airway obstruction in some cases.

2.3.1 OPEN AIRWAY AND MAINTAIN

You can open an airway and maintain it by using the following steps —

Step 1	Check if the victim has a partial or complete airway obstruction. If they can cough or speak, allow them to clear the obstruction naturally. Stand by, reassure the victim, and be ready to clear their airway and perform mouth-to-mouth resuscitation should they become unconscious.
	If their airway is completely obstructed, administer abdominal or chest thrusts until the obstruction is cleared. See **CHOKING** (Page 2-8).
Step 2	Using a finger, quickly sweep the victim's mouth clear of any foreign objects, broken teeth, dentures, sand.
Step 3	Using the jaw thrust method, grasp the angles of the victim's lower jaw and lift with both hands, one on each side, moving the jaw forward. 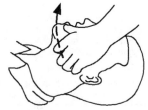
	For stability, rest your elbows on the surface on which the victim is lying. If their lips are closed, gently open the lower lip with your thumb.
Step 4	With the victim's airway open, pinch their nose closed with your thumb and forefinger and blow two complete breaths into their lungs. Allow the lungs to deflate after the second inflation and perform the following steps: • Look for their chest to rise and fall. • Listen for escaping air during exhalation. • Feel for flow of air on your cheek.
Step 5	If the forced breaths do not stimulate spontaneous breathing, maintain the victim's breathing by performing mouth-to-mouth resuscitation
Step 6	There is danger of the victim vomiting during mouth-to-mouth resuscitation. Check the victim's mouth periodically for vomit and clear as needed

 Cardiopulmonary resuscitation (CPR) may be necessary after cleaning the airway, but only after major bleeding is under control.

2.3.2 CONTROL BLEEDING

In a survival situation, you must control serious bleeding immediately because replacement fluids normally are not available and the victim can die within a matter of minutes. External bleeding falls into the following classifications (according to its source) —

Arterial	Blood vessels called arteries carry blood away from the heart and through the body. A cut artery issues bright red blood from the wound in distinct spurts or pulses that correspond to the rhythm of the heartbeat. Because the blood in the arteries is under high pressure, an individual can lose a large volume of blood in a short period when damage to an artery of significant size occurs. Therefore, arterial bleeding is the most serious type of bleeding. If not controlled promptly, it can be fatal.
Venous	Venous blood is blood returning to the heart through blood vessels called veins. A steady flow of dark red, maroon, or bluish blood characterizes bleeding from a vein. You can usually control venous bleeding more easily than arterial bleeding.
Capillary	The capillaries are the extremely small vessels that connect the arteries with the veins. Capillary bleeding most commonly occurs in minor cuts and scrapes. This type of bleeding is not difficult to control.

You can control external bleeding by direct pressure, indirect (pressure points) pressure, elevation, digital ligation, or tourniquet.

Direct Pressure

The most effective way to control external bleeding is by applying pressure directly over the wound. This pressure must not only be firm enough to stop the bleeding, but it must also be maintained long enough to "seal off" the damaged surface.

If bleeding continues after 30 minutes, apply a pressure dressing. A thick dressing is applied directly over the wound and held in place with a tight bandage. It should be tighter than an ordinary compression bandage but not so tight that it impairs circulation. Once you apply the dressing, do not remove it, even when the dressing becomes blood soaked.

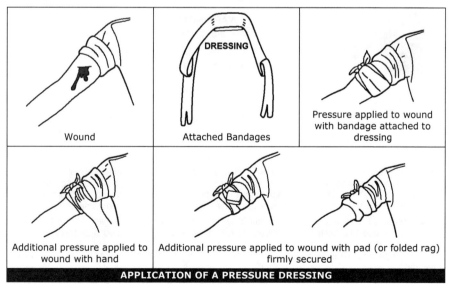

Wound	Attached Bandages	Pressure applied to wound with bandage attached to dressing
Additional pressure applied to wound with hand	Additional pressure applied to wound with pad (or folded rag) firmly secured	

APPLICATION OF A PRESSURE DRESSING

Make fresh, daily dressing changes and inspect for signs of infection.

Elevation

Raising an injured extremity as high as possible above the heart's level slows blood loss by aiding the return of blood to the heart and lowering the blood pressure at the wound. However, elevation alone will not control bleeding entirely; you must also apply direct pressure over the wound. When treating a snake bite however, keep the extremity lower than the heart.

Pressure Points

A pressure point is a location where the main artery to the wound lies near the surface of the skin or where the artery passes directly over a bone.

You can use finger pressure on a pressure point to slow arterial bleeding until the application of a pressure dressing.

Pressure point control is not as effective for controlling bleeding as direct pressure exerted on the wound. It is rare when a single major compressible artery supplies a damaged vessel.

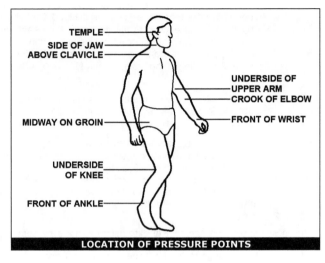

LOCATION OF PRESSURE POINTS

If you cannot remember the exact location of the pressure points, follow this rule: Apply pressure at the end of the joint just above the injured area. On hands, feet, and head, this will be the wrist, ankle, and neck, respectively.

WARNING!!!

Use caution when applying pressure to the neck.

Too much pressure for too long may cause unconsciousness or death.

Never place a tourniquet around the neck.

Digital Ligation

You can stop major bleeding immediately or slow it down by applying pressure with a finger or two on the bleeding end of the vein or artery. Maintain the pressure until the bleeding stops or slows down enough to apply a pressure bandage, elevation, and so forth.

Tourniquet

Use a tourniquet only when direct pressure over the bleeding point and all other methods did not control the bleeding. If you leave a tourniquet in place too long, the damage to the tissues can progress to gangrene, with a loss of the limb later. An improperly applied tourniquet can also cause permanent damage to nerves and other tissues at the site of the constriction.

If you must use a tourniquet, place it around the extremity, between the wound and the heart, 5 to 10 cm above the wound site. Never place it directly over the wound or a fracture. Use a stick as a handle to tighten the tourniquet and tighten it only enough to stop blood flow. When you have tightened the tourniquet, bind the free end of the stick to the limb to prevent unwinding.

After you secure the tourniquet, clean and bandage the wound. A lone survivor should not remove or release an applied tourniquet. In a buddy system, however, the buddy can release the tourniquet pressure every 10 to 15 minutes for 1 or 2 minutes to let blood flow to the rest of the extremity to prevent limb loss.

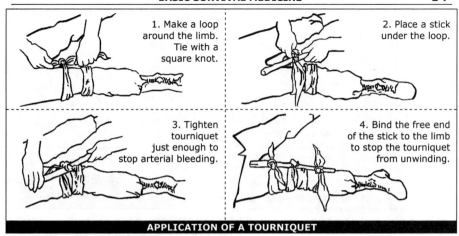

1. Make a loop around the limb. Tie with a square knot.

2. Place a stick under the loop.

3. Tighten tourniquet just enough to stop arterial bleeding.

4. Bind the free end of the stick to the limb to stop the tourniquet from unwinding.

APPLICATION OF A TOURNIQUET

2.3.3 PREVENT AND TREAT SHOCK

Shock stuns and weakens the body. When the normal blood flow in the body is upset, death can result. Early identification can be life saving. Look out for the following symptoms —

• Sweaty but cool skin (clammy skin).	• Confusion.
• Paleness of skin.	• Faster than normal breathing.
• Restlessness, nervousness.	• Blotchy or bluish skin (especially around mouth or lips).
• Thirst.	
• Loss of blood.	• Nausea and/or vomiting.

Regardless of which symptoms appear, the treatment is the same.

If the victim is conscious, treat as follows —

- Place them on a level surface with the lower extremities elevated 15 to 20 cm (6 to 8 in).
- If you are unsure of the best position, place the victim perfectly flat. Once the victim is in a shock position, do not move them.
- Maintain body heat by insulating the victim from the surroundings and, in some instances, applying external heat. Don't let them overheat or get chilled.
- If wet, remove the victim's wet clothing as soon as possible and replace with dry clothing.
- Improvise a shelter to insulate the victim from the weather.
- Use warm liquids or foods, a pre-warmed sleeping bag, another person, warmed water in canteens, hot rocks wrapped in clothing, or fires on either side of the victim to provide external warmth.
- If the victim is conscious, slowly administer small doses of a warm salt or sugar solution, if available.
- If the victim is unconscious or has abdominal wounds, do not give fluids by mouth.
- Have the victim rest for at least 24 hours.
- If you are a lone survivor, then lie in a depression in the ground, behind a tree, or any other place out of the weather, with your head lower than your feet.
- If you are with a buddy, reassess your patient constantly.

If the victim is unconscious, treat the same as above with the following differences —

- Place them on their side or abdomen with their head turned to one side to prevent choking on vomit, blood, or other fluids.
- Do not elevate extremities
- Do not administer fluids

2.3.4 CHOKING

If a person is choking, determine first whether they can speak. If they can still speak then encourage them to cough. At this point the person still has a good air exchange and you should not yet interfere with their attempts to clear the obstruction. They may indicate by giving the universal sign for choking.

Listen for high pitch sounds when the victim breathes or coughs – this indicates poor air exchange. If there is poor exchange or no breathing – immediately call for help and deliver manual thrusts.

There are two types of manual thrusts – the abdominal thrust (aka the Heimlich manoeuvre), and the chest thrust. The chest thrust is used for a pregnant woman, when the casualty has an abdominal wound, or is too large for you to get your arms around them.

These procedures can be done with the casualty standing or sitting.

UNIVERSAL CHOKING SIGN

Abdominal Thrust Procedure (Heimlich Manoeuvre)

- Get behind the casualty and wrap your arms around their waist.
- Make a fist with one hand and grasp it with the other. The thumb side of your fist should be against the casualty's abdomen – in the midline and slightly above the navel, but well below the tip of the breastbone.
- Press the fists into the abdomen with a quick backward and upward thrust
- Each thrust should be delivered slowly and distinctly, with the intent of ejecting the object.
- Continue performing abdominal thrusts until the obstruction is expelled or the casualty becomes unconscious.
- If they lose consciousness, proceed with steps to **Open Airway and Maintain** (Page 2-4).

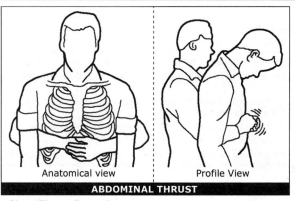

Anatomical view   Profile View

ABDOMINAL THRUST

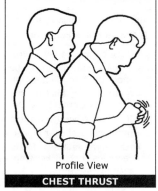

Profile View

CHEST THRUST

Chest Thrust Procedure

This is an alternate technique for pregnant women, people with abdominal injuries, or people too large for the abdominal thrust. The technique is similar but with a few key differences —

- Get behind the casualty and wrap your hands around their chest.
- Make a fist with one hand place the thumb side of your fist in the middle of the breastbone (take care to avoid the tip of the breastbone and the margins of the ribs).
- Grasp your fist with your other hand and exert thrusts
- Each thrust should be delivered slowly and distinctly, with the intent of ejecting the object.
- Continue performing chest thrusts until the obstruction is expelled or the casualty becomes unconscious.
- If they lose consciousness, proceed with steps to **Open Airway and Maintain** (Page 2-4).

2.4 BONE AND JOINT INJURY

You may face bone and joint injuries that include fractures, dislocations, and sprains.

2.4.1 FRACTURES

There are basically two types of fractures: open and closed. With an open (or compound) fracture, the bone protrudes through the skin and complicates the actual fracture with an open wound. After setting the fracture, treat the wound as any other open wound. The closed fracture has no open wounds. Follow the guidelines for immobilization, and set and splint the fracture.

The signs and symptoms of a fracture are pain, tenderness, discoloration, swelling deformity, loss of function, and grating (a sound or feeling that occurs when broken bone ends rub together).

The dangers with a fracture are the severing or compression of a nerve or blood vessel. For this reason minimum manipulation should be done, and with caution. If the area below the break becomes numb, swollen, cool to the touch, or pale, and the victim shows signs of shock, a major vessel may have been severed. You must control this internal bleeding. Rest the victim for shock, and replace lost fluids.

Often you must maintain traction during the splinting and healing process. You can effectively pull smaller bones such as the arm or lower leg by hand. You can create traction by wedging a hand or foot in the V-notch of a tree and pushing against the tree with the other extremity. You can then splint the break.

Very strong muscles hold a broken thighbone (femur) in place making it difficult to maintain traction during healing. You can make an improvised traction splint using natural material as follows –

Step 1	Find two forked branches at least 5 cm thick. Measure one from the patient's armpit to 20-30 cm past their unbroken leg. Measure the other from the groin to 20-30 cm past the unbroken leg. Ensure that both extend an equal distance beyond the end of the leg.
Step 2	Pad the two splints. Notch near the ends and lash a 20-30 cm cross member made from a 5 cm diameter branch between them.
Step 3	Using available material (vines, cloth, rawhide), tie the splint around the upper portion of the body and down the length of the broken leg. Follow the splinting guidelines.

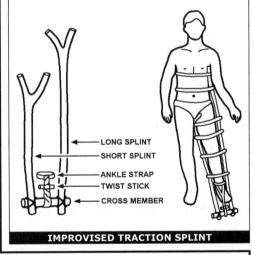

LONG SPLINT
SHORT SPLINT
ANKLE STRAP
TWIST STICK
CROSS MEMBER

IMPROVISED TRACTION SPLINT

Step 4	With available material, fashion a wrap that will extend around the ankle, with the two free ends tied to the cross member.
Step 5	Place a 10 x 2.5 cm stick in the middle of the free ends of the ankle wrap between the cross member and the foot. Using the stick, twist the material to make the traction easier.
Step 6	Continue twisting until the broken leg is as long as or slightly longer than the unbroken leg.
Step 7	Lash the stick to maintain traction.

2.4.2 POOR CIRCULATION AFTER INJURY - LEECHES

Leeches can be used where there is poor circulation to an area of the body after an injury. Poor circulation can lead to sepsis, which will lead to gangrene and amputation. Consider a crushed arm where blood is not flowing to the fingers, placing leeches on the fingers will draw blood through until normal circulation is restored.

Leeches secrete an anticoagulant that prevents blood from gumming up in injured parts during healing. They also have a natural antibiotic that they release into the bloodstream. Replace fat leeches with skinny ones during the treatment.

2.4.3 DISLOCATIONS

Dislocations are the separations of bone joints. These can be extremely painful and can cause an impairment of nerve or circulatory function. You must place these joints back into alignment as quickly as possible.

Signs and symptoms of dislocations are joint pain, tenderness, swelling, discoloration, limited range of motion, and deformity of the joint. You treat dislocations by reduction, immobilization, and rehabilitation.

Reduction or "setting" is placing the bones back into their proper alignment. You can use several methods, but manual traction or the use of weights to pull the bones is the safest and easiest. Once performed, reduction decreases the victim's pain and allows for normal function and circulation. Without an X-ray, you can judge proper alignment by the look and feel of the joint and by comparing it to the joint on the opposite side.

Immobilization
Immobilization is splinting the dislocation after the dislocated limb has been popped back into place. You can use any material at hand for a splint or you can splint an extremity to the body. The basic guidelines for splinting are —

• Splint above and below the fracture site.
• Pad splints to reduce discomfort.
• Check circulation below the fracture after making each tie on the splint.

To rehabilitate the dislocation, remove the splints after 7 to 14 days. Gradually use the injured joint until fully healed.

2.4.4 SPRAINS

The accidental overstretching of a tendon or ligament causes sprains. The signs and symptoms are pain, swelling, tenderness, and discoloration (black and blue). When treating sprains —

• Rest the injured area.
• Apply ice for 24 hours, then heat after that.
• Use compression-wrapping and/or splinting to help stabilize. If possible, leave the shoe on a sprained ankle unless circulation is compromised.
• Elevate the affected area.

2.5 BITES AND STINGS

Insects and related pests are hazards in a survival situation. They not only cause irritations, but they are often carriers of diseases that cause severe allergic reactions in some individuals.

Ticks	Can carry and transmit diseases, such as the Lyme disease.
Mosquitoes	May carry malaria, dengue, and many other diseases.
Flies	Can spread disease from contact with infectious sources. They are causes of sleeping sickness, typhoid, cholera, and dysentery.
Fleas	Can transmit plague.
Lice	Can transmit typhus and relapsing fever.

If you get bitten or stung, do not scratch, it might become infected. Inspect your body at least once a day to ensure there are no insects attached to you. If you find ticks attached to your body, cover them with a substance, such as Vaseline, heavy oil, or tree sap, which will cut off their air supply. Without air, the tick releases its hold, and you can remove it.

Take care to remove the whole tick. Use tweezers if you have them. Grasp the tick where the mouth parts are attached to the skin. Do not squeeze the tick's body. Wash your hands after touching the tick. Clean the tick wound daily until healed.

Bee and Wasp Stings

If stung by a bee, immediately remove the stinger and venom sac, if attached, by scraping with a fingernail or a knife blade. Do not squeeze or grasp the stinger or venom sac, as squeezing will force more venom into the wound. Wash the sting site thoroughly with soap and water to lessen the chance of a secondary infection.

Relieve the itching and discomfort caused by insect bites by applying —

• Cold compresses.	• Coconut meat.
• A cooling paste of mud and ashes.	• Crushed cloves of garlic.
• Sap from dandelions.	• Onion.

Spider Bites

The black widow spider is identified by a red hourglass on its abdomen. Only the female bites, and it has a neurotoxic venom. Severe local pain rapidly develops which gradually spreads over the entire body and settles in the abdomen and legs. Abdominal cramps and progressive nausea, vomiting, and a rash may occur. Weakness, tremors, sweating, and salivation may occur. Anaphylactic reactions can occur. Symptoms begin to regress after several hours and are usually gone in a few days. Treat for shock. Be ready to perform CPR. Clean and dress the bite area to reduce the risk of infection.

The funnelweb spider is a large brown or grey spider found in Australia. The symptoms and the treatment for its bite are the same as for the black widow spider.

Tarantulas are large, hairy spiders found mainly in the tropics. Most do not inject venom, but some South American species do. They have large fangs. If bitten, pain and bleeding are certain, and infection is likely. Treat a tarantula bite as for any open wound, and try to prevent infection. If symptoms of poisoning appear, treat as for the bite of the black widow spider.

Scorpion Stings

Scorpions are all poisonous to a greater or lesser degree. There are two different reactions, depending on the species —

• **Severe local reaction**, with pain and swelling around the area of the sting. Possible prickly sensation around the mouth and a thick-feeling tongue.

• **Severe systemic reaction**, with little or no visible local reaction. Local pain may be present. Systemic reaction includes respiratory difficulties, thick-feeling tongue, body spasms, drooling, gastric distension, double vision, blindness, involuntary rapid movement of the eyeballs, involuntary urination and defecation, and heart failure. Death is rare, occurring mainly in children and adults with high blood pressure or illnesses.

Treat scorpion stings as you would a black widow bite.

Snake Bites

The chance of a snakebite in a survival situation is rather small, if you are familiar with the various types of snakes and their habitats. However, you should know how to treat a snakebite. Failure to treat a snakebite properly can result in needless tragedy.

The primary concern in the treatment of a snakebite is to limit the amount of eventual tissue destruction around the bite area.

A bite wound, regardless of the type of animal that inflicted it, can become infected from bacteria in the animal's mouth. With non-poisonous as well as poisonous snakebites, this local infection is responsible for a large part of the residual damage that results.

Snake venoms not only contain poisons that attack the victim's central nervous system (neurotoxins) and blood circulation (hemotoxins), but also digestive enzymes (cytotoxins) to aid in digesting their prey. These poisons can cause a very large area of tissue death, leaving a large open wound. This condition could lead to the need for amputation if not treated.

Shock and panic in a person bitten by a snake can also affect the person's recovery. Panic can speed up the circulation, causing the body to absorb the toxin quickly.

Before you start treating a snakebite, determine whether the snake was poisonous or non-poisonous. Bites from a non-poisonous snake will show rows of teeth. Bites from a poisonous snake may have rows of teeth showing, but will have one or more distinctive puncture marks caused by fang penetration. Symptoms of a poisonous bite may be spontaneous bleeding from the nose and anus, blood in the urine, pain at the site of the bite, and swelling at the site of the bite within a few minutes or up to 2 hours later.

Breathing difficulty, paralysis, weakness, twitching, and numbness are also signs of neurotoxin venoms. These signs usually appear 1.5 to 2 hours after the bite.

If you determine that a poisonous snake bit an individual, take the following steps —

- Reassure the victim and keep them still.
- Set up for shock and force fluids or give an intravenous (IV).
- Remove watches, rings, bracelets, or other constricting items.
- Clean the bite area.
- Maintain an airway (especially if bitten near the face or neck) and be prepared to administer mouth-to-mouth resuscitation or CPR.
- Use a constricting band between the wound and the heart.
- Immobilize the site.
- Remove the poison as soon as possible by using a mechanical suction device or by squeezing.
- If possible, shove the bite affected body part inside the stomach of a freshly dead animal – the acid will draw out some of the venom. Dogs have especially strong stomach acid.

Do not —

- **Use mouth suction** – even with no sores in your mouth, you will still absorb venom
- **Make any incisions at the bite site** – Cutting opens capillaries that in turn open a direct route into the blood stream for venom and infection.
- Break open the large blisters that form around the bite site.
- Give the victim alcoholic beverages or tobacco products.
- Give morphine, opiates, or other central nervous system depressors.
- Put your hands on your face or rub your eyes, as venom may be on your hands. Venom may cause blindness.

After caring for the victim as above, take the following actions to minimize local effects —

- If infection appears, keep the wound open and clean.
- Use heat after 24 to 48 hours to help prevent the spread of local infection. Heat also helps to draw out an infection.
- Keep the wound covered with a dry, sterile dressing.
- Have the victim drink large amounts of fluids until the infection is gone.

2.6 WOUNDS

Wounds could be open wounds, skin diseases, frostbite, trench foot, and burns.

2.6.1 OPEN WOUNDS

Open wounds are serious in a survival situation, not only because of tissue damage and blood loss, but also because they may become infected. By taking proper care of the wound you can reduce further contamination and promote healing. Clean the wound as soon as possible after it occurs by —

- Removing or cutting clothing away from the wound.
- Looking for an exit wound if a sharp object, gun shot, or projectile caused a wound.

- Thoroughly cleaning the skin around the wound.
- Rinsing (not scrubbing) the wound with large amounts of water under pressure. You can use fresh urine if water is not available.

The "open treatment" method is the safest way to manage wounds in survival situations. Do not try to close any wound by suturing or similar procedures. Leave the wound open to allow the drainage of any pus resulting from infection. As long as the wound can drain, it generally will not become life-threatening, regardless of how unpleasant it looks or smells.

Cover the wound with a clean dressing. Place a bandage on the dressing to hold it in place. Change the dressing daily to check for infection.

To treat an infected wound

- Place a warm, moist compress directly on the infected wound. Change the compress when it cools, keeping a warm compress on the wound for a total of 30 minutes. Apply the compresses three or four times daily.
- Drain the wound. Open and gently probe the infected wound with a sterile instrument.
- Dress and bandage the wound.
- Drink a lot of water.

Continue this treatment daily until all signs of infection have disappeared.

If you do not have antibiotics and the wound has become severely infected, does not heal, and ordinary **Debridement** (Page 2-17) is impossible, consider maggot therapy —

- Expose the wound to flies for one day and then cover it.
- Check daily for maggots.
- Once maggots develop, keep wound covered but keep checking daily.
- Remove all maggots when they have cleaned out all dead tissue and before they start on healthy tissue. Increased pain and bright red blood in the wound indicate that the maggots have reached healthy tissue.
- Flush the wound repeatedly with sterile water or fresh urine to remove the maggots.
- Check the wound every four hours for several days to ensure all maggots have been removed.
- Bandage the wound and treat it as any other wound. It should heal normally.

Raising Sterile Maggots

If using maggots as micro-surgeons, raise sterile maggots if at all possible. The possibility of developing something like tetanus is too great a risk. This is achieved by placing some rotting meat inside a jar, then covering the jar with a fine cloth or gauze. Flies will swarm around the jar and lay eggs on the gauze.

Before the eggs hatch into maggots, immerse the cloth in a dilute antiseptic or weak salt-water solution to sterilise the eggs. Then raise the maggots on sterile food. The next generation eggs will produce sterile maggots.

2.6.2 SKIN DISEASES AND AILMENTS

Although boils, fungal infections, and rashes rarely develop into a serious health problem, they cause discomfort and you should treat them.

Boils

Apply warm compresses to bring the boil to a head. Then open the boil using a sterile knife, wire, needle, or similar item. Thoroughly clean out the pus with soap and water. Cover the boil site, checking it periodically to ensure no further infection develops.

Fungal Infections

Keep the skin clean and dry, and expose the infected area to as much sunlight as possible. Do not scratch the affected area. During the Southeast Asian conflict, soldiers used antifungal powders, lye soap, chlorine bleach, alcohol, vinegar, concentrated salt water, and iodine to treat fungal infections with varying degrees of success. As with any "unorthodox" method of treatment, use it with caution.

Rashes

To treat a skin rash effectively, first determine what is causing it. This determination may be difficult even in the best of situations. Observe the following rules to treat rashes —

- If it is moist, keep it dry.
- If it is dry, keep it moist.
- Do not scratch it.

Use a compress of vinegar or tannic acid derived from tea or from boiling acorns or the bark of a hardwood tree to dry weeping rashes. Keep dry rashes moist by rubbing a small amount of rendered animal fat or grease on the affected area.

Remember, treat rashes as open wounds and clean and dress them daily. There are many substances available to survivors in the wild or in captivity for use as antiseptics to treat wound —

Iodine tablets	Use 5 to 15 tablets in a litre of water to produce a good rinse for wounds during healing.
Garlic	Rub it on a wound or boil it to extract the oils and use the water to rinse the affected area.
Salt water	Use 2 to 3 tablespoons per litre of water to kill bacteria.
Bee honey	Use it straight or dissolved in water.
Sphagnum moss	Found in boggy areas worldwide, it is a natural source of iodine. Use as a dressing.

Frostbite

This injury results from frozen tissues. Light frostbite involves only the skin that takes on a dull, whitish pallor. Deep frostbite extends to a depth below the skin. The tissues become solid and immovable. Your feet, hands, and facial areas are particularly vulnerable to frostbite.

When with others, prevent frostbite by using the buddy system. Check your buddy's face often and make sure that they check yours. If you are alone, periodically cover your nose and lower part of your face with your mittens.

Above all – Move! Keep moving as much as surroundings will allow. Stomp. Jump. Slap arms across chest. Blow on hands. Stuff hands under clothing (inside pants or under armpits). Wriggle toes. Arch your feet. Bend ankles. Make faces. Cup hands on face. Button up clothing. Shout. Loosen tight clothing. Pull ears, nose and lips. Clench fists. Bend and unbend fingers and toes. Make vigorous love to a tree. Move and keep moving.

Do not –

- Try to thaw the affected areas by placing them close to a fire. Gently rub them in lukewarm water. Dry the part and place it next to your skin to warm it at body temperature.
- Spill gasoline on bare skin.
- Touch metal in freezing cold.
- Sit on snow – sit on anything else.
- Shove snow-laden gloves into pockets.
- Chafe or rub sore skin.

Keep working until you are warm and sheltered.

Trench Foot

This condition results from prolonged exposure to wet or damp conditions at a temperature just above freezing. The nerves and muscles sustain the main damage, but gangrene can occur. In extreme cases the flesh dies and it may become necessary to amputate.

The symptoms usually include blisters, reddened skin, inflammation and the presence of dead skin that peels and falls off. The symptoms are often intensified by extreme pain when the feet are warmed after cold exposure.

To treat trench foot before gangrene occurs, soak the feet in warm water for five minutes, cleaned, dried thoroughly and dressed in warm dry socks. Clean socks should be placed on the feet daily and the feet should be checked regularly for wounds, which can lead to infection.

The best prevention is to keep your feet dry. Carry extra socks with you in a waterproof packet. Dry wet socks in the air or against your body. Wash feet daily and put on dry socks.

Burns

The following field treatment for burns will relieve the pain somewhat. It seems to help speed healing, and offers some protection against infection —

- First, stop the burning process. Put out the fire by removing clothing, dousing with water or sand, or by rolling on the ground. Cool the burning skin with ice or water.
- Soak dressings or clean rags for 10 minutes in a boiling tannic acid solution (obtained from tea, inner bark of hardwood trees, or acorns boiled in water).
- Cool the dressings or clean rags and apply over burns.
- Treat as an open wound.
- Replace fluid loss.
- Maintain airway.
- Treat for shock.
- Consider using morphine or opiates if you have some, unless the burns are near the face.

2.7 ENVIRONMENTAL INJURIES

Heatstroke, hypothermia, diarrhoea, and intestinal parasites are some of the environmental injuries you could face.

Heatstroke

Heatstroke is the breakdown of the body's heat regulatory system (body temperature more than 40.5°C (105°F). Other heat injuries, such as cramps or dehydration, do not always precede a heatstroke. Signs and symptoms of heatstroke are —

• Swollen, beet-red face.	• Reddened whites of eyes.
• Victim not sweating, with hot red dry skin	• Rapid pulse
• Difficulty breathing	• Strange behaviour / confusion
• Agitation / disorientation	• Seizure
• Unconsciousness or delirium, which can cause pallor, a bluish colour to lips and nail beds (cyanosis), and cool skin.	

By this time the victim is in severe shock. Cool the victim as rapidly as possible by dipping them in a cool stream. If one is not available, douse the victim with urine, water, or at the very least, apply cool wet compresses to all the joints, especially the neck, armpits, and crotch and head. Heat loss through the scalp is great so a wet cloth on the head will help a lot.

In desert areas, cooler ground can be found by digging a trench about 1 foot deep and having the victim lie in that. Keep the victim shaded.

Expect, during cooling —

• Vomiting.	• Shouting.
• Diarrhoea.	• Prolonged unconsciousness.
• Struggling.	• Rebound heatstroke within 48 hours.
• Shivering.	• Cardiac arrest – be ready to perform CPR.

Treat for dehydration with lightly salted water (0.25 teaspoon per 1 litre).

Hypothermia

Hypothermia is defined as the body's failure to maintain a temperature of 36°C (97°F). Exposure to cool or cold temperature over a short or long time can cause hypothermia. Dehydration and lack of food and rest predispose the survivor to hypothermia.

Unlike heatstroke, you must <u>gradually</u> warm the hypothermia victim. Get the victim into dry clothing. Replace lost fluids, and warm them.

Stage 1	The first stage of hypothermia is a progressive decline of coordination. Described as "the 'umbles" – the victim mumbles, fumbles and stumbles. This indicates a 1-3°C loss in core temperature. Get the victim dry, warm and out of the wind.
Stage 2	The second stage is uncontrollable shivering. You should immediately build a fire and apply heat – you can use warm stones or a water bottle with warm water – to the groin, head, neck, and sides of the chest. If you have a tent, zip the victim inside and boil water to humidify the air.
	If you have no source of heat- force the victim to move around. This generates more heat than shivering
Stage 3	If the shivering stops and the victim is increasingly disorientated and can't stand or walk without your help, severe hypothermia has set in – a very serious situation. All efforts should be made to limit heat lost and rewarm the victim and external help should be sought if at all possible.

If hypothermia has begun and there is no sufficient heat source, a non-hypothermic person can lie naked with the victim, wrapped in blankets. A hypothermic person cannot generate body heat on their own until they recover so no amount of blankets alone will work.

Diarrhoea

A common, debilitating ailment caused by a change of water and food, drinking contaminated water, eating spoiled food, becoming fatigued, and using dirty dishes. You can avoid most of these causes by practicing preventive medicine. If you get diarrhoea, however, and do not have anti-diarrhoeal medicine, one of the following treatments may be effective —

• Limit your intake of fluids for 24 hours.

• Drink one cup of a strong tea solution every 2 hours until the diarrhoea slows or stops. The tannic acid in the tea helps to control the diarrhoea. Boil the inner bark of a hardwood tree for 2 hours or more to release the tannic acid.

• Make a solution of one handful of ground chalk, charcoal, or dried bones and treated water. If you have some apple pomace (the remains of fleshy fruit after pressing for oil or juice) or the rinds of citrus fruit, add an equal portion to the mixture to make it more effective. Take 2 tablespoons of the solution every 2 hours until the diarrhoea slows or stops.

Intestinal Parasites

You can usually avoid intestinal parasites if you take preventive measures. For example, never go barefoot. Never eat uncooked meat or raw vegetables contaminated by raw sewage or human waste used as a fertilizer. However, should you become infested and lack proper medicine, you can use home remedies. Keep in mind that these home remedies work on the principle of changing the environment of the gastrointestinal tract. The following are home remedies you could use —

Salt water	Dissolve 4 tablespoons of salt in 1 litre of water and drink. Do not repeat this treatment.
Tobacco	Eat 1 to 1.5 cigarettes. The nicotine in the cigarette will kill or stun the worms long enough for your system to pass them. If the infestation is severe, repeat the treatment in 24 to 48 hours, but no sooner.
Kerosene	Drink 2 tablespoons of kerosene but no more. If necessary, you can repeat this treatment in 24 to 48 hours. Be careful not to inhale the fumes. They may cause lung irritation.
Hot peppers	Peppers are effective only if they are a steady part of your diet. You can eat them raw or put them in soups or rice and meat dishes. They create an environment that is prohibitive to parasitic attachment.

2.8 FIELD SURGERY

These procedures should never be attempted if professional help is at all possible. They are only provided for a reference in a scenario where external medical help is non-existent. Do not take these procedures lightly. Incorrect implementation WILL result in serious injury or death.

Before any of these procedures are undertaken, your group – including the patient – should discuss the pros, cons, risks and the actual procedure at length. Have all materials and tools sterilised, razor sharp and on hand before you start and make sure everyone participating understands what is going to happen.

If possible, practice on a dead animal beforehand to know what to expect when dealing with the muscles, nerves, blood vessels and other tissue. Visual and tactile feedback is important.

2.8.1 WOUND DEBRIDEMENT

Following injury from severe puncturing or a bullet, soft tissue wounds may need debridement.

This means removal of dead tissue, and other foreign bodies, such as metal or bone fragments, pieces of wood, clothing, skin, hair etc.

High velocity projectiles such as bullets can cause shock waves that disrupt and destroy tissues as far as several inches away from the missile tract.

Incomplete debridement increases the risk of infection and complications such as gangrene and can result in death.

Tissue Layers

The main layers of body tissue consist of the epidermis, dermis, hypodermis and muscle.

Debridement Method

Normally, skin incisions for debridement in the arms and legs are made parallel to the bone.

Starting at the wound, use a scalpel to incise the skin, long enough to expose injured tissues. Then make another incision in the opposite direction.

Try not to cut deeper than the skin to avoid damaging healthy tissue. If the wound or incisions involves a joint,

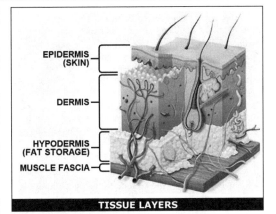

EPIDERMIS (SKIN)

DERMIS

HYPODERMIS (FAT STORAGE)

MUSCLE FASCIA

TISSUE LAYERS

Epidermis	This is the outer skin. It is the foremost defence against disease and infection.
Dermis	The dermis is a layer of skin between the epidermis and hypodermis. Structural components include collagen and elastic fibres.
Hypodermis	Also called subcutaneous tissue or superficial fascia, this layer is used mainly for fat storage.

obtain consultation if possible as some incisions over joints are better than others.

Normally, very little if any skin needs to be removed. Skin that is shredded can be removed, as well as any crushed and obviously necrotic (dead) skin.

After you are through the skin, use scissors and tissue forceps to isolate and incise the hypodermis down to the muscle fascia. Do not put your fingers in the wound. There may be razor sharp metal or glass fragments that can cut you. Try to work each layer one at a time. This will help prevent further injury to healthy tissue.

As you work down through the wound, remove any loose foreign bodies and cut away any damaged or necrotic tissue. Be careful not to sever any major blood vessels. Fatty tissue can hide nerves so be careful not to sever any nerves if you can avoid it.

Sterile irrigation fluid such as saline or lightly salted distilled water should be poured into the wound periodically to help float out clots and foreign matter. Gauze sponges will help to keep the wound clear for you to see. Good lighting and assistance is essential.

Once through the hypodermis and muscle fascia, you will be able to visualise the underlying muscles. Devitalised (necrotic) muscle is characterised by —

- Poor colour   – dark like liver, rather than beefy red.
- Poor consistency   – mushy like jelly, rather than firm.
- Poor contractility   – when you pinch healthy muscle with forceps, it will contract.
- Poor circulation   – it doesn't bleed when cut.

Devitalised muscle must be removed. Muscles can't absorb oxygen like other tissue, and if deprived will die quickly. Pick up a small piece of devitalised muscle with the forceps and excise it with the scissors. Look at the cut muscle edge – if it is oozing bright red blood then you have probably removed enough muscle in that area.

The goal is to remove all dead tissue while leaving as much health tissue as possible.

Most oozing will simply stop on its own or with gentle direct pressure. Care must be taken not to sever large blood vessels, be prepared beforehand to clamp and close. Use a fine thread, such as cotton or un-waxed dental floss (split the fibres), to close the vessel. Try to clamp just the bleeding point and not the surrounding tissue. Sterilise the thread by boiling beforehand.

Yellow or white fat in the wound is a sign that nerves are nearby. Nerves are always well padded so observe carefully. If the fat is intact you should leave it alone. Severing a nerve will only bring more misery to your patient. This is why you should practice on a dead animal beforehand, taking note of the structure of the tissue, nerves, blood vessels, muscle, tendons and bones. You are trying to avoid future infection, while ending up with a functioning limb.

After all dead tissue and foreign objects are removed, pack the wound loosely with gauze and cover with a loose dressing. Wounds that require debridement are rarely closed immediately, but left open for inspection several days later. Closure may be done then but only by an experienced medical professional.

To summarise, the basic principles of debridement are —

- Obtain good exposure with anaesthetic, an adequate incision, good lighting and assistance.
- Incise (remove) the tissue, exposing the underlying muscle.
- Excise devitalised muscle until the remaining muscle is healthy.
- Continue to work downward into the wound, layer by layer, debriding as you go and trying to avoid the nerves and blood vessels that commonly run between the muscle layers.
- Try to preserve as much normal tissue as possible and try not to injure the nerves.
- Attempting to close these wounds is usually a very bad idea.

2.8.2 FIELD AMPUTATION

In the absence of antibiotics, infection from wounds, compound fractures and other injuries may result in life threatening infections. Amputation may be the only option.

General Guidelines for amputation	Indications for amputation
• Field amputations are difficult and different from normal amputations.	• Massive gangrene.
• The amputation must include all dead, contaminated and bruised tissue.	• Overwhelming local infection that endangers life despite antibiotic therapy and surgical measures.
• Stump infection is very dangerous.	• Established death of a limb.
• Use a tourniquet for surgery.	• Massive injuries in which structures of the limb are obviously non-viable.
• Leave enough soft tissue to cover bone.	
• Do not underestimate muscle swelling post procedure.	• Secondary haemorrhaging. (When a wound starts to bleed several days after an injury which otherwise seems healed).
• Never attempt primary closure of the stump. This should only ever be done by an experienced surgeon.	• Limbs which are severely crushed or which otherwise have bone, muscle, skin and nerves in a state beyond separation.
• Amputations are done at the lowest level possible. All attempts should be made to save the knee and elbow joints.	• Limbs with anaesthetic terminus (death of tissue due to incorrect use or too high a dosage of anaesthetic).

The most acceptable method for amputations in field conditions is as follows —

Step 1	Place a tight tourniquet above the amputation point to restrict blood flow. You can make this extra tight because circulation to the limb to be removed is not an issue.
Step 2	An incision is made around the limb through the skin and fat. This incision is made at the lowest viable level. This layer is allowed to retract, exposing the muscles.
Step 3	Go around the limb, cutting the muscle bundles as you go. The muscles are cut near the point where the first layer retracted, but a little further toward the body. As you cut the muscles, they will retract toward the body. As blood vessels are encountered they are cut and tied with sutures, sewn shut, tied with strong fine thread (such as un-waxed dental floss), cauterized or closed by any non-intrusive means possible. Anything used to close the vessel should be sterilised by boiling first. Major nerves should be cut at the highest level possible.
Step 4	Place upward pressure on the skin, fat and muscle mass to push it toward the body and further expose the bone. Cut the bone off at this higher level. The surgical wound should resemble an inverted cone. The idea is to leave as much flesh and skin to cover the stump of the bone to provide natural cushioning once it is healed.
Step 5	Apply bone wax to the end of the bone to prevent oozing. If bone wax is not available, any wax will do as long as it is properly sterilised. As a last resort, pine pitch can be used, but use sparingly. See **Natural Glues** (Page 9-10)
Step 6	Place a layer of fine mesh gauze over the wound and pack the recess loosely with fluffed gauze. Place a stockinette over the stump and secure using adhesive.
Step 7	Wrap the stump with elastic bandages (ace wraps) using compression. Apply about 2.5 kg (5 pounds) traction to pull the skin and muscles over the stump. Continued traction will result in secondary closure over the stump. The elastic bandage needs to be tight enough to hold it, but without restricting circulation.

If bandages are not available, cut cloth into strips and sterilise thoroughly before the procedure. Non-elastic materials will not provide the same traction as 'ace-wraps' so will need to be bound tighter. This will reduce circulation so will need to be loosened for five minutes out of every 12 to 15.

If the skin starts to turn blue/white or grey, then it is bandaged too tightly. The natural colour of healthy tissue is pink. Watch the colour of the area and watch for bleeding.

If pain killers such as pethidine, morphine or opiates are available, administer before and after the operation. Separate the first few doses after surgery by at least 15 minutes to make sure you see the effect on the poor patient. You don't want them to OD after that ordeal.

Watch the temperature, respiration and the wound itself very carefully in the first 24 hours.

2.9 FIELD DENTISTRY

The basics of dentistry can be broken down into 7 areas —

2.9.1 PREVENTATIVE DENTISTRY

Before finding yourself in a primitive living situation make sure you are brushing and flossing daily and getting regular checkups and appropriate treatments. When access to professional dental care is impossible, daily brushing and flossing is essential.

2.9.2 SCALING AND CLEANING

Regular brushing and flossing will minimise plaque build-up but it will still occur. Plaque is mineralised deposits at the edges of teeth and gums. It is difficult to remove with simple brushing, but can be removed by simply scraping off with a sterilised scaler or dental pick.

2.9.3 DENTAL PAIN AND INFECTION

Standard Dental First Aid

This treatment is standard for many conditions. Symptoms are managed with oral anti-inflammatories, pain medication, local anaesthetic, cold packs, saline gargles and a soft diet.

Dental Pain

Pulpitis	**Inflammation of the dental pulp (toothache)**
	This pain is often referred to the surrounding area or other teeth. It can be difficult for the patient to identify the offending tooth. The tooth is usually not sensitive to agitation, but may be sensitive to heat, cold or sweets.
	Usually there is an obvious cause, such as a large cavity. Management is by standard dental first aid.
Periapical Inflammation	**Inflammation, but not infection, at the apex (root base)**
	The offending tooth is usually easy to locate. The tooth may protrude a bit and/or cause pain with chewing or agitation.
	Management is by standard dental first aid.
Aphthous Ulcers	**Lesion on oral mucus membrane – cause unclear**
	There are often multiple ulcers lasting 7 to 15 days. May be triggered by trauma or stress. Manage with standard dental first aid. Topical steroids may shorten healing time.
Muscle Pain and Spasm	**Chewing muscle dysfunction**
	This can be caused by teeth grinding, jaw clenching, heavy chewing. Manage by muscle rest, soft diet and anti-inflammatories.
Other Causes	Other causes of dental pain include infections (discussed below), facial nerve pain, herpes zoster, vascular pain-migraine, sinus pain and referred pain.

Infections

Herpes Labialis (viral)	**Cold sores on lips, tongue, gingival, palate**
	Often triggered by sunburn, stress and trauma. The patient often has a tingle of pain before a lesion appears. Manage with standard dental first aid.
Oral Candidiasis (fungal)	**Thrush, caused by the overgrowth of yeast normally found in the mouth**
	Often seen in the very ill, those with a weak immune system, or those recently taking antibiotics. It looks like white spots or patches in the mouth, may have a 'cottage cheese' appearance and can be rubbed off.
	The patients' mouth and throat are often very sore and red. Manage by eliminating sources of re-infection (boil toothbrushes in salty water and air dry) and with anti-fungal medication.

Bacterial Infections

Many different organisms present in the oral cavity can cause infections. An Infection can be life threatening if it spreads to deep tissues or into the brain. Fever, local swelling and lymph node swelling is common.

Apical Abscess/ Cellulitis	**Infection of the pulp extending down to the bone and gum.**
	The gum and tooth base appear normal. This is an infection at the very apex of the roots that has eaten through the thin bone of the jaw. Indications include fever, pain, often an abscess/pus pocket or swelling where the gum tissue meets the lip. No sensitivity to heat or cold.

	Management is by incision and drainage through the gum to the level of the bone. Dental first aid should be applied and antibiotics may be required. Extraction of the tooth will be necessary if treatment is unsuccessful.
Gingival/ Periodontal Abscess	**Infection between the gum and tooth**
	The abscess is usually on the cheek side. The tooth is usually sensitive to agitation, but not heat or cold. Manage with incision, draining and dental first aid. Antibiotics are usually not necessary.
Pericoronitis	**Infection of the gum overlying a partially erupted tooth**
	Common in wisdom teeth. Muscle spasms in the chewing muscles are common. It is managed by cleaning out between the tooth and gum and dental first aid measures. Antibiotics are usually not necessary.
	At times removal of some of the redundant gum tissue may be helpful.
Deep Tissue/ Fascia Infections	Any oral infection can spread quickly through tissues to other areas in the neck causing tissue breakdown, bleeding and obstruction of the airway.
	Immediate incision and drainage is required along with aggressive antibiotic therapy. This is potentially life threatening and help should be sought if at all possible.

When to use antibiotics

Dental abscesses are best treated by drainage of any collection present. Antibiotics should be used in patients who are systematically unwell – high temperatures, chills, shakes, nausea, vomiting or gross local swelling.

Penicillin 500mg 4 times daily or Erythromycin 500mg 3 times daily are usually acceptable antibiotics. Broader spectrum drugs or colloidal silver can also be used.

2.9.4 DRILLING AND FILLING

Cavities in teeth cause pain either because they allow infection into the inside of the tooth, or they expose nerve endings in the pulp of the tooth.

It is fairly easy to provide a temporary filling which covers the hole and protects exposed nerves. There is commercially available filling materials but if these aren't available consider using candle wax, pine tree resin, aspirin, hot pepper, tooth paste, or ginger root in the cavity.

Permanent fillings are more complicated and usually require the cavity to be opened up. The surface hole is usually too small, while there is a larger decayed area below. The cavity is opened up and cleaned with a dental drill.

A 'Dremel' type tool can be used for a dental drill. Use a thin diamond-tipped bit rather than a traditional drill bit. You want to 'route' out the cavity rather than drilling deep into it. Be sure to sterilise the bit first.

If you don't have a suitable drill, improvisation of one will be extremely difficult, especially because a low-rpm drill will be more painful for the patient. In this case, extraction of the tooth is probably the better option. Some cavities can be cleaned out with a scraping tool, if there is a large cavity in the tooth and is easily accessible.

This method should not be used when —

- There is presence of swelling or pus near the tooth.
- If the hole is too deep and the core/pulp of the tooth exposed.
- If the tooth has been painful for a long time, there may be a chronic infection of the pulp.
- The cavity cannot be easily reached, because of position or the size of the hole.

Finding a permanent filling material will be difficult. Gold is one option. After drilling and cleaning the cavity, a small crumpled ball of a very thin gold film is placed in the cavity. It is slowly tapped and molded into place with a dental pick. This is more difficult than it sounds.

Another option is to fill the cavity with candle wax, then top off with pine pitch. This won't be permanent but may last many years.

2.9.5 DENTAL TRAUMA

Below is a list of common dental trauma.

Crown Chip	**Small lines or 'crazing' in the enamel.** These are harmless
Simple Crown and/or Root Fracture	**The tooth is fractured, but no pulp is exposed** This is usually not a problem, but the tooth can be cold sensitive. Smooth rough edges with a nail file and remove small fragments.
Complicated Crown and/or Root Fracture	**The pulp is exposed but the root is intact** Remove and fragments and flush the area thoroughly with saline. If the pulp has been exposed for more than 24 hours, remove about 2 mm of the pulp tissue. Seal the exposed area with filling material. Extraction may be needed if pain continues or infection develops.
Intrusion	**The tooth is driven deeper into the socket** Use dental first aid measures. Long term survival of the tooth is poor so extraction may be the best option.
Extrusion	**The tooth is partially pulled out of the socket** Gently replace into the socket. Have the patient bite down gently to ensure the tooth is all the way in. Apply dental first aid measures and extract if pain continues or infection develops.
Tooth Loss	**The tooth is knocked completely from the socket** Do not touch the root segment or scrub the tooth or socket. Rinse the tooth and socket in saline until clean. If immediate replacement is not possible, store in saline, milk or saliva. This will usually not work if after 24 hours. Apply dental first aid.
Primary (baby) Teeth Injuries	**Normally these are not repaired unless needed** Apply dental first aid and consider extraction if pain continues or infection develops.

2.9.6 DENTAL EXTRACTIONS

Before antibiotics, this was the main treatment for dental infections. An infection in the root of the tooth was treated by pulling the tooth and allowing it to drain.

The basic principle is to loosen the tooth from the gum and the jaw, then gently rocking back and forward until loose enough to be removed. The key point is gentle rocking rather than simple pulling. The process however can be a lot more complicated.

Firstly, it will be very painful. Without local anaesthetic, the only option may be the patient blacking out from the pain itself. Secondly, without the proper instruments, gripping the tooth will be difficult. Any solid gripping instrument, such as a pair of pliers can be used if the tips are wrapped in gauze or padded in some other way.

Extreme care must be taken not to shatter the tooth with the gripping device during extraction. This will make it impossible to remove the entire tooth and will result in complications such as infections.

2.9.7 DENTAL PROSTHETICS

Without the ability to chew food, survival will be a lot more difficult. You should take all measures to prevent running out of teeth.

Historically porcelain was used to manufacture dentures, but other materials may be used in a survival situation such as metal, bone and even animal and human teeth properly shaped to fit.

2.10 PREGNANCY AND CHILDBIRTH

2.10.1 PREGNANCY

Signs of pregnancy
- The woman misses her period (often the first sign).
- 'Morning sickness' (nausea or feeling you are going to vomit, especially in the morning). This is worse during the second and third months of pregnancy.
- She may have to urinate more often.
- The belly gets bigger and the breasts get bigger or feel tender.
- Dark areas on the face, breasts and belly – often called the 'mask of pregnancy'.

Normal position of the baby after 9 months.

BABY POSITION

How to Stay Health during Pregnancy
- Eat enough to gain weight regularly – especially if you are thin. Eat plenty and eat well. The body needs plenty of proteins, vitamins, and minerals, especially iron. If possible, use iodized salt to decrease the chances of stillbirth or retardation. But use any salt sparingly to avoid other problems, such as swelling of the feet.
- Keep clean. Bathe or wash regularly and brush your teeth every day.
- In the last month of pregnancy, it is best not to use a vaginal douche and to avoid sexual contact to keep from breaking the bag of water and causing an infection.
- Continue to work and get exercise, but try not to get too tired.

Minor Problems during Pregnancy

Burning or Pain in the pit of the stomach or chest	Eat only small amounts of food at a time and drink plenty of water. Try to sleep with the head and chest lifted up with pillows or blankets. Antacids may help, so may sucking hard candy.
Swelling of the Feet	Rest at times during the day with your feet up. Avoid salty foods. Swelling of the feet usually comes from the pressure of the baby in the last months. It is worse when anaemic or malnourished.
Anaemia or Malnutrition	To make a baby healthy, a woman needs to eat well. If she is very pale and weak she needs more protein and foods with iron (beans, nuts, chicken, milk, cheese, eggs, meat, fish, dark green leafy vegetables). Take iron pills if available, to strengthen the blood and resist dangerous bleeding after childbirth. If possible take iron pills with folic acid and vitamin C. Vitamin C helps the body process the iron.
Swollen Veins (varicose veins)	This is common due to the weight of the baby pressing on the veins that come from the legs. Put your feet up often, as high as you can. If the veins get very big, wrap them with an elastic bandage or elastic stockings. Take them off at night.
Piles (haemorrhoids)	These are varicose veins in the anus. They result from the weight of the baby. To ease the pain, kneel with the buttocks in the air, or sit in a warm bath.
Constipation	Drink plenty of water. Eats fruits and food with a lot of natural fibre, such as cassava or bran. Get plenty of exercise. Do not take strong laxatives.

KNEEL LIKE THIS TO RELIEVE HAEMORRHOIDS

Danger Signs in Pregnancy

Bleeding	If a woman bleeds during pregnancy, even a little, this is a danger sign. She could be having a miscarriage or an ectopic pregnancy (where the baby develops outside the womb). If possible seek professional help.
	Bleeding late in pregnancy (after 6 months) may mean the afterbirth is blocking the birth opening. Without expert help the woman may bleed to death. Do not do a vaginal exam or put anything inside her vagina.
	Seek professional help if at all possible.
Severe Anaemia	The woman is weak, tired and has pale or transparent skin. If not treated she may die from blood loss at childbirth. If anaemia is severe, a good diet won't correct this in time. Take pills of iron salts and seek a health worker.
Toxaemia of Pregnancy	Swelling of the feet, hands and face, with headaches, dizziness and sometimes blurred vision are symptoms of toxaemia, or poisoning of the pregnancy. Sudden weight gain and high blood pressure are also signs.

To treat toxaemia of pregnancy –

- Stay quiet and in bed.
- Eat foods rich in protein, but with little salt.
- If she does not get better quickly, or has trouble seeing – get professional help – her life is in danger.

During the last 3 months of pregnancy, if you have trouble seeing, and if your face and hands begin to swell, you may be suffering from toxaemia of pregnancy.

If only your feet swell, it is probably not serious but watch for other signs. Use very little salt in your diet.

To help prevent toxaemia of pregnancy, eat nutritious food with plenty of protein, and only use a little salt.

Growth and Position of the Baby in the Womb

The womb should grow at a steady rate of about two fingers higher every month. At 4 1/2 months it is usually at the position of the naval.

If the womb seems too big or grows too fast, it may mean she is having twins. It can also mean the womb has more water than normal, if so, it can be difficult to feel the baby inside.

Too much water in the womb means greater risk of severe bleeding during childbirth.

9 MONTHS
7 MONTHS
5 MONTHS
3 MONTHS

POSITION OF THE WOMB

Baby's Heartbeat and Movement

After 5 months listen for the baby's heartbeat and check for movement. You can put your ear to the belly or use a fetoscope. A fetoscope can be carved from wood or made from fired clay.

If the baby's heartbeat is heard loudest below the naval in the last month, the baby is head down

If the baby's heartbeat is heard loudest above the naval, it is head up, and may be a breech birth.

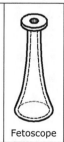

Fetoscope

CHECKING BABY'S HEARTBEAT AND POSITION

A baby's heart beats about twice as fast as an adult's. If you have a watch then count baby's heartbeats. It should be around 120-160 beats per minute.

If less than 120, then something is wrong, or you may have counted the woman's by accident. Check her pulse to be sure. The baby's heartbeat is often hard to hear.

Month 2 – 3	Tiredness, nausea and morning sickness.
Month 4	Womb at the level of the naval.
Month 5	Baby's heartbeat and first movements.
Month 7 – 9	Some swelling of feet, constipation, heartburn, varicose veins, shortness of breath, frequent urination.
Last Week	Baby moves lower in belly.
TYPICAL SYMPTOMS OF PREGNANCY	

2.10.2 PREPARING TO GIVE BIRTH

This is a list of things you should try to have ready well before the baby is ready to be born –

- A lot of very clean cloths or rags
- Soap (antiseptic if possible)
- A new razor blade (for cutting the umbilical cord), or at least a very sharp knife, or clean rust-free scissors (sterilised by boiling).
- Rubber or plastic gloves sterilised by boiling
- A bowl for washing hands

- Clean cotton wad
- Sterile gauze or patches of very clean cloth for covering the naval.
- Two ribbons or strips of clean cloth for tying the cord before cutting.
- Both patches and ribbons should be wrapped in paper and baked in an oven to sterilise.
- A bowl for catching the afterbirth

Birth is a natural event. In general, the less the midwife or birth attendant does, the more likely everything will go well. If you have a fever, cough, sore throat, sores or infections, it is better for someone else to deliver the baby.

Ensuring the Baby is in a Good Position

To make sure the baby is head down, the normal position for birth, check for the head as follows.

- Have the mother breathe out all the way
- With the thumb and two fingers, push just above the pelvic bone.
- With the other hand, feel the top of the womb.

The baby's butt is larger and wider, the head is small, hard and round.

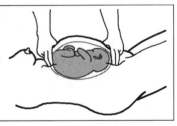

- Push gently from side to side, first with one hand, and then the other.

If the baby's butt is pulled gently sideways, the whole body will move too.

But if the head is pushed gently sideways, it will bend at the neck and the back will not move.

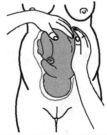

If the baby is still high in the womb you can still move it a little, but if it has dropped down (engaged), you cannot.

A woman's first baby sometimes engages 2 weeks before labour begins. Later babies may not engage until labour begins.

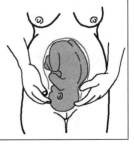

Signs that Show Labour is near

- A few days before labour begins, usually the baby moves lower in the womb. This lets the mother breathe easier, but may have to urinate more often because of pressure on the bladder. In the first birth this can be up to four weeks before delivery.
- A short time before labour begins, some thick mucus may come out, or some mucus may come out 2-3 days before labour. It is often tinted with blood. This is normal.

- The contractions (sudden tightening of the womb) or labour pains may start several days before childbirth. At first the contractions are far apart – several minutes or even hours. When the contractions become stronger, regular and more frequent, labour is beginning.
- Some women may have 'practice contractions' weeks prior to labour. This is normal. In rare cases, a woman may have false labour, this happens when contractions become frequent, but then stop. Sometimes walking, a warm bath or resting will calm the contractions if they are false, or bring on childbirth if they are real.
- The bag of water that holds the baby usually breaks with a flood of liquid sometime after labour has begun. If the water breaks before contractions start, this usually means the beginning of labour. After the water breaks the woman should keep very clean. To prevent infection, avoid sexual contact, do not sit in a bath of water, and do not douche.

The first stage of labour usually lasts 10 to 20 hours or more for a first birth, and 7 to 10 hours for a later birth. Do not try to rush this stage, reassure the mother that it is normal.

The mother should keep her bowels and bladder empty. During labour she should urinate often, and drink plenty of water or other liquids. If labour is long, she should also eat lightly. During labour the mother should change positions often and get up and walk around occasionally. Do not lie flat on the back for long periods of time.

2.10.3 GIVING BIRTH

During the first stages of labour, the midwife or birth attendant should wash the mother's belly, genitals, buttocks and legs with soap and warm water. Spread clean sheets or towels on the bed and replace them if they get dirty.

The midwife should **not** massage or push on the belly. The mother should push or bear down at this time. The mother should take <u>slow</u>, regular breaths between contractions. Strong pains are normal and will help to push the baby out.

The second stage of labour, when the baby is being born, is usually easier than the first and should not last longer than 2 hours. During contractions the mother pushes down with all her strength. Between contractions she may seem very tired or half asleep. This is normal. If the child comes slowly after the water breaks the mother can double her knees while doing one of the following –

| SQUATTING | SITTING PROPPED UP | KNEELING | LYING DOWN |

When the birth opening of the mother stretches and the baby's head begins to show, the midwife should have everything ready. At this point the mother should try <u>not</u> to push hard, so the head comes out more slowly. This helps prevent tearing of the opening.

In a normal birth, the midwife <u>never</u> needs to put a hand or finger inside the mother. When the head comes out, the midwife can support it, but must never pull.

NORMALLY THE BABY IS BORN HEAD FIRST LIKE THIS

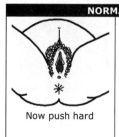 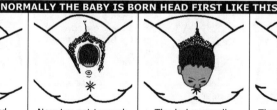  

| Now push hard | Now try not to push hard. Take many short fast breaths. This helps to prevent tearing. | The baby usually comes out face down. If there are feces in the mouth or nose, clean it immediately. | Then the baby turns to one side so the shoulders can come out |

All the force should come from the mother, the midwife should never pull on the head or twist or bend the baby's neck.

The third stage of labour is between when the baby is born and the afterbirth (placenta) comes out.

Usually the placenta comes out 5 minutes to an hour after the baby. In the meantime, care for the baby.

Care of the Baby after Birth

IF THE SHOULDERS GET STUCK WHEN THE HEAD IS OUT

The midwife can take the baby's head and lower it very carefully, so the shoulder can come out.

Then she can raise the head a little, so the other shoulder can come out.

Immediately after the baby comes out –

- Put the baby's head down so that mucus comes out of the mouth and throat. Keep it this way until it begins to breathe.

- Keep the baby below the level of the mother until the cord is tied. This way, the baby gets more blood and will be stronger.

- If the baby does not begin to breathe straight away, rub its back with a towel or cloth.

- If the baby still does not breathe, clear mucus out of its nose and throat with a suction bulb or clean cloth wrapped around a finger. In a pinch you can place your mouth over baby's mouth and nose, and gently suck to remove mucus.

- If the baby has not begun to breathe one minute after birth, start mouth-to-mouth breathing immediately.

PUT BABY'S HEAD DOWN

- Wrap the baby in a clean, <u>warm</u> cloth. It is important not to let the baby get cold. Note that **a newborn baby cannot produce body heat very well**, so a cold blanket will not do.

How to Cut the Cord

When a child is born, the umbilical cord pulses and is blue and fat. **Wait**.

After a while, the cord becomes thin and white, and stops pulsing. Now tie in two places with very clean strips of cloth, string, or ribbon. These should have been ironed or heated in an oven.

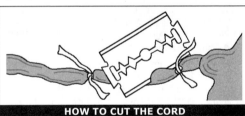

HOW TO CUT THE CORD

Cut the cord with a clean unused razor blade, or a very sharp knife or pair of scissors that has been sterilised by boiling for 10 minutes. Ensure your hands are cleaned with soap. Always cut the cord close to the body of the newborn. Only leave about 2 cm (just under an inch) attached to the body. These precautions help prevent tetanus.

Care of the Cut Cord

Keep the cord stump clean and dry. Always wash your hands before touching the cord stump. If the cord becomes dirty or has a lot of dried blood on it, clean it gently with medical alcohol, strong drinking alcohol, or with gentian violet.

Do not put anything else on the cord stump. Dirt and dung are especially dangerous. If the baby is wearing diapers, keep the diaper folded below the cord.

The cord stump usually falls of 5 to 7 days after birth. There may be a few drops of blood or smooth mucus where the cord falls off. This is normal. But if there is a lot of blood, seek help.

Clean the Newborn Baby

Use a warm damp cloth to gently clean away and blood or fluid. It is best NOT to bathe the baby until the after the cord drops off, then bathe daily in warm water using mild soap.

Feeding

Place the baby at its mother's breast as soon as the baby is born. If the baby nurses, this will help to make the afterbirth come out sooner, and also to prevent or control heavy bleeding.

Delivery of the Placenta (Afterbirth)

Normally the placenta comes out 5 minutes to an hour after the baby is born, but sometimes can be delayed for many hours. When the afterbirth comes out, examine it to make sure it is complete. If it is torn and there seems to be pieces missing, get medical help.

If the placenta is delaying in coming, but the mother is not losing much blood – do nothing. **Do not pull on the cord**. Sometimes the placenta will come out if the mother squats and pushes a little.

If the mother is losing blood, feel the womb through the belly. If it is soft, massage the womb carefully until it becomes hard. This should make it contract and push out the placenta.

If the placenta does not come out soon and bleeding continues, push downward on the top of the womb very carefully, while supporting the bottom of the womb ->

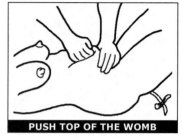

PUSH TOP OF THE WOMB

To help prevent or control heavy bleeding, let the baby suck the mother's breast.

If the baby will not suck, have the father (if possible) gently pull and massage the mother's nipples. This will cause her to produce a hormone (pituitrin) that helps control bleeding.

2.10.4 GIVING BIRTH ALONE

It is not uncommon for women to give birth at home, unassisted. In modern society, many women still give birth alone – even in hospitals, due to staff shortages or other issues. It is important to know what to expect. Even if it is not your first, no two labours are exactly alike.

Dangers of Giving Birth Alone

Because it is possible to mistake labour as frequent urges to urinate or move your bowels, there are many cases of bathroom babies. If you are having a premature baby, or usually have easy deliveries, then misinterpreting labour as toilet urges is more of a risk.

If you have some form of anaesthetic or narcotics, resist the urge to take them. When the baby is being passed through the birth canal, you will be in a naturally semi-conscious state, but when delivery completes, a survival-instinct rush of adrenaline is provided. This is necessary to allow the mother to do what she needs to do in the first few moments of birth.

The Point of Delivery

At this point is it important to sit up and attend to your new born. You need to make sure the cord is not wrapped around your baby's neck. If so, gently pick up the baby and carefully unwind it from the cord. Don't pull on the cord or do anything that will tighten it.

If your baby's face is covered by intact membranes, otherwise known as 'in the veil', you must break it to allow the baby to breath. Do not panic as the cord will supply oxygen for about 5 minutes after birth. However, if the baby's face is blue, then it really needs to breathe NOW.

If your baby is still not breathing, hold it upside down and give it a gentle slap on the buttocks or bottoms of the feet. This will help move any goo that may be still in the nose and mouth.

When you are sure the baby is breathing, the next step is to make sure it doesn't chill. Wrapping in a cool blanket won't help as babies don't make heat well at first and will lose heat to the blanket. Have the blankets warmed if possible, or put the naked baby inside your clothing next to your warm body, making sure the head has access to air.

To encourage your baby to nurse, touch the side of its mouth to your nipple. If you can get it to nurse, this will warm it and the act of sucking will help move any mucus in the mouth.

By this time you will have probably delivered the afterbirth, which will have the cord attached. There is no rush with the cord, make sure the other priorities are met first. Wait until there is no more pulse in the cord, then tie it at two points – one close to the belly, and one a few cm down. Then cut between the two knots. Leave the floppy end as is, it will dry up and fall off in due time. Ensure the tool you use to cut the cord is thoroughly cleaned to prevent infection.

3 WATER PROCUREMENT

Water is one of your most urgent needs in a survival situation. You can't live long without it, especially in hot areas where you lose water rapidly through perspiration. Even in cold areas, you need a minimum of 2 litres of clean water each day to maintain efficiency.

More than three-quarters of your body is composed of fluids. Your body loses fluid as a result of heat, cold, stress, and exertion. To function effectively, you must replace the fluid your body loses. So, one of your first goals is to obtain an adequate supply of water.

3.1 WATER SOURCES

Almost any environment has water present to some degree. This table lists possible sources of water in various environments. It also provides information on how to make the water potable (drinkable).

SOURCES OF WATER AND MEANS OF OBTAINING AND/OR MAKING DRINKABLE

Frigid Areas	Snow and ice	Melting: **DO NOT** eat snow or ice without melting! Eating snow and ice can reduce body temperature and lead to more dehydration.
		Snow and ice are no purer than the water from which they came.
		Sea ice that is grey or opaque is salty. Do not use without desalting it. Sea ice that is clear with a bluish colour has little ice in it.
At Sea	Seawater	Use desalination kit or still. **NEVER** drink straight seawater, ever.
	Rain	Catch in tarps or containers. If the tarp or containers have become encrusted with salt, wash in seawater first. Very little salt will remain.
	Sea Ice	See above remarks for frigid areas.
Beach	Ground	Dig a hole deep enough to allow water to seep in, or fill a container with seawater. Heat rocks in a fire and drop in water. Absorb steam with cloth and wring out.
		Fresh water can often be obtained by digging behind sand dunes. Normally water is found at 1 – 3 metres.
	Sandstone cliffs	Freshwater soaks can sometimes be found on the seaward side of sandstone cliffs. These are usually indicated by a fault or crack in the cliff, plus a gathering of ferns and mosses.
Desert	Ground	• In valleys and low areas • concave banks of dry river beds • at foot of cliffs or rock outcrops • at first depression behind first sand dune of dry desert lakes • wherever you find damp surface sand • wherever you find green vegetation	Dig holes deep enough to allow water to seep in. In a sand dune belt, any available water will be found beneath the original valley floor at the edge of dunes.
	Cacti	Cut off the top of a barrel cactus and mash, squeeze or suck the pulp. **CAUTION!** Do not eat pulp. Suck out juice and discard. Without a machete, cutting into a cactus is difficult because of the long spines and tough rind.
	Depressions or holes in rocks	Periodic rainfall may collect in pools, seep into fissures, or collect in holes in rocks. Water can be obtained from fissures or porous rock with a length of flexible tubing.

Condensation on metal	Extreme temperature variations between night and day may cause condensation on metal surfaces.
	Use a flat piece of metal or plastic to scrape the droplets over the edge and collect in a container. Alternatively use cloth to absorb water, and then wring or suck the water from the cloth.

Following are signs to watch for in the desert to help you find water:

- All trails lead to water. You should follow in the direction in which the trails converge. Signs of camps, campfire ashes, animal droppings, and trampled terrain may mark trails.
- Flocks of birds will circle over water holes. Some birds fly to water holes at dawn and sunset. Their flight at these times is generally fast and close to the ground. Birds tracks or chirping sounds in the evening or early morning sometimes indicate that water is nearby

If you do not have a canteen, a cup, a can, or other type of container, improvise one from plastic or water-resistant cloth. Shape the plastic or cloth into a bowl by pleating it. Use pins or other suitable items – even your hands – to hold the pleats.

If you do not have a reliable source to replenish your water supply, stay alert for ways in which your environment can help you.

DO NOT use the following fluids as a substitute for water —

Alcohol	Dehydrates the body, depletes motor skills, reaction time and judgement.
Urine	Despite what you may have seen in German pornography, it is never a good idea to drink urine. It contains harmful body wastes and is about 2 percent salt.
Blood	Is salty and consider a food; therefore, requires additional body fluids to digest. Blood may also transmit disease.
Seawater	Is about 4 percent salt. It takes about 2 litres of body fluids to rid the body of waste from 1 litre of seawater. Therefore, by drinking seawater you deplete your body's water supply, which can very quickly cause death.

Heavy dew can provide water. Tie rags or tufts of fine grass around your ankles and walk through dew-covered grass before sunrise. As the dew is absorbed, wring the water into a container. Repeat the process until you have a supply of water or until the dew is gone.

Bees or ants going into a hole in a tree may point to a water-filled hole. Siphon the water with plastic tubing or scoop it up with an improvised dipper. You can also stuff cloth in the hole to absorb the water and then wring it from the cloth.

Water sometimes gathers in tree crotches or rock crevices. Use the above procedures to get the water. In arid areas, bird droppings around a crack in the rocks may indicate water in or near the crack.

3.1.1 WATER FROM VEGETABLE SOURCES

Green bamboo thickets are an excellent source of fresh water. Water from green bamboo is clear and odourless. To get the water, bend a green bamboo stalk, tie it down, and cut off the top. The water will drip freely during the night. Old, cracked bamboo may contain water.

Note – The water should be purified before drinking.

Wherever you find banana or plantain trees, you can get water. Cut down the tree, leaving about a 30-centimeter stump, and scoop out the centre of the stump so that the hollow is bowl-shaped. Water from the roots will immediately start to fill the hollow. The first three fillings of water will be bitter, but succeeding fillings will be palatable. The stump will supply water for up to four days. Be sure to cover it to keep out insects.

Some tropical vines can give you water. Cut a notch in the vine as high as you can reach, then cut the vine off close to the ground. Catch the liquid in a container or your mouth.

Many trees can be used for water no matter how dry conditions are. The best way to get water from a tree is to drain the roots. Do this by digging them up at dawn when the tree has finished its night dew-collecting. Cut them at a 45° angle into 1 meter lengths (3 feet) and hang them over a container.

WATER FROM GREEN BAMBOO

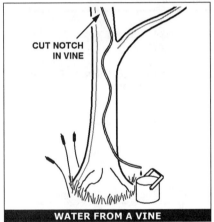

CUT NOTCH IN VINE

WATER FROM A VINE

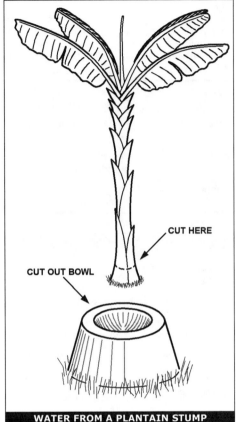

CUT HERE

CUT OUT BOWL

WATER FROM A PLANTAIN STUMP

You can get water from plants with moist pulpy centres. Cut off a section of the plant and squeeze or smash the pulp so that the moisture runs out. Catch the liquid in a container.

Fleshy leaves, stems, or stalks, such as bamboo, contain water. Cut or notch the stalks at the base of a joint to drain out the liquid.

Plant roots may provide water. Dig or pry the roots out of the ground, cut them into short pieces, and smash the pulp so that the moisture runs out. Catch the liquid in a container. Use a piece of bark or other material to create a 'gutter' for collection.

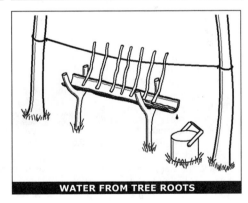

WATER FROM TREE ROOTS

CAUTION – Do not drink the water from roots or vines if it is sticky, milky or bitter tasting. Do not let the water-sap mixture stand as it may contain natural sugars and can ferment. Use it immediately.

The milk from green (unripe) coconuts is a good thirst quencher. However, the milk from mature coconuts contains oil that acts as a laxative. Drink in moderation only.

In the tropics you may find large trees whose branches support air plants. These air plants may hold a considerable amount of rainwater in their overlapping, thickly growing leaves. Strain the water through a cloth to remove insects and debris.

The following trees can also provide water —

Palms	Palms, such as the buri, coconut, sugar, rattan, and nips, contain liquid. Bruise a lower frond and pull it down so the tree will "bleed" at the injury.
Travellers tree	Found in Madagascar, this tree has a cuplike sheath at the base of its leaves in which water collects.
Umbrella tree	The leaf bases and roots of this tree of western tropical Africa can provide water.
Boabab	This tree of the sandy plains of northern Australia and Africa collects water in its bottlelike trunk during the wet season.

Frequently, you can find clear, fresh water in these trees after weeks of dry weather.

3.2 STILL CONSTRUCTION

You can use stills in various areas of the world. They draw moisture from the ground and from plant material. You need certain materials to build a still, and you need time to let it collect the water. It takes about 24 hours to get 0.5 to 1 litre (1 to 2 pints) of water.

3.2.1 ABOVEGROUND STILL

To make the aboveground still, you need a sunny slope on which to place the still, a clear plastic bag, green leafy vegetation, and a small rock.

To make the still –

- Fill the bag with air and 3/4 full of green vegetation.
- Remove all hard sticks or sharp spines that might puncture the bag.
- Place a weight in the bag.
- Close the bag and tie the mouth securely as close to the end of the bag as possible to keep the maximum amount of air.
- If you have a piece of tubing, a small straw, or a hollow reed, insert one

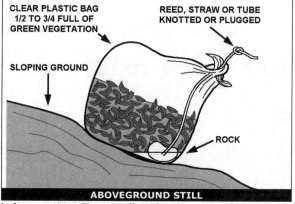

ABOVEGROUND STILL

end in the mouth of the bag before you tie it. Then tie off or plug the tubing so that air will not escape. This tubing will allow you to drain out condensed water without untying the bag.

- Place the bag, mouth downhill, on a slope in full sunlight. Position the mouth of the bag slightly higher than the low point in the bag.
- Settle the bag in place so that the rock works itself into the low point in the bag.

To get the condensed water from the still, loosen the tie around the bag's mouth and tip the bag so that the water collected around the rock will drain out. Then retie the mouth securely and reposition the still to allow further condensation.

Change the vegetation in the bag after extracting most of the water from it. This will ensure maximum output of water.

3.2.2 BELOWGROUND STILL

To make a belowground still, you need a digging tool, a container, a clear plastic sheet, a drinking tube, and a rock.

Select a site where soil will contain moisture (such as a dry stream bed or a low spot where rainwater has collected). Sunlight must hit the site most of the day.

To construct the still —

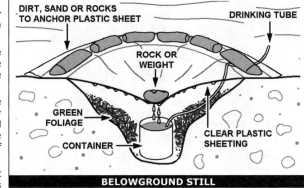

BELOWGROUND STILL

- Dig a hole about 1 meter (3 ft) across and 60 cm (2 ft) deep.

- Dig a sump in the centre of the hole to fit the container. Place the container in.

- Anchor the tubing to the container's bottom by forming a loose overhand knot in the tubing. Pull the other end over the lip of the hole.

- Place the plastic sheet over the hole, covering its edges with soil, sand or rocks to hold it in place.

- Place a weight in the centre of the plastic sheet. Make sure it doesn't puncture the plastic.

- Lower the plastic sheet into the hole until it is about 40 cm (15 in) below ground level. It now forms an inverted cone with the rock at its apex. Make sure that the cone's apex is directly over your container. Also make sure the plastic cone does not touch the sides of the hole because the earth will absorb the condensed water.

- Put more soil on the edges of the plastic to hold it securely and prevent moisture loss.

- Prevent moisture from evaporating from the tube by folding the end over and tying.

- You can use plants as a moisture source. If so, dig out additional soil from the sides of the hole to form a slope on which to place the plants.

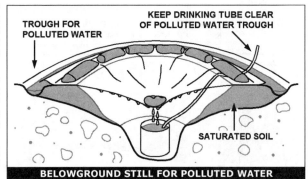

BELOWGROUND STILL FOR POLLUTED WATER

If polluted water is your only source, dig a small trough outside the hole about 20 cm (8 in) from the still's lip. Dig the trough about 20 cm deep and 8 cm (3 in) wide.

Pour the polluted water in the trough. Be sure you do not spill any polluted water around the rim of the hole where the plastic sheet touches the soil.

The trough holds the polluted water and the soil filters it as the still draws it through.

The water then condenses and drains into the container. This works well with salt water.

You will need at least three stills to meet your individual daily water intake needs.

3.2.3 COOKING POT STILL

If you have the materials, a cooking pot still can be improvised —

- Place a small container in the centre of a cooking pot. Place a rock or other heavy item in the small container so it does not float.

- Pour contaminated water around the small container. Only put in enough to fill the small container. Too much water will bubble up ('spew') into the small container.

- Place the lid of the pot upside-down on the top or fashion an inverted lid from aluminium foil. Plastic sheet or wrap can also be used if weighed down and tied on with cord.
- Place the pot on a fire and wait for the water to boil and collect in the container. If using plastic for the lid, wait until the fire dies to coals to prevent the plastic melting.

3.2.4 PRECAUTIONS FOR DISTILLED WATER

When drinking distilled water exclusively there is a long term danger of nutrients absorbing into the water and leaching from your body. This is only a danger if your food intake is almost zero over many months. In this situation add a small amount of sea salt or sea water (you should barely taste it) to all the water you drink. Sea salt is an excellent source of vitamins and minerals. Multivitamin tablets will also be of great help but cannot last forever.

3.3 WATER PURIFICATION

Rainwater collected in clean containers or in plants is usually safe for drinking. However, heavy pollutants in the atmosphere such as iron ore dust or volcanic ash may render all water sources unhealthy. Ideally all water sources should be distilled. At the very least boil and filter your water until the rain runs clear again.

Non-contaminated water can be purified by —

- Using water purification tablets. (Follow the directions provided).
- Placing 5 drops of 2 percent tincture of iodine in a canteen full of clear water. If the canteen is full of cloudy or cold water, use 10 drops. (Let the canteen of water stand for 30 minutes before drinking).
- Boiling water for 5 minutes will kill any virus or bacteria that you are likely to encounter.
- Clorox Bleach. Use 2 drops per litre (quart). 8 drops per 4 litres (gallon). 1/2 teaspoon per 20 litres (5 gallons). Double these amounts for cloudy water. Let stand for 30 mins.

By drinking polluted water you may contract diseases or swallow organisms that can harm you. Examples of such diseases or organisms are —

Dysentery	Severe, prolonged diarrhoea with bloody stools, fever, and weakness.
Cholera & typhoid	You may be susceptible to these diseases regardless of inoculations.
Flukes	Stagnant, polluted water – especially in tropical areas – often contains blood flukes. If you swallow flukes, they will bore into the bloodstream, live as parasites, and cause disease.
Leeches	If you swallow a leech, it can hook onto the throat passage or inside the nose. It will suck blood, create a wound, and move to another area. Each bleeding wound may become infected.

3.4 WATER FILTRATION DEVICES

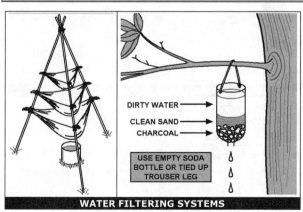

DIRTY WATER →
CLEAN SAND →
CHARCOAL →

USE EMPTY SODA BOTTLE OR TIED UP TROUSER LEG

WATER FILTERING SYSTEMS

If water is muddy it can be cleared by letting it stand for 12 hours. If it is polluted or stagnant, it must be filtered.

To make a filtering system, place layers of filtering material such as sand, crushed rock, charcoal, or cloth in bamboo, a hollow log, a soda bottle, or cloth.

Remove the odour from water by adding charcoal from your fire. Charcoal will absorb a lot of the impurities so remove it from the water. Let the water stand for 45 minutes before drinking it.

4 FOOD PROCUREMENT

After water, your most urgent requirement is food. In contemplating virtually any survival situation, the mind immediately turns to thoughts of food. Unless the situation occurs in an arid environment, even water, which is more important to maintaining body functions, will almost always follow food in our initial thoughts.

4.1 ANIMALS FOR FOOD

Unless you have the chance to take large game, concentrate your efforts on the smaller animals, due to their abundance and ease of preparation. You don't need to know all of the animals that are suitable as food. Few are poisonous, and make a smaller list to remember.

What is important is to learn the habits and behavioural patterns of classes of animals. Animals that are excellent for trapping, that inhabit a particular range and occupy a den or nest, that have somewhat fixed feeding areas, and those that have trails leading from one area to another. Larger, herding animals, such as elk, caribou roam vast areas are somewhat more difficult to trap. Also, you must understand the food choices of a particular species.

You can, with few exceptions, eat anything that crawls, swims, walks, or flies. The first obstacle is overcoming your natural aversion to a particular food source. People in starvation situations will eat everything imaginable. A person who ignores a healthy food source due to a personal bias is risking their own survival.

A highly nutritious and abundant source of food is insects and worms. Do not overlook this valuable resource. See **Critters for Food** (Page 4-4) for details.

4.1.1 MAMMALS

Mammals are an excellent protein source and (arguably) the tastiest food. There are some drawbacks to obtaining mammals. When trying to lay low, others may detect any traps or snares placed on land. All mammals have teeth and nearly all will bite in self-defence. Even a squirrel can inflict a serious wound and any bite presents a serious risk of infection. Also note that a mother can be extremely aggressive in defence of her young, and any animal with no route of escape will fight, ferociously, when cornered.

All mammals are edible; however, some arctic creatures have toxic levels of vitamin A in their livers. The platypus, native to Australia and Tasmania, is an egg-laying, semi-aquatic mammal that has poisonous glands. Scavenging mammals, such as the opossum, may carry diseases.

4.1.2 REPTILES

Reptiles are a good protein source and are relatively easy to catch. You should cook them, but in an emergency, you can eat them raw. Their raw flesh may transmit parasites, but because reptiles are cold-blooded, they do not carry the blood diseases of the warm-blooded animals.

The box turtle is a common turtle that you should not eat. It feeds on poisonous mushrooms and may build up a toxic poison in its flesh. Cooking does not destroy this toxin. Avoid the hawksbill turtle, found in the Atlantic Ocean, because of its poisonous thorax gland. Poisonous snakes, alligators, crocodiles, and large sea turtles present obvious hazards to the survivor.

4.1.3 CRUSTACEANS

Freshwater shrimp range in from 0.25 – 2.5 cm (1/10 to 1 in). They can form rather large colonies in mats of floating algae or in mud bottoms of ponds and lakes.

Crayfish are active at night, but you can locate them in the daytime by looking under and around stones in streams. You can also find them by looking in the soft mud near the chimney like breathing holes of their nests. You can catch crayfish by tying bits of offal or internal organs to a string. When the crayfish grabs the bait, pull it to shore before it has a chance to release the bait.

You find saltwater lobsters, crabs, and shrimp from the surf's edge out to water 10 meters deep. Shrimp may come to a light at night where you can scoop them up with a net. You can catch lobsters and crabs with a baited trap or a baited hook. Crabs will come to bait placed at the edge of the surf, where you can trap or net them. Lobsters and crabs are nocturnal and caught best at night.

4.1.4 MOLLUSCS

This class includes octopuses and freshwater and saltwater shellfish such as snails, clams, mussels, bivalves, barnacles, periwinkles, chitons, and sea urchins. You find bivalves similar to freshwater mussel and terrestrial and aquatic snails worldwide under all water conditions.

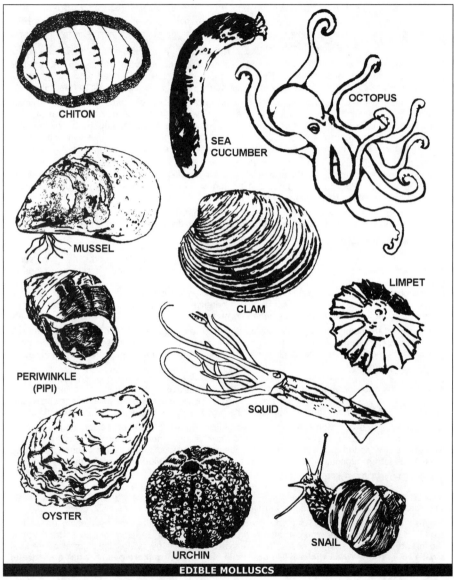

CHITON

SEA CUCUMBER

OCTOPUS

MUSSEL

CLAM

LIMPET

PERIWINKLE (PIPI)

SQUID

OYSTER

URCHIN

SNAIL

EDIBLE MOLLUSCS

River snails or freshwater periwinkles are plentiful in rivers, streams, and lakes of northern coniferous forests. These snails may be pencil point or globular in shape.

In fresh water, look for molluscs in the shallows, especially in water with a sandy or muddy bottom. Look for the narrow trails they leave in the mud or for the dark elliptical slit of their open valves.

Near the sea, look in the tidal pools and the wet sand. Rocks along beaches or extending as reefs into deeper water often bear clinging shellfish. Snails and limpets cling to rocks and seaweed from the low water mark upward. Large snails, called chitons, adhere tightly to rocks above the surf line.

Mussels usually form dense colonies in rock pools, on logs, or at the base of boulders.

 CAUTION – Mussels may be poisonous in tropical zones during the summer! Mussels should open when you cook them – if they don't, do not eat them.

Steam, boil, or bake molluscs in the shell. They make excellent stews in combination with greens and tubers.

CAUTION – Do not eat shellfish that are not covered by water at high tide!

4.1.5 BIRDS

All species of birds are edible, although the flavour will vary considerably. You may skin fish-eating birds to improve their taste. As with any wild animal, you must understand birds' habits to have a chance of capturing them. You can take pigeons and some other species from their roost at night by hand. During the nesting season, some species will not leave the nest even when approached. Knowing where and when the birds nest makes catching them easier.

Birds tend to have regular flyways going from the roost to a feeding area, to water, and so forth. Careful observation should reveal where these flyways are and indicate good areas for catching birds in nets stretched across the flyways. Roosting sites and waterholes are some of the most promising areas for trapping or snaring.

TYPES OF BIRDS	FREQUENT NESTING PLACES	NESTING PERIODS
Inland birds	Trees, woods, or fields	Spring and early summer in temperate and artic regions; year round in the tropics
Crane and herons	Mangrove swamps or high trees near water	Spring and early summer
Some species of owls	High trees	From summer to early autumn
Ducks, geese, and swans	Tundra areas near ponds, rivers, or lakes	Spring and early summer in arctic regions
Some sea birds	Sandbars or low sand island	Spring and early summer intemperate and artic regions
Gulls, auks, murres, and cormorants	Steep rocky coasts	Spring and early summer in temperate and arctic regions

Nesting birds present another food source – eggs. Remove all but two or three eggs from the clutch, marking the ones that you leave. The bird will continue to lay more eggs to fill the clutch. Continue removing the fresh eggs, leaving the ones you marked.

4.1.6 AMPHIBIANS

Frogs and salamanders are easily found around bodies of fresh water. Frogs seldom move from the water's edge. At the first sign of danger, they plunge into the water and bury themselves in the mud and debris. There are few poisonous species of frogs. Avoid any brightly coloured frog or any that have a distinct "X" mark on their back. Do not confuse toads with frogs. You normally find toads in drier environments. Several species of toads secrete a poisonous substance through their skin as a defence against attack. Therefore, to avoid poisoning, do not handle, eat or lick toads.

Salamanders are nocturnal. The best time to catch them is at night using a light. They can range in size from a few cm (1 in) to well over 60 cm (2 ft) in length. Look in water around rocks and mud banks for salamanders.

4.1.7 FISH

Fish represent a good source of protein and fat. They offer some distinct advantages to the survivor or evader. They are usually more abundant than mammal wildlife, and the ways to get them are usually silent. To be successful at catching fish, you must know their habits. For instance, fish tend to feed heavily before a storm. Fish are not likely to feed after a storm when the water is muddy and swollen. Light often attracts fish at night. When there is a heavy current, fish will rest in places where there is an eddy, such as near rocks. Fish will also gather where there are deep pools, under overhanging brush, and in and around submerged foliage, logs, or other objects that offer them shelter.

There are no poisonous freshwater fish. However, the catfish species has sharp, needle like protrusions. These can inflict painful puncture wounds that quickly become infected.

Cook all freshwater fish to kill parasites. Also cook saltwater fish caught within a reef or within the influence of a freshwater source as a precaution. Any marine life obtained farther out in the sea will not contain parasites because of the saltwater environment. You can eat these raw.

Certain saltwater species of fish have poisonous flesh. In some species the poison occurs seasonally in others, it is permanent. Examples of poisonous saltwater fish are the porcupine fish, triggerfish, cowfish, thorn fish, oilfish, red snapper, jack, and puffer. The barracuda, while not actually poisonous itself, may transmit ciguatera (fish poisoning) if eaten raw.

4.2   CRITTERS FOR FOOD

Insects are the most abundant form of life on earth. They are easy to find and catch and contain more protein per weight than beef, chicken, pork or lamb. Many insects are far cleaner than other animals as they only eat clean vegetable matter. Compare this to the diet of bottom-feeders like crabs, lobsters, catfish and sharks that eat foul decomposing matter.

4.2.1 WHAT TO AVOID

You should avoid eating creatures with the following characteristics –

- Insects that sting or bite. (their larvae is OK)
- Insects that are covered in hair.
- Insects that are brightly coloured.
- Insects that are already dead.

- Spiders and anything else with 8+ legs.
- Disease carrying creatures like Flies, mosquitoes, ticks, caterpillars.
- Any insect with a strong odour.

The above list will exclude some critters that are edible, erring on the safe side. Bees and wasps are OK after a good boiling. The poison is a protein which breaks down at boiling temperatures, the stinger will also soften.

Large tarantulas are safe to eat and taste much like crab. Throw them straight on a bed of coals to cook them and burn off the hairs. Be sure to suck or split the meat from their legs.

CAUTION – Be aware when eating a new type of insect that there may be an unknown allergy.
So try only one new type of insect at a time and in small amounts.

4.2.2 PREPARING INSECTS TO EAT

Although most insects can be eaten raw, it is advisable to cook them. Cooking will improve the taste, and minimise the risk of illness. Any insect with a hard outer shell (grasshoppers, crickets, beetles etc) absolutely must be cooked because they tend to carry parasites.

Mixing bugs in with other edibles will disguise the look and mask the taste, especially if spices are used. You can also grind cooked insects into a paste or powder to use with other foods.

Preparing for Cooking

To prepare insects for cooking, it is easier if they are dead first. This can be easily achieved by wrapping a bunch of them in a porous material (like cheesecloth) and dunking them under water for a minute or ten. This will also rinse off extraneous dirt and possible pesticides.

Once dead, remove all the parts that are not suitable for eating such as heads, wings and legs.

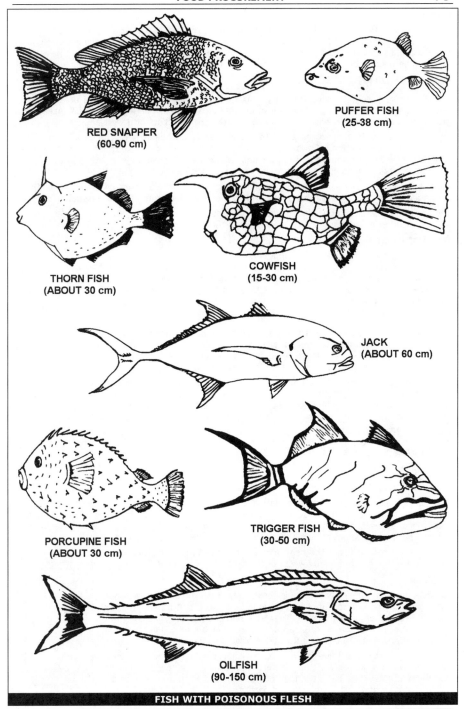

RED SNAPPER
(60-90 cm)

PUFFER FISH
(25-38 cm)

THORN FISH
(ABOUT 30 cm)

COWFISH
(15-30 cm)

JACK
(ABOUT 60 cm)

PORCUPINE FISH
(ABOUT 30 cm)

TRIGGER FISH
(30-50 cm)

OILFISH
(90-150 cm)

FISH WITH POISONOUS FLESH

Insect Flour

To make insect flour, the first step is to dry them thoroughly in an oven on a medium heat – around 90°C (200°F). Let them dry until they are brittle and can be easily crushed. Then grind them using a grain mill, coffee grinder, blender, mortar & pestle or whatever you have. This flour can be used in breads, soups, stews or anything you can imagine.

4.2.3 ACQUIRING INSECTS

Insects are very easy to find. The best places are generally dark, undisturbed areas such as under rocks or logs. Rotting wood will often contain termites, beetles and grubs. Areas with grass, soil and vegetation will contain more insects than mud flats or desert areas.

The golden rule of food procurement is to never expend more energy catching food than it will return upon consumption. If food is scarce, always be on the lookout for insects. Keep a container with you as you go about your daily activities and grab bugs as you see them. This way you are not expending any extra time or energy and can collect quite a few over time.

Indians would drive herds of grasshoppers across a field toward another group who would wait with dried grass in a row across the field, which they would light and fry the insects on site.

People in Bali catch dragonflies by dipping strips of palmwood in sticky sap. By running through rice fields and waving the sticks through the air, dragonflies would stick to the sap.

Aquatic Insects

To find aquatic insects look under underwater rocks, especially in shallow, fast moving water. Upturn the rocks and get ready with a net. In deeper water use a cloth between two poles under water. Place the net downstream, and then start kicking over rocks upstream to disturb the insects. Aquatic bugs also make excellent bait for fishing – especially if you can keep them alive while fishing with them.

Raising Insects

Mealworms and crickets are easy to raise and can be bought pre-SHTF from pet stores and bait shops. Shop-bought insects are usually fed sawdust or newspaper or some other packing material, so before you eat them, feed them grain or starve them for a few days to remove these products from the insects' bodies. They are not harmful, but will affect the taste.

For insects you find in the wild that you wish to cultivate, feed them what they like to eat. This will probably be the vegetation where you find them. Again, if you starve them for 24 hours or more before eating, this will empty their intestinal tracts and improve the taste, though this is not required.

4.2.4 INSECT GUIDE

Mealworms

Mealworms are a good insect for beginners to start on, both for raising and eating. Prepare a flat tub with a lid (plastic is recommended) and spread about 2 cm (1 in) of oats or other grain on the bottom. Add a hard vegetable – such as a carrot or potato to serve as a water source.

They will require frequent, but minimal care. Replace the vegetables before they dry out, or begin to develop mold, and be patient. Mealworms that you buy will be in the larval stage and can take months to develop. A beginners 'farm' will start with about 200 mealworms, a survival farm may require about 5000. Reptile food stores can supply this.

If you are concerned about the possibility of ants infesting your grain, float the tub in a tray or larger tub with a layer of soapy water at the bottom.

Maggots

Maggots are relatively easy to acquire especially in warm climates, and not difficult to catch. A trap can be made out of a large softdrink bottle by cutting the top off and inverting it in the bottle as shown. Place some smelly bait at the bottom of the trap and soon it will be full of flies that will be trapped and have no choice but to lay maggots inside.

FLY TRAP

Once enough maggots have been collected, harvest them from the trap and rinse them thoroughly in salty water. Then they can be cooked. Fry or boil them and they will have the look of wild rice and even a similar taste. When mixed with other food you would barely even know they are there.

Worms

You can find worms by digging in soil in areas with vegetation. Worms like to collect around the roots. We've all seen worms crawling along the ground after a rain, so don't let these critters go to waste. Worms can be eaten raw but they must be soaked (live) in water first to drown them. This will also force them to purge their contents so you won't be eating dirt with the worms.

Grasshoppers

Grasshoppers are a favourite the world over. They are nutritious like most other insects, they also taste good, are abundant and easy to capture. They can be boiled into a soup or dried or fried. Do not eat them live as they can carry parasitic worms.

Crickets

Crickets are easy to raise, but are adept escape artists. They can be kept in a container with tall sides and a tight-fitting lid. A tall enclosure can be made with two plastic tubs – stack one on top of the other and cut the bottom out of the top tub. Seal up any gaps between the two. The taller the enclosure is, the less chance of escape when you open the lid.

Line the bottom of the enclosure with about 5 cm (2 in) soil. The crickets will use the soil to lay eggs. Place water and cotton balls in a shallow dish (so the crickets do not drown). Place food in another dish. Crickets eat almost anything – small nymphs prefer soft food like fruit or lettuce, dry dog food is good for larger crickets.

Place some crumpled paper or something to create hiding places. Frequently add as many crickets as you can and apply misting water to the potting soil. Be sure to keep the food supply fresh, and discard any old food.

Ants

If you boil ants, this will remove the formic acid which they contain. Black ants have a slightly sweet taste, and can even be used to sweeten tea. Experiment.

Beetles

Beetles account for about 40% of the worlds' know insect population. The larvae of some beetles have a very high fat and protein content. These larvae are very tasty.

Wasps and Bees

Pound these creatures first, and then boil them for 2 minutes or more. Their poison is a protein which breaks down with heat. Their larvae are very edible.

Tarantulas

Be careful with these spiders. Tarantulas have barbed 'urticating' hairs on its body which it flings in the face of a chasing predator. Handle the spider carefully, dead or alive. Rub off the hairs of a cooked tarantula before eating – but not with your bare hands. Bald patches on the spider are a sure sign that the creature has these hairs and is not shy about using them.

4.3 TRAPS AND SNARES

For an unarmed survivor, or when the sound of a rifle shot could be a problem, trapping or snaring wild game is a good alternative. Several well-placed traps have the potential to catch much more game than a man with a rifle is likely to shoot. To be effective with any type of trap or snare, you must —

- Be familiar with the species of animal you intend to catch.
- Be capable of constructing a proper trap.
- Not alarm the prey by leaving signs of your presence.

You must determine what species are in a given area and set your traps specifically with those animals in mind. Look for the following –

- Runs and trails.
- Tracks.
- Droppings.

- Chewed or rubbed vegetation.
- Nesting or roosting sites.
- Feeding and watering areas.

Position your traps where you know animals pass through. Determine if it is a 'run' or 'trail.' A trail will show use by several species and will be rather distinct. A run is usually smaller and less distinct and will only contain signs of one species. A perfect snare will not catch anything if haphazardly placed. Animals have bedding areas, waterholes, and feeding areas with trails between. You must place snares and traps around these areas to be effective.

It is important not to create a disturbance that will alarm the animal and cause it to avoid the trap. If you must dig, remove all fresh dirt from the area. Most animals will instinctively avoid a pitfall-type trap. Prepare the various trap parts away from the site, carry them in, and set them up. Such actions make it easier to avoid disturbing the vegetation, thereby alerting the prey. Do not use freshly cut, live vegetation to construct a trap or snare. It may 'bleed' sap that has an odour the prey can smell. It is an alarm signal to the animal.

You must remove or mask the human scent around the trap you set. Although birds do not have a developed sense of smell, nearly all mammals depend on smell even more than on sight. Even the slightest human scent on a trap will alarm the prey and cause it to avoid the area. Actually removing the scent from a trap is difficult but masking it is relatively easy. Use the fluid from the gall and urine bladders of previous kills. Do not use human urine. Mud, particularly from an area with plenty of rotting vegetation, is also good. Use it to coat your hands when handling the trap and to coat the trap when setting it.

Most animals know the smell of burned vegetation and smoke. It is only when a fire is actually burning that they become alarmed. Therefore, smoking the trap parts is an effective means to mask your scent. If one of the above techniques is not practical, and if time permits, allow a trap to weather for a few days and then set it. Do not handle a trap while it is weathering. When you position the trap, camouflage it as naturally as possible to prevent detection by others and to avoid alarming the prey.

Traps or snares placed on a trail or run should use channelisation. To build a channel, construct a funnel-shaped barrier extending from the sides of the trail toward the trap, with the narrowest part nearest the trap. Channelisation should be inconspicuous to avoid alerting the prey. As the animal gets to the trap, it cannot turn left or right and continues into the trap. Few wild animals will back up, preferring to face the direction of travel.

A channel does not have to be an impassable barrier. It only has to be inconvenient to go over or through. For best effect, the channel should reduce the trails width to just slightly wider than the targeted animal's body. Maintain this constriction at least as far back from the trap as the animals body length, then start widening toward the mouth of the funnel.

4.3.1 USE OF BAIT

Baiting a trap or snare increases your chances of catching an animal greatly. When catching fish, you must bait nearly all the devices. Success with an unbaited trap depends on its placement in a good location. A baited trap can actually draw animals to it.

The bait should be something the animal knows. This bait, however, should not be so readily available in the immediate area. For example, baiting a trap with corn in the middle of a corn field would not be likely to work. Likewise, if corn is not grown in the region, a corn-baited trap may arouse an animal's curiosity, but under such circumstances, it may not go for the bait.

Bait that works well on small mammals is peanut butter, another is Vegemite. Salt is also good. When using such baits, scatter bits of it around the trap to give the prey a chance to sample it and develop a craving for it. The animal will then overcome some of its caution before it gets to the trap.

If you bait a trap for one species but another takes the bait without being caught, try to determine what the animal was. Then set a proper trap for that animal, using the same bait.

4.3.2 TRAP AND SNARE CONSTRUCTION

Traps and snares crush, choke, hang, or entangle the prey. A single trap or snare will commonly incorporate two or more of these principles. The mechanisms that provide power to the trap are almost always very simple. The force of gravity, the tension of a bent sapling, or the struggling animal itself provides the power.

The heart of any trap or snare is the trigger. When planning a trap or snare, ask yourself how it should affect the prey, what is the source of power, and what will be the most efficient trigger. Your answers will help you devise a specific trap for a specific species. Traps are designed to catch and hold or to catch and kill. Snares are traps that incorporate a noose to accomplish either function.

Simple Snare

A simple snare consists of a noose placed over a trail or den hole and attached to a stake.

If the noose is some type of cordage placed upright on a game trail, use small twigs or blades of grass to hold it up. Consider filaments from spider webs for holding nooses open because they are strong and difficult to see.

Make sure the noose is large enough to pass freely over the animal's head. As the animal continues to move,

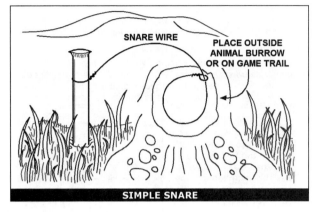

SNARE WIRE · PLACE OUTSIDE ANIMAL BURROW OR ON GAME TRAIL

SIMPLE SNARE

the noose tightens around its neck. The more the animal struggles, the tighter the noose gets.

This type of snare usually does not kill the animal. If you use cordage, it may loosen enough to slip off the animal's neck. Wire is therefore the best choice for a simple snare.

Drag Noose

Use a drag noose on an animal run.

Place forked sticks on either side of the run and lay a sturdy beam across them.

Tie the noose to the cross-beam and hang it at a height above the animal's head. Nooses designed to catch by the head should never be low enough for the prey to step into with a foot.

As the noose tightens around the animal's neck, the animal pulls the cross member from the forked sticks and drags it along. The surrounding vegetation quickly catches the cross member and the animal becomes entangled.

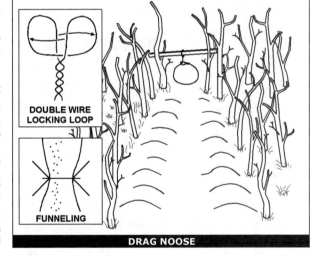

DOUBLE WIRE LOCKING LOOP

FUNNELING

DRAG NOOSE

Noosing Wand

A noose wand is useful for capturing roosting birds or small mammals. It requires a patient operator. This is more a weapon than a trap.

It consists of a long pole

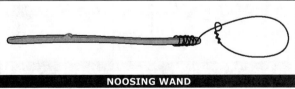

NOOSING WAND

with a slip noose of wire or stiff cordage at the small end. To catch an animal, you slip the noose over the neck and pull it tight. You can also place it over a den hole and conceal yourself nearby. When the animal emerges from the den, jerk the pole to tighten the noose and capture the animal. Carry a sturdy club to kill the prey.

Snare-wire

If you don't have snare wire, enamelled copper wire is cheap and strong and will not corrode over time. Due to the coating the wire is rather shiny so consider coating it with mud or hiding it in debris. You can find wire like this in old transformers, motors, alternators, ignition coils. Most modern electronic equipment will have some coils or transformers inside. Pre-SHTF ask for winding wire in a store (such as Radio Shack or Jaycar) and they'll know what you mean.

Twitch-up

A twitch-up is a flexible sapling, which, when bent over and secured with a triggering device, will provide power to a variety of snares. Select a hardwood sapling along the trail. A twitch-up will work much faster and with more force if you remove all the branches and foliage.

Twitch-up Snare

A simple twitch-up snare uses two forked sticks, each with a long and short leg. Bend the twitch-up and mark the trail below it. Drive the long leg of one forked stick firmly into the ground at that point.

Ensure the cut on the short leg of this stick is parallel to the ground. Tie the long leg of the remaining forked stick to a piece of cordage secured to the twitch-up. Cut the short leg so that it catches on the short leg of the other forked stick.

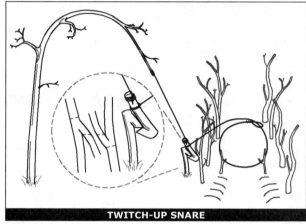

TWITCH-UP SNARE

Extend a noose over the trail. Set the trap by bending the twitch-up and engaging the short legs of the forked sticks. When an animal catches its head in the noose, it pulls the forked sticks apart, allowing the twitch-up to spring up and hang the prey.

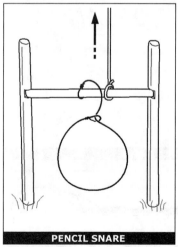

PENCIL SNARE

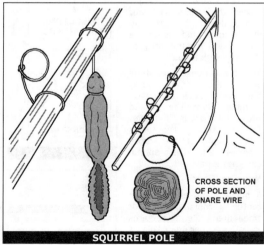

CROSS SECTION OF POLE AND SNARE WIRE

SQUIRREL POLE

Pencil Snare

Set this snare in a game trail. Like a drag noose or simple snare it is effective when you can channel your prey into the loop. Use a bent sapling or improvise to provide the upwards tension. When the animal runs through the loop, the horizontal stick will release from the notches in the vertical poles.

Squirrel Pole

A squirrel pole is placed against a tree in an area showing a lot of squirrel activity. Place nooses along the top and sides of the pole so that a squirrel trying to move along the pole will have to pass through one or more of them.

Position the nooses (5 to 6 cm in diameter) about 2.5 cm off the pole. Place the top and bottom wire nooses 45 cm from the top and bottom of the pole to prevent the squirrel from getting its feet on a solid surface. If this happens, the squirrel will chew through the wire.

Squirrels are naturally curious. After a period of initial caution, they will try to go up or down the pole and will get caught. They will soon fall from the pole and strangle. Others will soon follow and, in this way, you can catch several squirrels. You can place multiple poles to increase the catch.

Ojibwa Bird Pole

An Ojibwa bird pole is a snare used by Native Americans for centuries. To be effective, place it in a relatively open area away from tall trees. For best results, pick a spot near feeding areas, dusting areas, or watering holes.

Cut a pole about 2 meters long and trim away all limbs and foliage. Do not use resinous wood such as pine that may glue parts of the trap together. Sharpen the upper end to a point, and then drill a small diameter hole 5 to 7.5 cm down from the top. Cut a small stick 10 to 15 cm long and shape one end so that it will almost fit into the hole. This is the perch.

Plant the long pole in the ground with the pointed end up. Tie a small weight, about equal to the weight of the targeted species, to a length of cordage.   Or lash a twitch-up as shown to create the tension.

Pass the free end of the cordage through the hole, and tie a slip noose that you lay on the perch.

Tie a single overhand knot in the cordage and place the perch against the hole. Allow the cordage to slip through the hole until the overhand knot rests against the pole and the top of the perch. The tension of the knot against the pole and perch will hold the perch in position.

OJIBWA BIRD POLE

Spread the noose over the perch, ensuring it covers the perch and drapes over on both sides. As soon as the bird lands, the perch will fall, releasing the knot and allowing the tension to pull the noose tight around the bird's feet, capturing it. Note – if there is too much tension, it will cut the bird's feet off, allowing it to escape, miserable.

'Figure-4' Deadfall

The figure-4 is a trigger used to drop a weight such as a large log or rock onto a prey and crush it. The type of weight should be heavy enough to kill or incapacitate the prey.

Construct using three notched sticks. These notches hold the sticks together in a figure-4 pattern when under tension.

This trap can be difficult to set so consider other deadfalls before relying on this one.

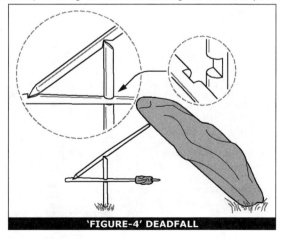

'FIGURE-4' DEADFALL

'Figure-9' Deadfall

A forked stick is placed vertically on the ground. Carve a notch to accept the bait-stick. Bend a sapling around as shown to support the deadfall weight and provide the trigger.

Paiute Deadfall

This deadfall uses a piece of cordage, a top stick and a catch stick.

Tie one end of cordage to the lower end of the top stick. Tie the other end to a stick about 5 cm long. This is the catch stick. Bring the cord halfway around the vertical stick with the catch stick at a 90° angle. Place the bait stick with one end against the drop weight, and the other against the catch stick.

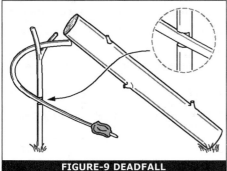

FIGURE-9 DEADFALL

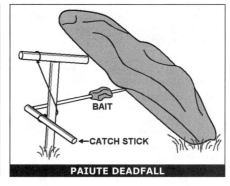

BAIT

←CATCH STICK

PAIUTE DEADFALL

Split-stick Deadfall

To build this trap, take a strong pole and cut it in two pieces. Carve a notch in each of the pieces for a stick to slot into. This trap is very unstable and will trip with only a slight movement of the bait-stick.

With all deadfall traps, it is best to make sure the weight falls directly over the bait, crushing only the head of the prey. Try not to crush other organs, such as the bladder, which will ruin the catch.

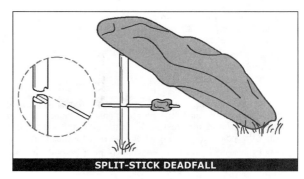

SPLIT-STICK DEADFALL

Beaver Press

This trap is time consuming to construct, but it is semi-permanent and reusable.

The area surrounding the bait-stick is confined by stakes in the ground, or anything else you can find. This area should be only large enough to contain the target animals head. Ideally the weight will fall on the targets neck.

The deadfall weight is held by a vertical stick balanced on the bait-stick. When the bait-stick is disturbed, the vertical stick moves and releases the weight.

GUIDES FOR DEADWEIGHT

BEAVER PRESS

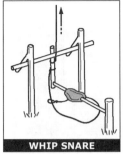
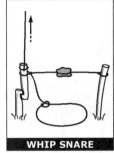

WHIP SNARE | **WHIP SNARE** | **LEVER TWITCH-UP**

Whip Snare

The classic whip snare uses a twitch-up to whip the prey into the air out of reach of predators and away from the ground so it can't pull itself free. The snare is activated when the prey tries to take the bait, pulling the bait rod off the toggle which releases and pulls the snare loop up.

A second whip snare is shown using notched pegs. The flyaway peg is attached to the twitch-up, the snare loop and wire with bait attached. The second peg should be loose in the ground so it releases with the snare loop.

The snare loop should be placed wide enough on the ground to ensure the prey is caught no matter how it approaches the bait.

Alternates to Twitch-Up

If a suitable sapling for a twitch-up is unavailable where you would like to place a trap, many alternatives are available. A heavy weight can be suspended over a tree limb, or a weighted lever may be improvised. A bungee cord can also be used if available.

Treadle Spring Snare

Use a treadle snare against small game on a trail. Dig a shallow hole in the trail. Then drive two forked sticks into the ground on either side of the hole, on the same side of the trail. Make sure the forks are pointed down.

Tie one end of cordage to a twitch-up or weight suspended over a tree limb. Bend the twitch-up down, or raise the suspended weight to determine where to tie to a 10 cm or so trigger stick.

Tie to the stick about half-way along the cordage leaving enough length to form a noose with the rest.

Find two fairly straight

SAPLING

LINE PRESSURE ON TRIGGER STICK HOLDS HORIZONTAL BAR IN PLACE

ANIMAL TRAIL

TREADLE SPRING SNARE

sticks that span the forks. Place one stick under the forks and the other below that. Hold the sticks in place with the trigger stick under tension from the twitch-up or suspended weight. Adjust the bottom stick so that it will barely hold against the trigger.

Place several sticks over the hole with one end on the lower horizontal stick and the other on the ground on the other side of the hole. Place enough sticks so an animal is sure to step on one. Open and spread the noose over the entire trap.

When an animal steps on a stick, the bottom horizontal stick falls and releases the trigger stick. The tension will then pull the noose tight, snaring the animal.

Because of the disturbance on the trail, an animal will be wary. You must therefore channel the trail into your trap and be sure to mask your scent.

Bow Trap

A bow trap is dangerous to man as well as animals. To construct this trap, build a bow and anchor it to the ground with pegs.

Adjust the aiming point as you anchor the bow. Lash a toggle stick to the trigger stick. Two upright sticks driven into the ground hold the trigger stick in place at a point where the toggle stick will engage the pulled bow string.

Place a catch stick between the toggle stick and a stake driven into the ground. Tie a trip wire or cordage to the catch stick and route

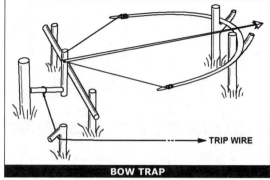

BOW TRAP

it around stakes and across the game trail where you tie it off. When the prey trips the trip wire, the bow will fire an arrow into it. A notch in the bow serves to help aim the arrow.

BOTTLE TRAP

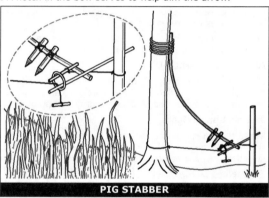

PIG STABBER

Bottle Trap

A bottle trap is a simple trap for mice and voles. Dig a hole 30 - 45 cm deep that is wider at the bottom than at the top. Make the top of the hole as small as possible. Place a piece of bark or wood over the hole with small stones under it to hold it up 2.5 - 5 cm off the ground.

Mice or voles will hide under the cover to escape danger and fall into the hole. They cannot climb out because of the wall's backward slope.

CAUTION – Be careful when checking this trap – it is an excellent hiding place for snakes.

Pig Stabber

To construct the pig stabber, select a sturdy pole about 2.5 meters long. At the smaller end, firmly lash several small stakes. Lash the large end tightly to a tree along the game trail.

Tie a length of cordage to another tree or stake across the trail. Tie a sturdy, smooth stick to the other end of the cord. From the first tree, tie a trip wire or cord low to the ground, stretch it across the trail, and tie it to a catch stick.

Make a slip ring from vines or other suitable material. Encircle the trip wire and the smooth stick with the slip ring. Place one end of another smooth stick within the slip ring and its other end against the second tree. Pull the smaller end of the spear shaft across the trail and position it between the short cord and the smooth stick. As the animal trips the trip wire, the catch stick pulls the slip ring off the smooth sticks, releasing the spear shaft that springs across the trail and impales the prey against the tree.

4.4   KILLING DEVICES

There are simple devices that you can help you obtain small game. The rabbit stick and the spear are such devices. More are described in **Weapons Tools and Equipment** (Chapter 9)

Rabbit Stick

One of the simplest and most effective killing devices is a stout stick as long as your arm, from fingertip to shoulder, called a "rabbit stick." You can throw it overhand or sidearm with considerable force. It is very effective against small game that stops and freezes as a defence.

Spear

For construction and use of a spear, see **Spearfishing** (Page 4-17).

4.5   FISHING DEVICES

You can make your own fishhooks, nets and traps and use several methods to obtain fish.

4.5.1   IMPROVISED FISHHOOKS

Fishhooks can be made from pins, needles, wire, small nails, or any piece of metal, wood, bone, coconut shell, thorns, flint, seashell, tortoise shell or a combination of these.

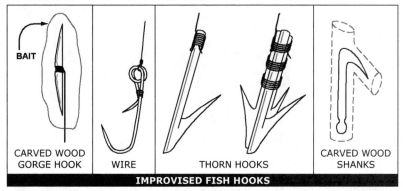

BAIT CARVED WOOD GORGE HOOK	WIRE	THORN HOOKS	CARVED WOOD SHANKS

IMPROVISED FISH HOOKS

To make a wooden hook, cut a piece of hardwood about 2.5 cm long and about 6 mm in diameter to form the shank. Cut a notch in one end in which to place the point. Place the point (piece of bone, wire, or nail) in the notch. Hold the point in the notch and tie securely so that it does not move out of position. This is a fairly large hook. To make smaller hooks, use smaller material.

A gorge is a small shaft of wood, bone, metal, or other material. It is sharp on both ends and notched in the middle where you tie cordage. Bait the gorge by placing a piece of bait on it lengthwise. When the fish swallows the bait, it also swallows the gorge.

4.5.2   IMPROVISED FISHING LURES

Lures can be improvised from any material that will attract the attention of fish. Foil can be fashioned around hooks into the shape of a small fish. Plastic bags or cloth can be torn into strips and attached to the lure to give the impression of tentacles. Sometimes a piece of colourful cloth attached to a hook will catch fish in the right place.

Lures can be carved from wood with hooks lashed to the body. These can be painted or decorated with foil, plastic, colourful feathers or whatever is on hand.

When using lures, cast them out to where there is evidence of fish (visual evidence or splashing in the water) and pull them in at a steady rate. Lures need to move to attract attention. Sometimes the movement of water will do this for you.

4.5.3   LIVE BAIT

When using live bait, be careful not to pierce the spine of the bait fish. Loop the hook under and around the spine to ensure the bait does not become incapacitated.

4.5.4 STAKEOUT

A stakeout is a fishing device you can use in a hostile environment.

To construct a stakeout, drive two supple saplings or reeds into the bottom of the lake, pond, or stream with their tops just below the water surface.

Tie a cord between them

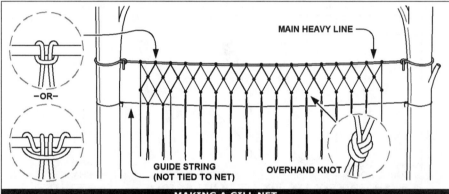

STAKEOUT

and slightly below the surface. Tie two short cords with hooks or gorges to this cord, ensuring that they cannot wrap around the poles or each other. They should also not slip along the long cord – use butterfly or dropper loops in the main line. Bait the hooks or gorges.

4.5.5 GILL NET

You can make a gill net using heavy cord for the main line and thinner cord for the netting.

MAKING A GILL NET

String the main line tightly between two trees or similar upright supports. Attach the thinner cord at even spaces along the line. Each length of thin cord should be approximately 3 times the depth of the desired net, and then doubled over and tied with larks head or prussik knots.

After all of the double vertical lines are tied to the main line, start tying them as shown. The left strand of one vertical line is tied to the right strand of the next one with an overhand knot.

To keep the rows even, tie a guideline to the trees, behind the net you are working on. Move this string line down as you complete each row.

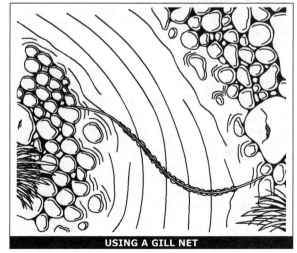

USING A GILL NET

Use the gill net as shown in a bottleneck of a stream. If necessary, channel fish into the gill net using rocks or logs.

4.5.6 CHOP FISHING

At night, in an area with a good fish density, you can use a light to attract fish. Then, armed with a machete or similar weapon, you can gather fish using the back side of the blade to strike them. Do not use the sharp side as you may cut them in two pieces and end up losing some of the fish.

4.5.7 SPEARFISHING

If you are near shallow water where the fish are large and plentiful, you can spear them. To make a spear, cut a long straight sapling and sharpen the end to a point or attach a knife, jagged piece of bone, or sharpened metal.

You can also make a spear by splitting the shaft a few inches down from the end and inserting a piece of wood to act as a spreader. You then sharpen the two separated halves to points.

To spear fish, find an area where fish either gather or where there is a fish run. Place the spear point into the water and slowly move it toward the fish. Then, with a sudden push, impale the fish on the stream bottom.

BAMBOO   METAL   BONE

IMPROVISED SPEARPOINTS

Do not try to lift the fish with the spear, as it with probably slip off and you will lose it. Hold the spear with one hand and grab and hold the fish with the other. Do not throw the spear, especially if the point is a knife. You cannot afford to lose a knife in a survival situation.

Be alert to the problems caused by light refraction when looking at objects in the water. You can compensate for this by moving through the water with the tip submerged.

4.5.8 FISH TRAPS

You may trap fish using several methods. Construct fish baskets by lashing several sticks together into a funnel shape. Close the top, leaving a hole large enough for the fish to swim in, but difficult to swim out. The bait should be suspended in the centre of the basket so fish and crustaceans cannot pick at it from the outside.

You can also use traps to catch saltwater fish, as schools regularly approach the shore with the incoming tide and often move parallel to the shore.

Pick a location at high tide and build the trap at low tide. On rocky shores, use natural rock

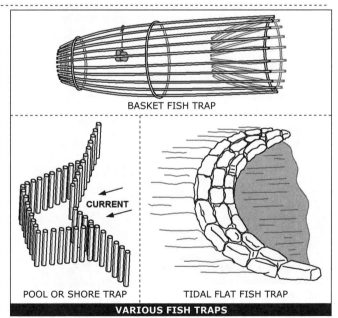

BASKET FISH TRAP

CURRENT

POOL OR SHORE TRAP

TIDAL FLAT FISH TRAP

VARIOUS FISH TRAPS

pools. On coral islands, use natural pools on the surface of reefs by blocking the openings as the tide recedes. On sandy shores, use sandbars and the ditches they enclose.

Build the trap as a low stone wall extending outward into the water and forming an angle with the shore.

Arrowhead Fish Trap

This is a permanent trap which will provide ample supply of fish in all seasons under ideal conditions.

It is suitable for coastal areas where the difference between high tide and low tide is 1-2 metres.

Select a site where the beach slopes evenly. Run a fence of wire netting that will be above the high water mark and will have at least 30 cm water at the low water mark. If wire netting is not available, poles can be used as long as they are close together and hammered in deep enough to hold steady with the movement of the water.

From the low water end run the 'arrowhead' back towards the high water end at about 45°, up to about the mid water mark. Complete construction as pictured. Clear the trap at low tide, taking only the fish that you need. Leave the rest alive in the trap. Some will undoubtedly escape at high tide, but others will remain trapped.

Tidal Rockpool Trap

These traps are useful on rocky shorelines. Find a site where there are rockpools that are well covered at high tide, and almost dry at low tide. Bait the pool heavily with crushed up shellfish and things like that.

Build a wall at the normal opening that will be well covered at high tide and above the water at low tide. The wall can be made from rocks, driftwood or other available material.

The fish with gather to feed at night during a high tide and will remain trapped when the water level drops. You can them gather them by hand or with a net.

Drum Net Fish Trap

A drum net is a cylindrical wire cage with inverted cone-shaped entrances at each end. These entrances allow easy entry for the fish, but make it difficult to escape.

You can place the trap mid-stream, or dropped into a deep river pool or anywhere where fish regularly feed.

Almost any bait will do. Stinky inedible meat or fish works well. If possible suspend the bait in the centre of the trap so fish and other creatures must enter to feed, rather than pick it out through the mesh.

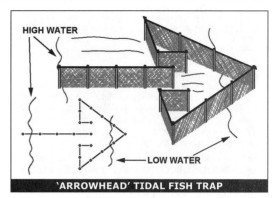

'ARROWHEAD' TIDAL FISH TRAP

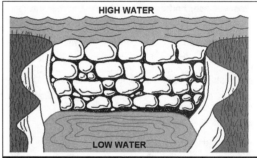

TIDAL ROCKPOOL TRAP

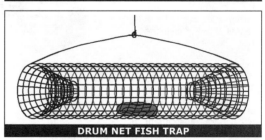

DRUM NET FISH TRAP

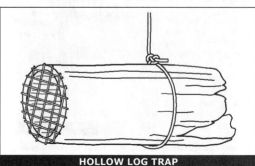

HOLLOW LOG TRAP

Hollow Log Trap

This trap can work because most fish cannot swim backwards. Cover a hollow log at one end with netting or other material which allows water to flow through freely. Make sure the log is not large enough to allow fish to turn around. Tie a rope securely towards the open end so when you pull it upwards, the fish is forced toward the netting. When you pull it up, do so in one smooth motion. Don't forget to bait it.

Crayfish or Yabby Snare

Make a circle out of heavy gauge wire about 30-50 cm in diameter. Keep it rigid with two crosspieces of equally heavy material. Tie a series of running nooses, no more than 5 cm diameter, around the perimeter. Heavy nylon fishing line is a good material to use.

Tie the bait to the centre and fix three or four cords to the outside and to a central rope to drop in and pull the trap up. If necessary, use heavy stones to weigh the trap down, although a bit of movement can help with snaring the prey.

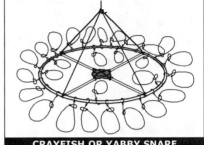

CRAYFISH OR YABBY SNARE

4.5.9 FISH POISON

Another way to catch fish is by using poison. Poison works quickly and allows you to remain concealed while it takes effect. It also enables you to catch several fish at one time. Some plants that grow in warm regions of the world contain rotenone, a substance that stuns or kills cold-blooded animals but does no harm to people who eat the animals.

ANAMIRTAS COCCULUS

This woody vine grows in southern Asia and on islands of the South Pacific.

Crush the bean-shaped seeds and throw them in the water.

CROTON TIGLIUM

This shrub or small tree grows in waste areas on islands of the South Pacific. It bears seeds in 3-angled pods.

Crush the seeds and throw them into the water.

BARRINGTONIA

These large trees grow near the sea in Malaya and parts of Polynesia. They bear a fleshy one-seeded fruit. Crush the seeds and bark and throw into the water.

DERRIS ELLIPTICA

This large genus of tropical shrubs and woody vines is the main source of commercial rotenone.

Grind the roots into a powder and mix with water. Throw a large quantity of the mixture into the water.

DUBOISIA	TEPHROSIA
 This shrub grows in Australia and bears white clusters of flowers and berrylike fruit. Crush the plants and throw them into the water.	 This species of small shrubs, which bears beanlike pods, grows through-out the tropics. Crush or bruise bundles of leaves and stems and throw them into the water.

OTHER SOURCES

- **LIME:** You can get lime from commercial sources and in agricultural areas. You may produce your own by burning coral or seashells. Throw the lime into the water.
- **NUT HUSKS:** Crush green husks from butternuts or black walnuts then throw into the water.

SOURCES OF FISH POISON

The best place to use rotenone is in ponds or the headwaters of small streams containing fish. Rotenone works quickly on fish in water 20°C (70°F) or above. The fish rise helplessly to the surface.

It works slowly in water 10 - 20°C (50 - 70°F) and is ineffective in water below 10°C (50°F).

4.6　PREPARATION OF FISH AND GAME

You must know how to prepare fish and game for cooking and storage in a survival situation. Improper cleaning or storage can result in inedible flesh.

Fish

Do not eat fish that appears spoiled. Cooking does not ensure that spoiled fish will be edible. Signs of spoilage are:

- Sunken eyes.
- Strange odour.
- Suspicious colour. (Gills should be red to pink. Scales should be a pronounced shade of grey, not faded).
- Dents stay in the fish's flesh after pressing it with your thumb.
- Slimy, rather than moist or wet body.
- Sharp or peppery taste.

1. GRIP THE DEAD SNAKE FIRMLY BEHIND THE HEAD

2. CUT AT LEAST 15 cm BEHIND THE HEAD

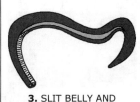

3. SLIT BELLY AND REMOVE INNARDS

4. SKIN

CLEANING A SNAKE

Eating spoiled or rotten fish may cause diarrhoea, nausea, cramps, vomiting, itching, paralysis, or a metallic taste in the mouth. These symptoms appear suddenly, one to six hours after eating. Induce vomiting if symptoms appear.

Fish spoils quickly after death, especially on a hot day. Prepare fish for eating as soon as possible after catching it. Cut out the gills and large blood vessels that lie near the spine. Gut fish that is more than 10 cm long. Scale or skin the fish.

You can impale a whole fish on a stick and cook it over an open fire. However, boiling the fish with the skin on is the best way to get the most food value. The fats and oil are under the skin and, by boiling, you can save the juices for broth. You can use any of the methods used to cook plant food to cook fish. Pack fish into a ball of clay and bury it in the coals of a fire until the clay hardens. Break open the clay ball to get to the cooked fish. Fish is done when the meat flakes off. If you plan to keep the fish for later, smoke or fry it. To prepare fish for smoking, cut off the head and remove the backbone.

Snakes

To skin a snake, first cut off its head and bury it. Then cut the skin down the body 15 - 20 cm. Peel the skin back, then grasp the skin in one hand and the body in the other and pull apart. On large, bulky snakes it may be necessary to slit the belly skin. Cook snakes in the same manner as small game. Remove the entrails and discard. Cut the snake into small sections and boil or roast it.

Birds

After killing the bird, remove its feathers by either plucking or skinning. Remember, skinning removes some of the food value. Open up the body cavity and remove its entrails, saving the craw (in seed-eating birds), heart, and liver. Cut off the feet. Cook by boiling or roasting over a spit. Before cooking scavenger birds, boil them at least 20 minutes to kill parasites.

4.6.1 SKINNING AND BUTCHERING GAME

Bleed the animal by cutting its throat. If possible, clean the carcass near a stream. Place the carcass belly up and split the hide from throat to tail, cutting around all sexual organs. Remove the musk glands to avoid tainting the meat.

For smaller mammals, cut the hide around the body and insert two fingers under the hide on both sides of the cut and pull both pieces off.

Remove the entrails from smaller game by splitting the body open and pulling them out with the fingers.

Do not forget the chest cavity. For larger game, cut the gullet away from the diaphragm.

Roll the entrails out of the body. Cut around the anus, and then reach into the lower abdominal cavity, grasp the lower intestine, and pull to remove.

Remove the urine bladder by pinching it off and cutting it below the fingers. If you spill

CUT THE HIDE OUT AROUND THE BODY

INSERT TWO FINGERS UNDER THE HIDE ON BOTH SIDES OF THE CUT AND PULL BOTH PIECES OFF.

SKINNING AND BUTCHERING SMALL GAME

urine on the meat, wash it to avoid tainting the meat.

Save the heart and liver. Cut these open and inspect for signs of worms or other parasites. Also inspect the livers colour – it could indicate a diseased animal. The liver's surface should be smooth and wet and its colour deep red or purple. If the liver appears diseased, discard it. However, a diseased liver does not indicate you cannot eat the muscle tissue.

Cut along each leg from above the foot to the previously made body cut. Remove the hide by pulling it away from the carcass, cutting the connective tissue where necessary. Cut off the head and feet.

Cut larger game into manageable pieces. First, slice the muscle tissue connecting the front legs to the body. There are no bones or joints connecting the front legs to the body on four-legged animals.

Cut the hindquarters off where they join the body. You must cut around a large bone at the top of the leg and cut to the ball and socket hip joint. Cut the ligaments around the joint and bend it back to separate it.

Remove the large muscles (the tenderloin) that lie on either side of the spine. Separate the ribs from the backbone. There is less work and less wear on your knife if you break the ribs first, then cut through the breaks.

Cook large meat pieces over a spit or boil them. You can stew or boil smaller pieces, particularly those that remain attached to bone after the initial butchering, as soup or broth. You can cook body organs such as the heart, liver, pancreas, spleen, and kidneys using the same

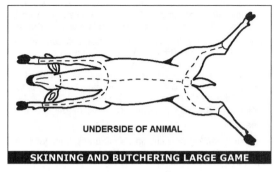

UNDERSIDE OF ANIMAL

SKINNING AND BUTCHERING LARGE GAME

methods as for muscle meat. You can also cook and eat the brain. Cut the tongue out, skin it, boil it until tender, and eat it.

4.6.2 SMOKING MEAT

To smoke meat, prepare an enclosure around a fire. The fire does not need to be big or hot. The intent is to produce smoke, not heat.

Do not use resinous wood in the fire because its smoke will ruin the meat. Use hardwoods to produce good smoke. The wood should be somewhat green. If it is too dry, soak it. Cut the meat into thin slices, no more than 5 cm thick (2 in), and drape them over a framework. Make sure none of the meat touches another piece. Keep the poncho enclosure around the meat to hold the smoke and keep a close watch on the fire. Do not let the fire get too hot. Meat smoked overnight in this manner will last about 1 week. Two days of continuous smoking will preserve the meat for 2 to 4 weeks. Properly smoked meat will look like a dark, curled, brittle stick and you can eat it without further cooking. You can also use a pit to smoke meat.

TEEPEE SMOKER

SMOKING IN A COVERED PIT

4.6.3 DRYING MEAT

To preserve meat by drying, cut it into 6 mm (1/4 in) strips, going with the grain. Hang the meat strips on a rack in a sunny location with good air flow. Make sure the strips of meat do not touch each other and there is plenty of airflow between the strips.

Keep the strips out of the reach of animals and cover them to keep blowflies off. Allow the meat to dry thoroughly before eating. Properly dried meat will have a dry, crisp texture and will not feel cool to the touch.

4.6.4 OTHER PRESERVATION METHODS

You can also preserve meats using the freezing or brine and salt methods.

Freezing

In cold climates, you can freeze and keep meat indefinitely. Freezing is not a means of preparing meat. You must still cook it before eating.

Brine and Salt

You can preserve meat by soaking it thoroughly in a saltwater solution. The solution must cover the meat. You can also use salt by itself. Wash off the salt before cooking.

Corning Meat

To corn meat use a large pot, preferably stainless steel (never aluminium). Place 3 cups of salt in the pot and enough hot water to dissolve the salt. Add enough cold water to fill the pot half way and allow the mixture to cool.

Rinse the meat with clean water and place in the brine solution. Cover the mixture with the lid upside down to push the meat completely under the liquid. Weigh the lid down.

After 5 days, remove and rinse the meat with clean water, replace the brine solution with a fresh batch and return the meat. Let this stand for another 10 days.

This meat will keep refrigerated for up to a week when complete, and can be consumed at anytime during the corning process. Rinse with clean water first.

4.7 FOOD DRYING

Drying or dehydration, the oldest method of food preservation, reduces moisture necessary for bacterial growth that eventually causes deterioration.

Successful dehydration depends upon a slow steady heat supply to assure that food is dried from the inside to the outside. Drying is also an inexact art. Size of pieces, relative moisture, and the method selected all affect the time required to dehydrate a food adequately.

4.7.1 METHODS OF DRYING

Foods may be sun dried with or without a solar dehydrator, in a gas or electric oven, or with a portable electric dehydrator. Dehydrators with thermostats provide better control over poor weather conditions and food quality than sun drying. An effective solar dehydrator is the shelf above the back seat of a car. Clotheslines are another popular drying rack.

Sun Drying

Prepared foods are placed on drying trays. Stainless steel screening and thin wood are good materials for trays. Do not use aluminium, galvanized, copper, fibreglass, or vinyl screening. Place trays of food away from dusty roads and yards. Elevate them at least 2.5 cm (1 in) above the table with spools or bricks to allow good air circulation below the food.

Cover the food with a muslin or cheesecloth tent to protect it from insects. Dry fruits and meats in direct sunlight – move trays periodically to assure direct sun exposure. Place vegetables in the shade to prevent excessive colour loss. If rain threatens or food requires more than one day to dry, cover or place the food in a sheltered area.

To destroy insects or their eggs that may be on sun-dried foods and to remove additional moisture in thicker pieces, heat foods in a 65°C (150°F) oven for 30 minutes

Oven Drying

Either build trays as described for sun drying or convert oven racks to drying racks by stretching muslin or cheesecloth across the oven rack. Secure with toothpicks or long sewn stitches. Alternate the trays in the oven periodically to assure even drying.

Set oven control at its lowest setting, but not below 60-65°C (140-150°F). If using an electric oven, wedge a potholder or stick between oven and door to allow a 1" opening. Moisture from the drying food will vent through this opening. Close the door on a gas oven, as into vent will permit moisture to escape.

Dehydrator

There are two types of dehydrators: solar and electric. For each type of dehydrator, prepare food and place on racks. If using a solar dehydrator, adjust the position of the food throughout daylight hours to keep in direct sunlight.

Follow manufacturer's instructions for the electric dehydrators. When purchasing an electric dehydrator, select one that has a thermostat to regulate temperature and a fan to circulate air.

Vegetables

Choose tender vegetables. Wash, remove any damaged areas, and cut into even pieces. Blanch, and then chill as though preparing for the freezer. **Note:** Do not blanch mushrooms, onions, or sweet peppers.

To blanch in boiling water, use 4 litres (1 gal) of boiling water for each 0.5 kg (1 lb) of food. Immerse vegetable into the boiling water using a wire basket or mesh bag, cover the pot and boil the recommended time (see table). Blanching water may be reused until it becomes cloudy. Drain vegetables thoroughly.

To steam blanch, place a few cm (1 in) of water in a pot and bring to a rolling boil. Suspend thin layer of vegetables in basket or loose cheesecloth bag. Cover and steam blanch.

Fruit

Choose firm, mature fruit. Wash, peel if desired, remove any damaged areas, and cut into even-sized pieces or slices. Some fruits require little or no pre-treatment. However, pre-treat apples, apricots, bananas, cherries, peaches, and pears by one of the following methods to reduce vitamin and flavour loss, browning, and deterioration during storage.

Immerse fruit in a solution of one of the following to a gallon of water: 1 tbsp of sodium bisulphate or 2 tbsp of sodium sulphite or 4 tbsp of sodium metabisulphite. These pre-treatment mixtures are available from some grocery stores, pharmacies, and wine-making shops. Soak fruit pieces for 5 min. and fruit halves for 15 min.

Note: Approximately 5% of asthmatics are sensitive to sulphites. Use one of the following pre-treatment's if sulphites present a potential health problem:

1	Dip fruit in a commercial ascorbic acid/water mixture from the grocery store. Follow manufacturer's instructions when preparing and using the solution.
2	Steam-blanch fruit for 5-6 min. Water blanch fruit for 4-5 min. (see information on water and steam blanching above).
3	Dip fruit in a saline solution of 2-4 tbsp of salt and 4 litre (1 gal) of water for 10-15 min.

Meat

Choose lean cuts of meat. Partially freeze and remove all visible fat. Slice with the grain of the meat into strips, 2.5 cm (1 in) wide, 1.2 cm (1/2 in) thick and 20-25 cm (8-10 in) long.

Pound strips flat to tenderize and season with salt, chilli, or other desired flavours. Marinate and refrigerate overnight for additional tenderness and flavour. Popular marinades include teriyaki, sweet and sour, soy, Worcestershire, and chilli sauces.

Fish

Slice filets into thin strips. Place strips in a dish or enamel pan. Salt strips using 4 tbsp. salt per kg. Refrigerate overnight. Oven or dehydrator drying is preferable to sun drying fish.

Drying Times

Drying times vary widely because of the method selected and the size and amount of moisture in food pieces. Sun drying requires the most time; an electric dehydrator requires the least. Vegetables take from 4-12 hours to dry; fruits take 6-20 hours. Meats require about 12 hours. Making raisins from grapes may require days/weeks when dried outside.

When testing foods for dryness, remove a piece from the centre of the drying tray and allow it to come to room temperature. Fruits and meat jerky should be leathery and pliable; vegetables should be brittle.

4.7.2 HANDLING DRIED FOODS

Conditioning Dried Foods

Food should be conditioned for a week before being packaged for long-term storage. To condition food, place it in a container such as a cloth sack or a clear, covered container and allowing any remaining moisture to redistribute itself through the fruit.

If using a clear, covered container, watch for moisture beads. If water droplets form, continue drying food. If using a cloth bag, hang it in a convenient location and shake the bag daily to redistribute food and moisture.

Storing Dried Foods

Place dried food in freezer-weight plastic storage bags, press out the air, and then put in containers with a tight-fitting lid. Store dried foods in a cool, dark and dry area.

Dried foods store well at room temperature for a month. Refrigerate foods if they will be used within three months. Freeze foods for storage periods between three months and one year. Foods should be used within one year.

Check for moisture by shaking the container several times during the first week after drying. If moisture appears, then the food needs to be returned to the dehydrator for further drying.

Do not place warm produce into storage containers, as condensation will form causing mould and mildew. Allow food to cool before storing.

Using Dried Foods

Dried meat, commonly called jerky, is normally not re-hydrated and is eaten in the dried state. Dried meats and vegetables used in soups re-hydrate during the cooking process.

Re-hydrate vegetables by soaking them in 1 1/2 to 2 cups of water for each cup of dried vegetable. If necessary, add more water during the soaking process. Heat and eat.

Cover dried fruit with boiling water and let stand for 5 min. Drain. Dried fruit may also be steamed for 3-5 min. until plump. Fruits may be eaten immediately or used in a recipe.

Making Fruit Leather

Fruit leathers, also called fruit roll ups, can be made from almost all fruits or combinations of fruits. However, peaches, apricots, cherries, and nectarines are ideal. Pears and apples, sufficiently softened, also work well.

Wash well, peel (if desired), cut into pieces, and puree fruit in a blender. Sweeten to taste with sugar or honey. Spread evenly, no more than 5 mm (1/4 in) deep, on a cookie sheet. Spray the cookie sheet lightly with a vegetable shortening or cover with plastic paper.

If using plastic paper, tape edges down to prevent them from folding into the puree. Dry fruit leather until it is slightly tacky to the touch. When dried, lift leather (including plastic paper if used), and roll or cut into small sections and roll. Storage recommendations are the same as those described previously.

Nutritional Value of Dried Foods

Dried foods retain their protein, mineral and vitamin A content fairly well if soaking water is also consumed. Because they are concentrated into a small mass, dried foods can also be high in calories. It's important to brush teeth after eating dried fruit because they stick to the teeth.

4.7.3 FOOD DRYING GUIDE

VEGETABLES				
VEGETABLE	PREPARATION	BLANCHING TIME*	COOLING TIME*	DRYNESS TEST
Asparagus	Wash thoroughly. Halve large tips.	4-6	4-5	leathery to brittle
Green Beans	Wash. Cut in pieces or strips.	2-3	2	very dry brittle
Beets	Cook as usual. Cool & peel. Cut into shoe-string strips 1/8" thick.	included in cooking		brittle, dark red
Broccoli	Trim, cut as for serving Wash. Quarter stalks lengthwise.	3-4	2	crisp, brittle
Brussels Sprouts	Cut in half length-wise through stem.	7-8	5-6	tough to brittle
Cabbage	Remove outer leaves quarter and core. Cut into strips 3mm (1/8") thick.	3	2	crisp to brittle
Carrots	Select crisp, tender vegetables. Wash. Cut off roots and tops, peel. Cut in slices or strips 3mm (1/8") thick.	3-4	4	tough to brittle
Cauliflower	Prepare as for serving.	5-6	4-5	tough to brittle
Celery	Trim stalks. Wash stalks and leaves thoroughly, Slice stalks.	2-3	2-3	very brittle
Green Chilli Peppers	Wash. To loosen skins, cut slit in skin, then rotate over flame 6-8 min. or scald in boiling water. Peel and split pods. Remove seeds and stem.	none		crisp, brittle, medium green

VEGETABLES

VEGETABLE	PREPARATION	BLANCHING TIME*	COOLING TIME*	DRYNESS TEST
Red Chilli Peppers	Wash. String whole pods together with needle and cord or suspend in bunches, root side up in area with good air circulation.	none		shrunken, dark red pods, flexible
Corn, on the Cob	Husk, trim, blanch until milk in corn is set.	3-5	3	brittle
Corn, cut	Prepare as for corn on the cob, except cut the kernels from the cob after blanching.	3-5	3	brittle
Eggplant	Wash, trim, cut into 1/4" slices.	3-4	3-4	leathery to brittle
Horseradish	Wash, remove small roots and stubs. Peel or scrape roots. Grate.	none		brittle, powdery
Mushrooms (see below)	Scrub. Discard tough woody stalks. Slice tender stalks 1/4" thick. Peel large mushrooms, slice. Leave small mushrooms whole.	none		dry and leathery
Onions	Wash, remove outer "papershells", tops and root ends, slice 1/8-1/4".	none		very brittle
Parsley and other herbs	Wash thoroughly. Separate clusters. Discard long or tough stems. Dry on trays or hang in bundles in area with good circulation.	none		flaky
Peas	Shell.	3-4	3	hard
Peppers, Pimentos	Wash, stem. Remove core and seeds. Cut into 1/4"-1/2" strips or rings.	none		tough to brittle
Potatoes	Wash, peel. Cut into 1/4" shoe-string strips or 1/8" thick slices.	7-9	6-7	brittle
Spinach, Kale, Chard, Mustard	Trim and wash very thoroughly. Shake or pat dry to remove excess moisture.	2-3 'til wilted	2	crisp
Squash, winter	Cut or break into pieces. Remove seeds and cavity pulp. Cut into 1" wide strips. Peel rind. Cut strips crosswise into pieces about 1/8" thick.	3	1-2	tough to brittle
Squash, Summer, Banana	Wash trim, cut into 1/4" slices	3	1-2	leathery to brittle
Tomatoes	Steam or dip in boiling water to loosen skins. Chill in cold water. Peel. Slice 1/2" thick or cut in 3/4" sections.	none		crisp

Blanching time is in minutes, with steam. Cooling time is in minutes, with cool water. Blanching times are for 3,000-5,000 ft. Times will be slightly longer at higher altitudes, or if the quantity of vegetable is large.

Dry in thin layers on trays to desired state of dryness.

WARNING: The toxins of poisonous varieties of mushrooms are not destroyed by drying or by cooking. Only an expert can differentiate between poisonous and edible varieties.

FRUITS

FRUIT	PREPARATION	PRE-TREATMENT	DRYING PROCEDURE
Apples	Wash, pare and core. Cut in rings or slices 1/8-1/4" thick or cut in quarters or eighths Coat with ascorbic acid solution to prevent darkening (uses 2 1/4 tsp/cup water).	Choose one: Soak 5 min in sodium sulphite solution. Steam-blanch 3-5 min., depending on size and texture. Or do nothing.	Arrange in single layer trays, pit side up. Dry until soft, pliable and leathery with no moist area in centre when cut.

FRUITS			
FRUIT	PREPARATION	PRE-TREATMENT	DRYING PROCEDURE
Apricots (firm, fully ripe)	Wash. Cut in half and remove pit (do not peel). Coat with ascorbic acid solution to prevent darkening during preparation (1 tsp/cup).	Choose one: Soak 5 min. in sodium sulphite solution. Steam blanch 3-5 min.	Arrange in single layer trays, pit side layer up. Pop the cavity up to expose more flesh to air. Dry until soft pliable and leathery with no moist area in centre when cut.
Bananas (firm, ripe)	Peel. Cut in 1/8" slices	No treatment necessary; may dip in lemon juice.	Arrange in single layer on trays. Dry until tough and leathery.
Berries (firm)	Wash. Leave whole or cut in half.	No treatment necessary; may dip in boiling water 15-30 sec., to crack skins. Steam blanch 30 sec. to 1 min.	Spread in layer not more than two berries deep. Dry until hard and berries rattle when shaken on trays.
Cherries (fully ripe)	Wash. Remove stems and pits.		Arrange in single layer on trays. Dry until tough, leathery and to slightly sticky.
Citrus peel	Choose thick-skinned. Wash. Thinly peel outer 1/16-1/8" of the peel; avoid white bitter part.		Arrange in single layers on trays. Dry at 130ºF 1-2 hours, then 120ºF degrees until crisp.
Figs (fully ripe)	Wash or clean with damp towel. Peel dark-skinned varieties if desired. Leave whole if small or partly dried on tree; cut large fig in halves or slices.		Arrange in single layer on trays. Dry until leathery and pliable.
Grapes (seedless varieties)	Wash, sort, leave whole on stems in small bunches, if desired, May also remove stems.		Spread in thin layer on trays. Dry until pliable and leathery with no moist centre.
Melons (mature, firm and heavy for size)	Wash. Remove outer skin, any fibrous tissue and seeds. Slice 1/4-1/2" thick.		Arrange in single layer on trays. Dry until leathery and pliable with no pockets of moisture.
Nectarines and Peaches (ripe, firm)	Peel. Cut in half and remove pit. Cut in quarters or slices if desired. Coat with ascorbic acid solution to prevent darkening during preparation (1-tsp/cup)		Arrange in single layer on trays pit side up. Turn halves over when visible juice disappears. Dry until leathery and somewhat pliable.
Pears	Wash. Pare, if desired. Cut in half lengthwise wash and core. Cut in quarters or eighths or slice 1/8-1/4" thick. Coat with ascorbic acid solution to prevent darkening during preparation (1-tsp/cup)		Arrange in single layer on trays pit side up. Dry until springy and suede like with no pockets of moisture.
Plums and prunes	Wash. Leave whole if small; cut large fruit into halves (pit removed) or slices	Arrange in single layer on trays pit side up, cavity popped out. Dry until pliable and leathery; pit should not slip when squeezed if prune not cut.	

4.7.4 FREEZE DRYING AT HOME

If you don't mind waiting a week you can experiment with freeze drying at home.

You will need a tray, preferably perforated. Something like a cake-cooling rack or a metal mesh tray is perfect. You can use a cookie sheet or a plate, but it will take longer.

Now you will need something to freeze dry. Three good candidates are apples, potatoes and carrots (Apples have the advantage that they taste OK in their freeze-dried state). With a knife, cut your apple, potato and/or carrot as thin as you can (try all three if you have them). Cut slices paper thin if you can. The thinner you cut, the less time the experiment will take. Then arrange your slices on your rack or tray and put them in the freezer. You want to do this fairly quickly, or your potato and/or apple slices will discolour.

In half an hour look in on your experiment. The slices should be frozen solid.

Over the next week look in on your slices. The water in the slices should sublimate away. That is, the water in the slices will convert straight from solid water to water vapour, never going through the liquid state (this is the same thing that mothballs do, going straight from a solid to a gas). After a week or so (depending on how cold your freezer is and how thick the slices are) your slices will be completely dry. To test apple or potato slices for complete drying, take one slice out and let it thaw. It will turn black quickly if not completely dry.

When all of the slices are completely dry, what you have is freeze-dried apples, potatoes and carrots. You can "reconstitute" them by putting the slices in a cup or bowl and adding a little boiling water (or add cold water and microwave). Apples you can eat in their dried state or you can reconstitute them. What you will notice is that the reconstituted vegetables look and taste pretty much like the original! That is why freeze drying is a popular preservation technique.

4.7.5 SAFELY MAKING JERKY

You can safely make jerky without deadly bacteria such as e-coli by pre-cooking it.

1	Slice the meat into long pieces that are a maximum 6 mm (1/4 in) thick. Some people find it easier to slice meat that is partially frozen. Slicing across the grain will result in a tenderer jerky. Remove all visible fat. It is not necessary to completely freeze the meat to kill parasites when this pre-cooking method is used.
2	Prepare a marinade in a large saucepan. Make enough marinade to cover all the meat strips; the amount will vary with the amount of jerky you make and the saucepan you choose. A general guideline is 1 - 2 cups marinade for each one pound batch of meat. Some marinade recipes (all include water): • soy sauce, liquid smoke and cayenne pepper • soy sauce, garlic salt, lemon pepper • soy sauce, liquid smoke, worchester sauce • soy sauce, salt, pepper, minced garlic • teriyaki sauce, salt, worchester sauce, onion powder • salt and water. It'll do. Experiment with what you have on hand.
3	Bring the marinade to a full rolling boil over medium heat. Add a few meat strips, making sure that they are covered by the marinade. Return to a full boil.
4	Using tongs, immediately remove meat from the marinade to prevent over-cooking. Repeat the immersion process until all meat has been given the heat treatment.
5	Place precooked strips on drying racks with a small space between each strip. Dry in dehydrator at 70°C (160°F) for 3-4 hours, then lower temperature to 60°C (140°F) for about another 4 hours or until dry. If drying in a household oven, the times tend to be longer; plan on about 8 hours at 70°C and then more time at 60°C. It is important that the temperatures not be higher, because you want to dry the meat for safety, not just cook it. Bacteria require moisture to grow so completely dry jerky is important for safety.
6	To test for dryness, remove a piece from the dryer, cool it, then bend it. It should crack but not break and there should be no moist spots. Package air tight (so moisture cannot re-enter the meat) and store at room temperature for a couple of months, or freeze for longer storage. Longer storage at room temperature is associated with off flavours.

5 SURVIVAL USE OF PLANTS

After solving the problems of finding water, shelter, and food, you will have to consider the use of plants you can eat. In a survival situation you should always be on the lookout for familiar wild foods and live off the land whenever possible.

You must not count on being able to go for days without food as some sources would suggest. Even in the best situation, maintaining health through a complete and nutritious diet is essential to maintaining strength and peace of mind.

You must learn as much as possible beforehand about the flora of the region where you will be operating. Plants can provide you with medicines in a survival situation. Plants can supply you with weapons and raw materials to construct shelters and build fires. Plants can even provide you with chemicals for poisoning fish, preserving animal hides, and for camouflaging yourself and your equipment.

5.1 EDIBILITY OF PLANTS

Plants are valuable sources of food because they are widely available, easily procured, and, in the proper combinations, can meet all your nutritional needs.

WARNING!!!

The critical factor in using plants for food is to avoid accidental poisoning. Eat only those plants you can positively identify and you know are safe.

Absolutely identify plants before using them as food. Poison hemlock has killed people who mistook it for its relatives, wild carrots and wild parsnips.

At times you may find yourself in a situation for which you could not plan. In this instance you may not have had the chance to learn the plant life of the region in which you must survive. In this case you can use the **Universal Edibility Test** (Page 5-3) to determine which plants you can eat and those to avoid.

It is important to be able to recognize both cultivated and wild edible plants in a survival situation. Most of the information in this chapter is directed towards identifying wild plants because information relating to cultivated plants is more readily available.

Remember the following when collecting wild plants for food —

- Plants growing near occupied buildings or along roadsides may have been sprayed with pesticides. Wash them thoroughly. In highly developed countries with many automobiles, avoid roadside plants, if possible, due to contamination from exhaust emissions.

- Plants growing in contaminated water or in water containing Giardia lamblia and other parasites are contaminated themselves. Boil or disinfect them.

- Some plants develop extremely dangerous fungal toxins. Do not eat any fruit that is starting to spoil or showing signs of mildew or fungus.

- Plants of the same species may differ in their toxic or subtoxic compounds content because of genetic or environmental factors. One example of this is the foliage of the common chokecherry. Some chokecherry plants have high concentrations of deadly cyanide compounds while others have low concentrations or none. Avoid any weed, leaves, or seeds with an almond like scent, a characteristic of the cyanide compounds.

- Some people are more susceptible to gastric distress than others. If you are sensitive in this way, avoid unknown wild plants. If you are extremely sensitive to poison ivy, avoid products from this family, including any parts from sumacs, mangoes, and cashews.

- Some edible wild plants, such as acorns and water lily rhizomes, are bitter. These bitter substances, usually tannin compounds, make them unpalatable. Boiling them in several changes of water will usually remove these bitter properties.

- Many valuable wild plants have high concentrations of oxalate compounds, also known as oxalic acid. Oxalates produce a sharp burning sensation in your mouth and throat and damage the kidneys. Baking, roasting, or drying usually destroys these oxalate crystals.

The corm (bulb) of the jack-in-the-pulpit is known as the "Indian turnip," but you can eat it only after removing these crystals by slow baking or by drying.

WARNING!!!

Do not eat mushrooms in a survival situation! The only way to tell if a mushroom is edible is by positive identification. There is no room for experimentation. Symptoms of the most dangerous mushrooms affecting the central nervous system may show up after several days have passed when it is too late to reverse their effects.

5.1.1 PLANT IDENTIFICATION

By learning the different types of leaves, roots and leaf arrangements, you can more efficiently identify plants and catalogue any wild foods, or other plants of interest you may discover.

The basic leaf margins are toothed, lobed, and toothless or smooth.

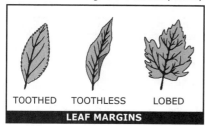

TOOTHED   TOOTHLESS   LOBED

LEAF MARGINS

These leaves may be lance-shaped, elliptical, egg-shaped, oblong, wedge-shaped, triangular, long-pointed, or top-shaped.

The basic types of leaf arrangements are opposite, alternate, compound, simple, and basal rosette.

The basic types of root structures are the bulb, clove, taproot, tuber, rhizome, corm, and crown. Bulbs are familiar as onions and, when sliced in half, will show concentric rings.

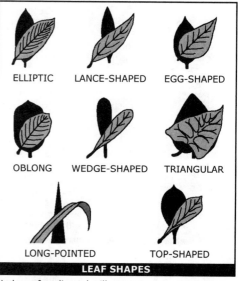

ELLIPTIC   LANCE-SHAPED   EGG-SHAPED

OBLONG   WEDGE-SHAPED   TRIANGULAR

LONG-POINTED   TOP-SHAPED

LEAF SHAPES

Cloves are those bulblike structures that remind us of garlic and will separate into small pieces when broken apart. This characteristic separates wild onions from wild garlic.

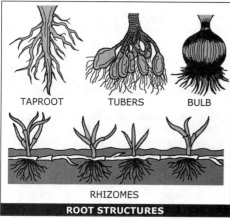

TAPROOT   TUBERS   BULB

RHIZOMES

ROOT STRUCTURES

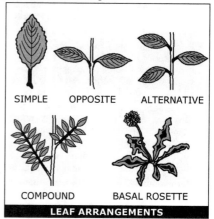

SIMPLE   OPPOSITE   ALTERNATIVE

COMPOUND   BASAL ROSETTE

LEAF ARRANGEMENTS

Taproots resemble carrots and may be single-rooted or branched, but usually only one plant stalk arises from each root. Tubers are like potatoes and daylilies and you will find these structures either on strings or in clusters underneath the parent plants.

Rhizomes are large creeping rootstock or underground stems and many plants arise from the "eyes" of these roots. Corms are similar to bulbs but are solid when cut rather than possessing rings. A crown is the type of root structure found on plants such as asparagus and looks much like a mop head under the soil's surface.

Learn as much as possible about plants you intend to use for food and their unique characteristics. Some plants have both edible and poisonous parts. Many are edible only at certain times of the year. Others may have poisonous relatives that look very similar to the ones you can eat or use for medicine.

5.1.2 UNIVERSAL EDIBILITY TEST

There are many plants throughout the world. Tasting or swallowing even a small portion of some can cause severe discomfort, extreme internal disorders, and even death. Therefore, if you have the slightest doubt about a plant's edibility, apply the Universal Edibility Test before eating any portion of it.

1	Test only one part of a potential food plant at a time.
2	Separate the plant into its basic components – leaves, stems, roots, buds, and flowers.
3	Smell the food for strong or acid odours. Remember, smell alone does not indicate a plant is edible or inedible.
4	Do not eat for 8 hours before starting the test.
5	During the 8 hours you abstain from eating, test for contact poisoning by placing a piece of the plant part you are testing on the inside of your elbow or wrist. Usually 15 minutes is enough time to allow for a reaction
6	During the test period, take nothing by mouth except purified water and the plant part you are testing.
7	Select a small portion of a single part and prepare it the way you plan to eat it.
8	Before placing the prepared plant part in your mouth, touch a small portion (a pinch) to the outer surface of your lip to test for burning or itching.
9	If after 3 minutes there is no reaction on your lip, place the plant part on your tongue, holding it there for 15 minutes.
10	If there is no reaction, thoroughly chew a pinch and hold it in your mouth for 15 minutes. Do not swallow.
11	If no burning, itching, numbing, stinging or other irritation occurs during the 15 minutes, swallow the food.
12	Wait 8 hours. If any ill effects occur during this period, induce vomiting and drink a lot of water.
13	If no ill effects occur, eat 1/4 cup of the same plant part prepared the same way. Wait another 8 hours. If no ill effects occur, the plant part as prepared is safe for eating.

CAUTION – Test all parts of the plant for edibility, as some plants have both edible and inedible parts. Do not assume that a part that proved edible when cooked is also edible when raw. Test the part raw to ensure edibility before eating raw. The same part or plant may produce varying reactions in different individuals.

Before testing a plant for edibility, make sure there are enough plants to make the testing worth your time and effort. Each part of a plant (roots, leaves, flowers, and so on) requires more than 24 hours to test – this also means separate testing for cooked and uncooked parts. Do not waste time testing a plant that is not relatively abundant in the area.

Remember, eating large portions of plant food on an empty stomach may cause diarrhoea, nausea, or cramps. Two good examples of this are such familiar foods as green apples and wild onions. Even after testing plant food and finding it safe, eat it in moderation.

You can see from the steps and time involved in testing for edibility just how important it is to be able to identify edible plants.

To avoid potentially poisonous plants, stay away from any wild or unknown plants that have —

- Milky or discoloured sap.
- Beans, bulbs, or seeds inside pods.
- Bitter or soapy taste.
- Spines, fine hairs, or thorns.

- Dill, carrot, parsnip, or parsley like foliage.
- "Almond" scent in woody parts and leaves.
- Grain heads with pink, purplish, or black spurs.
- Three-leaved growth pattern.

Using the above criteria as eliminators when choosing plants for the Universal Edibility Test will cause you to avoid some edible plants. More important, these criteria will often help you avoid plants that are potentially toxic to eat or even touch.

5.1.3 MYTHS ABOUT BUSH FOODS

The following is a list of misconceptions about bush foods that are **wrong** —

- If it tastes good it's edible – wrong!
- If it smells good it's edible – wrong!
- Cooking destroys toxins that are harmful – wrong! Although heat can destroy some toxins.
- If the fruit or any other part of the plant is edible, the whole plant is edible – wrong! Many plants have edible and highly poisonous parts.
- If other animals eat them they are okay for humans – wrong!

5.1.4 SEAWEEDS

One plant you should never overlook is seaweed. It is a form of marine algae found on or near ocean shores. There are also some edible freshwater varieties. Seaweed is a valuable source of iodine, other minerals, and vitamin C.

 CAUTION – Large quantities of seaweed in an unaccustomed stomach can produce a severe laxative effect.

When gathering seaweeds for food, look for living plants attached to rocks or floating free. Seaweed washed onshore any length of time may be spoiled or decayed. You can dry freshly harvested seaweeds for later use.

Its preparation for eating depends on the type of seaweed. You can dry thin and tender varieties in the sun or over a fire until crisp. Crush and add these to soups or broths. Boil thick, leathery seaweeds for a short time to soften them. Eat them as a vegetable or with other foods. You can eat some varieties raw after testing for edibility.

5.1.5 PREPARATION OF PLANT FOOD

Although some plants or plant parts are edible raw, you must cook others to be edible or palatable. Edible means that a plant or food will provide you with necessary nutrients, palatable means that it actually is pleasing to eat. Many wild plants are edible but barely palatable. Learn to identify, prepare, and eat wild foods.

Methods used to improve the taste of plant food include soaking, boiling, cooking, or leeching.

- Leeching is done by crushing the food (for example, acorns), placing it in a strainer, and pouring boiling water through it or immersing it in running water.
- Boil leaves, stems, and buds until tender, changing the water if necessary to remove any bitterness.
- Boil, bake, or roast tubers and roots. Drying helps to remove caustic oxalates from some roots like those in the Arum family.
- Leach acorns in water if necessary to remove the bitterness. Some nuts such as chestnuts are good raw, but taste better roasted.
- You can eat many grains and seeds raw until they mature. When hard or dry, you may have to boil or grind them into meal or flour.
- The sap from many trees, such as maples, birches, walnuts, and sycamores, contains sugar. You may boil these saps down to thick syrup for sweetening. It takes about 35 litres of maple sap to make one litre of maple syrup!

5.2 PLANTS FOR MEDICINE

In a survival situation you will have to use what is available. In using plants and other natural remedies, positive identification of the plants involved is as critical as in using them for food. Proper use of these plants is equally important.

Terms and Definitions

The following terms, and their definitions, are associated with medicinal plant use —

Poultice	A poultice can simply be crushed leaves or other plant parts, possibly heated, applied to a wound or sore either directly or wrapped in cloth.
	A poultice can be made into a paste by grinding or crushing plant parts and mixing with water – usually heated before or during mixing. You can thicken the paste by using agents such as flour or oatmeal.
	The mixture is then held to the affected area with cloth or gauze.
Infusion or tea	The preparation of medicinal herbs for internal or external application. You place a small quantity of a herb in a container, pour hot water over it, and let it steep (covered or uncovered) before use.
Decoction	The extract of a boiled down or simmered herb leaf or root. You add herb leaf or root to water. You bring them to a sustained boil or simmer to draw their chemicals into the water. The average ratio is about 28 to 56 grams (1 to 2 ounces) of herb to 0.5 litre of water.
Expressed juice	Liquids or saps squeezed from plant material and either applied to the wound or made into another medicine.
Tincture	A tincture is the infusion of dried, powdered or fresh herbs in alcohol, glycerine or vinegar. The idea of a tincture is not to produce intoxication, but to provide and preserve the strongest form of a herb's properties.
	To produce a tincture, place the herbs inside a glass jar and pour enough to cover the herbs completely. Continue to pour alcohol (rum or vodka works well, otherwise vinegar or glycerine) to fill the jar half way.
	Store in a cool dark place for up to two weeks. Shake the jar at least once a day. After two weeks, strain the tincture through cheesecloth or muslin and store. Tinctures remain potent for up to two years.
	Most tincture remedies call for one tablespoon to be consumed at mealtimes. See **Vinegar** (Page 9-24) for details on making vinegar.

Many natural remedies work slower than the medicines you know. Therefore, start with smaller doses and allow more time for them to take effect. Some will act more rapidly than others.

5.2.1 SPECIFIC REMEDIES

Sedatives	Get help in falling asleep by brewing a tea made from mint leaves or passionflower leaves.
Haemorrhoids	Treat them with external washes from elm bark or oak bark tea, from the expressed juice of plantain leaves, or from a Solomon's seal root decoction.
Constipation	Relieve constipation by drinking decoctions from dandelion leaves, rose hips, or walnut bark. Eating raw daylily flowers will also help.
Worms, Intestinal parasites	Using moderation, treat with tea made from tansy (Tanacetum vulgare) or from wild carrot leaves.
Gas and cramps	Use a tea made from carrot seeds as an antiflatulent; use tea made from mint leaves to settle the stomach.
Diarrhoea	Drink tea made from the roots of blackberries and their relatives to stop diarrhoea. White oak bark and other barks containing tannin are also effective. However, use them with caution when nothing else is available because of possible negative effects on the kidneys. You can also stop diarrhoea by eating white clay or campfire ashes. Tea made from cowberry or cranberry or hazel leaves works too.

Antihemorrhagics	Make medications to stop bleeding from a poultice of the puffball mushroom, from plantain leaves, or most effectively from the leaves of the common yarrow or woundwort (Achillea millefolium).
Antiseptics	Use to cleanse wounds, sores, or rashes. You can make them from the expressed juice from wild onion or garlic, or expressed juice from chickweed leaves or the crushed leaves of dock. You can also make antiseptics from a decoction of burdock root, mallow leaves or roots, or white oak bark. All these medications are for external use only.
Itching	Relieve the itch from insect bites, sunburn, or plant poisoning rashes by applying a poultice of jewelweed (Impatiens biflora) or witch hazel leaves (Hamamelis virginiana). The jewelweed juice will help when applied to poison ivy rashes or insect stings. It works on sunburn as well as aloe vera.
Fevers	Treat a fever with a tea made from willow bark, an infusion of elder flowers or fruit, linden flower tea, or elm bark decoction.
Colds and sore throats	Treat these illnesses with a decoction made from either plantain leaves or willow bark. You can also use a tea made from burdock roots, mallow or mullein flowers or roots, or mint leaves.
Aches, pains, and sprains	Treat with externally applied poultices of dock, plantain, chickweed, willow bark, garlic, or sorrel. You can also use salves made by mixing the expressed juices of these plants in animal fat or vegetable oils.
Antifungal washes	Make a decoction of walnut leaves or oak bark or acorns to treat ringworm and athlete's foot. Apply frequently to the site, alternating with exposure to direct sunlight.

5.3 MEDICINAL PLANT GUIDE

This section lists common plants and their use as medicine, as well as a definition of terms.

Onion

Onion contains sodium, potassium, calcium, iron, phosphorous, and small quantities of vitamins like A, B1, B2 and C. Onions are also an excellent source of sulphur which is essential to the body.

As a medicine, onion is recommended raw.

The onion is an energizer. It is useful for edemas (dropsy), cirrhosis, pleurisy, and it has antiseptic features.

Internally:
- To treat an excess of uric acid, leave two crushed onions overnight in 500ml of boiling water. In the morning, filter and drink with lemon juice and honey.
- Diarrhoea: boil 200 grams of onion leaves for 10 minutes in a litre of water (it will boil down). Consume half a litre of the liquid daily.
- Cough, bronchitis: cut 3 onions in half and boil for 10 minutes in 500ml of water. Filter, sweeten with honey and drink half a cup daily.
- Diabetes: Consume raw (best) or cooked onion with all 3 meals, daily for a week. Repeat this every 3 months. It works on the pancreas.

Externally:
- For a mild burn, apply crushed onion mixed with a pinch of salt.
- Freckles: crush an onion and leave it in apple vinegar for 4 hours. Apply and massage. Onion juice and warm water is also effective.
- Abscess, furuncle: Cut a ripe onion and apply on the swollen parts and hold for 10-15 minutes. Repeat this 4 or 5 times a day.
- Haemorrhoids: cut the onion in halves, wash it in warm water, let it cool and apply on the painful spot.

Garlic

The main therapeutic qualities of garlic describe it as being antiseptic, antibacterial, stimulating digestion, reducing high blood pressure, a glandular regulator, a diuretic and even a cancer deterrent.

The active compounds of garlic are volatile oil, the mixture of sulphide and allyl oxide in an almost pure state, very important mineral antibiotic components (sulphur, iodine, zinc, and manganese), vitamins B and C.

- Garlic can be made into an antiseptic vinegar, useful in the treatment of wounds, or simply a poultice can be made and applied.
- Consumption of raw garlic is effective against intestinal worms. If you're feeling kinky, a garlic enema is even more effective.
- Cases of bad acne can be helped by rubbing clove halves on it.

Mixtures:

- Ground and mixed in grease or oil: can be used as an ointment. Used for treating white tumours.
- A clove of garlic ground and mixed with camphorated oil: rubbed on the back and chest is effective against scabies, also used in treating asthenia and arthritis
- For wound treatment: Mix a solution of 10% garlic juice and 1-2% alcohol, or put 30g of ground garlic in 500ml of vinegar for 10 days.
- Garlic juice is useful in treating hypertension, infectious diseases, lung problems, tuberculosis, asthma, intestinal parasites.

Dandelion

Dandelion roots have been used to treat liver problems. Dandelion decoctions are used to treat kidney disease, swelling, skin problems, heartburn and upset stomach. Avoid if pregnant or breast feeding.

It has also been used to treat digestive disorders, appendicitis, and breast problems (such as inflammation or lack of milk flow). Herbalists often incorporate it into remedies for fever, boils, eye problems, diabetes and diarrhoea. Every part of the plant is edible.

Parts:

- The leaves produce a diuretic effect – useful in removing toxins, poor digestion or high blood pressure.
- The root is used to promote liver detoxification, while the leaves support kidney function.
- The roots act as an antiviral agent, appetite stimulant and digestive aid. It can be used to treat stomach problems.
- The flower is known to have antioxidant properties.

Internal Use:

- Decoct for lowering cholesterol levels: 15g of leaves and 15g of roots boiled in 1 litre of water for 30 minutes. Drink a cup before meals. Use the same remedy for liver disorders, with 25g leaves/25g roots.
- Obtain juice from hashed and pressed dandelions. If consumed immediately and in high quantities, it will purify the blood and enrich it with iron.
- To treat anorexia or constipation, boil 20g leaves and 20g roots in 1 litre of water for 20 minutes. Let this sit for 24 hours. Consume 1 cup before each meal.

External Use:

- To treat cataracts, decoct the whole herb. Boil 10g of leaves, roots, flowers and stalks in 750ml of water for 20 minutes. Use the fresh mixture to wash the area around the eye 4 or 5 times a day.
- A decoction of 15g of fresh flowers and leaves, boiled for 10 minutes in 500ml of water for 10 minutes can be used to attenuate freckles.

Rosemary 	Properties of rosemary include analgesic, antiseptic, antidepressant, anti-inflammatory, expectorant, antiviral, aphrodisiac, and disinfectant. Its active ingredients include choleric, antiseptic, diuretic and tonic aspects at the nervous level. Rosemary has calming effects working against fatigue, sadness, anxiety, calming muscle soreness, digestive pains and stress-induced indigestion. Rosemary consumption improves digestion, fights against obesity, liver disease, gastritis, cholesterolemia, bronchic asthma, edemas (dropsy) and adjusts fast heart beats caused by coffee or tobacco excess. Rosemary is extremely beneficial in cases of fainting, influenza, hangovers, asthma, bronchitis, cramps, constipation, cystitis, headaches, polyps, colds, cough, sinusitis or muscular pains.

Mixtures and Treatments:

- Tincture: Used in cases of indigestion, diabetes, vomit, stomachal atony, colics, liver congestion, icterus, chronic and painful inflammations of the biliary bladder, high cholesterol, insomnia, dizziness, headaches, irritability, convalescence, weak memory, asthenia, palpitations, asthma, and convulsive cough.

  A tablespoon, diluted in water is consumed before main meals.

  This is also used for sprains, swelling, arthritis and torticolis. Administer a teaspoon of tincture in 100 ml water three times a day.

- Essential Oil: Is analgesic, anti-inflammatory, anti-microbial, stimulates peripheral blood circulation, and prevents hair falling. Adding a few drops in a bath is also useful for cases of anxiety, headaches, debility, and weakness.

Warning:

Avoid during pregnancy, or in cases of epilepsy or hypersensitivity.

Sesame  Sesame plant Sesame seeds	Sesame seeds contain fat substances, antioxidants, sesamol, proteinic substances, arginine and cellulose, mineral substances and calcium. Sesame seeds have a high energetic value and stimulate virility. The white seeds can be eaten or cold pressed to obtain oil with a high therapeutic value and aphrodisiac effects, being used in massages. Sesame deters the development of tumours. It has anti-rheumatic, anti-cancer, anti-fungal and anti-bacterial effects. It can be used as a protein infusion in various nutrition affections, and also helps increase fertility.

Treatments:

- Sesame is recommended in treating insomnia.
- It helps detoxify the liver and kidneys, improving immune systems.
- The oil is used in treating gum bolls, gingivitis and paradontosis. Apply a few drops on the gums after brushing teeth. Massage the gums gently and repeat the treatment every evening for 3 months.
- Sesame oil has laxative effects.
- The leaves, rich in mucilaginous substances, are used in combination with other plants for treating dysentery and cholera.

Mixtures:

- Sesame Oil: Obtained through cold pressing. The oil must be heated carefully to preserve the aromatic compounds. The oil can also be obtained by pan-frying the seeds before being cold pressed. The pressing is done at 60-80 °C (140-175 °F).
- Sesame Milk: Prepare from a cup of sesame seeds, a quarter cup of honey and 3 cups of milk. Mix in a blender and consume cold.
- Sesame Flour: Rich in amino acids, calcium.

Yarrow 	White yarrow is usually taken as a tea made with 1 teaspoon of herb: • As a digestive aid – yarrow assists in relaxing the muscle tissue in the digestive tract – making it an antispasmodic. • The antispasmodic qualities can also be effective in treating menstrual cramps. • Yarrow has traditionally been used as a sedative. • It is also used as an anti-inflammatory, a pain reliever and an antiseptic. • If you crush the plant and rub it on your skin it will help to keep insects away. **Wound Treatment with Yarrow:** • Yarrow contains two chemicals that promote blood coagulation, making it useful for treating wounds on humans and animals. • Especially useful for saddle sores on horses.
Oregano 	Usually thought of as a culinary herb, oregano has also been used medicinally for thousands of years. **Oregano Tea:** This can be used to help with indigestion, bloating, flatulence, coughs, urinary problems, bronchial problems, headaches, swollen glands and to promote menstruation. Unsweetened tea can be used as a gargle or mouthwash. **Externally:** Oregano leaves can be pounded into a paste – add small amounts of hot water or tea to reach the proper consistency. Oatmeal may also be added for thickness. **Oil:** Oil can be made with oregano leaves to relieve toothache pain. Put a few drops on the affected tooth. It can also get rid of warts, any kind.
Cinnamon  Leaves of the tree Dried inner bark	In traditional Chinese medicine, cinnamon is used to treat colds, flatulence, nausea, diarrhoea, and painful menstrual periods. It is also believed to improve energy, digestion of dairy products, and circulation. Cinnamon is obtained from the inner bark of several trees of the *cinnamomum* genus. The tree is grown for two years, and then coppiced (they are cut off at the trunks, and allowed to form new shoots the next year). The shoots are harvested and the outer bark is scraped off. The thin (0.5 mm) inner bark is prised out in long rolls, and allowed to dry. Studies have shown cinnamon has benefits on blood sugar levels, therefore helpful for people suffering type 2 diabetes (adult onset). Take between 1/4 and 1 teaspoon of cinnamon daily. Cinnamon has been shown to have antibacterial and antifungal properties and is effective against Candida albicans – the fungus that causes yeast infections and thrush, and Helicobacter pylori – the bacteria that causes stomach ulcers. **Warnings:** People taking and medication that affects blood sugar or insulin levels shouldn't take therapeutic doses of cinnamon except under a doctor's supervision. At high levels, it can damage the liver. It can also thin the blood, so should not be taken with anti-clotting medication, or by people with bleeding disorders. Pregnant women should avoid high doses.

Aloe Vera 	Aloe vera (*aloe barbadensis*) has many medicinal properties useful for a variety of conditions such as burns, wounds, skin irritations and constipation. It is grown in most tropical and subtropical locations. **Treatments:** Burns: Aloe contains active compounds that can help alleviate pain and inflammation, and stimulate skin growth and repair. Aloe is best used for minor burns and skin irritations Herpes and Skin Conditions: Evidence suggests that aloe gel may improve symptoms of genital herpes and skin conditions such as psoriasis. **Mixtures:** Aloe Gel: to make aloe gel, slice off an outer leaf of the plant and simply scoop out the gel inside and blend. You can add powdered vitamin C and E for enhanced skin repair properties. You can also just slice open the outer leaves and apply directly.
Chilli Peppers 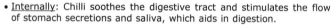 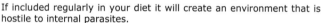	The main medicinal properties of chilli are derived from the capsaicin contained (this is what makes chilli hot). The pods can be used fresh, or dried and crushed. Generally the seeds are far hotter than the skin. Other components are vitamins E, C, and carotenoids. It is used to treat a variety of conditions including poor circulation, weak digestion, heart disease, chronic pain, sore throats, headache and toothache. **Treatments:** • Internally: Chilli soothes the digestive tract and stimulates the flow of stomach secretions and saliva, which aids in digestion. If included regularly in your diet it will create an environment that is hostile to internal parasites. • Topical: Apply a poultice of about 6 chillies (or a spoon of chilli powder) blended with milk and torn bread or oatmeal for an effective topical pain reliever for the treatment of arthritis pain, shingles, muscle pain and psoriasis.
Rose Hips 	Rose hips are the berry like fruits left behind after the bloom has died. They are typically red or orange, but may be dark purple to black in some species. They have a tangy, fruity flavour similar to cranberries. The Rugosa Rose plant is said to produce the tastiest rose hips. They may be used fresh, dried or preserved. Each hip comprises an outer fleshy layer containing seeds and fine hairs. The irritating hairs should be removed before using in a recipe. Certain species (such as dog rose and rugosa rose) contain high concentrations of vitamin C – up to 2% by weight when dry. They can be made into syrup for an effective source of vitamin C. **Treatments:** Rose hips contain high levels of antioxidant flavonoids with anti-inflammatory properties The anti-inflammatory properties of rose hips are shown to be useful in the treatment of knee or hip osteoarthritis. Rose hips also contain many compounds known to reduce the risk of cancer and cardiovascular disease. The hips of a dog rose are a traditional laxative and diuretic, and are useful in the treatment of influenza-like infections and various urinary tract disorders. No side effects are known when used in moderate amounts.

Spinach

Spinach contains a huge range of substances essential for the body. Because of this any diet that contains spinach leads to the strengthening of the body. Spinach is important as a survival food.

The magnesium contained helps prevent diabetes. Iodine helps treat skin diseases and strengthens the immune system. Vitamin K contributes to bone resistance, vitamin B improves cerebral activity, maintaining firmness of the skin and controlling insomnia. Potassium stimulates the heart muscle. Beta-carotene prevents sight problems.

Alimentary fibres, vitamins and minerals contained in spinach make it a good depurative and detoxifier. Toxins from animals that are rich in fat and protein are purged quickly. These fibres also prevent constipation and colon cancer, and regulate the body's cholesterol levels.

Mixtures and Treatments:

- Spinach Juice: Administering 0.5 lt of juice per day can cure even the most severe constipation. One fresh glass of spinach juice in the morning is good for nervous depressions and fatigue.

  The juice also helps in the recovery of diseased organs, helps with duodenal ulcer, pernicious anaemia, weakness, convulsions, deficiencies of the suprarenal glands or the thyroid gland, low and high blood pressure, limb inflammations, migraines, etc.

- Spinach Infusion: The infusion is used for increasing diuresis in kidney or bladder diseases. Obtain the mixture by pouring a cup of boiled water on one teaspoon of crushed spinach leaves. Cover for 15 minutes then filter. Consume two cups a day.

- Cataplasms: For external use, cataplasms can calm burns. The leaves are soaked in boiling olive or soybean oil and fastened with a bandage on effected areas. Apply two or three cataplasms a day.

Warning:

The consumption of spinach is not recommended for people who suffer hepatitis, rheumatism, gastric and intestinal inflammations, or for people on a diet without salt. Consume only moderately or not at all.

Ginger

Ginger has been used for centuries in Asian cooking and for therapeutic properties. Its green leaves – similar to spinach – can be used in salads, but the roots of the plant are where the medicinal benefits are.

Treatments:

- Digestive Aid: Ginger is an excellent herb for digestion. It helps break down proteins and rid the stomach and intestines of gas, and aids in digestion of fatty foods.

- High Blood Pressure: Ginger's warming properties relax the muscles surrounding blood vessels, improving and stimulating circulation.

- Nausea: Ginger has been shown to prevent and treat motion sickness, relax the stomach and relieve the feeling of nausea and morning sickness.

- Lowers Cholesterol: Ginger can lower cholesterol by reducing absorption in the blood and liver. It can also extract and reduce the levels of LDL (bad) cholesterol in the body.

- Anti-Inflammatory: Make ginger poultice with dried ginger powder mixed with warm water. Heat this mixture and stir into a paste. Dip pieces of cloth or linen into the mixture and apply to and massage the effected area of the body. Note – some side effects may include itching, rashes, swelling of the mouth and throat. Discontinue if so.

Brewed as tea, ginger induces sweating which helps fever run its course. It also tones and helps boost the immune system. For ginger tea, infuse 5 or 6 thin slices of root in boiled water.

Horseradish

Horseradish root

Horseradish leaves

The medical properties and uses include stimulant, laxative, rubefacient, diuretic, expectorant and antiseptic. If taken too often it can be emetic. It contains a large amount of sulphur and is a powerful stimulant, whether used internally or applied externally as a rubefacient.

Treatments:

Taken with oily fish or rich meat, it acts as an excellent stimulant to the digestive organs, to help with complete digestion. Useful in the treatment of dropsy. Also recommended in treating scurvy when there is little fever.

A poultice of the root can be used in the same fashion as mustard to treat bronchitis, asthma and pneumonia. This will also help in cases of sciatica, gout, joint-ache or hard swellings of the spleen or liver.

Direct application of poultice or freshly sliced root will help to alleviate insect stings and dental pain.

A gargle of horseradish infusion will help with tonsillitis.

Mixtures:

- Infusion: Mix 0.5 litre boiling water to 30 g horseradish, and 15 g crushed mustard seeds. Consume 2 to 3 tablespoons daily.

- Tincture: A compound spirit may be prepared with slices of the fresh root, orange peel, nutmeg, and fortified wine. This helps with digestion, as well as chronic rheumatism. Take 1 or 2 teaspoons daily after meals with 1/2 glass of water.

- Poultice: Cut only part of the root that you need, and grate. Mix with water to obtain a paste and apply to the effected area.

Turmeric

Turmeric root

Turmeric plant

Turmeric is a perennial plant of the ginger family. It is the root (rhizome) of this plant that is used as a spice and natural medicine. If not used fresh, the root is boiled for several hours and then dried in hot ovens and ground into a fine yellow powder.

Turmeric is a natural antiseptic, antibiotic, anti-inflammatory and antibacterial agent. It is a general immune system booster due to its high antioxidant capacity.

To obtain the most benefits from turmeric it is recommended that it be added to a regular diet, but no more than two or three teaspoons daily.

Treatments:

- Arthritis: Take internally to ease arthritic pain and inflammation.
- Pain Relief: Turmeric is a natural pain killer.
- Wounds: Use turmeric to treat wounds, cysts, eczema and other skin conditions. Make a poultice and apply directly. Note – it stains fabric.
- Cancer Prevention: A teaspoon a day can help to rid the body of cancer cells and protect the body from free radicals.
- Diabetes: It is recommended that those with type 2 diabetes, and those struggling to lose weight take 2 teaspoons a day.

Other Uses:

Turmeric is a natural liver detoxifier. It can also treat gallstones, indigestion, poor circulation, heart disease, anaemia, food poisoning and parasites. Traditionally it was used in Chinese medicine to treat depression.

When applied as a poultice, turmeric speeds up the healing of wounds and assists in remodelling of damaged skin.

Notes:

Taking too much turmeric can cause an upset stomach.

Thyme

Thyme herb

Thyme plant

Also known as brotherwort, traditionally the decoction of thyme (or the plant mashed and mixed with brandy) was held in the mouth against and aching tooth. It was also consumed for stomach aches. For wounds, place thyme together with its leaves against the wound, and pour warm water over for a few minutes.

Floral stalks are effective for paralysis or venereal diseases.

Pharmaceutical Properties:

Thyme is an intestinal antiseptic, choleretic/cholagogue, stomachic, expectorant, and an antiseptic for breathing pipes. It improves the function of the liver and kidneys, it is effective against parasitic worms, and it reduces intestinal spasms.

Mixtures:

- Tea: Place 1-2 teaspoons of plant in 250 ml boiling water. Cover for 10 minutes, after which it can be consumed in three rounds, before main meals.
- Externally: Place 100 g of finely chopped plant in 5 lt of boiling water. Cover for 15 minutes then filter directly into a bath tub. Lay in the bath for at least 20 minutes.

It can be used in the following medical conditions:

Abscesses, acne, lung disease, renal disease, thrushes, dizziness, anaemia, anorexia, burns, asthma, bloating, acute or chronic bronchitis, nervous contractions of the stomach and intestines, diarrhoea, dyspepsia, tooth ache, rheumatic pain, sciatic ashes, infected eczema, enteritis, enterocolitis, oral wounds, intestinal ferments, liver (stimulant), nausea, gout, haemorrhage, intestinal infections, ganglion sores, nipple sores, skin irritations, leucorrhoea, migraines and headaches, oral pemphigus, infected or running wounds.

Thyme administered in any form can destroy the staphylococcus and streptococcus and is useful in any type of infections with these germs. It has no side effects and can be administered to small children and pregnant women, even over long periods of time.

Warnings:

Do NOT overdose, because it can lead to gastro-intestinal disorders, nervous stimulation followed by depression and muscle strain.

Do NOT use in cases of gastritis, enteritis, esophagitis, or pancreatic failure.

Ginseng

Ginseng is a powerful anti-oxidant, anti-inflammatory, analgesic (pain relief), and anticonvulsant. It contains several steroid compounds that are very similar to anabolic steroids found naturally in the body.

Ginseng improves muscle tone, decreases blood sugar levels, and balances the metabolism as it regulates hormone levels.

It helps control diabetes, improves blood pressure and heart action, reduces cholesterol levels, and reduces mental confusion, headaches and weakness among the elderly.

Sometimes referred to as an aphrodisiac, it improves stamina and endurance, and can help prevent or reverse erectile dysfunction.

Ginseng regulates hormones and helps normalize menstruation.

Mixtures:

It can be made into tea or tinctures, or ginseng can simply be chewed or sucked on fresh and raw.

- Tea: Steep a slice of ginseng root in boiled water and cover for at least 5 minutes. Flavour with sugar, honey, cinnamon etc if desired.
- Tincture: Put a handful of dried ginger root in a jar and cover with vodka or gin. Let sit for a few weeks, then strain the liquid and store.

Basil

The medical properties of basil include antiseptic, anti-inflammatory, antimicrobial, antispasmodic, carminative, febrifuge, and expectorant, prevents vomiting, stimulates the adrenal cortex, and soothes itching.

The main use for basil in medicine is for its digestive and anti-gas properties. It is also recommended for treating stomach cramps, vomiting, constipation, headaches and anxiety.

Treatments:

- Basil tea can help with blood pressure, fever or flu. Tea will help a sore throat.
- Basil seed juice is good for liver, kidney and urinary problems.
- For eye troubles associated with pain or burning, mix the juice of basil leaves with honey. For swelling around the eye, apply a mixture of leaf juice and a pinch of alum to the affected area.
- Earache: Mix a tincture of camphor with strong basil juice. Administer a drop or two in the ear for instant relief.
- Epilepsy: Massage the body daily with the juice of the basil leaves. During loss of consciousness during an attack, grind 10 basil leaves and a little salt, and place this under the nostrils of the patient.
- Whooping Cough: Grind equal amounts of basil leaves and black pepper and add a little honey so as to have a consistency to make small tablets. These tablets, sucked slowly, should be taken four times a day. In the case of dry cough, take a mixture of equal amounts of the juices of basil seeds, ginger and onion. In the case of loose cough, add sugar.
- Bladder Stones: Make the patient sit on a steam bath prepared with about 100 g of basil blossoms to a litre of water. Do this daily for a week. Depending on the size and nature of calculi, they should dissolve and be flushed out with the urine.

Mixtures:

- Tea: When used as medicine, basil is usually taken as tea. Use 2 tablespoons of fresh herb, or 1 tablespoon of dried per cup, plus 1 for the pot. Cover the pot while boiling then let this steep for about 5 minutes covered. Strain before consuming. Sweeten with honey if desired.
- Seed Juice: Soak 1 teaspoon of basil seeds in water overnight. The next morning grind the seeds in the water with sugar and drink. Consume twice daily.

Cumin Seeds

Cumin seeds

Cumin flower

Cumin seeds can calm a number of digestive disorders such as morning sickness, indigestion, heartburn, ulcers, diarrhoea and flatulence.

Cumin is an antiseptic, anti-inflammatory, pain reliever.

Mixtures and Treatments:

Mix 1 cup of boiled water with 1 teaspoon of cumin seeds and 1 teaspoon of coriander. Allow to infuse for 20 minutes before drinking. This will relieve many digestive disorders.

Treat a sore throat or cough with tea made from cumin seeds and a slice of ginger. It's a great remedy for colds and flu.

Soothe skin irritations with a paste made from cumin seeds. Add some onion juice to crushed cumin seeds and grind into a paste. Apply to bites, boils, insect stings, even scorpion stings to reduce pain and inflammation.

Drinking 1 teaspoon of cumin seeds and 1 teaspoon of honey in a cup of warm milk will help in healthy development of an unborn baby.

Relieve insomnia by mixing 1 teaspoon of cumin seeds with the pulp of a ripe banana and consume before bed.

Mustard

White mustard
(brassica hirta)

Black mustard
(brassica negra)

Mustard has a laxative effect due to the presence of mucilage. The white seeded mustard has milder effects, being a source of vegetable oil and proteins, calcium, magnesium and potassium.

Combining it with warm water has the effect of increasing arterial pressure and stimulating blood circulation. Mustard also has anti-inflammatory properties.

Treatments:

- Mustard baths are useful for treating headaches, colds and coughs.
- Consuming a spoonful of mustard seeds 2 or 3 times a day can have laxative effects.
- Bronchitis, asthma and pneumonia are treated by applying a black mustard flour poultice on the chest area. Leave it as long as the burning sensation is strong, and then remove it and cover the area with a warm material.
- Intoxications can be treated by drinking a glass of water with a spoonful of black mustard powder, on an empty stomach if possible. This will induce vomiting, purging the toxic material.

Mixtures:

- Mustard flour: This is obtained by grinding or crushing the seeds. Keep it in dark containers and use within 2-3 weeks. Internally, the flour is administered in liquids such as water, milk or wine. Externally it is used in poultices.
- Poultice: Prepare this from 100g of mustard flour mixed with warm water – about 25-30°C until a soft paste is formed.

  Put the paste between two cloths and apply to the troubled area for about 15 minutes, then removed, possibly applying it elsewhere.

  For children or those sensitive to the irritation of mustard, prepare the poultice with 50g mustard flour, and 100g flax or other flour.
- Local wash: Used for treating rheumatism, colds, neuralgias or articulation inflammations. Place 25-30g of mustard flour in a small bag and run 2-3 litres of warm water (25-30°C).
- General Bath: For a general bath, use about 250g of mustard flour in a bag and stir it in the water. This bath should last only 30 minutes.

Warnings:

- Do not administer black mustard to children under 6.
- Administering mustard, black or white, for prolonged periods becomes irritating and toxic – especially in cases of individuals suffering dyspepsia, with a sensitive stomach or colon, or those that suffer from irritations of the urinary tract.

Coriander

Coriander was used by the ancient Greeks, ancient Egyptians and Chinese in their medicine. The whole herb is used to treat conditions such as nausea, toothache, hernias, measles, dysentery and piles.

It is antibacterial and antioxidant. It can be used to delay the spoilage of food, like other herbs with antioxidant properties. The leaves contain a higher concentration of antioxidants than the seeds.

It is usually taken as a tea infusion made from the leaves of the plant.

An effective diuretic can be made by mixing coriander seeds and cumin seeds in equal amounts and boiled to make tea. Cool before drinking.

Coriander will reduce the level of total cholesterol.

Coriander is a great help with the treatment of diabetes, due to its insulin-releasing and insulin-like activity.

Coriander can also relieve insomnia and anxiety.

Lavender

Dried lavender flowers are used to prepare a series of natural remedies with cicatrizing, antiseptic, calming and relaxing effects, as well as nerve stimulating effects. Lavender flowers contain tannin, a bitter substance, mineral substances and essential oils. They are used in cases of digestive disorder, in hypertension, cardiac afflictions, headaches, insomnia, depression, dizziness or bronchial asthma.

Treatments:

- For headaches, anxiety, rheumatism or distension – consume lavender flower tea.
- For insomnia, add some drops of lavender oil to the pillow. This is also useful for relieving stress and clearing nostrils – for this add 5 drops of oil to a vessel of hot water and inhale.
- The oil is a disinfectant of wounds and burns or ulcers. For sunburn, moisten the infected area with the oil mixed with mineral water.
- Use tincture to treat various throat infections, or as a mouthwash.
- Lavender vinegar has insecticide and anti-calcareous effects. Used for rheumatism or colds.

Mixtures:

- Lavender Tea: Prepare with two teaspoons of flowers to a cup of boiled water. Drink it hot and sweeten with honey.
- Tincture: Place 200g of dried flowers in 1 litre of alimentary alcohol and 0.5 litre of distilled water. Leave to macerate (soften) for 4 days, stirring occasionally.
- Concentrated Infusion: Prepare with 5 to 6 spoons of macerated herb in boiling water. Use to treat superficial burns and light wounds.
- Macerated Lavender: Place 40g of dried flowers in 1 litre of alcohol. Leave at room temperature for 2 weeks, stirring occasionally.
- Lavender Oil: Mix 20g of dried flowers with 20ml of alcohol. Place in a jar and mix in 200ml of olive oil and stir well. Place the jar in boiling water for 2 hours, stirring occasionally. Leave it covered for 2 days and filter through gauze. Store in a cool, dry place.
- Vinegar: Prepare vinegar with lavender flowers, mint and sage leaves, rose, savoury and juniper petals and macerate for 1 week in a litre of wine vinegar. Filter and top up to 1 litre with more vinegar.

Warning:

Do not use if you are suffering from hyperacid gastritis or hypertension. Use with caution during pregnancy or breastfeeding.

Fennel

flower

Fennel is a carminative tonic, a stomachic helping digestion. It helps with flatulence and stomach gas, heart problems and increases appetite.

Internal Use:

For stomach problems drink a mixture of 5 g of dried fruits in a cup of water. If you do this before meals it will increase your appetite.

As a diuretic it increases elimination of corporal liquids, helpful in cases of obesity, arthritis and heart illness associated with the accumulation of water in the body. Use a decoction of about 50 grams in a litre of water.

For bronchitis, coughs or chest pains, take 2 drops of essence or tincture dissolved in sugar after main meals. Do this for 3 days maximum.

A strong tea will help with menstruation and the pain that comes with it.

External Use:

For eye irritation, squeeze the juice from the tender plant onto gauze and apply to the eyes. This also with conjunctivitis. For retinal detachment or glaucoma, make a decoction of 40 grams per litre and apply with a towel.

For stomach pains, apply a cataplasm of boiled leaves to the stomach.

Echinacea

Stamens close up

Echinacea is used to stimulate the body's immune system. It is most commonly used in the treatment of the common cold. It can also be used in topically for the treatment of wounds and burns.

Historically it has been used as a general cure-all to treat conditions such as scarlet fever, syphilis, malaria, blood poisoning and diphtheria.

The above ground parts of the plant contain more immune-system activating substances than the roots, which contain high concentrations of volatile oils. Both parts of the plant are used in medicine.

The upper parts of the plant are used to treat colds, upper respiratory tract infections, urinary tract infections and slow healing wounds. The root of the plant is used for flu like infections.

Mixtures:

- Tea: Prepare with 1-2 grams of dried root or herb. Drink 3 times daily.
- Expressed Juice: Take 6-9 ml at a time, 3 times a daily.
- Tincture: Use the root or herb, or both. Use about 100g of root, or 200g of herb (or 50g/100g of each) and put in a large jar with about 1 litre of high-proof alcohol. Cap tightly and store for about 8 weeks. Shake daily for the first week, then every few days after that.

  Strain through cheesecloth and bottle. This is quite a lot, so scale down for smaller quantities. Use 2-3 ml three times daily.

For children, adjust doses according to the weight of the child, assuming a full dose for a 70 kg (150 lb) adult.

Warnings:

Do not take for more than a few weeks. If tingling or twitching or nerve disorders occur, discontinue use immediately. In rare cases it may cause allergic reactions ranging from a mild rash to anaphylaxis – a life threatening reaction causing the throat to tighten and restrict breathing.

Do NOT use if you suffer from tuberculosis, leukaemia, diabetes, multiple sclerosis, HIV or AIDS, or any auto-immune disorder. Use with extreme caution if you suffer from liver disorders.

When taken by mouth – especially in tincture form – echinacea may cause temporary numbing and tingling on the tongue. If this is not severe or long term, there is no cause for alarm.

Apples

Apples, as fresh fruit, contain between 83 to 93% water. Apples contain proteins, vitamins and minerals, in both the flesh and the skin, and are moderately acidic. The skin contains more vitamin C than the flesh.

The acidic quality of an apple helps the digestive system through reflex action invoking saliva and gastric secretions.

Treatments:

Apples eaten with the skin are slightly laxative, and will absorb toxins and micro-organisms from the intestines. Eaten without the skin, apples will help children with acute or chronic diarrhoea.

Apples are very effective at ridding the body of uric acid, which can lead to kidney stones and a type of arthritis known as gout.

For those with obesity, or diabetes – including infants, a diet including apples and tomatoes has been shown to have favourable results.

Ear pains can be alleviated by covering the ear with boiled apple flesh.

Apples will also help reduce high blood pressure and cholesterol.

Warnings:

Apple products such as iMac, iPhone, iPod or iPad should not be taken orally, although they may be used as a suppository.

Hibiscus

Hibiscus sabdariffa (roselle)

Calyces

Calyces dried

All of the *Hibiscus Sabdariffa* (Roselle) plant has uses in both food and medicine. It is also known as Chinese Rose or Chinese hibiscus.

Treatments:

- The leaves: Externally the leaves are antibacterial, emollient (moisturising) and have refrigerant properties – they will help to cool the body and is a useful treatment for heatstroke.

  Internally, a decoction of the leaves will help with coughs, menorrhagia (abnormally long and heavy menstrual periods), dysuria (painful urination), and will help with a headache.

  Make a poultice from the leaves and apply to burns, wounds, swellings or abscesses. This is also soothing for dry or sensitive skin.

- The Flowers: A tea made from the flowers can control chest and lung complaints such as bronchitis. It is an expectorant.

- The Sepals: The sepals are the red pointy 'sub-petals' of the Roselle flower (aka calyces). Hibiscus tea is made from these sepals and is drunk either hot or cold. This tea has properties which help to lower blood pressure, especially for people with type 2 diabetes.

  The tea is a stomachic, a mild diuretic, helps to lower cholesterol, and helps with liver problems and heart disease. It is high in vitamin C and helps boost the body's immune system against colds and flu. It is a powerful anti-oxidant and helps remove bacteria from the body, and to fight infections.

  A delicious syrup or cordial can be made by reducing 1 Kg sugar, 1 litre water and 200 g of Roselle calyces. This can be used directly on deserts or mixed with water for a quick and tasty drink.

- The Fruits: The berries left over after the flower has bloomed, similar to rose hips, are anti-scorbutic (preventing or curing scurvy).

- The Seeds: The seeds are 20% oil and high in vitamin E. They are diuretic and laxative. The seeds roasted can be used as a coffee substitute and is said to have aphrodisiac properties.

- The Root: This is edible, but fibrous and without much flavour.

- The Stem: A strong fibre obtained from the stem can be used to make a tough rope or cordage, known as rosella hemp.

Meadowsweet

Spiraea ulmaria

Filipendula ulmaria

Meadowsweet or *Spiraea ulmaria*, also known as Bridewort or its new botanical name *Filipendula ulmaria*, is part of the Rosaceae plant family.

The entire plant contains methyl salicylate and other salicylates in quantities consistent from plant to plant (unlike other plants that contain these compounds). Aspirin is a synthetic version of methyl salicylate.

The salicylates in this plant are a highly effective analgesic, anti-inflammatory, and fever reducer, without the side effects of aspirin. Other properties include antacid, antiseptic, astringent, diuretic, diaphoretic (it makes you sweat) and antibacterial.

It is very effective as treating stomach disorders in small amounts. It is a valuable treatment in diarrhoea – especially in children, imparting nourishment to the bowels. It is also effective against heart disease, dropsy, dysentery and strangury (painful frequent urination).

Mixtures:

- Usually administered by infusing 30 g (1 oz) of dried herb to 1/2 litre (1 pint) of water, then drinking it in doses of about 1/2 a cup.

- The tea of this plant was used by the Black Foot Indians as an enema and vagina douche to treat infections of the bowels and vaginal area.

Warnings:

In pure form, methyl salicylate is toxic. The lowest lethal does is 100 mg per kg of body weight for adults, and as little as 4 mg total for children.

Rhodiola Rosea 	This perennial plant grows in cold regions of the world including much of the Arctic, the mountains of Central Asia, the Rocky Mountains, the Alps, Scandinavia, Great Britain, Ireland and other places. Studies have shown this plant is effective in reducing depression, reducing fatigue, improving mental and physical performance and regulating serotonin and dopamine levels. It can also stimulate the nervous system, and prevent high altitude sickness. This is drug may help you to cope in a stressful situation, increasing productivity during the day and aiding in a restful sleep at night. Rhodiola is included among a class of plant derivatives called adaptogens which differ from chemical stimulants, such as nicotine, and do not have the same physiological effects. **Mixtures:** • Prepare a tea made out of the crushed <u>root</u> of the plant. Other parts of the plant are not indicated for consumption. **Warnings:** People who suffer disorders such as schizophrenia or bipolar disorder should generally avoid this herb. It may cause mood swings and hallucinations. Pregnant women should also avoid taking this herb.
Comfrey  *Symphytum x uplandicum*	While there are many varieties of comfrey, Russian Comfrey (Symphytum x uplandicum) is the variety most often used for medicine. Also known as Bruisewort, Blackwort, Knitbone and Healing Herb. It contains allantoin which is a natural compound that speeds up the replacement of body cells. Due to this, it has remarkable healing uses. **External Use:** • <u>Poultice:</u> The leaves can be applied directly to injuries to provide instant pain relief. It works well to reduce swelling and inflammation, it can help to speed up healing of torn tendons and ligaments, sprains, and can even aid in healing broken bones. It works very well to heal cuts, bruises, open wounds and sprains. Staph infections are killed quickly by applying salve or poultice. • <u>Salve:</u> Add some aloe vera gel to finely crushed comfrey leaves to form a salve. Apply this for the same ailments as the poultice above. • <u>Infusion:</u> Place 1/4 cup of crushed, dried leaves in 2 cups of boiling water. Let this steep for 10 minutes, and apply directly to the area. **Internal Use:** Some practitioners do not recommend the use of comfrey internally because it contains substances that can cause liver disease and eventual liver failure. Use sparingly if you do ingest it. • Boiling the crushed root provides a mild remedy for diarrhoea and gastro-intestinal problems. • Adding a small amount of comfrey leaves to water (2 teaspoon of dried leaf to a cup of boiling water) can help with a variety of bronchial complaints, particularly whooping cough. **Other Uses:** Comfrey is an excellent natural fertilizer for your garden, and can help speed up composting due to the high nitrogen content. For your garden, mix 1 part of finely chopped or blended comfrey leaves to 10 parts water and use as a liquid fertilizer. For your compost heap, use a 1 to 1 mix and pour over your compost heap. It a great source of potassium, and while growing, will extract nutrients from deep in the soil, beneath the roots of other plants.

Heather

Calluna vulgaris

Heather, also known as Scotch heather, has many traditional uses in medicine. The herb and flowers are usually taken as a tea to purify the blood, stimulate the metabolism, treat gastrointestinal disorders, and reduce gravel and inflammation of the urinary system.

Heather was used in Swedish traditional medicine to treat inflammatory diseases and wounds. It has many antimicrobial compounds and honey made from heather flowers has high antibacterial activity.

Taken internally, heather will help to ease cystitis, will suppress coughing and breathing disorders like bronchitis. It helps circulatory disorders, digestive disorders, gastrointestinal problems, urinary tract problems, laryngitis, and will help with high blood pressure. It aids sleepiness and relaxation. It is an appetite stimulant, and a diuretic.

Mixtures:

- Normal use is to infuse 1-2 grams of finely chopped herb and/or flower in boiled water for 10 minutes, then strain and consume. Heather tea is taken 3 times a day.
- A stronger infusion will treat urinary tract infections.
- A Benedictine monk believed that boiling the stems and drinking the brew for 30 days could dissolve kidney stones. He also recommended the patient bathe in heather water.

External Use:

- A warm poultice made from the leaves and flowers will help to ease insect bites, can be used to treat wounds, can help ease arthritis and chilblains, and has astringent properties.

Warning:

Due to the high tannin content of the leaves, prolonged use is not recommended and may damage the liver and alimentary canal.

Tomatoes

Tomatoes have been shown to help and prevent certain types of cancer, although it is unknown why. They decrease the risk of prostate, lung and stomach cancer, and may also prevent pancreatic, colorectal, oesophageal, oral, breast and cervical cancer.

Tomatoes, technically a fruit, are easy to grow and contain a wealth of vitamins and minerals and should be a regular part of your diet.

Cooking tomatoes rather than eating them raw increases its benefits in preventing cancer. Adding a little oil intensifies this even further.

Internal Benefits:

- Good for coronary heart health, reduces high blood pressure, prevents diarrhoea, and supports liver health.

External Use:

- Heals sunburn, soothes eye irritation, soothes wounds and sores, will help stop the stink of skunk when used with lemon juice.

5.3.1 NOTES

The pictures in this plant guide are not intended to be used for identification of wild plants. They are there so you can identify plants in your own garden, because you are a staunch survivalist and are actively growing these plants from properly sourced heirloom seeds. See **MEDICINE GROWING GUIDE** (Page 10-4) for details on growing most of the listed plants.

Wherever a specific botanical name is given for a plant, notes given are for that plant ONLY. Other species listed under the common name may contain no medicinal benefit at all, and may even be poisonous. Parts of the plant not listed for consumption, should not be consumed unless you know specifically otherwise.

When using herbal remedies pay careful attention to side effects and discontinue use if adverse reactions are noted. This guide is intended to be a helping hand where no other help is available. If you have access to professional help, please use it.

5.3.2 CROSS REFERENCE

key
x useful treatment
Ø do not use with condition
† do not use if pregnant
‡ caution if pregnant

	Aloe Vera	Basil	Chilli Peppers	Cinnamon ‡	Comfrey	Coriander	Cumin Seeds
abscesses							
acne							
arthritis (rheumatism)			x				
anorexia							
asthma		x					
bronchitis				x			
burns	x			x			
cataracts		x					
cirrhosis							
cholera							
colds				x			x
constipation	x						
coughs							x
dental pain			x		x		
diabetes			x	x	x		
diarrhoea				x	x		
distension							
dysentery					x		
dyspepsia							
earache		x					
eczema							
epilepsy		x					
eye problems							
edemas (dropsy)							
fever/flu		x					
flatulence		x		x			x
gastritis					x		
gout							
haemorrhoids							
headaches		x					
indigestion		x					x
influenza							
insomnia		x			x		
intestinal inflammation							
lung problems							
menstruation				x			
nausea				x		x	
pain relief					x	x	x
parasites			x				
pleurisy							
pneumonia							
psoriasis	x		x				
scabies							
sciatica							
scurvy							
shingles			x				
skin irritation	x						
sinusitis		x					

	Aloe Vera	Basil	Chilli Peppers	Cinnamon ‡	Comfrey	Coriander	Cumin Seeds
stomach aches							
stomach cramps		x					
stomach ulcers				x			x
stones		x					
throat problems							
thrush				x			
tonsillitis							
tuberculosis							
tumours							
urinary problems		x					
vomiting		x					
warts							
whooping cough		x			x		
worms			x				
wounds	x				x		
yeast infections				x			

USEFUL FOR

	Aloe Vera	Basil	Chilli Peppers	Cinnamon ‡	Comfrey	Coriander	Cumin Seeds
blood coagulation							
blood pressure							
blood sugar				x			
cardiovascular							
cholesterol						x	
circulation			x				
digestion	x	x	x				x
itching/irritation		x				x	x
immune system							
insect bites		x					x
insecticide							
liver/kidney function							

MEDICAL PROPERTIES

	Aloe Vera	Basil	Chilli Peppers	Cinnamon ‡	Comfrey	Coriander	Cumin Seeds
antibacterial			x		x		
anti-calcareous							
anticonvulsant							
antifungal			x				
anti-inflammatory		x			x		x
antioxidant						x	
antiviral	x						
antiseptic	x						x
antispasmodic	x						
choleretic							
cholagogue						x	
diuretic							
expectorant	x						
laxative							
sedative							
stimulant			x				
stomachic	x	x	x				x

key
x useful treatment
Ø do not use
   with condition
† do not use
   if pregnant
‡ caution if pregnant

	Dandelion†	Echinacea	Fennel	Garlic	Ginger	Ginseng	Heather	Hibiscus	Horseradish	Lavender‡	Meadowsweet	Mustard	Onion	Oregano	Rose Hips	Rosemary†	Sesame	Spinach	Thyme	Tomatoes	Turmeric	Yarrow
abscesses													x						x			
acne			x																			
arthritis (rheumatism)		x	x		x	x		x	x			x			x	x	Ø		x		x	
anorexia	x															x						
asthma			x					x				x			x							
bronchitis		x				x		x														
burns	x												x						x	x		
cataracts	x																					
cirrhosis													x									
cholera															x	x						
colds				x				x				x			x							
constipation	x			x											x	x	x					
coughs		x		x			x					x	x	x	x							
dental pain				x				x						x		x						
diabetes		Ø			x								x								x	
diarrhoea			x								x		x							x		
distension										x												
dysentery											x					x	x					
dyspepsia												Ø							x			
earache																						
eczema																			x		x	
epilepsy																Ø						
eye problems	x	x																		x		
edemas (dropsy)							x				x		x			x						
fever/flu	x	x			x	x																
flatulence		x												x								
gastritis						x			Ø								Ø	Ø				
gout								x					x						x			
haemorrhoids													x									
headaches					x	x		x	x	x						x			x			
indigestion														x	x						x	
influenza					x										x	x						
insomnia					x					x						x	x					
intestinal inflammation																		Ø				
lung problems													x			x			x			
menstruation		x			x		x															x
nausea					x														x			
pain relief					x					x	x					x					x	x
parasites				x																		
pleurisy												x										
pneumonia								x				x										
psoriasis																						
scabies				x																		
sciatica								x														
scurvy							x	x														
shingles																						
skin irritation																				x	x	
sinusitis			x										x			x						

key
x useful treatment
Ø do not use with condition
† do not use if pregnant
‡ caution if pregnant

	Dandelion†	Echinacea	Fennel	Garlic	Ginger	Ginseng	Heather	Hibiscus	Horseradish	Lavender ‡	Meadowsweet	Mustard	Onion	Oregano	Rose Hips	Rosemary †	Sesame	Spinach	Thyme	Tomatoes	Turmeric	Yarrow
stomach aches		x									x								x			
stomach cramps															x							
stomach ulcers																		x				
stones				Ø		x															x	
throat problems								x	x													
thrush																						
tonsillitis								x														
tuberculosis				x																		
tumours				x																		
urinary problems	x						x	x				Ø	x	x	x							
vomiting															x							
warts														x								
whooping cough																						
worms				x													x					
wounds	x	x								x									x		x	x
yeast infections																						

USEFUL FOR

	Dandelion†	Echinacea	Fennel	Garlic	Ginger	Ginseng	Heather	Hibiscus	Horseradish	Lavender ‡	Meadowsweet	Mustard	Onion	Oregano	Rose Hips	Rosemary †	Sesame	Spinach	Thyme	Tomatoes	Turmeric	Yarrow
blood coagulation					x																	x
blood pressure			x	x	x	x					Ø				x							
blood sugar					x																	
cardiovascular										x		x			x						x	
cholesterol	x				x			x														
circulation					x										x							
digestion	x		x	x	x		x		x	x		x	x	x					x		x	x
itching/irritation																						
immune system	x				x			x											x		x	
insect bites							x		x													
insecticide									x													
liver/kidney function	x				x			x				x		x				x	x		x	

MEDICAL PROPERTIES

	Dandelion†	Echinacea	Fennel	Garlic	Ginger	Ginseng	Heather	Hibiscus	Horseradish	Lavender ‡	Meadowsweet	Mustard	Onion	Oregano	Rose Hips	Rosemary †	Sesame	Spinach	Thyme	Tomatoes	Turmeric	Yarrow
antibacterial		x					x	x			x	x									x	
anti-calcareous									x													
anticonvulsant					x																	
antifungal												x										
anti-inflammatory					x	x									x	x					x	x
antioxidant	x							x							x		x				x	
antiviral	x																					
antiseptic		x							x			x			x						x	x
antispasmodic																						x
choleretic																			x			
cholagogue																			x			
diuretic	x	x	x				x	x			x				x	x		x				
expectorant		x							x						x				x			
laxative												x			x		x					
sedative						x	x															
stimulant		x							x									x				
stomachic	x	x	x	x			x	x	x		x		x	x					x		x	x

5.3.3 MEDICAL TERMS AND DEFINITIONS

MEDICAL CONDITIONS	
Abscesses	An abscess is a collection of pus that has formed in a cavity in tissue where an infection has developed – usually caused by bacteria or parasites. Can be caused by foreign materials such as splinters, bullets wounds or injecting needles.
Anaemia	Anaemia is a decrease of the number of red blood cells in the body or less than the normal quantity of haemoglobin in the blood. Anaemia results in lack of oxygen in organs (hypoxia).
	It is characterized by feelings of weakness and fatigue, and sometimes a paleness of the skin. Anaemia can be caused by lack of iron in the diet.
Bronchitis	This is inflammation of mucous membranes in the airways that carry air from the trachea to the lungs.
	Acute bronchitis is characterized by a development of a cough, with or without mucous that is coughed up through the respiratory tract. Chronic bronchitis produces a cough – often worse after waking, with mucous that lasts three or more months in a year for at least two years.
	Other symptoms may include wheezing, shortness of breath, sore throat, runny nose, pleurisy. The yellow-green mucous may have blood.
Cataracts	A cataract is a cloudiness in the normally transparent part of the eye. This can cause a decrease in vision and may lead to eventual blindness.
Cholera	Cholera is an infection of the small intestine that causes a large amount of watery diarrhoea. Cholera comes from drinking contaminated food or especially water. It has also been associated with shellfish, especially raw oysters. Symptoms include abdominal cramps, dry skin, excessive thirst, lethargy/tiredness, dry eyes, nausea, rapid pulse, vomiting.
Distension	Gastric distension is bloating of the stomach when air is pumped into it. This may happen when someone is performing CPR. It can cause the contents of the stomach to rise up and spill down into the lungs.
	Abdominal distension is usually described as gas or bloating and gives the feeling of being uncomfortably full. It can be caused by diabetes, dyspepsia, constipation, food poisoning. Women often suffer from it during menstruation.
Dysentery	Dysentery refers to a group of gastrointestinal disorders characterized by inflammation of the intestines, in particular the colon. Symptoms include abdominal pain and cramps, and frequent passage of watery diarrhoea containing blood and mucus.
Dyspepsia	Dyspepsia is also known as an upset stomach, or indigestion. It is characterized by chronic or recurring pain in the upper abdomen, a feeling of fullness. It can also be accompanied by bloating, belching, nausea or heartburn.
Eczema	An acute or chronic inflammation of the skin. It is characterized by redness, itching and the outbreak of lesions that may discharge matter and become encrusted and scaly. It is not contagious.
Edemas (dropsy)	This is an accumulation of fluids in the circulatory system or in tissues between the body's cells. It is sometimes characterized by swelling where an indent in the skin will remain after pressure is applied.
Gastritis	Gastritis generally refers to inflammation of the lining of the stomach, causing burning or discomfort. Not to be confused with common symptoms of upper abdominal discomfort, gastritis can lead to ulcers and sometimes more serious complications.

Gout	Gout is a form of acute arthritis that causes severe pain and swelling in the joints. It most commonly affects the big toe, but may also affect the heel, ankle, hand, wrist or elbow. It usually comes on suddenly and goes away after 5-10 days, and can keep reoccurring.
Haemorrhoids (piles)	A haemorrhoid is an area around the anus where veins become swollen and the tissue swells, causing itching and pain. They can be internal, external or mixed.
Hypertension	High blood pressure.
Pleurisy	This is an inflammation of the lining surrounding the lungs. Infections are the most common cause. The main symptom is a sharp stabbing pain in the chest that gets worse when deep breathing.
	Other symptoms can include shortness of breath, cough, fever and chills, unexplained weight loss, sore throat, diarrhoea, vomiting blood.
Pneumonia	This is an inflammatory condition of the lungs, or when the lungs fill with fluid. The main cause is infection from bacteria, viruses, fungi, or parasites. Symptoms include cough, chest pain, fever and difficult breathing. It is most commonly treated with antibiotics.
Psoriasis	Psoriasis is a condition that causes skin cells to mature faster than the body can shed the dead cells. This causes raised patches of dead skin on the arms, back, chest, elbows, legs, nails, buttocks and scalp.
	This non-contagious disease is characterized by inflamed legions covered with silvery-white scabs of dead skin.
Scabies	Scabies is a fairly contagious infection caused by a tiny mite about 0.3 mm long. The female burrows into the skin and lays eggs. The eggs hatch and the babies rise to the surface, mate, and repeat the cycle.
	The intense itching is caused by a reaction between the skin and feces.
Sciatica	Sciatica is a pain in the sciatic nerve. This nerve runs from the lower part of the spinal cord down the back of the leg to the foot.
	Injury or pressure to this nerve can cause a sharp or burning pain that radiates from the lower back or hip. Sometimes this pain follows the path of the nerve to the foot.
Scurvy	Scurvy is a condition caused by lack of vitamin C. Symptoms include tiredness, muscle weakness, joint and muscle aches, a rash on the legs and bleeding gums. It's common amongst people deprived of fresh fruits and vegetables for long periods of time – most notably, sailors.
Shingles	Shingles (herpes zoster) is a painful, blistering skin rash due to the varicella-zoster virus, the virus that causes chickenpox.
Thrush	A contagious disease caused by a fungus. It occurs most often in infants and children, characterized by small whitish eruptions on the mouth, throat and tongue. Usually accompanied by fever and diarrhoea.
Tonsillitis	Tonsillitis is an inflammation of the tonsils caused by viral or bacterial infection. Symptoms include red and/or swollen tonsils, white or yellow patches on the tonsils, sore throat and painful swallowing.
	Bacterial tonsillitis is treated with antibiotics. There is no known treatment to shorten the duration of viral tonsillitis.
Whooping Cough	This is a highly contagious bacterial disease. The symptoms are initially mild, and then develop into severe coughing fits, which produce a high-pitched "whoop" sound in infected babies and children when they inhale air after coughing. The incubation stage is typically 7 to 10 days, with the coughing stage lasts approximately 6 weeks.

TREATMENTS

Analgesic	A pain reliever.
Antibiotic	An antibiotic is a substance that kills or slows growth of bacteria, such as penicillin. Colloidal silver is a wide spectrum antibiotic.
Anti-inflammatory	A substance that reduces inflammation, which can reduce pain, as opposed to other analgesics that work by affecting the nervous system.
Antiseptic	A substance that kills micro-organisms on external surfaces of the body.
Anti-spasmodic	This is a treatment that reduces muscle spasms. Cannabis (marijuana) is a highly effective anti-spasmodic. Peppermint oil is also effective.
Carminative	A carminative is a herb or preparation that prevents formation, or helps to expel, gas in the intestinal tract (ie, flatulence).
Cholagogue	A cholagogue is a medicinal agent which promotes the discharge of bile from the system, purging it downward.
Choleretic	Choleretics are substances that increase the volume of secretion of bile from the liver as well as the amount of solids secreted.
Diuretic	This is a treatment that increases output of urine. All diuretics reduce the amount of water in the body. They can be used to treat heart failure, liver cirrhosis, hypertension, and certain kidney diseases.
Expectorant	An expectorant or mucolytic agent is any agent which dissolves thick mucus and is usually used to help relieve respiratory difficulties.
Febrifuge	These are treatments that are used to help reduce fever. If one does not have a fever, they will normally not lower body temperature. Aspirin and ibuprofen are febrifuges.
Rubefacient	A rubefacient is a topical treatment which produces redness of the skin by causing dilation of the capillaries and an increase in blood circulation. It can sometimes help acute or chronic pains, although its effectiveness is debated.
Stomachic	A stomachic medicine is one that serves to tone the stomach, improving its function and increasing appetite.

5.4 MISCELLANEOUS USES OF PLANTS

- Make dyes from various plants to colour clothing or to camouflage your skin. Usually, you will have to boil the plants to get the best results. Onion skins produce yellow, walnut hulls produce brown, and pokeberries provide a purple dye.
- Make fibres and cordage from plant fibres. Most commonly used are the stems from nettles and milkweeds, yucca plants, and the inner bark of trees like the linden. Rope making is discussed in detail in **Making Ropes and Cord** (Page 7-1).
- Make fish poison by immersing walnut hulls in a small area of quiet water. This poison makes it impossible for the fish to breathe but doesn't adversely affect their edibility.
- Make tinder for starting fires from cattail fluff, cedar bark, lighter knot wood from pine trees, or hardened sap from resinous wood trees.
- Make insulation by fluffing up female cattail heads or milkweed down.
- Make insect repellents by applying the expressed juice of wild garlic or onion to the skin, by placing sassafras leaves in your shelter, or by burning or smudging cattail seed hair fibres.
- Plants can be your ally as long as you use them cautiously. The key to the safe use of plants is positive identification whether you use them as food or medicine or in constructing shelters or equipment.

6 FIRECRAFT

In many survival situations, the ability to start a fire can make the difference between living and dying. Fire can provide warmth and comfort, keep insects and animals at bay, cook and preserve food, and also many advanced uses.

You can use fire to purify water, sterilize bandages and provide protection from animals. You can also use fire to produce tools and weapons.

Fire can also cause problems. Others can detect the smoke and light. Remember to weigh your need for fire against your need to avoid detection.

6.1 SITE SELECTION AND PREPARATION

Look for a dry spot that —

- Is protected from the wind.
- Is suitably placed in relation to your shelter.
- Will reflect heat in the direction you desire.
- Has a supply of wood or other fuel available.

If you are in a wooded or brush-covered area, clear the brush and scrape the surface soil from the spot you have selected. Clear a circle at least 2 metres in diameter so there is little chance of the fire spreading.

If time allows, construct a fire wall using logs or rocks. This wall will help to reflect the heat where you want it. It will also reduce flying sparks and cut down on the amount of wind blowing into the fire. However, you will need enough wind to keep the fire burning.

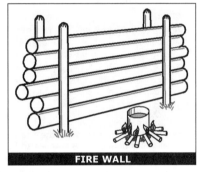

FIRE WALL

 CAUTION – Do not use porous rocks, such as sandstone or rocks found in a river bed as they may explode with quite some force when heated.

In some situations, you may find that an underground fireplace will best meet your needs. It conceals the fire and serves well for cooking food. To make an underground fireplace or Dakota fire hole —

- Dig a hole in the ground.
- On the upwind side of this hole, poke or dig a large connecting hole for ventilation.
- Build your fire in the hole as illustrated.

If you are in a snow-covered area, use green logs to make a dry base for your fire. Trees with

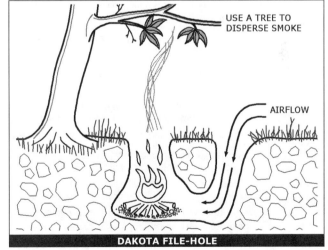

USE A TREE TO DISPERSE SMOKE

AIRFLOW

DAKOTA FILE-HOLE

wrist-sized trunks are easily broken in extreme cold. Cut or break several green logs and lay them side by side on top of the snow. Add one or two more layers. Lay the top layer of logs opposite those below it.

6.2   FIRE MATERIAL SELECTION

You need three types of materials to build a fire – tinder, kindling, and fuel.

Tinder

Tinder is dry material that ignites with little heat – a spark starts a fire. The tinder must be absolutely dry to be sure just a spark will ignite it. If you only have a device that generates sparks, **Char Cloth** (Page 6-11) will be almost essential.

Other materials suitable for tinder is birch bark, dried grasses, fine wood shavings, bird down, waxed paper, cotton fluff from clothing. Dried fungi are excellent if finely powdered. Where insects such as wood wasps have been boring into trees, the fine dust they produce is good tinder. Powdery bird and bat droppings can be used. The inside of birds nests are usually lined with down feathers and ignite easily.

It is critical that your tinder stays bone dry. It is a good idea to carry tinder in a waterproof container. Always keep an eye out for dry tinder to collect.

Kindling

Kindling is the wood used to raise the flames from tinder so that larger and less combustible materials can be burned. The best kindling is small dry twigs and softer woods. Kindling that contains resin is even better.

Don't collect kindling straight from the earth, it is almost always damp. Instead take it from standing deadwood. Many healthy trees will have dead twigs still attached to their trunks. If the outside is damp, shave it until the dry core is reached.

Fuel

Fuel is less combustible material that burns slowly and steadily once ignited. Use dry wood from standing trees to build the fire up. As a general rule, the heavier the wood is, the more heat it will produce – this applies to both dead and green wood. Mixing green and dead wood makes a long lasting fire – especially useful at night.

Hardwoods such as hickory, beech or oak burn well, provide a lot of heat and lasts for a long time as hot coals. They keep a fire going through the night.

Softwoods tend to burn too fast and give off sparks. The worst spark emitters are cedar, alder, hemlock, spruce, pine, chestnut and willow.

Note that damp wood can sometimes be an advantage as the smoke it produces will keep flies, midges and mosquitoes at bay. It will also make the fire last longer.

6.2.1 OTHER FUELS

In areas where wood is scarce, other forms of fuel must be found.

Animal Droppings	These make excellent fuel. Dry the droppings thoroughly for a good smokeless fire. You can mix them with grass, moss and leaves.
Peat	Peat is often found in well-drained moors. It is soft and springy underfoot and may be exposed on the edges of rocky outcrops – looking black and fibrous. It is easy to cut with a knife. Peat needs good ventilation when burning.
	Cut blocks of peat and stack with plenty of air in between each block to dry.
Oils	If you have oils around that you have no other use for you can burn it. This includes diesel, anti-freeze, hydraulic fluid, motor oil and other materials.
	In very cold areas drain oil from an engine sump before it congeals. If you have no container, drain it on the ground and use later in the solid state.
	Mix petrol with sand and burn it in a container as a stove, or dig a hole and make a fire-pit.
Animal Fats	These can be used with a wick in a ventilated tin to make a stove. Bones add bulk when fat is being burned as a fire. Sometimes this is the only fuel available in polar regions.

6.3   HOW TO BUILD A FIRE

There are several methods for laying a fire, each of which has advantages. The situation you find yourself in will determine which fire to use. Prepare the fireplace carefully. Choose a site that is sheltered, especially from high winds.

Teepee

To make this fire, arrange the tinder and a few sticks of kindling in the shape of a tepee or cone. Light the centre. As the tepee burns, the outside logs will fall inward, feeding the fire. This type of fire burns well even with wet wood.

KINDLING

Pyramid

To lay this fire, place two logs or branches parallel on the ground. Place a solid layer of small logs across the bottom logs. Add three or four more alternating layers of logs or branches, each layer smaller than the layer below it.

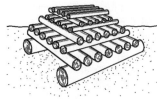

Light a fire on top of the pyramid. As the fire burns, it will ignite the logs below it. This gives you a fire that burns downward, requiring no attention overnight.

There are several other ways to lay a fire that are quite effective. Your situation and the material available in the area may make another method more suitable.

Platform Fire

If the ground is wet or covered with snow, the fire must be built on a platform. Make this from a layer of green logs covered with a layer of earth or stones.

Beware of using porous rocks such as sandstone or those found on riverbeds, as they may explode.

Temple Fire

If the land is swampy or the snow is deep, a raised platform is needed. This is known as a temple fire.

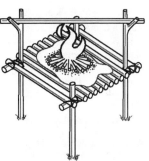

- This consists of a raised platform built of green timber.
- Four uprights support cross pieces in their forks.
- Across them place a layer of green logs and cover them with several inches of earth or sand.
- Light the fire on top of this.
- A pole across upper forks on diagonally opposite uprights can support cooking pots.

Reflectors

A single fire outdoors will only heat one side of you, requiring constant turning when it's very cold, as one side bakes and the other freezes. You can light two or three fires and sit in the middle of them, but this requires a lot of fuel and, no matter which way the wind is blowing, will cover you with smoke. Instead, build one fire and use reflectors.

FIRE REFLECTORS

Snake Hole Fire

This is a shielded fire that produces a good draught and burns almost anything when lit.

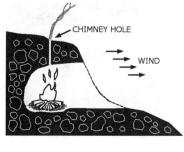

In the side of a firm earth bank, excavate a decent sized chamber. Drive a stick down from above to create a chimney. Remove the dirt that falls below and light a fire in the chamber.

It's good for burning rubbish and for smoke preserving meat and fish. The fire entrance is best placed downwind in windy conditions.

Burning Oil and Water

This mixture makes one of the hottest of all fires and will burn almost anything.

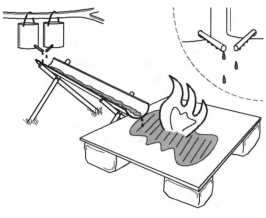

Take two tin cans and pierce a hole near the bottom in each. Fit a tapered stick into the holes to govern flow rate.

Fill one container with oil and one with water. Adjust the tapered plugs to provide a suitable flow rate.

Try about 2-3 drops water to 1 drop oil.

Light a fire underneath a metal plate to get it hot. Once hot, the mixture is extremely volatile.

Light it above the plate.

6.3.1 COOKING FIRES

These cooking fires are also good for heating.

Yukon Stove

This fire, once lit, will burn almost anything.

It takes a lot of effort to build but if you are in a permanent or semi-permanent setup, it is worth it.

The whole structure gives off good heat which lasts for ages due to the thermal mass of the stones and earth used to make it, and the top can be used for cooking.

Dig a circular hole about 30cm (1 ft) deep with a channel on one side leading down to it – basically a Dakota fire hole.

Set up rocks around the edge of the main hole and build up a funnel, gradually sloping inwards.

When you near the top, let the upper courses begin to open out again.

Seal the spaces between the rocks with earth or clay as you build it up.

Light the fire first in the channel. When it gets going, push it beneath the chimney.

Fuel is fed through the top of the chimney and the rate of burning is controlled by opening or closing the top.

This fire leaves very little ash and will burn a very long time before it needs clearing out.

Trench Fire

This fire is sheltered from strong wind by being below ground. Dig a trench deep enough to contain the fire and a layer of rocks to line the bottom. Even when the fire has died down, the rocks will remain hot and make an excellent grill.

A spit across the embers is great for roasting

Hobo Stove

This stove provides a good source of heat which several people can huddle around and its top can be used for cooking. To make it you need something like a 5 gallon or larger oil or chemical drum.

Punch holes in the bottom, and punch a ring of holes around the side of the drum near the bottom. Cut out a panel on one side through which to stoke the fire.

Punch holes in the top if to be used for heating, but make them on the upper part of one side if you don't want smoke coming through the top. Set the whole drum on a ring of stones so that there is plenty of draught between.

6.4 COOKING

When food is heated it loses nutritional value – the more heat the greater the loss – so nothing should be cooked longer than necessary to make it palatable unless it is suspect and being cooked to kill germs and parasites, or to neutralise poisons.

Boiling vegetables destroys their vitamin C content and roasting meat removes its all-important fat, but we are used to eating our food cooked and a hot meal is invaluable for morale. It would take great discipline to eat many things raw that you had not previously considered foods, but a frog, grubs or rats do not seem so bad once cooked.

Cooking requires a slow heat. Use the flame for boiling water then let the fierce flames die down to embers and hot ash for cooking.

Boiling

Cooking in boiling water requires a container. In the absence of proper cooking gear, tin cans and metal boxes are ideal. Make a handle, hang them from a pot support, or use pliers or improvised tongs to remove them from the fire.

Puncture holes in pots can be repaired by hammering in small plugs of wood – they will swell when wet.

A thick length of bamboo will also hold liquid well. Containers can be built from birch bark, but be careful that it doesn't boil dry. In a pinch you can also dig a hole, heat rocks up and place these in the water.

Roasting

Roasting meat cooks in its own fat. The easiest method is to skewer the meat on a spit and turn it over hot embers, or beside a blazing fire. Continually turning the meat keeps the fat moving over the surface.

Roasting makes a tasty meal, but has two disadvantages. Valuable fat is lost unless a drip tray is placed beneath the spit. Roasting by a fierce fire can cook and seal the outside, the inner flesh remaining uncooked, leaving harmful bacteria alive.

A slow roast is preferable, and you can slice off outer meat as it cooks, and keep the remaining meat cooking to ensure all the meat is cooked properly. The dangers of bacteria are too great to risk eating undercooked meat.

Baking

You need an oven for baking which will take some time and resources to improvise, but if you have such luxuries, an oven is well worth the effort.

A large food tin or metal box with a hinged lid is ideal for an improvised oven.

Make sure the lid does not seal airtight or pressure may build and cause an explosion.

Stand the tin on some rocks so that a fire can be lit beneath.

Build up rocks and earth – or better, clay – around back and sides to cover it.

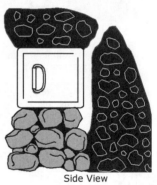

Front View   Side View

But make sure you leave a gap behind it for smoke and heat to move around the back. Use a stick to make a chimney hole from above to the space at the back.

Steaming

Steaming does not overcook so preserves nutrition. It is an excellent way of cooking fish and green vegetables. Fresh young leaves take very little cooking. The food needs to be suspended in the steam, out of the boiling water.

Make a simple steamer by punching holes in a can and suspending it inside a larger can, or putting a pile of rocks or such above the water level to keep the inner can above the water.

Cover the outer can so that that steam has a chance to circulate, but not so tightly so that it is sealed or pressure may build up causing an explosion.

The sections of bamboo also make a good improvised steamer. Make a small hole between the sections, but big enough so the bottom section can be filled with water from the top.

Make a lid for the top, but not too tight. Water from the bottom will boil and produce steam to cook food in the top section.

Cooking in clay

Wrapping food in clay is a method that requires no utensils and offers a tasty alternative even when you have them. Wrap the food in a ball of thick clay – about an inch, and place on the hot embers of a fire. The heat radiates trough the clay which protects the food from burning.

Animals must be cleaned and gutted first but need no be prepared in any other way. When the clay is removed, a hedgehog's spines or fish scales will remain embedded on it. The feathers of small birds will also be removed by the clay, but the feathers are insulating and may prevent the meat from being thoroughly cooked.

Hangi Method

This is another way of cooking without utensils. It requires kindling, logs and round logs about the size of a fist. Do not use soft, porous or flaky stones that may explode when heated.

Dig an oval-shaped hole with round sides 45-60 cm (18-24 in) deep and set up a well-formed tee-pee fire in the bottom, but do not light it yet.

Lay logs across the hole, then place another layer at right angles to the, interspersing them with stones. Make another layer of logs and build up five or six more layers, topping the whole construction off with stones.

When the kindling is set alight, the logs will burn, heating the stones above them, until eventually it all falls into the pit. Remove the burning embers and ash and place food on top of the hot rocks, meat in the centre and vegetables toward the outside edge.

Make sure the food does not touch the earth on the outside.

Lay saplings across the hole, and place sacking, leaves and so forth on top of them. Cover the lot with the earth you excavated to keep the heat in.

The hole now acts like a pressure cooker. After about 1 to 2 hours, remove the cover – your meal is cooked.

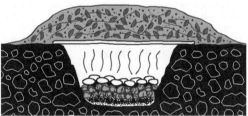

6.4.1 COOKING UTENSILS

Tongs

Choose two branches, both with a natural curve and lash them together so that they want to spring apart at the free ends. Or use a tapering piece of wood between them under the lashings to hold them apart. If one has a forked end, this will provide a better grip.

Pot Rods

Simple pot rods can be improvised by driving a sturdy fork into the ground near the fire – but not too close that it catches fire. Rest a much longer stick across it and hold it down with heavy rocks, or drive it deep into the ground.

Cut a groove near the tip to prevent pots from hanging off. The stick could also be used to skewer a piece of meat or root vegetables.

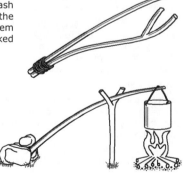

Swinging Pot Holder

This can be made from two forked sticks and a firm upright driven securely into the ground. Bind the branches together so the forks fit in opposite directions on the upright.

The cantilever action will maintain the height you set it at when it is weighted, and a push sideways will swing the pot away from the flames.

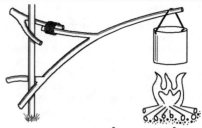

Variable Pot Hook

When cooking over a fire it is often necessary to vary the height to prevent burning or to maintain heat as the fire dies.

This hanging device will allow you to control the height.

Cut a strong piece with several branches from a small tree or bush and trim the branches to about 10 cm (4 in). Strip off any bark that may hide rotten branches, and may flake off into your container.

Bamboo Cup

Cut a section of bamboo just below a natural joint and then cut just below the next joint up. Smooth the edges to prevent splinters.

Spoon

Start with a flattish piece of wood and scribe a spoon shape into it with the point of your knife. Then whittle away to the required shape. Do not rush as this will result in mistakes.

6.5 HOW TO LIGHT A FIRE

Always light your fire from the upwind side. Make sure to lay your tinder, kindling, and fuel so that your fire will burn as long as you need it. Igniters provide the initial heat required to start the tinder burning. They fall into two categories: modern methods and primitive methods.

6.5.1 MODERN METHODS

Matches

Make sure these matches are waterproof. Also, store them in a waterproof container along with a few dependable striker pads. NOTE – matches suck. Forget them. Stock lighters instead.

Cigarette Lighters

A stock of everyday cigarette lighters will serve you well. The French Bic brand is recommended because of their reliability, availability and ease of drying. In some countries they come with a metal strip over the flint wheel to make it difficult for children to light them. This strip can give some protection against water, but should be removed if you need to dry it.

Try to keep them dry, but if they do happen to get wet it is a simple task to get them sparking, even if they have been fully submersed. Put the flint to your lips and suck air through it, then flick the flint wheel a few times (without pressing on the gas), and repeat this procedure until you get a spark.

Convex Lens

Use this method only on bright, sunny days. The lens can come from binoculars, camera, telescopic sights, or magnifying glasses. Angle the lens to concentrate the sun's rays on the tinder.

Hold the lens over the same spot until the tinder begins to smoulder. Gently blow or fan the tinder into flame, and then build up a fire around it.

Metal Match (or Firesteel)

Place a flat, dry leaf under your tinder with a portion exposed. Place the tip of the metal match on the dry leaf, holding the metal match in one hand and a knife in the other.

Scrape your knife against the metal match to produce sparks. The sparks will hit the tinder. When the tinder starts to smoulder, proceed as above.

This works far better with a carbon-steel knife or striker than with a stainless steel one.

Battery

Use a battery to generate a spark. Attach a wire to each terminal. Scrape the wires together near the tinder to create sparks. Be careful not to let the terminals weld together. If this happens then quickly and sharply pull them apart. A short circuited battery is dangerous.

Gunpowder

If you have ammunition, carefully extract the bullet from the shell casing, and use the gunpowder as tinder. A spark will ignite the powder. Be extremely careful when extracting the bullet from the case.

Chemical Methods

These mixtures can be ignited by grinding with rocks or putting them under the friction point in a fire drill.

Mix carefully and avoid contact with metal. Make sure you keep them dry.

CHEMICAL	(FORMULA)	(RATIO)
Potassium chlorate and sugar *(found in some throat tablets)*	$KClO_3$ + sugar	mix 3:1
Potassium permanganate and sugar *(may be part of your survival kit)*	$KMnO_4$ + sugar	mix 9:1
Sodium chlorate and sugar *(sodium chlorate is a weed killer)*	$NaClO_3$ + sugar	mix 3:1

6.5.2 PRIMITIVE METHODS

The fire creating methods employed by our early ancestors are not beyond a survivor. However, they are exhaustive and require practice to work. This is why tools such as cigarette lighters should be carried, so primitive methods can be practised before these run out.

Flint and Steel

The direct spark method is the easiest of the primitive methods to use. The flint and steel method is the most reliable of the direct spark methods. Strike a flint or other hard, sharp-edged rock edge with a piece of carbon steel (stainless steel will not produce a good spark).

This method requires a loose-jointed wrist and practice. When a spark has caught in the tinder, blow on it until spreads and bursts into flames.

This takes a LOT of practice, and you must of course know how to source the correct rock, if you plan to stock items of this nature, buy some high quality firesteel, also known as a metal-match.

Fire-Plow

The fire plow requires a straight base of softwood and a shaft of hardwood. To use this method, cut a

HARDWOOD

SOFTWOOD

FIRE-PLOW

straight groove in the base and plow the blunt tip of the shaft up and down the groove. The plowing action of the shaft pushes out small particles of wood fibres. Then, as you apply more pressure on each stroke, the friction ignites the wood particles.

Bow and Drill

The technique of starting a fire with a bow and drill is simple, but you must exert much effort and be persistent to produce a fire. You need the following items to use this method —

Socket	The socket is an easily grasped stone or piece of hardwood or bone with a slight depression in one side. Use it to hold the drill in place and to apply downward pressure.
Drill	The drill should be a straight, seasoned hardwood stick about 2 cm in diameter and 25 cm long. The top end is round and the low end blunt (to produce more friction).
Fire board	Its size is up to you. A seasoned softwood board about 2.5 cm thick and 10 cm wide is preferable. Cut a depression about 2 cm from the edge on one side of the board. On the underside, make a V-shaped cut from the edge of the board to the depression.
Bow	The bow is a resilient, green stick about 2.5 cm in diameter and a string. The type of wood is not important. The bowstring can be any type of cordage. You tie the bowstring from one end of the bow to the other, without any slack.

To use the bow and drill, first prepare the fire lay. Then place a bundle of tinder under the V-shaped cut in the fire board. Place one foot on the fire board.

Loop the bowstring over the drill and place the drill in the pre-cut depression on the fire board. Place the socket, held in one hand, on the top of the drill to hold it in position.

Press down on the drill and saw the bow back and forth to twirl the drill. Once you have established a smooth motion, apply more downward pressure and work the bow faster.

FIRE DRILL CONSTRUCTION

This action will grind hot black powder into the tinder, causing a spark to catch. Blow on the tinder until it ignites.

If there are problems with the cord from slipping on the drill, an alternative the Egyptians used involves a hole through the drill.

The cord is slipped through the hole and one end is wrapped around the drill a few times. The cord will not slip as the drill turns.

USING THE DRILL

Fire Piston

Used by many people in South-East Asia, a fire piston is a device that creates heat by rapid compression of air. This device was also discovered and used by pirates before matches.

When a piston is rammed into a cylinder, the air temperature rises quickly.

This temperature rise can be sufficient to light a piece of tinder placed on the piston.

These can be made from a cylinder of bone or hollow bamboo. The piston is made from wood or bone.

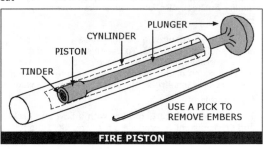

PLUNGER
CYNLINDER
PISTON
TINDER
USE A PICK TO REMOVE EMBERS

FIRE PISTON

To use the device –

- Place a small piece of tinder on the end of the piston.
- Place the piston in the end of the cylinder.
- Ram the piston in **hard** and **fast** with the palm of your hand. It may be easier to place the cylinder on the ground or against something hard like a rock or tree.
- Pull the piston out and check the tinder. If the tinder is not lit, place the piston back cylinder **immediately** and try again. The initial strike may have heated the tinder to just below the point of lighting.
- You may need to use a picker to pull the lit tinder out of the cylinder.

The approximate dimensions of a fire piston are as follows —

Cylinder	Length	10 – 15 cm
	Outside diameter	2.5 cm
	Inside diameter	1 – 2 cm
Piston	Total length	10 – 15 cm
	Shaft length	8 – 10 cm
	Piston head length	2 – 2.5 cm

The piston head should be a snug fit inside the cylinder but allowed to move freely. If necessary a tighter seal may be made by wrapping a single layer of cotton thread a few mm wide around the piston head. Vaseline, oil, grease or animal fat should be used to lubricate the cotton gasket.

If constructed properly, the piston should hit the bottom and spring back up slightly. It also should make a 'pop' noise when you pull it out.

6.5.3 CHAR CLOTH

Char cloth is cotton that has been heated to become blackened, but not to the point of combustion. It is useful tinder in starting fires, especially with primitive methods such as spark methods, friction methods or a fire piston.

To create char cloth you need a small tin that is fairly air tight, such as a tobacco tin. Place a small hole in the top from 1 to 5 mm for gasses to escape. Cut the cloth into small squares and place them neatly inside. Do not pack them tightly. The cloth must be 100% cotton.

Place the tin on a small fire or glowing coals and soon it will start smoking. Wait until it is finished smoking and carefully remove it from the fire. Wait until the tin is cool before opening it because if oxygen rushes in, it will ignite immediately.

When finished it should be completely black, not brown, if not just put it back on the fire. If it is crumbly then it is overdone and useless. It should be fairly soft and not too fragile.

Carefully remove and store in a watertight container, or just leave in the tin for later.

6.5.4 FIRE WITH DAMP MATERIALS

Creating fire when all the available materials are wet is a difficult task, and all the more important when you are cold and soaking. It is not impossible however.

To gather kindling to start the fire, snap dead twigs from trees rather than collect them from the ground. A fuzz-stick can also be used. To create a fuzz-stick, take a dead branch about 1-2 cm in diameter that is relatively dry. Strip any bark off with a knife to further remove any moisture. Then start cutting curly slivers into the stick. The wood inside will be dry.

Once a small fire is burning, keep feeding it dry kindling and surround it with larger fuel to dry that. When that fuel is dry, feed it into the fire and continue until you have a suitable fire. Keep stacking damp wood around the fire to ensure you have fuel.

CREATING A FUZZ STICK

Friction Methods with Damp Materials

If you are trying to use friction to light a fire and your tools are damp, you face a very difficult challenge. If you have a dry cloth or towel, dry the equipment off as best as you can before you start.

You will not get it started in one go with the wet material but you can get it to start smoking by applying a lighter effort than usual. If you use too much pressure, the wood will be eaten away, rather than just the moisture being drawn out.

Once smoke is produced, rest for a few seconds until the smoke stops then repeat. Doing this will eventually draw moisture from the wood to a point where you can get an ember.

6.5.5   FIRE WITH AN EMPTY LIGHTER (AKA PRISON MATCH)

If you have a disposable cigarette lighter that has run out of gas but is still producing a spark, you can still get several fires from it. If you turn the striker slowly, it will grind small shavings from the flint, rather than sparking it. You need something to collect these shavings. A piece of tissue paper is ideal.

Turn the striker slowly for a few revolutions, and then tap the filings out of the lighter. Repeat this process until you get a noticeable pile. About 1 cubic mm is required. This will take quite some time, so be patient.

FILINGS

TISSUE PAPER 'PRISON MATCH'

If using tissue paper – with the pile of filings in the centre, fold and twist carefully so the filings are contained in a small pocket. Now flick the striker near this pocket and the spark will ignite the shavings and tissue.

If you don't have tissue paper – carefully pack dry tinder around the pile while keeping the shavings exposed. Flick the striker to ignite the pile and tend very carefully to the small and brief flame produced.

6.5.6   FIREWOOD TYPES

There are many things which make some woods burn hotter than others - rate of growth, resin content, age of tree, part of tree, structure of the wood itself. As a general rule, woods that are good for making friction fires make bad firewood, since they are low density and resin-less.

The best woods include oak, hickory, madrone, manzanita, mesquite, and other dense hardwoods. The worst woods include pine sapwood and many other softwoods and willow, although these make good kindling.

Wet wood burns cooler than dry wood, but burns relatively longer. Heart wood burns hotter than sapwood in general. Rotten wood is good for producing smoke, but not heat or light.

Charcoal burns hotter than the wood it was made from as the volatile gases which produce flames burn at a relatively low temperature. So your coals are the hottest part of the fire, not the flames. Light comes from the burning gases.

6.6   HELPFUL HINTS

- Use non-aromatic seasoned hardwood for fuel, if possible.
- Collect kindling and tinder along the trail.
- Add insect repellent to the tinder.
- Keep the firewood dry.
- Dry damp firewood near the fire.
- One you have a fire going, dry some kindling to take with you for later.
- If you have firelighters, remember you don't need to use a whole firelighter for each fire.
- Bank the fire to keep the coals alive overnight. Mixing in green wood will slow burning.
- Carry lighted punk, when possible.
- Be sure the fire is out before leaving camp. It is better to bury it under sand or soil rather than to douse with water. The water will dry out and the fire will rekindle, as well as creating a lot of smoke.
- Do not select wood lying on the ground for friction methods. It may appear to be dry but generally doesn't provide enough friction.

7 ROPES AND KNOTS

One of the most basic needs in a primitive living situation is the skilful use of knots and lashings. From creating fishing line and nets, animal snares, building shelters, creating bridges, climbing and general tasks, the uses are endless.

Although modern day rope is extremely cheap and strong, emergencies can arise. It is therefore important not on only to commit at least a few knots to memory, but how to make or improvise rope from natural materials.

7.1 SUITABLE MATERIALS

Almost any fibrous material can be spun into decent rope. Materials between 30 – 60 cm or more can be used. If a group of people are employed to the task, large ropes of up to 10 cm diameter, with breaking strains of over 1000 kg can be made.

Breaking Strains

Using a 3-lay, 3 cm diameter rope as a guide, the following list gives an idea of the strength of various materials. This is a general guide only, for safety in a critical application, test the ropes thoroughly beforehand.

Green grass	50 - 100	Kg
Bark fibre	200 - 700	Kg
Palm fibre	300 - 1000	Kg
Sedges	900 - 1000	Kg
Lianas (monkey vines)	250 - 300	Kg
Lawyer vine (*Calamus*) (10 mm unskinned)	- 500	Kg
MATERIAL STRENGTH GUIDE		

7.1.1 SELECTING MATERIALS

The proper materials for making rope must have the following qualities —

• It must have reasonably long fibre

• It must be strong

• It must be pliable and not snap when bent

• It must have grip so the fibres will bite into each other

There are three simple tests that can be applied to determine the suitability of the material –

• First pull on the material to determine its strength. If you can easily break it, it is of no use

• Twist the fibres between your fingers and roll the fibres together. Make sure the material does not snap apart.

• Finally, tie a knot in the material and slowly and gently pull it together. If it does not cut itself and can be pulled reasonably tight, it is suitable.

Many plants can be found with these qualities such as ground vines, most long grasses, water reeds, rushes and the inner bark of many trees and shrubs. Some fresh green material may be stiff, however if you pass them over hot flames for 30 seconds, often the sap will burst through some of the cell structures, making the material pliable.

Some seaweeds and members of the large aloe family may also be useful.

Gathering and Preparing Materials

Some plants may have high amounts of vegetable gum. Soaking these plants in water for several hours may remove this. A running stream is good if the material can be weighed down or contained. Boiling or drying thoroughly in the sun and teasing the fibres out can also work.

Some materials only have strength if used green. Such materials may include sedges, water rushes, grasses and liana vines. When harvesting, the plants should never be pulled out of the ground, but cut above ground level with a sharp knife or machete. Harvesting should only be done over a wide area. Never clear a site and only use the larger clumps to allow for regrowth.

In temperate areas fibre from the inner bark of some trees and shrubs is an excellent material to use. It is best to use when the tree is dead and the fibre dried out. If you absolutely must use material from a living tree, cut and test a small strip first. Then remove bark from branches only. Cut through to the sapwood, peel it off the tree and test the different layers. Unless it's oozing sap it is probably suitable, but should be soaked in water for a few hours then sun dried.

Palm fibre in tropical or sub-tropical regions is an excellent material. It is found at the junction at the leaf and the trunk.

Many types of vines are also very strong, and can be extremely long in ideal conditions. In the case of most vines usually only the skin is especially strong. If used as a complete vine they should therefore be used unskinned (leave the skin on).

If the vine skin itself is used for its fibre to make rope, the correct way to remove the skin is to bend the main stalk away from the split, rather than trying to pull a strand off from the main stalk.

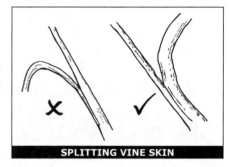

SPLITTING VINE SKIN

7.2 MAKING ROPE

Once suitable materials are identified and gathered in large enough quantities, rope can be made. Rope is made by creating cord from the fibres first, then combining three or more cords into rope in the same manner. This can be repeated to make even thicker rope.

7.2.1 MAKING CORD WITH YOUR HANDS

Gather the fibres into loose bunches of strands of reasonably even thickness. Twist each of these strands clockwise. The twist will hold the fibres in the strand. As a rough rule, the strands should be about 1 mm with about 15 – 20 fibres per strand. Thicker strands will generally produce weaker cord.

Without letting the strands untwist, group two, three or four together and twist them together in an anti-clockwise direction. They will tend to twist together naturally so ensure they do so evenly.

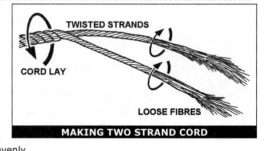

MAKING TWO STRAND CORD

Work down the length twisting the unlaid fibre bunches together clockwise, feeding in more fibre as you go, and twisting the strands together anti-clockwise. Make sure the strands are of an even thickness, with an even twist and even tension. This takes quite some practice so don't expect to get it right first go, especially when making fine strong cord.

Normally two or more people are required to spin and lay cord. It is a community effort, especially if a lot of rope is needed. It is possible for one person to make cord by twisting the strands by running a flat hand along the thigh, with the fibre between the hand and thigh. The other hand is free to feed in more fibre. This method is very quick but takes time to master.

7.2.2 SETTING UP A ROPEWALK

Cord can be made into rope by laying several cords together in the same manner as the cord was made. An easy way to do this is with a ropewalk.

When spinning ropes of 10 metres or more, it is necessary to support the length with crossbars every few metres. This prevents the cord sagging on the ground and getting snagged with twigs and dirt on the ground.

The crossbars should be smooth and free of twigs and loose bark that may interfere with the spinning of the cord.

A crank at the laying end is turned to lay the strands together. A connecting bar between the cranks at the spinning end allows one person to spin all cranks simultaneously. If the rope is correctly laid, the fibres should lay horizontally along the rope.

When you need to make a very long rope, it can be made in sections. The sections are made one at a time and placed aside until the last section is made. The strands are then spliced together. When splicing the sections, stagger the strands to ensure the join is smooth.

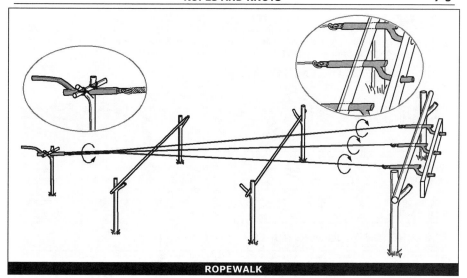

ROPEWALK

The spinners can be made from natural sticks, thick bent wire or constructed. A connecting bar at the spinning end allows one person to spin all cords simultaneously. This handle is turned in a reverse direction to the handle at the opposite end, to twist the strands together. These strands are laid by a feeder working down the rope.

It is necessary for both ends to work together because the act of laying the strands will take some of the original twist out.

If the rope is well laid then the strands will lay lengthways across the rope.

If a rope is needed which is too long to be laid on a single ropewalk, sections of the complete rope are made one at a time. When a section is complete, coil it at the single crank end until the next section is complete. Then splice the two sections together and continue as needed. See **Rope Splices** (Page 7-13).

When a rope is complete, pass it quickly over a fire to remove loose fibres. This will make the rope smoother and more professional.

Do not attempt to rush rope making. The turners must turn evenly and smoothly while putting their weight on the rope as the layer advances up the rope laying the strands side by side.

POOR VS GOOD ROPE LAY

When making the initial cord, take time to make sure the fibres are fed and twisted evenly.

This takes a lot of practice to do quickly. A poorly spun rope will be bulgy, uneven and weak at points. The breaking strain can be as little as a quarter of the potential strength. Expect a three people team to take at least 2 hours to spin 20 metres of rope at first.

CAUTION: When your rope is made, always test it before you use it in critical applications such as climbing or making bridges.

Rope Wrenches

These simple tools are used near the point where the rope is being laid to aid in separating the rope strands evenly. They can be carved or cut or made by more simple means. The notches should be smoothed to ensure the rope does not catch as it passes through.

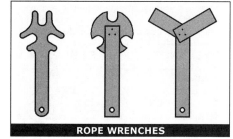

ROPE WRENCHES

7.3 KNOTS

Knots are a hard won technology. While it is adequate to know only a few, it is well worth practising a range of different knots and committing them to memory.

7.3.1 KNOTS FOR THE ENDS OF A ROPE

Thumb Knot
Simple knot used for a stopper at the end of a rope or a grip. AKA a granny knot.

Overhand Knot
Makes a larger grip than the thumb knot and is easy to untie.

Figure Eight
Same use as the thumb knot but more ornamental.

In these images the free (F) end is shown as being closed, where the standing (S) or secured end is shown open.

7.3.2 KNOTS FOR JOINING ROPES

Sheet Bend
This is used to join two ropes of unequal thickness. The thicker rope is the bend.

Double Sheet Bend
Similar to the sheet bend more secure. Useful for wet ropes.

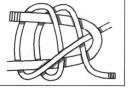

Crossover Sheet Bend
A very secure way to join ropes.

Use it in windy conditions where flapping may undo the bend.

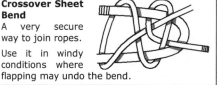

Carrick Bend
This is used for secure joining of two even ropes. It can be used on steel cables.

It is easily undone and does not jam.

Reef Knot
Used to securely join two ropes of equal thickness together. Note the position of the free and standing ends.

Thief Knot
Tied to appear as a reef knot, it was used to detect entry, as it would be retied as a reef knot.

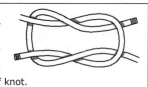

Stopper Hitch
This is used to fasten a rope to another rope (or bar) on which there is already strain. When the hitch is pulled tight the attached rope will not slip, and tension on the main rope can be taken on the attached rope. Can be useful for climbing.

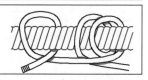

7.3.3 KNOTS TO MAKE LOOPS IN ROPE

Bowline
A sturdy loop that will not close in on its self.

Bowline on a Bight
A double loop that will not close on it's self.

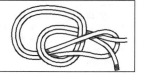

Thumb Eye Knot

This method of creating a loop is quick and effective, but it can jam and be difficult to untie.

Flemish Eye Knot

This loop is less likely to jam than the overhand eye knot. Basically a figure-8. This knot can be used on fishing line.

Crabbins Hitch

This eye knot is very sturdy. It doesn't tend to cut it's self or pull out. NOTE: the loop will pull closed under tension.

Manharness

This is useful for making a series of loops in a rope without a free end.

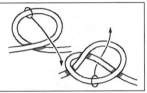

Butterfly Loop

The butterfly loop is sturdier than the man-harness loop. It is easier to untie and resists jamming. Two methods of tying it are shown. This knot is also useful for fishing line.

7.3.4 KNOTS FOR FASTENING ROPES

Slippery Hitch

A knot that can be released quickly in an emergency. It holds secure as long as there is tension on the standing end.

Clove Hitch

For securing a rope to a spar. If pulled taut this hitch will not slip on smooth surfaces. Useful for starting or ending lashings.

Boat Knot

This is a method of securing a rope to a pin or small piece of wood on a boat. It is quickly released.

Double Boat Knot

A bight is passed through the ring and a spike. Removing the spike will release the knot.

Rolling Hitch

To fasten a rope to a spar. This is a very secure hitch.

Be sure to cinch it up tight.

Timber Hitch

For securing a rope to square timber, round logs etc. A good starting knot for lashings.

Hallard Hitch

For fastening a rope to a spar. The sketch shows the hitch open. When pulled tight and the hitches closed it is neat and secure.

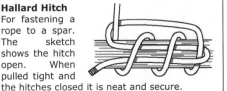

Noose Hitch

A quick and easy method of securing a rope to a beam.

Can be made more secure with an overhand knot.

Cats Paw Hitch

For securing a rope to a hook or beam. Easy to tie to an open hook.

Can be tied to a closed loop if you feed it through.

Larks Head

Use to secure a rope to a ring. It can be made more secure with a thumb knot.

Double Larks Head

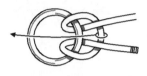  

The bight is first made then the ends are passed through it. This knot is very secure.

Sailor's Backhand Knot

Used to secure rope to a ring or beam.

Very similar to the rolling hitch.

Kellick Hitch

Good for fastening to a stone that will hold in rocky sea floors where an anchor might foul.

It is a timber hitch finished off with a half hitch.

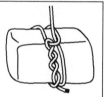

Tom Fool's Knot

Formed by making two overlapping loops and then pulling the inner loops through the outside.

This is useful for improvising carry handles.

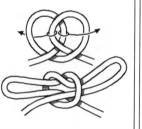

Barrel Sling

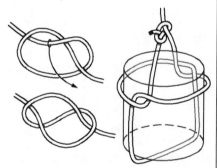

Use to securely hold a drum or log. Form the loop as shown, insert the barrel, and tie around the standing rope with a bowline.

7.3.5 SHORTENING ROPES

Sheepshank

A knot to quickly shorten the length of a rope. By inserting toggles in the end bights as shown, the sheepshank is secured from slipping.

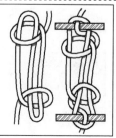

Twist Knot

The rope is laid out as shown and then the strands are braided together.

A spike is inserted between the ropes in the centre to hold the braid secure.

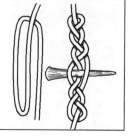

7.3.6 FISHING KNOTS

When tying knots in fishing line, pulling the knot tight will produce friction – which will weaken the line. To prevent this, lubricate the knot with some saliva before cinching closed.

Knots to Terminate Tackle

Uni Knot

This knot is easy to tie and useful for many purposes.

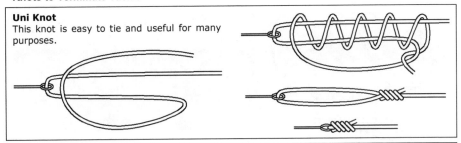

Palomar Knot

The Palomar knot is regarded as the strongest known fishing knot, and is very easy to tie.

To feed the loop through the eye, it is easier to feed a single line through the eye, and then pass it back through. If you plan ahead, it is often possible to tie a whole rig using this knot.

Make sure you pass the loop completely over the hook or ring before you cinch the knot tight.

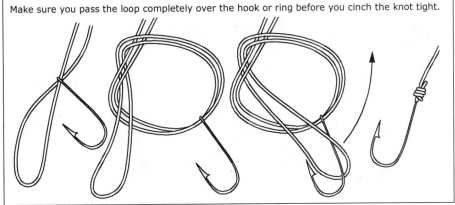

Dropliner's Knot

This knot is usually used to attach hooks to commercial droplines, though is useful for other purposes. It is strong on anything from light to heavy lines.

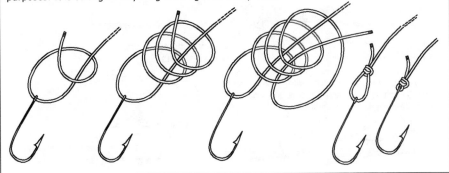

Clinch (or Blood) Knot

A good knot for attaching light line to hooks or rings. It is the strongest of its type.

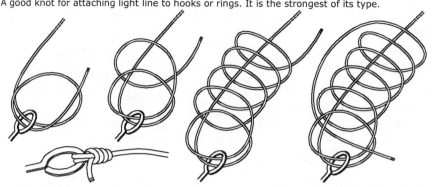

Snell (or Snood) Knot

This knot is used to tie to hooks that have open eyes (such as ganged hooks), or no eye (such as an improvised hook). Form the loop as shown and hold at the top. Wrap the loop around the hook and tag several times. Pull the tag (A) against the mainline (B) to cinch the knot.

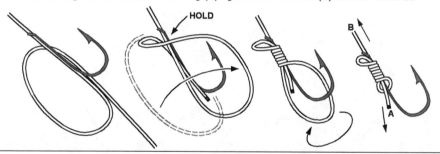

Knots to Tie Line to Line

Uni Knot

This is tied in exactly the same manner as the uni knot for joining tackle, but done to each line. It is suitable for joining lines of equal or different thickness.

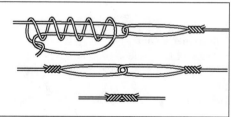

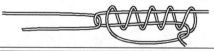

Albright Knot

This is a great knot for joining lines of unequal diameters or materials (like tying mono to braid). The less flexible material is represented by the thicker line.

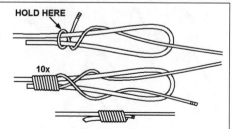

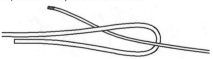

Shock Leader Knot

This is a small and compact knot useful for joining heavy leaders to light lines. Particularly suitable to repetitive castings as the knot will resist damage as it passes through the runners.

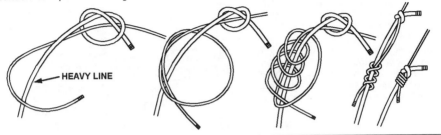

HEAVY LINE

Knots to Tie Loops in Line

You can use the Flemish Eye Knot, a doubled over Overhand Knot, or a Butterfly Loop to tie loops in fishing line. Two more loops, specific to fishing, are shown below.

Dropper Loop

Often used when the sinker is at the bottom of the rig, or when you have many hooks on one line. This is an easy loop to tie in the middle of a line.

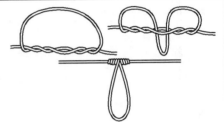

Harrison's Loop

Introduced by writer, Rod Harrison. This loop is useful for attaching lures to a leader.

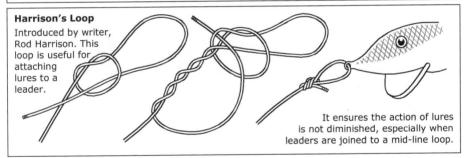

It ensures the action of lures is not diminished, especially when leaders are joined to a mid-line loop.

Tying Line to a Reel

Use this knot to tie a line to a reel. As with all fishing knots, lubricate it before cinching tight.

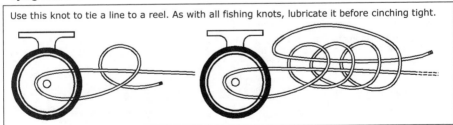

7.3.7 MISCELLANEOUS KNOTS

Honda Knot

This is a knot that gives a free-running noose, but it gives a clear circular loop suitable for throwing – it is a lasso.

You may find a use for this lasso in many ways. However, in a situation where you only have a few lengths of rope, it would be unwise to spend much too time and energy trying to catch animals in this way.

It takes a lot of practice and when you really need the rope it may be worn and damaged from your lassoing efforts.

However, it is worth making one to experiment so you have the skill ready should you need it.

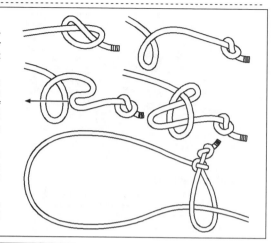

Marlin Spike Hitch

This is an instant, but temporary, knot for securing a mooring line to a post, or for dragging over the top of any upright peg or pole.

It is particularly useful when tightening lashings.

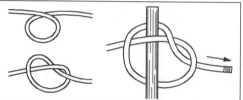

Truckers Hitch

Use this knot to cinch down a load on a car, trailer, horse, or for other situations where tension is needed. This pulley-like action allows the rope to be pulled extra tight.

Start with a slippery half-hitch to make a loop. Make a turn around a bar or ring etc with the free end, and then pull through the loop and pull to tighten. Finish with two half-hitches.

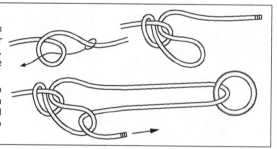

Tape Knot

This is a useful knot for joining flat materials such as leather or webbing straps, tape and even for joining sheets or other fabrics.

Make an overhand knot in the end of one tape – do not pull it tight. Then feed the other tape through so if follows the shape of the first knot exactly. The live ends should be well clear of the knot so they will not slip back when you tighten it.

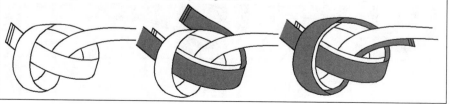

7.4 LASHINGS

There are several types of lashings that are commonly used —

- Square Lashing
- Diagonal Lashing
- Sheer Lashing
- Figure of Eight Lashing

A square lashing is most commonly used and is used when the spars will try to slide over each other regardless of the angle that they cross.

A diagonal lashing is used when the spars have to be pulled together or when they tend to spring apart from each other. A good example is the cross-brace of a framework.

Sheer lashing has two purposes, for joining two poles end to end, and for making 'sheer legs', where the spars are opened to form an inverted 'V'.

Figure of eight lashing is sometimes known as the round, or tripod lashing. It is used to bring three spars together to form a tripod.

The usual way to start a lashing is with a clove hitch or timber hitch. If using a timber hitch, it is important to pull straight through the eye and not back from it. Pulling back can cut the lashing material.

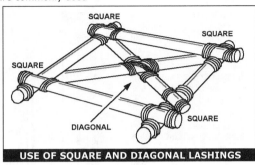

USE OF SQUARE AND DIAGONAL LASHINGS

SHEER LASHINGS

FIGURE OF EIGHT

Square Lashing

This is used to join poles at right angles.

1. Start with a clove or timber hitch below the crossbar.

2. Lash tight around upright and cross bar about four times.

Instead of laying each turn towards the outside of the previous turn, run each turn of lashing towards the INSIDE on the spar you started the lashing, and towards the OUTSIDE on the other bar.

3. Make about two or three 'frapping' turns (not shown) around the lashing to pull it taut.

Secure with a clove hitch or two half hitches.

Diagonal Lashing

This is used for bracing or joining spars at irregular angles.

1. Start with a timber hitch or clove hitch.

2. Tightly run about three or four full turns vertically.

Pass rope under top spar and make about four turns horizontally.

3. Make two or three frapping turns to pull the lashing taut.

Secure to the pole with a clove hitch or two half hitches.

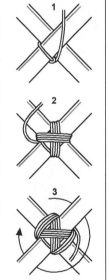

Sheer Lashing

(For increasing the length of a spar)

It is important to have a good overlap of a quarter to a third of the overall length.

Start with a clove hitch or timber hitch around both spars near the end of the overlap.

Continue with six to ten turns around both spars. Finish with a clove hitch around the second spar.

To tighten, insert small wedges inside the turns, or make three or four frapping turns around one side of the lashings to pull them in tight.

Add a second lashing to increase strength of the join.

Sheer Lashing

(For making 'sheer legs')

Line up the two butts of the spars.

Start with a timber hitch around one spar.

Continue with six to ten turns which are made firmly, but not too tight.

Make a couple of frapping turns between the two spars to tighten the lashings.

Finish with a clove hitch.

The sheer legs are opened out to tighten the lashings. It's possible to make the turns too tight so it may help to insert a small wedge between the spars before you start lashing.

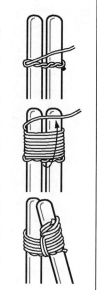

Figure of Eight Lashing

Lay three spars so that the centre spar goes in the opposite direction of the outer two. Start with a timber hitch or clove hitch on one of the outer spars.

Continue with about six turns which are taken loosely over and under the spars. Finish with a few loose frapping turns and a clove hitch.

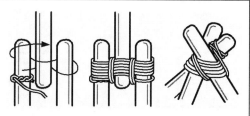

Wedges can be used before doing the lashing to enable even spacing, and to make sure you don't make the lashing too tight. Remove the wedges before spreading the legs out.

Transom Knot

This is a good knot to tie two sticks at right angles when you don't want a bulky lashing or you don't have a lot of material.

You can cut the ends off close to the knot.

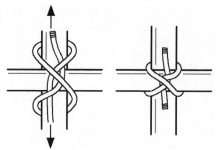

Chainstitch Lashing

This is a good lashing to use with soft or awkwardly shaped bundles. Start with a timber hitch and make the chain as illustrated. Finish with two half hitches.

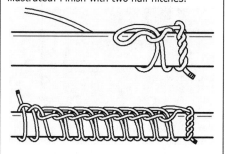

7.5 ROPE SPLICES

Splicing ropes together is sometimes preferable to knots or bends, especially when the rope needs to pass through a block and tackle or may otherwise get snagged. Splicing also looks a lot neater than a knot, no matter how well the knot is tied.

7.5.1 SHORT SPLICE

The simplest of all splices is known as the short splice.

To start this splice, unravel the strands of each rope about a hands length. Wrap some twine around the ropes to prevent further unravelling. You should also seize the ends of the strands to help with splicing.

If you are using nylon rope, melt the strands with a flame to secure them.

Butt the two ends of the ropes together as shown.

With a spike or short stick, work one of the strands up and feed a loose strand under it. The first strand must be run over the strand which it is next to, and under the next one.

Take the next free strand and loop it over the strand you previously lifted, and under the next one.

Continue around the rope until complete and then trim the ends.

The splice can be made neater by gradually thinning out the strands as you go, giving a taper to the splice. In this way the splice will not be much larger than the original rope and will not snag easily.

SHORT SPLICE

7.5.2 LONG SPLICE

This splice is stronger and neater than the short splice. If it is made well enough, the splice cannot be detected after a few days use.

To make this splice, unlay the strands about 1 or 2 metres. Then unlay one strand in each rope half as much again.

Place the middle strands together at A. Strands B and C will leave a groove from where they were unlaid at D and E.

LONG SPLICE

Take the two central strands, F and G, and lay them into the grooves until they meet at B and C. Be sure to keep them twisted tightly as you do so.

Take the strands H and J, and cut out half the fibres in each. Tie an overhand knot in the end and tuck them into the next lays as in a short splice. Do the same for strands B, C and F, G.

Finally stretch the rope tight, pull pound and roll the splice until smooth and round. Then trim off all the loose ends close to the rope.

7.5.3 EYE SPLICE

An eye splice is very easy to make and is handy in many ways. It is made the same way as the short splice, but the end of the rope is unlaid and then bent around and spliced into its own strands of the standing part.

7.5.4 CUT SPLICE

A cut splice is made in the same way as the short splice or eye splice. A short piece of rope is cut and each end of the rope is spliced into the centre of the standing rope to form a loop that closes shut when the rope is taut.

EYE SPLICE

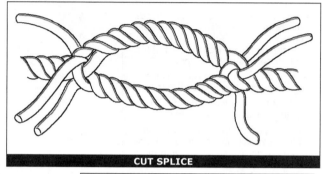

CUT SPLICE

7.5.5 CROWN SPLICE

A crown is useful for stopping the end of a frequently used rope from fraying.

Start off as shown in the diagram then pull the ends tight to cinch it up. Then tuck the strands in as with a short splice to complete the crown.

Taper the strands as you work down if you want a neater appearance to the crown.

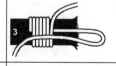

CROWN SPLICE

7.5.6 WHIPPING

Whipping is another way to stop the end of a rope from fraying. This is the practice of binding the end of a rope with thin twine.

Good whipping must be very tight and neat to be effective. If it is too slack it will work loose.

The same technique can also be used with rope or cordage to form comfortable grips to the end of axes or knives.

3	Form the loose end of the twine (a) into a loop and lay it back along the whipped section.

 1	Lay the length of twine along the side of the rope, leaving its end (a) projecting a hand's length beyond the rope's end.
4	Continue whipping, covering the loop until you have nearly reached the end of the rope. Pass the end (b) through the loop.

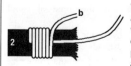 2	Wrap the twine (b) around the rope, working towards the end, covering the piece you have laid along it.
5	Pull the short end (a) to pull the loop and tighten the whipping. Trim the ends neatly.

8 SHELTERS

A shelter can protect you from the sun, insects, wind, rain, snow, hot or cold temperatures, and enemy observation. It can give you a feeling of well-being. It can help you maintain your will to survive.

In some areas, your need for shelter may take precedence over your need for food and possibly even your need for water.

The most common error in making a shelter is to make it too large. A shelter must be large enough to protect you and your equipment, but also small enough to contain your body heat, especially in cold climates.

8.1 SHELTER SITE SELECTION

When you start looking for a site, you must consider whether the site —

- Contains material to make the type of shelter you need.
- Is large enough and level enough for you to lie down comfortably.
- Provides protection against wild animals and rocks and dead trees that might fall.
- Is free from insects, reptiles, and poisonous plants.

You must also remember the problems that could arise in your environment. For instance —

- Avoid flash flood areas in foothills.
- Avoid avalanche or rockslide areas in mountainous terrain.
- Avoid sites near bodies of water that are below the high water mark.

8.2 BASIC SHELTERS

When looking for a shelter site, keep in mind the type of shelter (protection) you need. However, you must also consider –

- How much time and effort you need to build the shelter.
- If the shelter will adequately protect you from the elements (sun, wind, rain, and snow).
- If you have the tools to build it. If not, can you make improvised tools?
- If you have the type and amount of materials needed to build it.

To answer these questions, you need to know how to make various types of shelters.

8.2.1 SIMPLE LEAN-TOS AND TENTS

It takes only a short time and minimal equipment to build this lean-to. You need material such as a canvas or poncho, 3 - 4 meters of rope, two or three stakes about 30 cm long, and two trees or poles 2 - 3 metres apart. Ensure that the back of your lean-to will be into the wind.

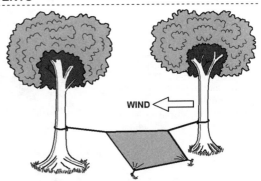

WIND

If you plan to use the lean-to for more than one night, or you expect rain, make a centre support for the lean-to. Make this support with a centre-pole, or a line attached to an overhanging branch.

 When at rest, you lose as much as 80 percent of your body heat to the ground. To reduce heat loss to the ground, place some type of insulating material, such as leaves, inside your shelter.

This simple tent protects you on two sides. Use a poncho, tarp or other material. Stake the edges and suspend a rope between two trees to support the centre. Or you can use a long pole lashed to the trees if you have one. A tarpaulin with eye holes is ideal.

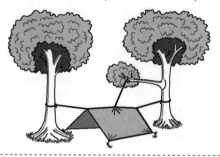

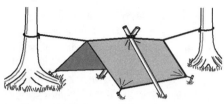

Another method for supporting the centre is to use an external A-frame. Use two long sticks, preferably one with a forked end, to form the A-frame. Drive the frame into the ground.

This simple one-person shelter can be built with one or three poles, one for the centre brace and two to hold down the sides.

The centre brace can be lashed around a tree, hooked on a fork, or suspended from above.

If you use logs to secure the sides, roll the material around the logs. Stake out or put a spreader between the poles to ensure they don't slide inwards.

An alternative is to dig trenches and bury the sides under dirt and rocks. This is especially effective in beach sand.

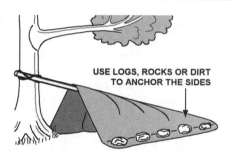

USE LOGS, ROCKS OR DIRT TO ANCHOR THE SIDES

8.2.2 FIELD-EXPEDIENT LEAN-TO

This type of shelter can be made if you are in an area with enough natural materials. It will take more time to construct than if you use a poncho or tarpaulin, but will be semi-permanent. It is pictured here with a fire reflector wall.

To make the lean-to –

- To start, lash a strong pole between two trees or upright beams at about chest height.

- You can also construct a frame from two forked sticks to hold this beam

- Lean four or five beams at an angle against the horizontal bar. This side should be positioned into the wind.

- Next lash crossbeams or vines to the angled beams.

- Cover the frame with brush, leaves, pine needles or grass. Start at the bottom and work your way up like shingling.

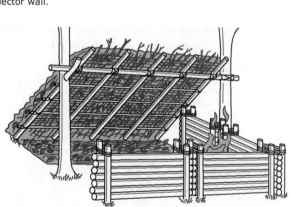

- Place a thick layer of straw, leaves or grass inside for bedding.

Adding a fire reflector –

If the weather is cold and time and resources allow, construct a fire reflector as shown. You can build the walls by placing upright stakes in the ground and stacking green logs in the space between. Lash the stakes together at the top to keep the wall in place.

For a stronger wall, use two stacks of logs between the upright stakes, with a cavity between the log stacks. Fill this cavity with dirt. This will increase the heat reflection of the wall, and retain heat througout the night.

8.2.3 SWAMP BED

In any area with standing water or continually wet ground, the swamp bed keeps you out of the water. When selecting such a site, consider the weather, wind, tides, and available materials.

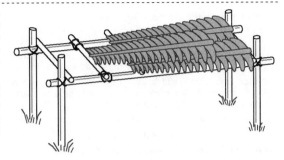

Consider the possibility of moving to another area. Being continually wet will adversely affect your health and wellbeing – not to mention you will generally be miserable and stressed.

To make a swamp bed –

- Cut four or six poles and drive them firmly into the ground so they form a rectangle. They should be far enough apart and strong enough to support your height and weight, to include equipment.
- Cut two poles that span the width of the rectangle.
- Secure these two poles to the upright poles. Be sure they are high enough above the ground or water to allow for tides and high water.
- Cut additional poles that span the rectangle's length. Lay them across the two side poles, and secure them.
- Cover the top of the bed frame with broad leaves or grass to form a soft sleeping surface.
- Build a fire pad by laying clay, silt, or mud on one comer and allow it to dry.

Another shelter designed to get you above and out of the water or wet ground uses the same rectangular configuration as the swamp bed. You very simply lay sticks and branches lengthwise on the inside of the upright poles until there is enough material to raise the sleeping surface above the water level.

8.2.4 ANCHORS

Proper selection of stakes and anchors is important especially in areas of soft soil, sand or snow. Strong winds and stormy weather can also necessitate strong anchors.

In order for stakes to be strong and not split when they are driven into the ground, select straight wood and sharpen them all round, like you would a pencil. A bevel on the head of the stake will prevent splitting.

If you are trying to anchor in soft soil, or you need extra strength, use the 1-2-3 anchor.

For sand or snow you will need to dig a trench about 30-50 cm deep (or more if stormy weather is expected). Tie the rope around the middle of a peg or log and fill the trench.

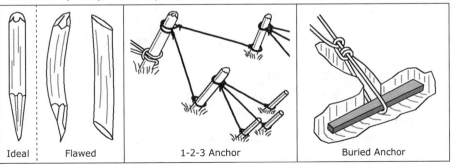

| Ideal | Flawed | 1-2-3 Anchor | Buried Anchor |

8.2.5 DEBRIS HUT

For warmth and ease of construction, this shelter is one of the best. When shelter is essential to survival, build this shelter first before you attempt a more difficult one.

To make a debris hut –

- Build it by making a tripod with two short stakes and a long ridgepole or by placing one end of a long ridgepole on top of a sturdy base, or by anchoring it to a tree at about waist height.
- Prop large sticks along both sides of the ridgepole to create 'ribs'. Ensure the ribbing is wide enough to accommodate your body and steep enough to shed water.
- Place finer sticks and brush cross-wise on the ribbing. These form a latticework that will keep the insulating material (i.e. grass, pine needles, and leaves) from falling through the ribbing into the sleeping area.
- Add light, dry, soft debris over the ribbing until the insulation is at least 50cm thick.
- Place a thick layer of insulating material inside the shelter.
- As a final step, add shingling material or branches on top of the debris layer to prevent the insulation from blowing away.

DEBRIS HUT CONSTRUCTION STEPS

8.2.6 TREE-PIT SNOW SHELTER

If you are in a cold, snow-covered area where evergreen trees grow and you have a digging tool, you can make a tree-pit shelter.

To make this shelter –

- Find a tree with bushy branches that provides overhead cover.
- Dig out the snow around the tree trunk until you reach the depth and diameter you desire, or until you reach the ground.
- Pack the snow around the top and the inside of the hole to provide support.
- Find and cut evergreen boughs. Place them over the top of the pit to give you additional overhead cover, and use them to line the bottom for insulation.

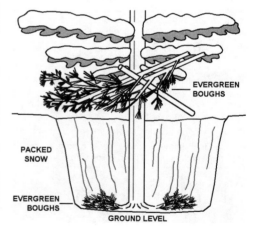

EVERGREEN BOUGHS

PACKED SNOW

EVERGREEN BOUGHS

GROUND LEVEL

8.2.7 BEACH SHADE SHELTER

This shelter protects you from the sun, wind, rain, and heat. It is easy to make using natural materials.

To make this shelter –

- Collect driftwood or other natural material to use as support beams and as a digging tool.
- Select a site that is above the high water mark.

- Scrape or dig out a trench running north to south so that it receives the least amount of sunlight. Make the trench long and wide enough for you to lie down comfortably.
- Mound sand on three sides.
- Lay support beams (driftwood or other material) that span the trench on top of the mound to form the framework for a roof. Line the inner side walls with wood if you can.

- Enlarge the shelter's entrance by digging out more sand in front of it.
- Use natural materials such as grass or leaves to form a bed inside the shelter.

8.2.8 BOUGH SHELTER

Look for branches that sweep to the ground or fallen trees that offer protection from the wind. A bough is a branch that comes off the main trunk.

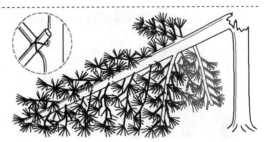

Ensure they are secure so they don't fall on you. If in doubt, secure them with lashing. Weave in other branches or debris to increase shelter.

Conifers are more suited to this technique than broad leaves.

8.2.9 NATURAL HOLLOW

A shallow depression in the earth will provide some immediate protection from wind, and can be a basis for construction of a shelter.

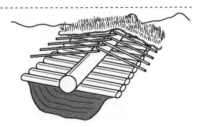

Take care in damp areas or on hills or you'll end up under water! Dig a channel to divert rain if needed.

Lay a few light logs across the hollow and then a larger bow across them. This will give pitch to short branches laid across the top to keep out rain. Finish with turf or twigs and leaves.

8.2.10 FALLEN TRUNK

A fallen trunk alone provides a good windbreak. To increase your shelter, scoop out a small hollow on the leeward side and construct a lean-to roof using whichever method is convenient.

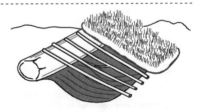

You could use thatching techniques to create a study and removable roof, or you can simply lay small branches and pile them up with debris and weighing it down dirt or turf.

8.2.11 STONE BARRIERS

If you dig or find a hollow for shelter, it will be more comfortable if you at least have room to sit up in it.

Building up a wall of stones around it the hollow and construct a roof using a suitable method.

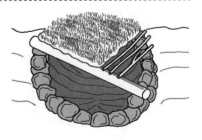

You can lay a log across the middle and lay smaller branches across that and pack it with foliage and turf, or you can create a removable thatched roof that covers the entire opening.

If you pack the walls with mud, this will add insulation and stop water from seeping into the hole.

8.2.12 SAPLING SHELTER

If you find a group of saplings, clear the ground between them and lash their tops together.

Use a thatching or a waterproof sheet weighed down with stones or logs.

A similar effect can be gained by driving pliable branches firmly in the ground.

SAPLING SHELTER

8.2.13 TARP SHELTERS

With a waterproof poncho, groundsheet or a piece of plastic sheeting or canvas (which should be included in even the smallest of survival kits) you can quickly and easily make a number of shelters which will offer protection until you can build something more permanent.

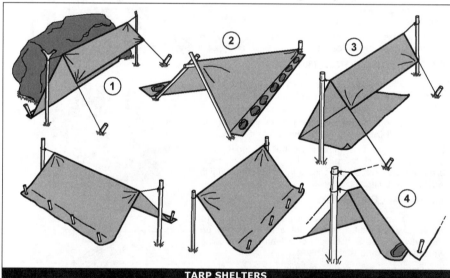

TARP SHELTERS

A trailer tarp is ideal because it has eyelets along the edge for attaching rope or driving stakes through. These tarps are also suitable for collecting water, unlike other plastic sheeting which may render your collected water poisonous – at least for the first few rains.

Make use of natural shelter (1) or make a triangular shelter with its apex pointed into the wind (2). Stake or weigh down edges with rocks, sand or clay. Loose soil is generally not heavy enough. If your sheeting is large enough, fold the sheet below you (3) running downhill so it keeps out surface water.

Use dry grass or bracken as bedding, or make a **Bed** (Page 8-19). Never lie on cold or damp ground. Even if the ground is dry when you sleep, it will be wet in the morning from dew.

A double shelter (4) is useful if your material is not totally waterproof (such as loosely woven canvas, or even a couple of blankets). Some water may seep through, but it will drip down the sides, not on your head. Avoid touching the inner surface of the shelter as this will create a pathway for the water to drip through.

This shelter is also useful in hot climates to insulate from the searing heat of the sun.

8.2.14 DESERT SHELTERS

In an arid environment, consider the time, effort, and material needed to make a shelter. If you have material such as a poncho or canvas, use it along with such terrain features as rock outcropping, mounds of sand, or a depression between dunes or rocks to make your shelter.

Using rock outcroppings –

- Anchor one end of your poncho (canvas, tarp, or other material) on the edge of the outcrop using heavy soil, rocks other weights.
- Extend and anchor the other end of the poncho so it provides the best possible shade.

In a sandy area –

- Build a mound of sand or use the side of a sand dune for one side of the shelter.
- Anchor one end of the material on top of the mound using sand or other weights.
- Extend and anchor the other end of the material so it provides the best possible shade.

> If you have enough material, fold it in half and form a 30 - 45cm (1 - 1.5 ft) airspace between the two halves. This airspace will reduce the temperature under the shelter.

A belowground shelter can reduce the midday heat as much as 16 - 22°C (30 - 40°F). Building it, however, requires more time and effort than for other shelters. Since your physical effort will make you sweat more and increase dehydration, construct it before the heat of the day.

To make this shelter –

- Find a low spot or depression between dunes or rocks. If necessary, dig a trench deep and long and wide enough for you to lie in comfortably.
- Pile the sand you take from the trench to form a mound around three sides.
- On the open end of the trench, dig out more sand so you can get in and out of your shelter easily.
- Cover the trench with your material.
- Secure the material in place using sand, rocks, or other weights.

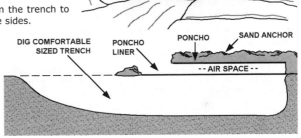

DIG COMFORTABLE SIZED TRENCH   PONCHO LINER   PONCHO   SAND ANCHOR   - - AIR SPACE - -

If you have extra material, you can further decrease the midday temperature in the trench by securing the material 30 - 45 cm above the other cover. This layering of the material will reduce the inside temperature 11 - 22°C (20 - 40°F).

Another type of belowground shade shelter is of similar construction, except all sides are open to air currents and circulation.

For maximum protection, you need a minimum of two layers of material. If you can, use a lighter material (preferably white) for the top layer, and a darker material (preferably black) for the inside layer.

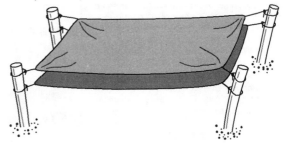

Use stakes, or pile rocks to create the height needed between the layers and between the ground and the inner layer. If you use stakes in sand, bury them deep or use a 1-2-3 anchor.

8.2.15 NATURAL SHELTERS

Do not overlook natural formations that provide shelter. Examples are caves, rocky crevices, clumps of bushes, small depressions, large rocks on leeward sides of hills, large trees with low-hanging limbs, and fallen trees with thick branches. However, when selecting a natural formation –

- Stay away from low ground such as ravines, narrow valleys, or creek beds. Low areas collect the heavy cold air at night and are therefore colder than the surrounding high ground. Thick, brushy, low ground also harbours more insects.
- Check for poisonous snakes, ticks, mites, scorpions, and stinging ants.
- Look for loose rocks, dead limbs, coconuts, or other natural growth than could fall on your shelter.
- Be aware of possible seismic activity in the area when exploring caves and rocky outcrops. Your shelter could become your tomb.

8.3   THATCHING

Materials suitable for thatching range from long grass, reeds, rushes, most of the long stalked ferns (such as bracken), palm leaves of all types and as a last resort, many pliant, leafy branches.

Long grass and reeds make a high quality roof when they are used dried rather than in their green state. It is advisable when using these materials to cut and stack them at the very start of your building project. This allows the material to dry out before being used.

If placed on the roof supports in their green state, grass and reeds will shrink and curl, allowing the rain to enter. All green materials will shrink and this will affect the lashings or stitches as well, causing them to become loose.

Green branches do not make a very efficient roof and should only be used in an emergency.

With most of the brackens it is advisable to use the material when it's green and sew it down tightly. This also applies if you are forced to use green branches.

Palm leaves are best for thatching when they are dead and dry. It is usual to find large amounts of them at the base of the tree. They are excellent material but can become brittle, especially in the summer heat.

The best time to collect palm leaves for shelter is early in the morning when the dead leaves have been softened by dew, or after rain. It is also advisable to soften the leaves with water before sewing them onto the thatching battens.

There are many times of thatching, each with their own peculiar advantages and application with certain types of material.

Principles of Watershed in Thatching

Thatch may be for shade or protection against rain. Thatching for shade is easy. Thatching for protection from wind and rain will be effective only if certain principles are observed. If the stitching interrupts the smooth, continuous course of the raindrops, the drops will travel along the stitching and the roof will leak. Thatch will never leak if the stitching is properly covered.

It is the quality of coverage, rather than the amount that makes a natural roof waterproof. Wind proofing however depends on the thickness and tightness of the thatch.

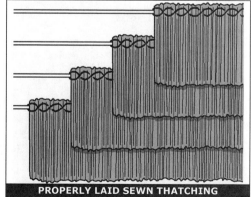

PROPERLY LAID SEWN THATCHING

8.3.1   SEWN THATCHING

Sewn thatching is started by stitching the first layer of thatch on the lowest thatching batten. The second layer must lie on top and completely cover the stitching below.

To sew thatching, make a thatching needle by cutting a dead, straight-grained stick about 2 cm thick and about 15 cm long. Sharpen one end and rub it as smooth as possible on a stone. Narrow the other end until it is about 5mm thick. Before doing this, however, cut an eye in this end. If you cut the eye first, it will not split out when the end is shaved down.

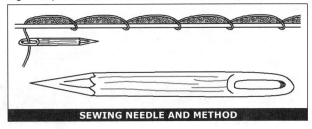

SEWING NEEDLE AND METHOD

Lay the thatching material with the butts toward the roof and the lower end on the lowest batten. Secure one end of the sewing material to the batten.

Thread the other end through the eye of the needle and sew the material to the batten.

To avoid holes where the sewing may tend to bunch the thatching together, push the needle through the thatch at an acute angle. Then push the thatch over the crossing of the stiches.

8.3.2 STICK THATCHING

With the stick thatch, ties about 60 cm apart are fastened onto the thatching batten. The thatching stick is tied down thus binding the material together.

This method of securing thatching is useful when long lengths of material for sewing are not available.

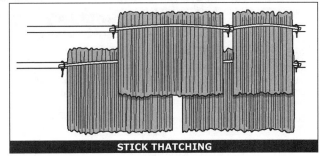

STICK THATCHING

As with sewn thatching, follow the principles of overlapping layers to cover the thatching stick. This will ensure a rainproof roof. This is not as secure (or windproof) as sewn thatching.

8.3.3 TUFT THATCHING

This is an excellent method if the material is fairly long (60 cm – 1 meter), and pliable. Reeds and sedges are very suitable.

- Gather the material into small sheaves about 3 mm or so thick.
- Bend the butt end over the thatching batten.
- Twist a few strands around the sheave a few times and push it through the bunched up material to hold it secure.
- The tuft is the slipped along the batten and the procedure continued until the batten is completed.

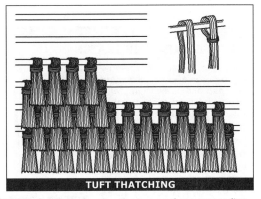

This thatch makes a very neat job from the inside. It is secure in strong weather and requires no tying material. If sedges or sharp sword grass is being used then protect your hands with socks to avoid cuts if gloves are not available.

TUFT THATCHING

It is important that the long, free ends of each tuft bundle overlap the two or three proceeding rows. Do not push the joining or knot end of these tufts up too tightly together.

There can be some space (say up to 2 cm) between the bent over ends on the battens. This space will be covered by the next row.

8.3.4 STALK THATCH

Any type of palm leaf, complete with stalk can be used for this type of thatching. It is both quick and efficient.

That stalks of the palms are woven through the thatch battens. The stalks are literally jammed between the battens and the pressure is sufficient to hold them in place.

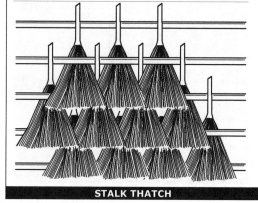

8.3.5 SPLIT STALK THATCH

This thatch is suitable for long pinnate leaves such as those found on date palms. The centre rib of each frond is split lengthways. The split ribs are tied together and secured to the ridge poles of the hut in an overlapping fashion. This eliminates the need for thatching battens unless extra strength is needed for the roof.

STALK THATCH

8.3.6 WOVEN THATCH

This is an alternative to the split stalk method if a lot of people are available and time is not a factor. The pinnate fronds are laid flat on the ground and the leaves from one side are laid over another and woven between the leaves opposite them. The stalk is the tied onto the framework of the hut.

You can also weave leaves directly over horizontal battens instead of tying to save cordage.

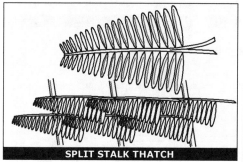

SPLIT STALK THATCH

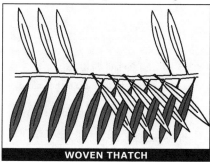

WOVEN THATCH

8.3.7 SEWN BATTEN THATCH

With long, broad leaves, they can be bent over the thatching battens and sewn in with lengths of split cane or other suitable material.

This can take a lot of time if the leaves are small.

The battens can be thatched before attaching to the framework.

If green material is used, make sure it doesn't curl as it dries by testing in the sun.

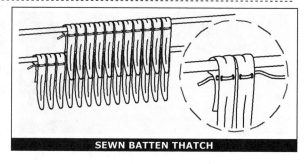

SEWN BATTEN THATCH

8.3.8 MAT WEAVE THATCHING

Long grass can be bunched and woven into large sheets. Any grass that is 30 cm (1 ft) or longer is suitable, as you can overlap the ends of short lengths to make a continuous bunch.

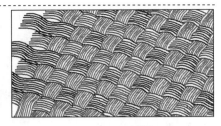

Weave these bunches together in a 'warp and weft' fashion. Very large sheets can be made.

You can use these mats as bedding, walls, or you can even lay a continuous piece over the top of an a-frame.

8.3.9 SHINGLE THATCHING

Birch bark is ideal for making shingles. Ring a birch tree with even 60 cm (2 ft) cuts and carefully remove the bark. Paperbark trees are also suitable for this as the watershed is excellent, the bark is easy to cut, and is very flexible. If using paperbark, use the whole ringed section as one flat piece rather than cutting it into slim shingles.

Across a frame, fix pairs of canes or creepers in closely spaced pairs. Upper ends of the shingles are gripped between the canes. The lower ends rest on top of those below. Stagger the shingles so the gaps between one row lie in the middle of the shingles on the row below – this will practically eliminate water leakage.

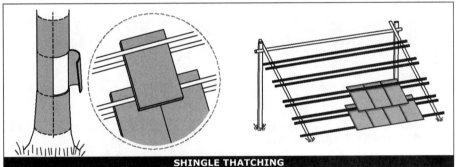

SHINGLE THATCHING

8.3.10 BAMBOO

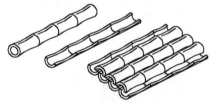

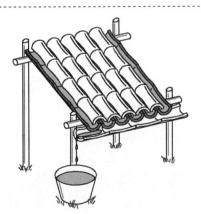

If you are lucky enough to have a supply of bamboo, you can use this versatile building material in many ways, even as roofing.

The giant form of bamboo can be found in damp places from India to China, and there are types native to Africa, Australia, and the southern United States.

Split bamboo vertically to make roofing and guttering to collect rainwater. The split stems are laid alternatively to interlock with one another form efficient and waterproof pantiles.

You can flatten split bamboo for smooth walls, floors or shelving by cutting vertically through the joints every cm or so around the circumference. It can then be flattened out.

8.3.11 RIDGE THATCHING

In thatching, the ridge of any hut must have the top row of stitching covered. Otherwise the hut will leak along the ridgeline.

This cap must therefore curl completely around the ridge pole, or better yet – a false ridge pole.

Alternatively it may stand up from the ridge. If it is bound tightly this will shed water efficiently. This is ideal for pyramid and circular huts.

With long material, two poles may be slung over the ridge pole with rope so that they lie on either side of it and hold the edges of the thatch down.

You can also lash poles to the top thatching battens to hold down the ridge material tight.

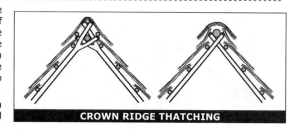

SLUNG POLE RIDGE THATCHING

TIED POLE RIDGE THATCHING

8.3.12 CROWN RIDGE

Another method is to sew ridge material on to three poles, one of which acts as a false ridge and the other two, sewn to the ends of the material, hang down about 50 cm on either side. This can be made on the ground and then hoisted up to cover the ridgepole.

If you like, you can simply make a crown of thatch without poles and place it over the top thatching.

CROWN RIDGE THATCHING

You may have to extend the wall thatching up above the top batten to make sure it is covered.

8.3.13 FLASHING AND GUTTERING

If a tree is being used as support for a shelter, or if one or more of the structural poles extend above the thatch line the roof, flashing may be required. Use thin rope to bind extra thatching material around the tree or pole. Continue this lashing several centimetres above the extra thatching to ensure water doesn't run down the pole.

Under some conditions it may be necessary to create a gutter to channel heavy rainfall away from your shelter. Guttering can be made from wide sheets of bark. Very wide leaves of some palms may also be laid so they overlap each other.

A more robust, and laborious material is hollowed out palm tree trunks. Large bamboo cane halves can also be used if the mid-sections are carved or hammered out.

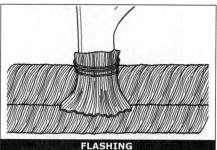

FLASHING

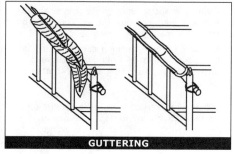

GUTTERING

8.4   SEMI PERMANENT SHELTERS

If the situation permits, more advanced dwellings can be constructed. For a large building job, a group of people should be organised into smaller sub groups each with different tasks —

- The building site needs to be cleared, and levelled if necessary. If shovels aren't available digging tools can be improvised from bush timber.
- Poles need to be cut and carried to the build site.
- If cordage needs to be made, consider the time required.
- Material for thatching needs to be cut and gathered first as it usually needs time to dry out.

8.4.1   FINE-WEATHER SHELTER

If conditions are favourable, a simple 'fine weather' shelter can be constructed by one or two people in a couple of hours.

The supporting poles should be buried for extra stability. The thatched side faces the prevailing winds, while the overhang will keep out a light shower.

This shelter obviously provides little to no protection in extreme conditions.

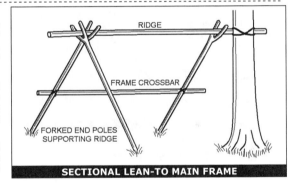

FINE WEATHER SHELTER

8.4.2   SECTIONAL LEAN-TO

Small one or two person huts can be constructed in an hour or two by making and thatching two or three frames from 2 metres in length by 1 meter high or larger as needed.

These frames are lashed onto two forked sticks and secured to a strong living tree by the ridgepole. The framework is simple to construct.

For the down pieces and the front eve, if you build one, select sticks with strong forks and cut to leave a hook at the end.

RIDGE

FRAME CROSSBAR

FORKED END POLES
SUPPORTING RIDGE

SECTIONAL LEAN-TO MAIN FRAME

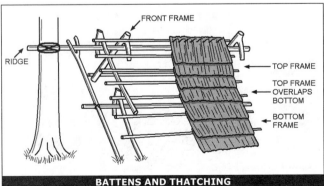

FRONT FRAME

RIDGE

TOP FRAME

TOP FRAME
OVERLAPS
BOTTOM

BOTTOM
FRAME

BATTENS AND THATCHING

Hang these sticks from the ridgepole and crossbar as supports to lash horizontal battens for thatching.

Ensure the end of the top frame projects well beyond the fork and the ridge.

This protects the top frame from weather and saves the work of ridge thatching.

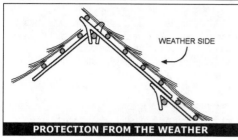

WEATHER SIDE

PROTECTION FROM THE WEATHER

8.4.3 PERMANENT LEAN-TO HUT

This permanent lean-to uses trees for the main supports and is simple to construct.

The ridge pole is held against the trees at about 3 metres high by two or more long forked poles, leaning at an angle from the ground to the ridge pole.

Lash crossbars (A) to the angled beams and to the trees. Make sure they are positioned correctly for the eve.

Lash eve bar (B) to crossbars (A). This should be lower than the ridge pole so the eve lies at an angle. Lash support beams (C) across the ridge pole and eve bar.

Lash rear wall support beam (D) to the angled beams at a suitable position. Hammer rear wall pegs into the ground and lash to beam (D).

This frame can be made very long and a front wall can be added by driving stakes into the ground and lashing to an extra beam under the eve.

When the frame is complete, add battens for thatching. The spacing will be dependent on the thatching material. A spacing of one quarter to one third of the length of material is a good rule of thumb.

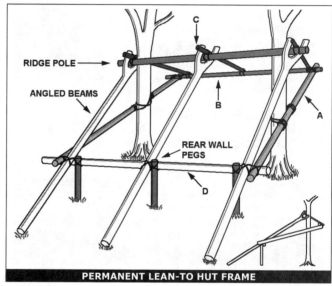

RIDGE POLE

ANGLED BEAMS

C

B

A

REAR WALL PEGS

D

PERMANENT LEAN-TO HUT FRAME

For extra security, bury the angled beams instead of just letting them rest on the ground.

8.4.4 TREE SWING SHELTER

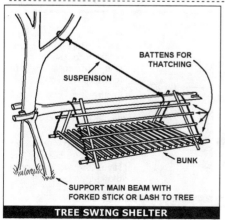

BATTENS FOR THATCHING

SUSPENSION

BUNK

SUPPORT MAIN BEAM WITH FORKED STICK OR LASH TO TREE

TREE SWING SHELTER

In areas that are swampy, or infested with snakes, a swinging bunk shelter can be made by a single person in a day.

The forked pole that supports the bunk must be very strong. The suspension line should be tied as high as practical, and preferably to the bottom of a fork.

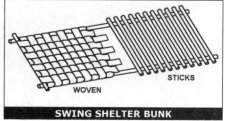

WOVEN

STICKS

SWING SHELTER BUNK

The frame poles from the thatch battens are lashed separately, with a square lashing, to the forked frame pole. For extra strength, lash some short sticks to either end of the frame. When thatching the frame, thatch one row on one side, then one row on the other. This will help strengthen the framework and keep it balanced.

The bunk is made separately and attached to the supporting forked pole. Its main frame is simply four frames lashed together. The centre of the bunk can be made with woven material or made with crossed sticks.

8.4.5 ROUND HUT

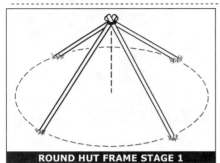

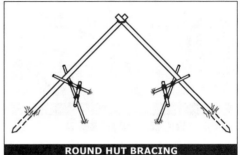

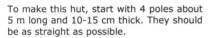

ROUND HUT BRACING

To make this hut, start with 4 poles about 5 m long and 10-15 cm thick. They should be as straight as possible.

Stage 1

Mark out a circular area of about 3 metres radius using a stake and rope. Dig holes about 30 to 50 cm deep to bury the main poles and use temporary braces as shown while the 4 main poles are lashed together at the peak. You will need a ladder, scaffold or monkey for this.

Stage 2

Once the 4 main poles are lashed tightly at the peak and stable, gather 8 poles of length equal to the main poles, although they may be thinner. Bury these at equal spacing around the perimeter and lash them tightly to the peak.

ROUND HUT FRAME STAGE 2

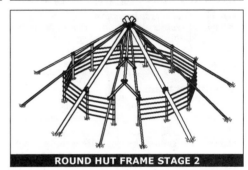

ROUND HUT STAGE 3

You need another pole for the doorway about 2/3 as long as the main poles, and 4 shorter poles to raise the arch.

Gather 12 short poles to drive vertically into the ground and lash to the diagonal beams. These will form the inside wall.

Attach thatching battens around the perimeter, leaving a gap for the doorway.

Stage 3 and Completion

Attach thatching battens around the roof and along the doorway arch. The battens should extend at least 2 spaces beyond the inside wall. Next the hut can be thatched. If the thatching battens are strong enough, you can stand on these while you thatch the section next to where you are standing. If your thatching is strong enough, you can stand on that as you work your way up to the top. Otherwise you can construct a long ladder to lean against the battens. Your weight will be distributed evenly. To thatch the peak, bend long material completely over the crown all the way around, and secure it with tight lashing.

8.4.6 LOG WALLS

Simple and sturdy walls can be built by stacking logs or large sticks between upright stakes, and filling the cavity with dirt. This provides excellent insulation and protection from the elements. Lash at the top if possible to ensure it stays tight.

This can be used as the basis of a larger structure, a sturdy barrier, or a simple wind block.

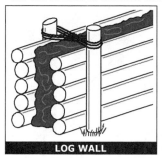

LOG WALL

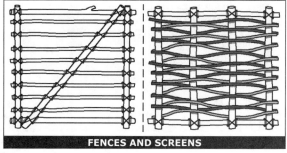

FENCES AND SCREENS

8.4.7 FENCES AND SCREENS

Screens can be made from springy saplings, small branches, plant stems or tough grasses. These can be the basis of fences and gates, a roof covering, doors etc.

Make the frame first from stronger, less pliable material, tie off the struts and weave in your material. If you are short on cordage, drive the stakes into the ground and weave in enough material to make a basic framework. When it is sturdy enough, remove from the ground and finish.

8.4.8 USEFUL HINTS

Materials for Lashing

Although in building larger structures, manufactured items such as rope, twine, special tools etc will be used. Some or all of these items may have to be improvised.

For lashings, sewing and tying, any ground or tree vine which has length, strength and pliability will serve. They should be tested for strength and pliability by tying a thumb knot in the vine and gently pulling it tight. If it snaps or cuts itself it is useless.

In addition to vines, the outer skin of long leaves of most palms can be used for ties. The inner bark of many shrubs and trees, alive or dead, also makes excellent lashing material. Strip down to the required thickness but watch for weak spots where it is likely to fray away.

Special Knots

Many of the sedges have length and strength and may be used for lashing and sewing work. Nearly all the bulrushes can serve as lashings.

Green materials require special knots. The usual start of a square lashing is with a clove hitch, but such a hitch on green material is useless. The natural springiness will cause the knot to open.

Always start a lashing with

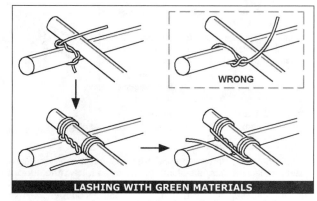

WRONG

LASHING WITH GREEN MATERIALS

a timber hitch and make sure that the free end passes straight through the eye and does not come back against it, as this will usually cause the material to cut itself.

8.4.9 DOORS AND WINDOWS

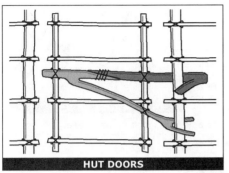

HUT DOORS

Fixtures such as doors and windows are easily added with very little extra work.

Windows can simply be two or three forked sticks cut off short before the fork with the long end protruding. Thatch battens are lashed to these forked sticks and the framework is lifted up and hung on one of these battens of the hut itself.

In the general thatching of a hut this window space is left clear. The window frame is thatched as a separate unit.

It is best to make the window frame wider than the window opening. There should be at least a 10 cm overlap of the frame and the window. The loose ends of the thatching above the window frames should be allowed to come on to the window's own thatch and should completely cover the sewing at the top.

Doors are also made and thatched separately. The hinge of the door can be made by several methods. In construction they are similar to a gate frame with the addition of two uprights lashed across the fork. To these two uprights, the horizontal thatching battens are secured.

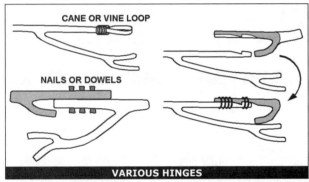

CANE OR VINE LOOP

NAILS OR DOWELS

VARIOUS HINGES

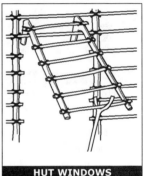

HUT WINDOWS

8.5 CAMPCRAFT

In a long term camp situation, life can become more comfortable and efficient by constructing some simple furniture, such as tables and chairs. It's time consuming, but good for morale.

8.5.1 TABLES

This solid camp table, with integrated seating, has been used for so long that the basic design has been incorporated into commercial patio and park furniture, seen everywhere.

To start the framework, select two forked sticks about 8-10 cm diameter. The length of the stake will depend on how hard you need to drive them into the ground to be secure.

Sharpen and drive the stakes into the ground so the prong of the fork is pointing outwards.

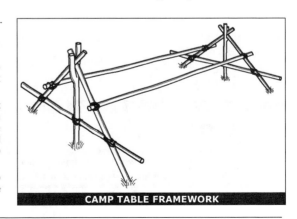

CAMP TABLE FRAMEWORK

Find and cut four strong, straight poles and place them into the crotch of the fork at a 45° angle to the uprights. Shave these cross-braces as shown so they fit neatly into the crotch.

Tightly lash the table and seat supports as shown, at a comfortable height. The framework is now complete.

To finish the table, find many straight long poles for the table and seat surfaces and lash them as shown. The surface poles can be squared off with a drawknife and plane, or can be split down the middle with a wedge, otherwise just accept a rounded, bumpy surface.

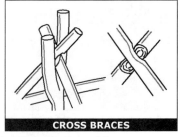

CROSS BRACES

If the seats show signs of sagging, construct an 'H' frame for support in the middle.

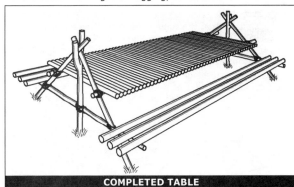

COMPLETED TABLE

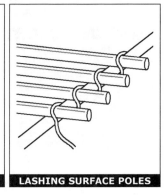

LASHING SURFACE POLES

Bracing in Soft Ground

If the ground is soft or sandy, additional bracing may be needed to stop the table from wobbling. Any wobble will lead to the table's premature destruction and you will have to reconstruct it.

Portable Table

If you don't want a table that is permanently fixed in one position, some extra bracing will eliminate the need for driving poles into the ground. The table can then be moved as needed.

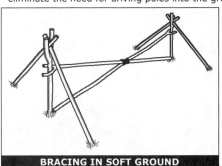

BRACING IN SOFT GROUND

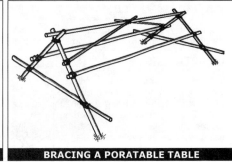

BRACING A PORATABLE TABLE

Keeping Things Level

If you don't have a spirit level, it is easy to construct shelters and benches that are level by using a plum. A plum is simply a piece of string with a weight attached. When the string is held the weight will point straight down and will provide a perfectly accurate vertical reference.

To find the horizontal level line, it is simply a matter of determining the 90° angle from the vertical. Almost any commercially made item will have 90° angles somewhere. If you are truly struggling for 90°, the human eye is very efficient at determining this angle.

CHAIRS

In the bush, any raised object becomes a seat but if you get tired of sitting on rocks and logs, you can make comfortable furniture with a little time and imagination.

At right is one design for a bush chair, remember to make it tall enough so you don't have the fork sticking in the back of your head.

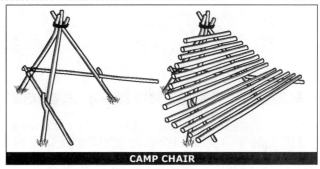

CAMP CHAIR

When selecting the poles for the seat and backing, position the wood so you don't have uncomfortable knots sticking into your butt, unless you like that sort of thing. If you have a drawknife or spokeshave you can plane the poles to create a somewhat flat surface.

Park Bench

This illustration of a simple park bench needs little explanation.

Drive the vertical poles deep enough into the ground to ensure stability, or add diagonal cross bracing.

If the bracing is strong enough the bench can be made to be portable.

8.5.2 BEDS

An hour of hard work is worth a good nights rest. Sleeping directly on the ground is not ideal and will drain heat out of your body very quickly.

A raised bed will eliminate the thermal coupling between your body and the ground and will also reduce the amount of small creatures crawling on you.

This design shows the basic framework for a raised camp bed. Select two large straight poles for the footing and peg them so they don't roll around.

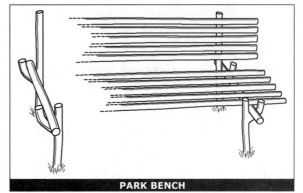

PARK BENCH

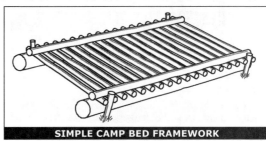

SIMPLE CAMP BED FRAMEWORK

The cross-poles can either be lashed directly to the bottom logs, or lashed to the two thinner upper poles, forming a moveable frame.

Bedding Material

As comfortable as sleeping on a grill of gnarly knot-ridden sticks would be, to complete the bed you need an ample layer of soft material, and a covering mat to hold it all together.

Just about any material can be used for the 'down' as long as it is soft and large enough so it doesn't slip through the grill. Dried grass, ferns, green leaves etc. Make sure this layer is thick enough to support your body weight and provide a soft, springy bed.

Next construct a mat out of reeds or long grass bundled and woven together with some cordage. This will prevent the loose material from being displaced during your sleep.

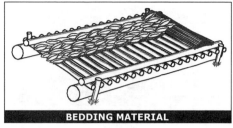

BEDDING MATERIAL

COVER MAT

Above Ground Camp Beds

Rocks or large logs can be used to raise a camp bed off the ground. Another method is to construct some A-frames, similar to those used for the camp table, and lash the bed framework to that.

RAISING A CAMP BED

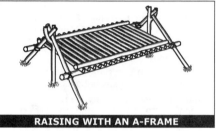

RAISING WITH AN A-FRAME

If you have some strong material such as canvas, the design can be greatly simplified by constructing a stretcher type bed. Canvas bags can be simply looped around the side supports. If you need to stitch the material, use a back-stitch and double or triple them.

STRETCHER BED

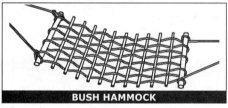

BUSH HAMMOCK

If you have enough spare rope, a hammock can be woven. Using sticks for the cross supports reduces the amount of rope needed. This design is both comfortable and strong.

Tree-Swing Shelter

A shelter and a bed can be incorporated into one design. Find or cut a large log with a fork and suspend it to a suitable tree as shown. The forked end may need to be lashed to the tree to prevent it from slipping upwards.

Next, construct the bunk in the same manner as a camp bed and suspend it to the large main pole with some strong rope.

Now horizontal beams can be lashed to the A-frame rope supports, and these can be thatched to provide a waterproof shelter.

This design is useful in swampy territory or areas that are prone to snakes. Be sure to make the shelter large enough so it is not difficult to enter.

BATTENS FOR THATCHING

SUSPENSION

BUNK

SUPPORT MAIN BEAM WITH FORKED STICK OR LASH TO TREE

TREE SWING SHELTER

8.6 LONG TERM SHELTERS

If the situation requires, and permits, you may consider building a larger, more robust shelter. Many options are available from the popular log-cabin to mud-brick, rammed earth and others.

Before commencing construction, the site should be well prepared and the materials should be collected and stored in advance.

8.6.1 FOUNDATIONS

Buildings such as rammed earth or mudbrick houses should be set on a solid foundation. This foundation does not need to cover the entire floor, only to bear the weight of the walls.

A trench 60 cm deep by 30 cm wide, lined all over with 4 cm of clay is enough to bear the weight. Large stones are then set into this clay and the footing continued with more clay and stones until a packed wall has been made that stands about 20 cm above ground level. The wall is raised to prevent water from damaging the walls. If you are in an area that is subject to flooding, a higher foundation may be required.

Clay is a good material to use because it is fairly resistant to moisture once tramped in and the

STONE FOUNDATIONS

building will require no damp course. Concrete can be used if available, but a damp course (water-proof barrier) will be required underneath.

8.6.2 RAMMED EARTH CONSTRUCTION

Earth buildings can either be constructed by making forms to contain the material, or by ramming it in blocks, forming bricks, and laying these in courses.

The material required for construction is earth, mixed with a proportion of clay, sand or other gritty particles. It should be free of organic materials such as tree roots.

Soil Properties

Any heavy loamy soil is suitable for rammed earth construction. The soil must have the right moisture content. To test the moisture content, roll some into a golf-ball sized lump and drop it from 30 cm. If it breaks up on contact, it is too dry and will need moisture to be added before ramming.

If it holds together after being dropped, apply a second test. Drop the ball from above your head. If it still holds together, it is too wet and will need to be dried out.

The soil should be tested for its clay-silt-sand ratio. There should be between 30% - 70% sand and 30% - 70% clay and silt. The ideal proportions are 50/50. You should take samples from various areas and test. You may combine soils from different areas to obtain the correct mix.

Testing Soil

To test soil, take a clear container about 10 cm high. Dry some of the test earth, crumble it and fill the container to the top. Then empty the container into another dish, and wash thoroughly in slowly running water until all the clay and silt washes over the rim.

Dry what remains and place back into the container. This will provide the sand ratio of the soil. Soil with too much clay will crack, but if the clay content is too low, the block will crumble. Soil that is heavy in clay however is suitable for mudbricks.

Strengthening Agents

The walls can be made with earth only, but adding binding agents such as dried grass or straw will increase the strength considerably. If bricks are to be made in molds, the binding agent should be cut in lengths to fit in the molds. If long walls are to be made, any reasonable length will do, but shorter lengths will mix better with the clay-sand material.

Small stones and river gravel can also be used. If using either straw or gravel, test blocks should be made, seasoned, and tested for strength and cracking before beginning construction. Make note of the materials and proportions used in each test block.

Forms and Molds

Forms can be made from a series of boards which are bolted together to allow the rammed earth wall to be built directly onto the buildings footing. Use threaded rods and nuts, or dowels with pins to hold the forms together so they can be taken apart when the wall is finished.

Alternatively, molds can be made and the earth rammed into them to make large blocks. After drying, these blocks can be laid in the same way as bricks.

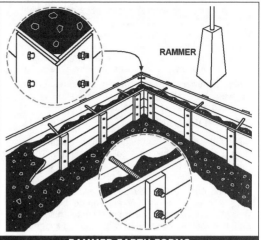

RAMMED EARTH FORMS

If forms are used, the most convenient size for filling is about 1 meter high and 2 metres long.

At the first level clamp the forms to the footings by driving poles into the earth and securing at the top of the forms.

Ramming Technique

When ramming, shovel about 10 cm of earth along the entire form and ram it down until it 'rings'. The ringing sound is distinctly different from the initial 'thuds' when starting to ram. When the first layer is 'ringing' throughout its entire length, the process is repeated.

Separate right-angle forms are needed for the corners and the earth should be rammed particularly hard in these sections. Each level of the wall should be allowed to cure for several days before the forms are removed and the next layer is started.

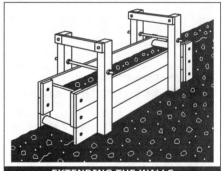

EXTENDING THE WALLS

Rammers generally weigh between 4 - 8 kg and have a large flat hardwood head. The handle should be about 1.5 metres long. For a wall 2.5 - 3 metres tall, 30 cm thick is sufficient. Higher walls should be 40 cm thick.

Incorporating pieces of wood into the structure during building will make it easier to attach fixtures such as doors and windows.

If molds are used to form bricks, they can be

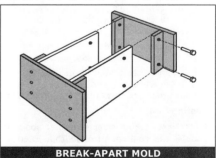

BREAK-APART MOLD

designed to break apart once a brick has been made. The bricks can cure without support.

The roof can be thatched or shingled, or can be made by laying a bed of logs which is then chinked with clay and covered with soil and sod. The angle should be at least 15° to allow for proper water shedding. Once the structure has been constructed and roofed, extra protection on the outside walls from rain can be applied. This can be a whitewash, lime-wash, a cow dung-mud render mix, bituminous paint or a cement render made from one part cement to two parts sand in a very liquid form.

8.6.3 SIMPLE LOG CABIN

If timber is plentiful and termites are not a problem, a log cabin can be built as a permanent shelter. Any type of log can be used as long as it is fairly straight and about 20 – 25 cm in diameter, and only minor tapering. A taper of 5 cm over a 5 meter log is acceptable. Two logs should be larger and heavier than the rest for use as bed logs.

Seasoning the Timber

If possible, cut down trees in early winter. The cooler temperatures allow for longer drying times, which reduces cracking and splitting. To season the logs, stack them on the ground with thinner logs as spacers between the courses to keep the main logs off the ground and provide the most airflow.

The bark should be partially peeled off with a drawknife if you have one. This will increase drying speed with only minimum splitting cracking. Season the wood for at least 1 – 2 years.

Construction

Find a clear flat area, or clear and level one, in a suitable place. The area should not be vulnerable to flooding or landslides and be out of view from possible intruders.

Lay the bed logs in the required position, ensuring they are square. If you measure diagonally from corner to corner, both measurements should be even. Bury the logs half their thickness deep.

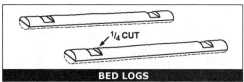

BED LOGS

Cut square notches in the bed logs quarter way through. Next select two logs for the first course of end logs and cut them to length if necessary. Cut two square notches a quarter way through so they slot into the bed logs.

The remaining logs are 'scarfed' into the lower rows by cutting round grooves half way through. This method of scarfing underneath the logs ensures water will automatically run down and not get trapped in the grooves.

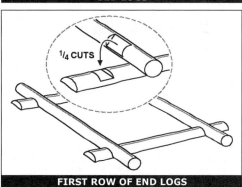

FIRST ROW OF END LOGS

Continue building in this manner to build up the walls. Alternate each row so the tapered end sits on the fat end of the previous row. Once the walls reach about waist height, cut the openings for doors and windows. The loose ends can be braced by cutting a vertical groove into the ends of the logs and inserting a thin pole to hold them in place.

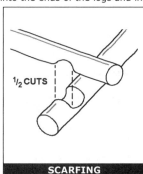

SCARFING

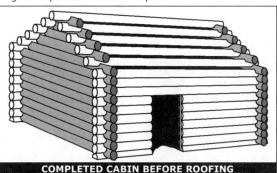

COMPLETED CABIN BEFORE ROOFING

Once the walls are high enough, form the apex for the roof by using shorter and shorter end logs. You can then finish with a thatched, shingled or sod roof. When complete, chink the cabin from the inside, using a clay/soil mixture. This will need to be reapplied from time to time.

8.6.4 OTHER CONSTRUCTION TECHNIQUES

There are many ways to build strong shelters and entire books have been written on each of the methods presented in this chapter. Choose a method that best suits your resources and requirements, even if that means combining two or more techniques.

It is best not to start too large, but rather build the minimum you require to improve your immediate situation and expand later on as your situation permits.

Adobe

Adobe is basically soil that has been moistened, formed into shape, and allowed to dry. Often chopped straw or other fibres are added for strength. The best adobe soil will have between 15% to 30% clay, with the rest of the mixture being sand or larger aggregate.

Too much clay will cause shrinkage and cracking when drying, too little will not be enough to bind the material properly. Adobe can be stabilised with a small amount of cement or asphalt emulsion to keep it intact when subject to excessive weather.

Sometimes adobe is shaped into uniform blocks that can be stacked like bricks to form walls, but more often is simply piled up over time to create a solid structure. It can be shaped into blocks by pouring into molds and rammed or simply left to dry. The walls should be about 50 cm (20 in) thick.

Occasional re-plastering will be required as the weather deteriorates the walls. Large eaves to protect the walls from the weather and a foundation to raise it off the ground will greatly reduce the need for maintenance.

Due to the high earth content, adobe has a large thermal mass and will hold heat or cold for a long time. Insulation can be provided with a second internal wall of light cob, described below.

Cob

Cob is similar to adobe, but there is a much higher percentage of long straw fibres mixed in and the clay content is between 10% to 20%. The mixture of clay, soil, coarse sand, straw and water is thoroughly mixed and beaten together. The stiff mud is then built up into walls while still wet, without the use of formwork or ramming.

The mixture is applied in courses, each of which is 'sewn' or 'woven' into the lower course while it is still pliable. As the walls are formed, frames for doors and windows and other fixtures such as wooden anchors benches are incorporated along the way.

Because of the weight of the material, the bottom courses must be allowed to dry before a new course can be added. This makes it hard to add more than about 30 cm (1 ft) per day. The walls should be about 50 cm (20 in) thick.

Due to the lack of mortar joints and the high percentage of fibres, cob houses are usually more resistant to earthquakes than their close cousin, adobe. They also have higher insulation, as opposed to thermal mass (holds heat or cold), because of the amount air trapped in the fibres.

Cob houses, like adobe, must be protected from the weather with generous eaves and a foundation. They should never be constructed in flood plains, well nothing should really.

Light Cob

A variation of cob is to use long straw fibres and coat them with enough clay mixture so that they stick together, but does not form a solid mass.

This material is then tamped into form and left to set before removing the formwork. This is useful for making interior walls that do not bear any weight. These walls offer a lot more insulation than traditional cob or adobe.

External walls can be made from this way if they are made thick enough, but some sort of frame would be needed as the light cob is not load bearing.

The walls can be rendered with a clay mixture once they are set.

Straw Substitute

If you don't have straw, many other natural materials can be substituted, such as dried reeds. Basically any material that is suitable for rope making will add the strength necessary if they are long enough, and abundant. See **Selecting Materials** (Page 7-1) for details.

If you are going to collect such materials, then your fist task should be gathering a large supply before you start construction as this will be time consuming.

9 WEAPONS, TOOLS & EQUIPMENT

A knife is your most valuable tool in a survival situation. You must always keep it sharp and ready to use. Imagine being in a survival situation without any weapons, tools, or equipment except your knife. You would probably feel helpless, but with the proper knowledge and skills, you can easily improvise needed items.

In survival situations, you may have to fashion any number and type of field-expedient tools and equipment to survive. Examples of tools and equipment that could make your life much easier are ropes, rucksacks, clothes, nets, and so on.

Weapons serve a dual purpose. You use them to obtain and prepare food and to provide self-defence. A weapon can also give you a feeling of security and provide you with the ability to hunt on the move.

9.1 CLUBS

You hold clubs, you do not throw them. As a field-expedient weapon, the club does not protect you from enemies. It can, however, extend your area of defence beyond your fingertips. It also serves to increase the force of a blow without injuring yourself. There are three basic types of clubs. They are the simple, weighted, and sling club.

Simple Club

A simple club is a staff or branch. It must be short enough for you to swing easily, but long enough and strong enough for you to damage whatever you hit. Its diameter should fit comfortably in your palm, but it should not be so thin as to allow the club to break easily upon impact. A straight-grained hardwood is best if you can find it.

Weighted Club

A weighted club is any simple club with a weight on one end. The weight may be a natural weight, such as a knot on the wood, or something added, such as a stone lashed to the club.

To make a weighted club, first find a stone that has a shape that will allow you to lash it securely to the club. If you cannot find a suitably shaped stone, you must fashion a groove or channel into the stone by a technique known as pecking. By repeatedly rapping the club stone with a smaller hard stone, you can get the desired shape.

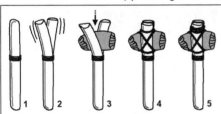

1. Wrap lashing around stick.
2. Split the end of the stick to meet the lashing.
3. Insert the stone in the split.
4. Lash securely above, below and across the stone.
5. Bind the split end of the stick tightly to secure the stone.

SPLIT-HANDLE TECHNIQUE

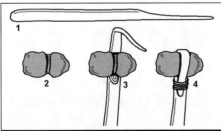

1. Find some hardwood about 1 m (3 ft) long and about 2.5 cm (1 in) thick. Shave the end to about half diameter.
2. Find a heavy stone with a groove, or chip away with another stone to make a groove.
3. Wrap the shaved end around the stone tightly in the groove.
4. Lash securely.

WRAPPED-HANDLE TECHNIQUE

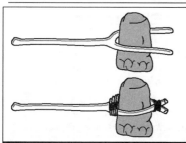

Find a suitable forked stick a heavy stone.

Lash securely at the crotch of the fork.

Insert the stone in the fork and lash the ends together tightly.

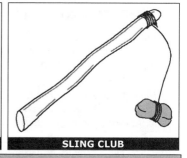

FORKED-BRANCH TECHNIQUE   **SLING CLUB**

9.2 EDGED WEAPONS

Knives, spear blades, and arrow points fall under the category of edged weapons. The following paragraphs will discuss the making of such weapons.

9.2.1 KNIVES

A knife is an invaluable tool used to construct other survival items. You may find yourself without a knife or you may need another type knife or a spear. To improvise you can use stone, bone, wood, or metal to make a knife or spear blade.

Stone

To make a stone knife, you will need a sharp-edged piece of stone, a chipping tool, and a flaking tool. A chipping tool is a light, blunt-edged tool used to break off small pieces of stone. A flaking tool is a pointed tool used to break off thin pieces of stone. You can make a chipping tool from wood, bone, or metal, and a flaking tool from bone, antler tines, or soft iron.

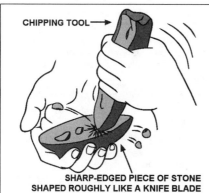

CHIPPING TOOL→

SHARP-EDGED PIECE OF STONE SHAPED ROUGHLY LIKE A KNIFE BLADE

1. SHAPE BLADE –

STRIKE GLANCING BLOWS NEAR EDGE TO GET EDGE THIN ENOUGH TO SHARPEN

FLAKING TOOL

2. SHARPEN BLADE –

PRESS DOWNWARD WITH FLAKING TOOL AT STONE EDGE OR PUSH FLAKING TOOL ALONG EDGE

NOTCHES FOR LASHING BLADE TO HILT

BLADE LASHED TO HILT (HARDWOOD, ANTLER, ETC)

MAKING A STONE KNIFE

Start making the knife by roughing out the desired shape on your sharp piece of stone, using the chipping tool. Try to make the knife fairly thin. Then, using the flaking tool, press it against the edges. This action will cause flakes to come off the opposite side of the edge, leaving a razor sharp edge. Use the flaking tool along the entire length of the edge you need to sharpen. Eventually, you will have a very sharp cutting edge that you can use as a knife.

Lash the blade to some type of hilt.

 Stone will make an excellent puncturing tool and a good chopping tool but will not hold a fine edge. Some stones such as chert or flint can have very fine edges, but will break easily.

Bone

You can also use bone as an effective edged weapon. First, select a suitable bone. The larger bones, such as the leg bone of a deer or another medium-sized animal, are best. Lay the bone upon another hard object. Shatter the bone by hitting it with a rock. From the pieces, select a suitable pointed splinter. You can further shape and sharpen this splinter by rubbing it on a rough-surfaced rock. If the piece is too small to handle, you can still use it by adding a handle to it. Select a suitable piece of hardwood for a handle and lash the bone splinter securely to it.

 Use the bone knife only to puncture. It will not hold an edge and it may flake or break if used differently.

Wood

You can make edged weapons from wood. Use these only to puncture. To make a knife using wood, first select a straight-grained piece of hardwood that is about 30 cm long and 2.5 cm in diameter. Fashion the blade about 15 cm long. Shave it down to a point. Use only the straight-grained portions of the wood. Do not use the core or pith, as it would make a weak point.

Harden the point by a process known as fire hardening. Dry the blade portion over the fire slowly until lightly charred. The drier the wood, the harder the point. After lightly charring the blade portion, sharpen it on a coarse stone. If using bamboo and after fashioning the blade, remove any other wood to make the blade thinner from the inside portion of the bamboo. Removal is done this way because bamboo's hardest part is its outer layer. Keep as much of this layer as possible to ensure the hardest blade possible. When charring bamboo over a fire, char only the inside wood; do not char the outside.

Metal

Metal is the best material to make field-expedient edged weapons. First, select a suitable piece of metal, one that most resembles the desired end product. Depending on the size and original shape, you can obtain a point and cutting edge by rubbing the metal on a rough-surfaced stone. If the metal is soft enough, you can hammer out one edge while the metal is cold. Use a suitable flat, hard surface as an anvil and a smaller, harder object of stone or metal as a hammer to hammer out the edge. Make a knife handle from wood, bone, or other material that will protect your hand.

Other Materials

You can use other materials to produce edged weapons. Glass is a good alternative to an edged weapon or tool. Obtain a suitable piece in the same manner as described for bone. Glass has a natural edge but is less durable for heavy work. You can also sharpen plastic – if it is thick enough or hard enough – into a durable point for puncturing.

9.2.2 SPEARS

Use the same procedures to make a spear blade as a knife blade. Select a shaft (a straight sapling) 1.2 - 1.5 metres long. The length should allow you to handle the spear easily and effectively.

To attach the blade to the shaft, split the handle, insert the blade, and then lash it tightly.

You can use other materials without adding a blade. Select a long straight hardwood shaft and shave one end to a point. If possible, fire-harden the point.

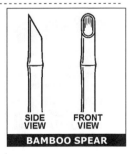

SIDE VIEW FRONT VIEW
BAMBOO SPEAR

Bamboo also makes an excellent spear. Starting 8 - 10 cm back from the end used as the point, shave down the end at a 45° angle. Remember, to sharpen the edges, shave only the inner portion.

9.3   OTHER EXPEDIENT WEAPONS

Anything that extends your reach and adds force to your blows can become a weapon. You can make other weapons such as the throwing stick, archery equipment, and the bola.

9.3.1   THROWING STICK

The throwing stick, commonly known as the rabbit stick, is very effective against small game. The rabbit stick itself is a blunt stick, naturally curved at about a 45-degree angle. Select a stick with the desired angle from heavy hardwood such as oak. Shave off two opposite sides so that the stick is flat like a boomerang. You must practice the throwing technique for accuracy and speed. First, align the target by extending the non-throwing arm in line with the mid to lower section of the target.

45-50 cm (18-20 in)

THROWING STICK

Slowly and repeatedly raise the throwing arm up and back until the throwing stick crosses the back at about a 45-degree angle or is in line with the non-throwing hip. Bring the throwing arm forward until it is just slightly above and parallel to the non-throwing arm. This will be the throwing stick's release point. Practice slowly and repeatedly to attain accuracy.

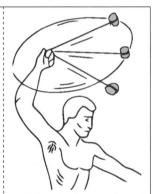

9.3.2   BOLA

The bola is weapon that is easy to make. It is especially effective for capturing running game or low flying birds in a flock.

To use the bola, hold it by the centre knot and twirl it above your head.

Join 3 cords and tie weights securely to the ends.

Hold by the knot and twirl the bola over your head. Release toward target.

BOLA

Release the knot so that the bola flies toward your target. When you release the bola, the weighted cords will separate. These cords will wrap around and immobilize the fowl or animal that you hit.

9.3.3   SLING

You can make a sling by tying two pieces of cordage, about 60 cm long, at opposite ends of a palm-sized piece of leather or cloth. Place a rock in the cloth and wrap one cord around the middle finger and hold in your palm. Hold the other cord between the forefinger and thumb. To throw the rock, spin the sling several times in a circle and release the cord between the thumb and forefinger. You will need practice to gain proficiency. The sling is very effective against small game.

9.4   ARCHERY EQUIPMENT

While it may be relatively simple to make a bow and arrow, it is not easy to use one. You must practice using it a long time to be sure that you will hit your target. Also, a field-expedient bow will not last very long before you have to make a new one. For the time and effort involved, you may well decide to use another type of field-expedient weapon.

It is often recommended that a bow should be longer than twice your draw length. A shorter bow may shoot a little faster and be more convenient to carry than a longer bow, but it may be more likely to fail. A longer bow may help you shoot more accurately, has a greater potential pull and will probably be a bit more durable.

Experiment with different materials to make a bow. Some of the most recommended bow woods are relatively dense and heavy. Light woods are generally not recommended.

Traditionally, nocks are cut near the tips of each end to hold the bow string. Instead of using cut nocks, the bow string can be stopped from slipping down the bow by applying a tight wrapping of cord or leather strapping around the end of the limb.

9.4.1 ARROWS

Select arrows from the straightest dry sticks available. The arrows should be about half as long as the bow. Scrape each shaft smooth all around. You will probably have to straighten the shaft. You can bend an arrow straight by heating the shaft over hot coals. Do not allow the shaft to scorch or burn. Hold the shaft straight until it cools.

You must notch the ends of the arrows for the bowstring. Cut or file the notch; do not split it. Fletching (adding feathers to the notched end of an arrow) improves the arrow's flight characteristics, but is not necessary on a field-expedient arrow.

9.4.2 ARROW POINTS

To make an arrow point, use the same procedures for making a stone knife blade. Chert, flint, and shell-type stones are best for arrow points. You can fashion bone like stone – by flaking. You can make an efficient arrow point using broken glass.

You can make arrowheads from bone, glass, metal, or pieces of rock. You can also sharpen and fire harden the end of the shaft. To fire harden wood, hold it over hot coals, being careful not to burn or scorch the wood.

9.4.3 SINGLE PIECE BOW

A good bow is the result of many hours of work. You can construct a suitable short-term bow fairly easily. When it breaks or loses its spring, you can replace it.

Select a hardwood stick about one meter long that is free of knots or limbs. Carefully scrape the large end down until it has the same pull as the small end. Careful examination will show the natural curve of the stick. Scrape from the side that faces you, or the bow will break the first time you pull it.

Dead, dry wood is preferable to green wood. To increase the pull, lash a second bow to the first, front to front, forming an "X" when viewed from the

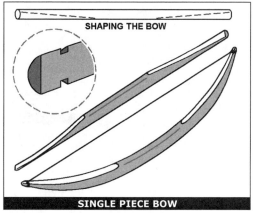

SHAPING THE BOW

SINGLE PIECE BOW

side. Link the tips of the bows with cordage and only use a bowstring on one bow.

9.4.4 BUNDLE BOW

A bundle bow is made up of sticks that are tied together in such a way to achieve a similar taper to a carved bow.

BUNDLE BOW

Three or more sticks of a similar diameter and fairly uniform thickness are bundled together to make a bow. The shortest stick should be around half the length of the longest one. The middle-sized stick should be about three-quarters the length of the longest one. Experiment to find the best direction for the pull of the bow.

Small saplings can be cut and seasoned or a suitable seasoned bamboo may perform a little better because of its comparatively low weight. Some varieties of bamboo seem to be quite unsuitable for this purpose. Old fibreglass or carbon fibre fishing rods can also be used.

9.5   LASHING AND CORDAGE

Many materials are strong enough for use as lashing and cordage. A number of natural and man-made materials are available in a survival situation. For example, you can make a cotton web belt much more useful by unravelling it. You can then use the string for other purposes (fishing line, thread for sewing, and lashing).

This subject is discussed in detail in **Making Ropes and Cords** (Page 7-1).

9.5.1   NATURAL CORDAGE SELECTION

Before making cordage, there are tests you can do to determine your materials suitability. First, pull on a length of the material to test for strength. Next, twist it between your fingers and roll the fibres together. If it withstands this and does not snap apart, tie an overhand knot with the fibres and gently tighten. If the knot does not break, the material is usable.

Sinew

An excellent natural material for lashing small objects is sinew. You can make sinew from the tendons of large game, such as deer. Remove the tendons from the game and dry them completely. Smash the dried tendons so that they separate into fibres. Moisten the fibres and twist them into a continuous strand. If you need stronger material, you can braid the strands. When you use sinew for small lashings, you do not need knots as the moistened sinew is sticky and it hardens when dry.

Plant Fibres

You can shred and braid plant fibres from the inner bark of some trees to make cord. You can use the linden, elm, hickory, white oak, mulberry, chestnut, and red and white cedar trees. After you make the cord, test it to be sure it is strong enough for your purpose. You can make these materials stronger by braiding several strands together.

Gather fibres in two groups and secure with knot	Twist both groups of fibres clockwise to form two strands	Twist both strands together anti-clockwise and tie off at end.

MAKING CORD FROM PLANT FIBRES

Rawhide

You can use rawhide for larger lashing jobs. Make rawhide from the skins of medium or large game. After skinning the animal, remove any excess fat and any pieces of meat from the skin. Dry the skin completely. You do not need to stretch it as long as there are no folds to trap moisture. You do not have to remove the hair from the skin. Cut the skin while it is dry. Make cuts about 6 mm wide. Start from the centre of the hide and make one continuous circular cut, working clockwise to the hide's outer edge. Soak the rawhide for 2 to 4 hours or until it is soft. Use it wet, stretching it as much as possible while applying it. It will be strong and durable when it dries.

9.6   CLOTHING AND INSULATION

You can use many materials for clothing and insulation. Both man-made materials and natural materials, such as skins and plant materials, are available and offer significant protection.

Animal Skins

The selection of animal skins in a survival situation will most often be limited to what you manage to trap or hunt. However, if there is an abundance of wildlife, select the hides of larger animals with heavier coats and large fat content. Do not use the skins of infected or diseased animals if at all possible. Since they live in the wild, animals are carriers of pests such as ticks, lice, and fleas. Because of these pests, use water to thoroughly clean any skin obtained from any animal. If water is not available, then at least shake out the skin thoroughly. As with rawhide, lay out the skin, and remove all fat and meat. Dry the skin completely. Use the hind quarter joint areas to make shoes and mittens or socks. Wear the hide with the fur to the inside for its insulating factor.

See **Tanning Animal Hides** (Page 9-8) for details on preparing animal hides.

Plant Fibres

Several plants are sources of insulation from cold. Cattail is a marshland plant found along lakes, ponds, and the backwaters of rivers. The fuzz on the tops of the stalks forms dead air spaces and makes a good down-like insulation when placed between two pieces of material. Milkweed has pollen like seeds that act as good insulation. The husk fibres from coconuts are very good for weaving ropes and, when dried, make excellent tinder and insulation.

9.7 COOKING AND EATING UTENSILS

Many materials may be used to make equipment for the cooking, eating, and storing of food.

Bowls

Use wood, bone, horn, bark, or other similar material to make bowls. To make wooden bowls, use a hollowed out piece of wood that will hold your food and enough water to cook it in. Hang the wooden container over the fire and add hot rocks to the water and food. Remove the rocks as they cool and add more hot rocks until your food is cooked.

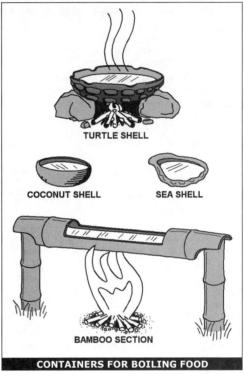

TURTLE SHELL

COCONUT SHELL   SEA SHELL

 CAUTION – Rocks with air pockets such as limestone and sandstone may explode while heating in the fire.

You can also use this method with containers made of bark or leaves. However, these containers will burn above the waterline unless you keep them moist or keep the fire low.

A section of bamboo works very well, if you cut out a section between two sealed joints.

 CAUTION – A sealed section of bamboo will explode if heated.

BAMBOO SECTION

CONTAINERS FOR BOILING FOOD

Forks, Knives, and Spoons

Carve forks, knives, and spoons from non-resinous woods so that you do not get a wood resin aftertaste or do not taint the food. Non-resinous woods include oak, birch, and other hardwood trees.

 Do not use trees that secrete a syrup or resin-like liquid on the bark or when cut.

Pots

You can make pots from turtle shells or wood. As described with bowls, using hot rocks in a hollowed out piece of wood is very effective. Bamboo is the best wood for making cooking containers.

To use turtle shells, first thoroughly boil the upper portion of the shell. Then use it to heat food and water over a flame.

Water Bottles

Make water bottles from the stomachs of larger animals. Thoroughly scrape out and flush the stomach out with water, then tie off the bottom. Leave the top open, with some means of fastening it closed.

9.8 TANNING ANIMAL HIDES

Tanning a hide will make it soft and suitable for clothing and many useful items. Start with a freshly-skinned hide from the animal. You will also need the brain for the tanning solution. An interesting quirk is that every animal has enough brains to tan its own hide.

9.8.1 SIMPLE TANNING

Fleshing the Hide

If the hide is not fresh, and the meat seems dry and stuck to the hide, soak it in water overnight. It will tend to float so weigh it down. Let it drip dry the next day.

Spread the hide fur side down on a flat log or other surface if available. If possible, stretch it taut and tack it down. Another method is to use a horizontal beam about naval height (a pole lashed between two trees). Lay the hide with the neck over the beam so you can hold it in place with body weight.

Take a dull scraping tool and begin scraping the muscle and fat tissue away until you see the pores of the skin. Be sure to scrape every square inch of the hide, including the edges.

De-hairing the Hide

If you chose to remove the hair from the hide, fill a large container with enough water to completely cover the hide. Mix up one cup of ashes with two cups cold water and stir it well. Stir this lye solution into the water then submerge the entire hide.

Keep it submerged until the hair begins to pull out easily. Stir the mixture and let the hide soak for a while longer until you can scrape a blunt scraping tool gently across the skin a few times and remove a strip of hair. At this point you can scrape all the hair off.

Once all the hair is removed, trim the hide so there are no thin edges.

Braining the Hide

Mix the animal brain with a small amount of water and mash into a smooth consistency. Once blended, mix about 0.5 kg (1 pound) of brains to 15 litres (4 gallons) of water. Another way to measure is about a large walnut size of brain to 1 1/2 cups water.

The water should be very warm, but not too warm to put your hands in, otherwise it will slow cook the hide and weaken it. Divide this mixture into two equal portions.

Begin to dip the hide in the warm solution. Wet the hide thoroughly and work with your hands. All parts of the hide should feel very slimy and smooth. If there are parts that do not feel slimy, gently pull on that part and let it absorb the brain solution.

Leave this to soak in the brain solution overnight, completely submerged and weighed down.

The next day, hang the hide up to dry. If it is a hot sunny day, do not leave it hanging too long once dry or it will be difficult to work later.

Once the hide is dry, place it in a container of clean water and let soak overnight again.

Softening

Begin to stretch your hide. Pull it side to side and head to tail over a beam. The back of an old chair works well. Stretch and buff it over the entire length of the hide. Continue doing this until dry. If the pelt dries tough in one some spots, reapply some brain solution, let it soak in and stretch until dry.

For larger pelts you can make a frame to stretch the hide over. This can be made with four poles lashed together, or two horizontal poles lashed between two trees. Cut slits in the edge of the hide about 2 cm in from the edge and about 1 cm long to lace the hide to the frame. Pull the hide as taut as you can in the frame.

Smoking

Smoke the hide for a few hours using a tepee setup. This will help reduce oxygen to the fire. Use old rotting wood that contains a lot of punkwood. Dampen the wood if necessary and check often for flare-ups. Don't use bark to create the smoke, the bark doesn't contain the oils necessary.

It shouldn't get too hot in the smoker or the hide will bake. Once smoking is complete trim the edges of the hide.

9.8.2 ADVANCED TANNING

This is a more involved process but will produce excellent quality leather. This method is very suitable for using large hides for clothing. To start, flesh, de-hair and brain the hide in the same manner as above.

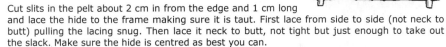

Pre-Stretching

This is the most important step. It should be done out of the sun and wind if possible as the stretching is best done when wet. You will need a frame to stretch the hide on. This can be made by lashing two horizontal poles between two trees. Make sure the frame is large enough to accommodate the hide as well as about 25 cm (10 in) of lacing on each side.

Cut slits in the pelt about 2 cm in from the edge and 1 cm long and lace the hide to the frame making sure it is taut. First lace from side to side (not neck to butt) pulling the lacing snug. Then lace it neck to butt, not tight but just enough to take out the slack. Make sure the hide is centred as best you can.

Work the hide from side to side (not neck to butt) with a flat rounded stick or paddle to stretch it out. The hide will whiten as you stretch it. Make sure you work the edges well before the rest of the hide as they tend to dry out first. If the edges become dry before being stretched, it will be harder to stretch the centre and the lacing holes may break and need to be recut.

As soon as the hide starts to become baggy, tighten the lacing making sure it's even. Make sure you tighten it as much as possible to prevent it from shrinking again. Work both sides of the hide. The hair side doesn't whiten as easily as the flesh side so work it really well.

Continue working the hide and pulling in the lacing until the hide won't stretch any further. Then start to really work the neck, the hips and along the back. The hide is thicker in these places and will still be wet.

Once the hide is dry it will be stiff and hard and sound hard when tapped. It can be stored in this state indefinitely as long as it is kept dry. Because of stretching in one direction only, the hide will be fatter and shorter. This will be rectified in the final stage.

Smoking

Smoke the hide for a few hours as above. Then you will need the second half of the brain solution you produced previously.

It is important to take the hide directly from the smoker into the brain solution. Warm the brain solution up and take the hide from the smoker into the brain solution. Submerge and soak this for an hour or so.

Woking the Hide

This step involves a long metal edge to scrape along the hide. The thin metal strips that bind palettes and large appliance packages work well. Use a length about 1.2 metres (4 ft) and nail each end to a vertical pole like a tall straight tree. Let the band bow out about 20 cm (8 in) so there is room to pull the hide through.

Place the hide container under the band so the solution runs into it. Pull the hide through the band back and hold by each end. Pull the hide back and forth to work out any rubbery feeling parts of the hide. Pay attention to the neck, hips and along the back. It should feel like a soft, thick wet towel.

This step makes sure the pores are open and accept as much brain solution as possible. It should take about 5 to 10 minutes if it was stretched properly. Once complete, place the hide back in the brain solution and let soak overnight.

Softening

Remove the hide from the solution and wring out as well as you can over a horizontal beam (do not scrunch it). Lace up and work the hide in the same manner as the pre-stretching. This time however, lace it up from neck to butt first tightly, then from side to side but only enough to take out the slack. You will not need to lace it up as tightly as in pre-stretching.

When you work it, work from neck to butt to restore the original shape of the hide. You should not need to work it as much as before if the pre-stretching was done well.

Leave this overnight, and then work it again just to relax it a bit and remove it from the frame.

The hide is ready for use, but you may smoke it again for colour.

9.8.3 MAKING RAWHIDE

You don't need brains to make rawhide. Basically the same as tanning but without the brain solution and usually the hair is removed. Whereas tanning is meant to keep the hide soft and flexible for use in clothing and crafts, rawhide is meant for toughness and strength.

The hide is fleshed and de-haired and usually cut into a rectangular shape. This can be stretched to soften the leather or made even tougher. For extra toughness soak in water and dry over a smoky fire and repeat several times. This can then be cut into patches, straps or any desirable shape.

9.9 NATURAL GLUES

Many excellent bonding agents can be found in nature.

9.9.1 PINE PITCH

Resin can be collected from the wounds of pine trees. Create a wound with a knife, axe or sharp stone and collect the orange resin a few days later.

- Grind down some charcoal between stones, or a stone and a flattened stick, like a cudgel.
- Place a flat rock onto a fire to warm it. Once warmed, place pieces of resin on the stone.
- When the resin starts to melt, scrape it into a heap. Add some beeswax if you have it. This will help keep the pitch pliable when cooled. The more beeswax, the more pliable it will be.
- Scrape any impurities to the side.
- Add some powdered charcoal to the resin and mix in.

You can use this immediately to bond things such as arrow heads to arrows, or you can let it cool and store for later. Simply re-heat when you want to use it.

9.9.2 BIRCH TAR

This method shows how to extract tar from the bark of a birch tree. It can be used as a wood preservative, adhesive and many other uses. The same method can be used to extract tar from other types of bark or wood.

You need tin with a lid. An old biscuit tin is ideal. Drill a hole in the bottom of this tin, about 1 cm (1/2 in) diameter. You will also need a smaller tin for collection, ie, a baked beans tin.

Collect your birch bark and start rolling it up into the large tin. You will need to cut it into strips that are as wide as the tin is high.

Stand it vertically as shown to ease drainage and pack in as much as is practical.

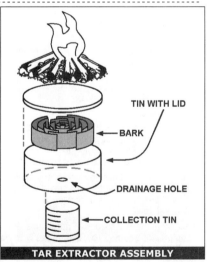

TIN WITH LID
BARK
DRAINAGE HOLE
COLLECTION TIN

TAR EXTRACTOR ASSEMBLY

BARK PACKED IN TIN

TIN CONTAINING BARK
COLLECTION TIN

TIN ASSEMBLY IN GROUND

Dig a hole deep enough for the collection tin and the top tin. Place the small collection tin in the hole and pack some dirt around it (pack it a few cm below the rim to prevent dirt spilling in when you remove it). Place the larger tin over this so the drainage hole is aligned to the centre of the collection tin.

Make sure the tins are flush together and pack dirt around the assembly so it doesn't move. Now light a fire on top of the tin. When heated, the bark inside will produce a thick vapour that has nowhere to go except down through the hole, when it will distil in the can beneath.

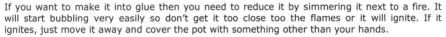

It takes a few hours for all the tar to be properly extracted, so keep the fire going for this time.

After a few hours when the fire has burnt out, carefully remove the top tin. Try not to get dirt in the collection tin. Make sure that the fire is completely out as the fumes are extremely flammable.

TAR-STICK

The tar will be very runny and can be used as a wood preservative in this state.

If you want to make it into glue then you need to reduce it by simmering it next to a fire. It will start bubbling very easily so don't get it too close too the flames or it will ignite. If it ignites, just move it away and cover the pot with something other than your hands.

Periodically dip a stick into the tar and let it cool to see how tacky it is. It may take a few hours before it starts to set on the end of the stick. When it does start to set, take the can away and let it cool for a while to see if it is hard enough.

While the tar is still warm and gooey, mould it on the end of a stick. When you need to use the tar-stick to glue something, hold the tar over a flame for a second or two to make it sticky again, and then apply. It sets very fast so you need to be quick.

9.9.3 GLUE FROM ANIMAL FAT

Make glue by placing hide scrapings and hooves into a pot with only enough water to cover them. Simmer for a few hours until thick and gluggy. Cover and/or add liquid as it boils away to prevent the mixture from burning. Stir occasionally. To create a finer consistency, skim off the scum that bubbles to the surface.

9.9.4 ICE GLUE

If it is below freezing and you need a temporary glue, to fix barbs to a spear for example, glue can be made from a mixture of ice and sawdust.

Mix up a paste of liquid water and sawdust and glob it around the objects to be joined. Once this mixture freezes, the glue is remarkably strong. It is easy to rework if necessary simply by wetting it, or applying fresh animal dung or anything else with moisture in it.

This glue is obviously useless if the ambient temperature rises above freezing point.

9.10 BASKET WEAVING

Baskets can be made from many materials, including but not limited to grasses, rushes, reeds, cane. Any fibrous material that is strong and does not snap when folded over (after it has been soaked for at least a day) should be suitable. Experiment if in doubt and it won't take long to find an acceptable weaving material.

When gathering the material, go for the longest pieces and try to match the thickness. Gather thicker pieces for the main stakes. You will need 16 main stakes per basket.

Any material that is shrinks when it dries will need to

WILLOWS FOR WEAVING

be dried before constructing your basket otherwise your basket will become loose and misshapen when it dries. Weaving material collected in winter may have less sap and leaves.

Once you have your material collected and dried, you will need to soak them in water to make them more flexible. Some material may take days.

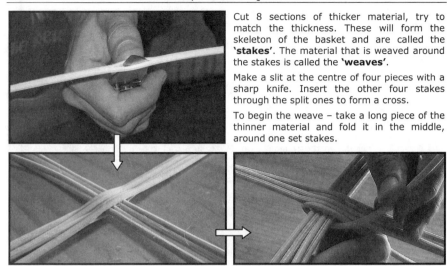

Cut 8 sections of thicker material, try to match the thickness. These will form the skeleton of the basket and are called the **'stakes'**. The material that is weaved around the stakes is called the **'weaves'**.

Make a slit at the centre of four pieces with a sharp knife. Insert the other four stakes through the split ones to form a cross.

To begin the weave – take a long piece of the thinner material and fold it in the middle, around one set stakes.

The following weaving technique is called 'twining'. To 'twine' around the base, simply twist the weavers around the stakes, swapping the top weaver with the bottom. The weavers should be twisted in the same direction every time.

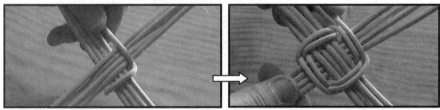

Weave around the stakes twice then open each stake out and weave around them individually to form an even spoke structure. Be sure to make the wraps tight to create a sturdy basket.

Remember to always twist the weavers in the same direction. This creates more grip on the stakes and therefore a stronger basket.

When you get to the end of a weaver, it's time to insert a new one. The new weaver is laid by the side of the old. The old ends will stick out and can be trimmed after a couple of new rows.

Adding a new weaver

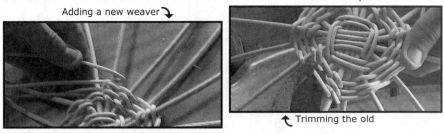

Trimming the old

Keep adding new weavers and building until the base is big enough. The stakes probably won't be long enough to complete the basket at this point, so push in new stakes alongside the old ones. Sharpen the end to make it easy to push through and give a neater overall finish.

Bend the new stakes upward and tie together to keep them in position. You can bend the short stakes up and weave into the basket, or simply cut them off.

TWINING THE SIDES

To begin twining the sides of the basket, insert two weavers into the base alongside the stakes as before.

Now bend these weavers to the right and begin weaving around the side uprights in the same manner as the base.

Add new weavers in the same manner as the base. Be sure to periodically compress the sides as you weave. This will add strength. ↘

↖ To finish the basket and add a proper rim, bend each stake to the right, and then weave it behind the next stake. Continue around the basket until all stakes are tucked in.

Now weave each end back under the next weaver on the right, skipping one. Continue around the rim. ↘

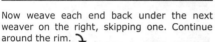

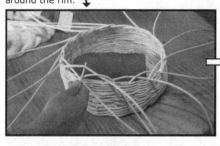

You can now trim the remaining ends of the weavers. If you don't need any handles, then your basket is complete! ↗

HANDLES

Handles are easy to add. The method is the same whether you are making two handles or a large one across the middle —

- Insert a weaver vertically into the basket through the rim. Make a sharp bend in the centre. Arc this weaver over to form the shape of the handle and thread it through the side of the basket, below a few weavers.

- Take the end and wrap it around and around the arc. When you get to the end, simply insert the end of the weaver next to the start.

- Repeat this process but start on the opposite side of the arc. Try to lay all four weavers in the same twist. That is one handle made, repeat if needed.

9.11 NETTING

Netting is an ancient handicraft of unknown origin. Making a net is simple once the basics are grasped. Netting can be very fine, or very coarse, depending on the needle, gauge and thread.

Experienced net makers don't need to use a gauge. A netting needle and gauge can be purchased, whittled from thin wood or shaped from plastic.

Tools Used

Nets can be made with no tools at all, but it will be made easier if you use a shuttle (netting needle) and gauge. Two types of shuttle are shown as well as a gauge.

The gauge is simply a tool that is made to be the intended size of the loops. A stick or a thumb will do.

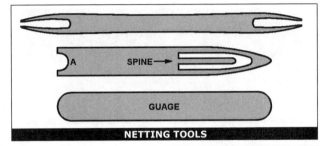

NETTING TOOLS

The foundation cord is usually made of thicker material. Tie the ends of this cord together to make a loop, and anchor the loop to a solid object.

Threading the Needle

If using a shuttle of the second type, fasten the thread to the spine and wind down over end A, and up over spine on the other side. Alternate from side to side, rotating the needle. Fill the needle leaving about 5 mm (1/4 in) at the tip of the spine free.

9.11.1 HOW TO NET

On the end thread coming from the needle, make a loop twice the width of the gauge tying it around the anchor loop. Place this knot in the middle of the left side and hold the gauge in the left hand as shown.

With the needle in the right hand, pass it through the loop from right to left, using the gauge to measure the space of the mesh.

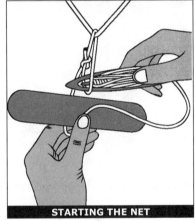

STARTING THE NET

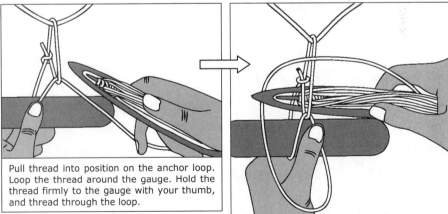

Pull thread into position on the anchor loop. Loop the thread around the gauge. Hold the thread firmly to the gauge with your thumb, and thread through the loop.

Loop twine down at right of first loop and hold with your thumb. Pass the needle under the first two strands, and over the third and fourth strands under gauge.

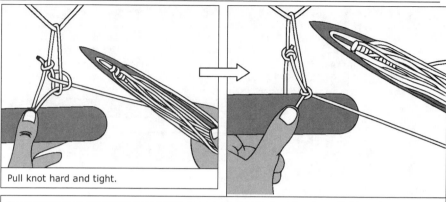

Pull knot hard and tight.

Do not remove your thumb from below the knot until the knot has been tightened.

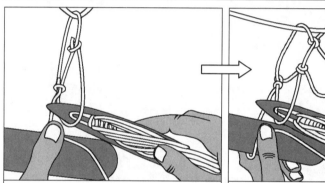

Remove the gauge and place the new knot on the left and repeat until the desired number of meshes have been made. The length depends on what is being made.

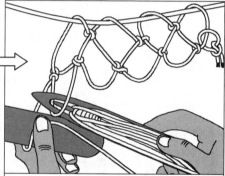

Now thread a heavy cord through the first row of meshes. This is the new anchor loop. Shorten the first anchor loop and leave tied on to locate the starting mesh.

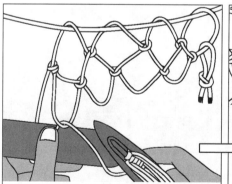

Now work across instead of down. Starting a knot at the first mesh, continue working across to the right until the row is complete.

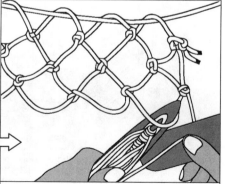

When the row is complete, change the needle to the left hand, and gauge to the right. Work this row right to left.

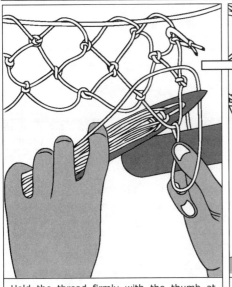

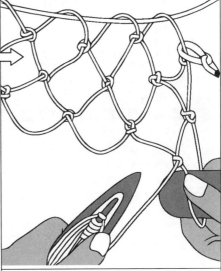

Hold the thread firmly with the thumb at bottom of the loop.

Continue working left to right across the row. Repeat alternate left and right rows until the net has reached the desired length.

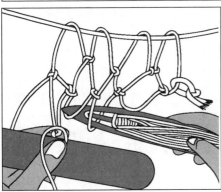

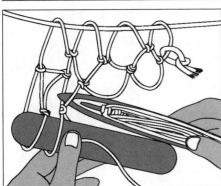

9.11.2 CHANGING MESH SIZE

If you want to make nets that get smaller or bigger, such as a cone shape or rounded, the mesh can be increased or decreased a row at a time.

Reducing the Mesh

To reduce the mesh at the end of a row, do not net the last mesh.

To reduce the mesh in the middle of a row, net 2 meshes at one time by sliding the needle through two loops instead of 1 and complete the knot.

Increasing the Mesh

To increase a mesh, make two knots in the same loop.

To Make a Triangle

Cast on required number of stitches, Decrease down to one stitch by joining the last two loops of every row with one knot.

9.11.3 NOTES

If you use a stranded rope for an anchor, you can use a long splice to close it into a loop.

You can use a double rope for the anchor, to make two loops. The opening of the net can then be closed by pulling each loop in opposite directions.

9.12 BLACK POWDER

Black powder is a mixture of saltpetre, charcoal and sulphur.

A mixture of only saltpetre and charcoal will still explode, however saltpetre and sulphur without charcoal doesn't burn at all. A recipe without sulphur yields a little less energy (Joules/g) but will also produce less smoke.

The addition of sulphur will also reduce the ignition point by around 100°C.

9.12.1 BASIC RECIPES

	parts saltpetre	parts coal	parts sulphur
• A good standard black powder	100 - (74.6%)	18 - (13.4%)	16 - (11.9%)
• A powder without sulphur	100 - (80.6%)	24 - (19.4%)	
Some Historical Recipes —			
• Marcus Graecus (ca. 1250)	100 - (69.0%)	33 - (22.8%)	12 - (8.28%)
• Canton of Zurich (1775)	100 - (75.0%)	16.7 - (12.5%)	16.0 - (12.5%)
• Swiss Army (1849)	100 - (75.0%)	17.3 - (13.0%)	16.0 - (12.0%)
• Modern Swiss black powder	100 - (75.0%)	20.0 - (15.0%)	13.3 - (10.0%)

9.12.2 CHARCOAL

To create good powder it is important to start with good charcoal. For this you need a tin can.

Drill a small hole in the top about 1 to 2 mm diameter. This needs to be large enough to allow gas to escape but small enough to prevent the entrance of air.

Build a decent fire and let it die to embers. Fill the can with pieces of wood 2 to 3 cm diameter.

The wood should be very dry and stripped of bark. Use young branches, not old wood or pieces from large split logs. Willow is the wood of choice, followed by grapevine, hazelwood, elder, laurel, and pine cones.

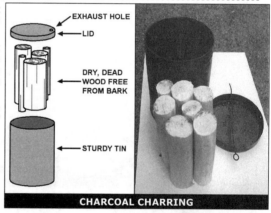

EXHAUST HOLE
LID
DRY, DEAD WOOD FREE FROM BARK
STURDY TIN

CHARCOAL CHARRING

WOOD GAS IGNITED

Partially bury the tin in embers and wait for wood gas to start being produced and escaping through the vent hole. Set this gas on fire – the flame is your indicator.

Note, if you light it too early the can may explode, so wear eye protection.

Frequently turn the can around.

When the flame is extinguished, remove the tin from the fire and cover the exhaust hole (eg with aluminium foil).

Wait until the can is cool before opening. If you open it hot and let oxygen in, the wood can spontaneously ignite.

The resulting charcoal is a lot smaller than the original wood. To store, you can grind coarsely and store in an airtight container.

CHARCOAL FINISHED

9.12.3 SALTPETRE

Saltpetre (potassium nitrate, KNO3) is the critical oxidising component of black powder.

Traditionally it was produced from mounds of soil, manure, urine and nitrogen-rich materials. The soil from cow barns and dung heaps were also often harvested. This soil is leeched and filtered through wood ashes to produce saltpetre.

Saltpetre can also be harvested directly from deposits that crystallise on stone or cave walls, or accumulations of bat guano in caves.

This image shows some saltpetre formed on a cellar wall of an old mill. Outside the house there was once a dung pit of a former horse stable.

SALTPETRE BRUSH

That sample was analysed and contained over 95% potassium nitrate – pure enough to grind and use without purification. It is advisable to filter however, as sand would abrade a barrel.

Ammonia from the decomposition of urea and other nitrogen-rich materials produces nitrates. These nitrates are converted to potassium nitrate by filtering through potassium carbonate (found in wood ashes).

Filter

Whether saltpetre crystals are harvested or grown, they should be filtered and purified. Wood ashes contain potassium carbonate, and will remove calcium and magnesium salts.

This filter can be used to filter saltpetre soil, or saltpetre-laden water. This is described later.

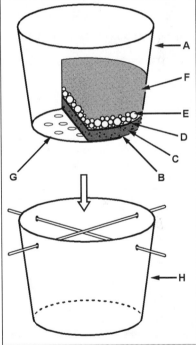

1	Take two buckets and drill or punch drainage holes (G) in the bottom of bucket (A).
	If you punch the holes – punch them from the inside so the burrs are on the outside.
2	Place a layer of fine cloth (B) over the holes. Make sure the cloth fully covers the bottom.
3	Place a layer of wood ashes (C) on top of the cloth. It should be 6 to 12 mm thick (1/4 to 1/2 in).
	Make sure there are no pieces of charcoal in the ash – this will remove the saltpetre.
	Make sure this layer is fairly thick and evenly packed. There should be no places where liquid can seep through unfiltered.
4	Place another layer of cloth (D)
5	Place a layer of pebbles or loose rocks (E) to hold the cloth/wood-ash sandwich in place.
	You can fill sand in the gaps in between these rocks to provide further filtration.
6	Finally, the saltpetre-rich soil or liquid (F) goes in the bucket. Fill to about 3/4.
7	Filter bucket (A) is then placed over the collection bucket (H). Use crossbeams or some other method of holding the bucket off the bottom.

A	Top Bucket
B	Piece of Fine Cloth
C	Layer of Wood Ashes
D	Piece of Fine Cloth
E	Pebbles and Sand Layer
F	Saltpetre soil
G	Drainage Holes
H	Collection Bucket

SALTPETRE FILTER

Large Scale Production – Heap Method

1	Gather a large amount of cow manure, planting soil, or both. Mix in some green plant life, dirt (anything but sand) and some burnt ashes. The ashes can come from burnt thistles, worm wood, tree bark, pinecones or just normal wood ashes. Make sure there are no pieces of charcoal as they will absorb the potassium nitrate.
	Traditionally the piles were around 1.5 metres high, 2 metres wide and about 5 metres or more long (5 x 7 x 15 feet). Set the pile on something waterproof if possible so the saltpetre doesn't seep into the ground, ply wood or clay is suitable.
	If possible, provide a roof for the heap to keep it out of the weather. Use a tarp tied to the side of a shed or see **Shelters** (Page 8-1) for hints on how to improvise something.
2	Pore lant (stale urine) over the pile at least once a week for 3 to 4 months or until thin light-yellowish crystals collect on the surface. Stop pouring the lant at this point and wait until a decent layer of saltpetre developing on the surface. This may get up to 10 cm (4 in) thick.
	It takes some experience to know what to look for. Saltpetre collects in light yellowish crystals. Production will take longer in dry climates.
3	Scrape off the top layer of saltpetre soil and filter it. When you see more crystals scrape off that layer. Continue until the pile needs replacing.
4	When you need a new saltpetre pile, use the soil from the old pile to get it started.

Filtration Method for Saltpetre Soil
To filter saltpetre soil, place the soil in the bucket above the layer of pebbles/sand. Fill the bucket up to about 3/4. Very slowly pour boiling water into the soil and wait for it to start leaching through. This will take some time.

Make sure the water passes through all of the soil so there are no dry spots. Keep pouring boiling water into the soil as it leeches through, but don't put more through than the bottom container will hold.

Let this water cool and settle for an hour or so. There will be a layer of sludge at the bottom as the sediment settles. Carefully drain off the top liquid and discard the sludge.

Boil this liquid to reduce it to saltpetre brine. Leave this brine to dry in the air. The crystals that remain when the water has evaporated is your potassium nitrate.

Small Scale Production – Straw Method

1	Fill a large container with hay and green plant matter. Pack the vegetation reasonably well. Then saturate with lant (stale urine). The container should be somewhat water proof. Leave it open, but protected from the sun and rain.
2	Continue pouring lant at least once a week for 3 to 4 months or until a thin layer of light-yellowish crystals appears. This takes longer in dry climates.
3	Stop pouring lant at this point and let the hay dry out and the crystals develop.
4	When it looks like no more crystals will develop, wash the crystals from the vegetation thoroughly in a container of warm water. Discard the vegetation, but keep the water.
5	Bring this water to the boil and filter through wood-ashes in the filter described.
6	Let this water dry out in the open air. The crystals that remain when the water has evaporated is your potassium nitrate.

Further Notes
- In the 1400's Swedish saltpetre boilers placed solid copper rods into the saltpetre brine as it was left to evaporate. The saltpetre crystals were scraped off the rods as they developed, and then the rods were placed back in the brine to collect more crystals.
- When you burn saltpetre, it will burn with a purple flame due to the presence of potassium.
- The same filtration techniques can be used to extract saltpetre from high-nitrate fertilizer.
- Adding lime to a heap will help control the pH to an optimum value of 7.2 to 7.8.
- Boiling water will dissolve 2 1/2 times its weight in potassium nitrate.

9.12.4 SULPHUR

Sulphur (S) is a chemical element with the following properties:

- Melting Point ....114°C
- Inflammation Point...............260°C
- Boiling Point ....444°C
- Specific Weight....................2.06g/ml

Sulphur is obtained by first mining it, then melting in the absence of air, and further purified by distillation. Sulphur in modern times comes from the petroleum industry. The extraction of sulphur from other sources is not trivial chemistry and will not be discussed here.

Either stock up on it, or make black powder without. The primary reason for sulphur is to reduce the ignition temperature (by around 100°C). Sulphur-less powder will produce less smoke, but flintlock and matchlock rifles will suffer misfires.

9.12.5 MIXING BLACK POWDER

Once you have your ingredients it's time to grind and mix them. A good tool to use is a mortar and pestle. In a pinch you could use a flat rock and a stout stick with a flattened end. If you have a mortar and pestle that is too smooth, make it rougher by grinding up something abrasive, like crude quartz sand.

Avoid using two rocks against each other to grind the ingredients as this may cause a spark.

1	Grind the ingredients separately, and grind in small amounts only. Grinding in smaller amounts is quicker than large amounts. The ingredients won't ignite, but don't smoke and make sure the tools you use to grind are non-sparking (ie, don't use metal on stone)
2	After grinding your ingredients mix them together to the recipe of your choice.
3	Grind this mixture well for about 10 minutes. Then add about 8% water in small amounts, rubbing and beating, until it is the texture of pottery clay. Pound and rub it for about 15 to 20 minutes more, then roll it into a ball. It should be about golf-ball sized.
	Note: You can mix the ingredients dry, but this will result in a slower burning powder. By adding water, the ingredients are homogenised causing a better burning.

Corning

To corn the black powder, take the dough that you formed into a ball and rub it through a sieve. An ordinary kitchen sieve with a mesh of about 1.5 mm will do. Spread the sifted flakes evenly on a piece of paper and let them dry.

Once the flakes have dried sift them again through the same sieve, using fingers to help. Separate the fine dust by sifting the powder through a fine sieve, such as a flour sifter. Add the discarded dust to the next batch of black powder so nothing is wasted.

Density of Homemade Black Powder

When you use this homemade black powder, you will need to use twice as much as a commercial powder.

This is not because the quality is lacking – it will be as good as or better than commercial powders – it is because it is only about half as dense.

Commercial powders are milled for much longer and under much higher pressure than possible with a mortar and pestle. Commercial powder is ground for hours using edge-mills with granite wheels that weigh several tons.

Because of this, you will encounter more fouling using home made powder and your weapons will require more frequent cleaning. Fouling is reduced by grinding the charcoal extremely fine.

GRINDING WET POWDER

FINAL PRODUCT ON 5mm GRID

9.13 CLEANING PRODUCTS

A sustained existence is aided greatly by keeping yourself and your environment clean.

9.13.1 MAKING LYE

Lye is a key ingredient in soap making and is also a useful product in itself, as it is caustic. It is made from fire ashes. To make stronger lye, use ashes from hardwoods if possible, such as oak, walnut or fruit wood. Softwoods like pine, fir and evergreens will yield a weaker solution.

1	You will need a barrel or other container with a small hole at the base. Place a non-metallic container under the hole to collect the lye.
2	Place clean rocks in the bottom of the container, then a generous layer of straw, hay or grass. Then add your ashes. You can let it accumulate over time until you have enough. The setup described for saltpetre filtration (Page 9-19) is also suitable.
3	Add water to the container (soft water, such as rainwater, is best) until water begins to run from the drainage hole – this may take a while.
4	When the water starts to drain, plug the hole with a cork or correctly shaped piece of wood and let the mixture soak for a few days. You can add more ashes and water when the first layer settles.
5	After 3 days, remove the plug and collect the trickle of lye in a non-metallic container.

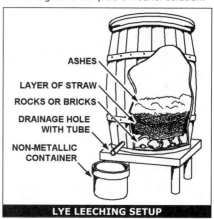

ASHES
LAYER OF STRAW
ROCKS OR BRICKS
DRAINAGE HOLE
WITH TUBE
NON-METALLIC
CONTAINER

LYE LEECHING SETUP

Lye Concentration

To test the density of the lye mixture, float an egg or potato in the liquid. A small portion should remain above water.

If it sinks, the lye is not strong enough for soap-making. To make it stronger you can leech it through more ashes, or boil it down.

Using Lye

You can use diluted lye as a cleaning fluid for washing animal housing and other problem areas. Dilute lye in warm water at about a 50:1 ratio for general cleaning.

9.13.2 FATS FOR SOAP

For quality soap with a clean odour, the grease must be clean. The best source is therefore from butchering, rather than from drippings. The grease should be pure and fresh (or frozen).

Mutton or goat fat is the hardest of all animal fats, followed by beef, and will make hard soap unless made with extra water or mixed in with softer fats, such as pig fat (lard), chicken fat, goose grease or vegetable fat. Pig fat makes a good soap. Poultry and vegetable fat is too soft alone and must be mixed with harder fats. Soap made from soft fats will require less water and take longer to dry. Adding coconut oil will make a very soft soap suitable for shaving.

Storing and Rendering Fats

Store your fat in a cool dry place, and use it as soon as you have enough. Un-refrigerated fat will keep for several weeks if kept cool and dry. Keep away from strong sources of odour.

Render surplus fat from butchering or trimming meat. Cut the fat into small pieces and place into a large pot with some water. Use about 1 litre (1 quart) of water for every 5 kg (10 lb) of fat. Place on a moderate heat and stir occasionally. When the fat is liquefied and the solids are brown and settling, carefully strain the fat. You may want to do this more than once.

Your soap will be as white as your fat is. If your fat is not pure enough, you may end up with smelly yellow soap. Let the fat cool and solidify, then scrape out and store with your other accumulated fat until you are ready to make soap with it.

9.13.3 MAKING SOAP

You need pure water free of chemicals that can combine with the lye. You should use 'soft water' rather than 'hard water'. Hard water means it has minerals dissolved in it. Rainwater and distilled water is soft, but almost all water from springs, wells and rivers is hard.

Saponification is a chemical process where fat and lye are brought together to form an alkali salt of fatty acids and glycerine – aka soap. This process can take several weeks to complete. Soon after it is made, soap may contain some free lye, but this will reduce with aging.

Lye	Fat	Water
0.25	2	0.75
0.5	4	1.5
0.75	6	2.25
1	8	3
SOAP MAKING PROPORTIONS		

Cold Process

The correct proportions (by volume) of basic ingredients to make soap are as follows:

For the best soap, use the correct temperatures and measures. Too much fat will make for an ineffective emulsifier, too much lye creates a harsh soap. The saponification needs to be complete as free fat can become rancid brown spots, and free lye can burn the skin.

Don't use steel, aluminium or cast iron containers to mix the ingredients. Use an earthenware, unchipped enamelled or 'ceramic on steel' container. Steel or aluminium under the enamel is OK. Mix outdoors as the mixing process produces heat and fumes that you can't see.

Stir evenly and in one direction only. Rapid addition of the ingredients will cause separation.

1	Place the cold water in your container. Slowly add your lye to the container and stir slowly and evenly until all crystals are dissolved. Use only a wooden spoon or stick to stir and be careful not to splash any on your skin.

Fat	Temp (°C)	Temp (°F)
Vege. oil	43-46	110-115
Bear	46	115
Goose	46	115
Pork	49	120
Beef	55	130
Deer	55	130
Sheep	55	130
FAT HEATING TEMPERATURES		

2	Let the solution cool as it will have heated during mixing. Cool to 21-24°C (70-75°F) for lard (pig fat) or 32-35°C (90-95°F) for all tallow soap.

3	While the water-lye solution is cooling, heat your fat in a separate container. Refer to the table above for the correct temperature depending for the type of fat you are using.
4	Pour the fat slowly into the lye-water when both are at the right temperature.
5	Stir evenly in one direction until you have soap. This usually takes about 15 minutes but can be anywhere from 5 minutes to an hour. If the ingredients are at the right temperature you should have no problem.
	If the mixture does not seem to be setting, you can try to put the mixing container in another container of cold water. If the soap starts setting on the edges, stir faster or even beat it. Soap starts out a dark colour and gets lighter as you beat it.
6	When all the lye and fat mix together, saponification happens. It starts with cloudiness in the mixture. When the consistency is like thick pea soup, it's time to pour.
	At this point drops from the mixing spoon will stand on the surface, and the spoon should be able to stand on it's own in the mixture. If you pour too soon, the soap may separate into two layers – a hard bottom layer and a top greasy layer.
7	Pour the mixture into molds or any suitable non-metallic container. Keep setting soap away from heat. it can take anyway from a few hours to several days for the soap to harden enough to be removed. Soaps with higher amounts of soft fats will take longer.
8	Let the soap dry at room temperature for about 2 weeks, but keep it from freezing because that will upset to curing process and makes a too soft soap. After 2 weeks the temperature is not as important, but you should still age it for a few months to remove as much free lye as possible.

9.13.4 VINEGAR

Vinegar is an extremely useful product in a primitive situation. Used as a general cleaner it will kill bacteria, it should be used in washing clothes for the same reason – at least occasionally. To disinfect surfaces and kitchen tools, use full strength vinegar and leave to sit for 30 minutes before wiping clean. For general cleaning, use a 50:50 diluted solution.

Vinegar can be made from apples (cider vinegar), grapes (wine vinegar), berries, other fruits or even a 10 percent sugar solution. The strength of the finished product is directly proportional to the sugar in the original solution. For this reason sweet apples usually make stronger vinegar than tart ones, although this is not always true – some sour apples contain a high proportion of sugar that is masked by acid content.

To Make Cider or Wine – First Fermentation

1 Use only fresh uncooked grape or other fruit juice with no preservatives. Preservatives will prevent it from turning into vinegar.

2 Fill a large container 3/4 full with the juice. There needs to be some airspace for the fermentation process. The container will need an airlock. These can be purchased from winemaking stores, or made.

To make one, take a rubber stopper with a hole through the middle and some beverage hose – wash this hose thoroughly first, preferably boiling it. Push the hose through the hole.

Take the other end of the hose and place it in another container half filled with water. Find some way of holding this hose in place – you can simply tie a weight to it.

If you don't have a rubber stopper you can improvise one out of a piece of corn cob cut to fit – seal the top of the corn with wax if you have it. You can also use a normal soda bottle lid with a hole drilled through it if you seal it up well, say with plastic wrap and electrical tape, our you can simply place the hose in the top of the bottle and seal up the neck in a similar way.

3 As the juice ferments, the carbon dioxide bubbles up through the water but no oxygen can reach the juice. The first fermentation will take 4 to 6 weeks at room temperature. It is not necessary to add yeast because of the wild yeasts that are always present. If you feel like it, human saliva is a source of yeast – best not to tell anyone your secret.

The grey foam that forms on top is excess yeast which is harmless.

When the bubbling stops, the sugar has all changed to alcohol – you have made hard cider. To turn this into vinegar – assuming you haven't already drunk it all in celebration, you need a second fermentation which will turn the alcohol into acetic acid.

To Make Vinegar – Second Fermentation

1 Unlike the first fermentation, which occurs through the liquid, the second fermentation takes place only on the surface. Different organisms are involved and they require oxygen. A large surface area in relation to the volume will speed the fermentation.

At this point, adding mother of vinegar will speed up the fermentation process. Place some on a piece of dried corn cob and float it in the cider. This is not necessary but will reduce the time required for the fermentation to start.

To make mother of vinegar, expose a 50:50 mixture of vinegar and cider to a temperature of 26°C (80°F) for a few days. The thin scum that forms on the surface is mother of vinegar.

2 Tie cloth over the opening of the container to admit oxygen, but keep out dust and bugs.

3 The time of the second fermentation depends on the spores present. All strains work best at a temperature of 21-26°C (70-80°F). Too low and the spores become dormant, to high and they die. This will take anywhere from 3 to 9 months.

10 Sustainable Gardening

A food producing garden will greatly enhance the wellbeing of a single survivor, or a group. Not only will it reduce the energy expended to hunt and forage for wild foods, a diverse garden will add to your overall health.

If you can't start a garden before disaster because of your current location, you may be able to start one later – either from seeds that you carry or propagated from wild plants in the area.

10.1 PLANNING A GARDEN

Before jamming all your seed in the ground, plan your garden and prepare the soil properly. A little forethought and preparation will go a long way towards a successful harvest.

10.1.1 CLIMATE CHANGE

First of all, do not presume the seasons in your area will remain unchanged. Many disaster scenarios such as asteroid strike, pole shift or global warming or cooling will bring drastic changes in the climate. Therefore it is suggested that you test before planting large crops.

For any given plant, sow a few seeds to determine the viability. If seed refuses to germinate, does not grow well or produces no seed, save your seeds and try again later. Stock a variety of seeds, even if they do not grow well or at all in your area now. Experiment cautiously – you may be surprised.

10.1.2 SECURITY

Your garden needs to be secure from intruders, of the four and two-legged variety. As always, choose a location that is out of view. A simple fence if made strong will keep most animals out of your plot, but may still attract wildlife.

If you are attracting unwanted wildlife and fear damage to your fence, a possible solution is a 'honey-pot'. Use the produce they are targeting as bait and position outside the fence – an easy target. Then set a suitable trap or snare. Consider this for two-legged intruders as well.

If you are being overrun by vermin or crawling insects, consider a small moat. If you are having a problem with flying insects, a smoky fire will keep these at bay, but may also give away your location. Birds are more difficult to keep out and will require netting, or a few cats. Perhaps a better solution is to provide something tastier, away from your crop.

10.1.3 SEEDS

The seeds you need to be stocking should be the heirloom variety. Commercial seeds are usually hybrids. Seed produced from hybrids may not come true. On seed packets, the 'F1' or 'F2' designator will indicate hybrid seeds. These seeds will not produce seed-producing plants, or plants at all, and you will not be able to produce any more food until you acquire more seeds.

10.1.4 PREPARING THE LOCATION

Vegetables grow best in an open, level area where the soil is loose, rich and well drained. If the soil is poor, mix in 10 cm of topsoil, peat moss, manure, seaweed, compost or leaf litter. Mix in some fertilizer to get you started if you have some. The more organic matter or topsoil you add, the better the soil will be. See **Composting** (Page 10-11).

Generally, avoid heavy clays, sandy soils and shaded areas. Most vegetables require at least 6 hours of direct sunlight a day. Chickens can help work weedy tough ground into suitable soil.

10.1.5 GARDEN LAYOUT

Keep the early vegetables such as lettuce, radishes and onions together. Tall-growing crops like sweet corn and tomatoes should be place further from the equator to prevent shading the smaller plants. (North in the Northern hemisphere, South in the Southern).

Plants that are self pollinated (like corn) should be planted in blocks of several short rows, rather than one long row. To stretch out the growing season, plant the same vegetables at intervals, rather than one large single planting.

10.1.6 PLANTING A GARDEN

When the first warm days of spring appear, allow for the sunshine and warmth to dry out the soil before trying to work it. You should be able to crumble a ball of dirt with your fingers. If it clings together it is still too wet and new roots will have a hard time pushing through the soil.

Prepare the soil at least 15 cm (6 in) deep, making sure all sod is turned over. Do this with a spade or plow. Shatter and slice each shovelful to break up the soil. Remove all weeds as you go to prevent them from competing with the vegetables. Finish by levelling smooth.

Planting the Seeds

Make a furrow for the seed using a stick for fine seeds, or hoe blade for larger seeds. Small seeds should be barely covered and large seeds should have no more than 2.5 cm (1 in) of soil. If the seeds are planted too deep they may not come up.

10.2 VEGETABLE GROWING GUIDE

This is a general guide only. Sowing times will vary greatly between different regions and climates. It also does not take into account the effects of climate change.

When direct planting with small seeds (eg carrots), bulk them out first by mixing with sand. You can help them pre-germinate by keeping them in moist sand for 2-4 days. When planting large seeds (eg peas, corn), soak them overnight. A weak seaweed solution or diluted worm water is good for this.

Try not to water directly on the leaves of plants susceptible to fungal diseases (tomatoes, cucumbers, pumpkins, zucchinis etc). If using overhead sprinklers, water in the early morning so water can evaporate during the day.

Summer Crops

In summer you should mulch your garden beds to keep the soil cool and moist. A 5 cm (2 in) layer of mulch will reduce the evaporation by over 70%. Don't lay down thick layers of material such as lawn clippings or sawdust that will pack down and form a barrier to water.

In days of extreme heat it may be necessary to physically protect the plants with some shade.

Winter Crops

Winter is usually the time to plant or prune soft fruits including strawberries, berries, currants etc. If your winter is mild you might start a number of crops in late winter rather than early spring. Such crops include artichokes, beetroot, cabbage, carrots, potatoes and radish.

Frost

If frost is an issue in your region, frost-sensitive vegetables such as capsicum, eggplant and tomatoes may need a glasshouse or warm spot to germinate and will usually need protection when planted out.

An alternative to a glasshouse can be improvised with a glass jar or clear plastic bottle with the top cut off and placed over the seedlings.

10.2.1 GENERAL PLANTING AND ROTATION GUIDE

Below is a simple guide for planting times which also describes a 5 year crop rotation scheme. See **Crop Rotation** (Page 10-7) for more information on this practice.

Plant	Spring			Summer			Autumn			Winter		Rotate*
Asparagus	ST									S	ST	- - 3 - -
Beans	S	S	S	S	S							1 - - - -
Beetroot	S	S	S	S	S	S						- - - 4 -
Broad Beans							S	S	S			1 - - - -
Broccoli			S	ST	ST	T	T					- - - - 5
Brussels Sprouts		S	ST	ST	ST	T	T					- - - - 5
Cabbage	ST	ST	ST	ST	ST	T	T					- - - - 5
Capsicum	S	S	S									- - 3 - -

Plant	Spring			Summer			Autumn			Winter			Rotate*
Carrots	S	S	S	S	S	S							- - - 4 -
Cauliflower			S	ST	ST	T	T						- - - - 5
Celery	S	ST	ST	T	T	S							- - - 4 -
Chicory				S	S	S	ST	T					-any-
Chilli	S	S	ST	T									- - 3 - -
Chives	S	S	S	S	S	S	ST	T	T				- 2 - - -
Chinese Cabbage				S	S	ST	T						- - - - 5
Coriander	S	S	ST	ST	T								- - - 4 -
Corn		S	ST	ST	T								-any-
Cucumber	S	S	ST	ST	T								-any-
Dill	S	ST	T	T									- - - 4 -
Eggplant	S	T	T										-any-
Endive			S	S	S	S	ST	T					-any-
Fennel	S	ST	T										-any-
Garlic							S	S	S				- 2 - - -
Kohlrabi				ST	ST	ST	ST	T					- - - - 5
Leeks	S	S	ST	ST	ST	T	T					S	- 2 - - -
Lentils	S	S	ST	T									1 - - - -
Lettuce	ST	ST	ST	ST	ST	ST	ST	ST				S	-any-
Melons	S	S	S										-any-
Onions	ST	T					S	S		S	ST	ST	- 2 - - -
Parsley	S	S	S	ST	ST	T	T	T					- - - 4 -
Parsnips	S	S	S	S	S	S							- - - 4 -
Peas	S	S	S	S	S	S						S	1 - - - -
Potatoes	S	S	S	S	S								- - 3 - -
Pumpkins	S	S	S										-any-
Radish	S	S	S	S	S	S							- - - - 5
Shallots	T					S	S	S	ST	ST	T	T	- 2 - - -
Silver beet	S	S	ST	ST	ST	T						S	- - - 4 -
Spinach	S	S										S	- - - 4 -
Squash	S	S	ST	ST									-any-
Swede		S	ST	ST	T								- - - - 5
Tomatoes	S	ST	ST	T	T								- - 3 - -
Turnips	S	S	S	ST	ST	T	T	T					- - - - 5

S Sow

T Transplant

* The rotate column refers to the order in which crops should be planted in a plot. For example, plants marked with **1** should be placed in one bed, and then next year use the same soil for plants marked **2** and so on...

Plants designated **−any−** can be planted anywhere in the rotation.

VEGETABLE GROWING GUIDE

10.3 MEDICINE GROWING GUIDE

Plant/Height	Propagation	Germination °C	°F	Days	Sun	Growth Type
Aloe about 30 cm divide in spring	division				O	perennial
	Aloe plants are very sensitive to frost. They like full sun or light shade, and fast draining soil. Water minimally during winter.					
Basil sow late winter	seed, cuttings, transplant	20°	70°	5-10	O	annual
	Protect from heavy wind, frost and too much sun. It likes moist but well drained conditions. Sow thinly and cover with about 6 mm (1/4 in) soil.					
Chilli sow mid spring	seed, transplant	20°	70°	~	O	ann./per.
	Chillies like a warm environment and well drained soil. Chillies like full sun, but if the sun is too harsh in your climate then shade is beneficial.					
Comfrey plant in spring or early autumn	seed, division	20°	70°	3-5	O	perennial
	Comfrey rarely sets seed and is best propagated from root division. Each broken piece of root has potential to sprout. Choose a permanent place that is sunny or with partial shade and loose, deep soil. It will thrive from sun to partial sun to near full shade.					
Coriander sow mid spring	seed, division	15°	60°	14-21	O	annual
	Prefers full sun, but benefits from shade in summer. Rake seeds into soil about 12 mm (1/2 in) deep, and then thin to 10 cm (4 in). Sow after last spring frost, blooms in midsummer.					
Cumin sow spring	seed, transplant	18-20°	65-70°	7-14	O	annual
	Sow the seeds about 6-12 mm (1/4 to 1/2 in) deep. Plant close together in a block rather than a row so they support each other. Cumin likes full sun and well drained soil, but does not need particularly rich soil.					
Dandelion sow early spring 5 to 90 cm	seed, division	10-20°	50-70°		O	perennial
	Dandelions prefer full sun or partial shade, and fertile well drained soil. Plant seeds in rows about 20 cm (8 in) apart, covered lightly or not at all.					
Echinacea sow mid spring up to 140 cm	seed	18-20°	65-70°	10-20	O	perennial
	Echinacea likes a sunny location and well drained soil. Sow 6mm (1/4 in) deep and 5 cm (2 in) apart. Thin to 50 cm (18 in) when 3 cm (1 in) tall.					
Fennel sow mid spring 120 cm	seed, division	15-20°	60-70°	6	O	annual
	Sow 15 cm (6 in) spacing about 3 mm (1/8 in) deep, in spring after the frost has passed. Fennel needs moist, fertile, well drained soil. It propagates well by seed but can also be divided by root or crown.					
Garlic sow late autumn 20 to 60 cm	seed, division	10-35°	50-95°	10-14	O	perennial
	Plant the cloves, point upwards, deep enough to just cover with soil. Plant on the shortest day, harvest on the longest is the rule. If you leave it to go to seed you will get self-sown plants the following year.					
Ginger plant late winter/ early spring 60 cm to 1 m	division	25-30°	75-85°		●	perennial
	Ginger loves a sheltered spot with filtered sunlight, warm weather, humidity and rich, moist soil (but not soggy) – it is a tropical plant. Get fresh rhizomes with well developed buds and soak overnight in water. Plant the ginger root with the buds facing up about 5 cm (2 in) deep.					
Ginseng sow mid autumn 45 to 60 cm	seed					perennial
	Ginseng takes at least 7 to 10 years to mature, but will produce for decades to come. This is a difficult herb to cultivate and this small space cannot give it justice. Research independently, or stock it.					
Hibiscus sow autumn 2 to 3 m	seed, cuttings	20-27°	70-80°	7-20	O	perennial
	Hibiscus likes about 6-8 hours sunlight a day, hates frost and likes to be planted alone. Plant seeds 6mm (1/4 in) deep in moist but not soggy soil.					
Horseradish plant spring up to 150 cm	division	10-25°	50-75°		●	perennial
	Plant root pieces that are 6 mm (1/2 in) diameter and about 15 cm (6 in) long, in autumn or very early spring. Harvest mid autumn or as needed. After the frost in autumn kills the leaves, harvest the roots for division. Plant them vertically in holes about 60 cm (2 ft) apart, 5 cm (2 in) deep.					

Plant/Height	Propagation	Germination			Sun	Growth Type
		°C	°F	Days		
Lavender	seed, cuttings, transplant	20-25°	70-75°	14-60	◯	perennial
sow late spring to early summer 30 to 45 cm	Lavender does not tolerate shade. It likes dry, well drained soil. Plant seeds or transplant about 30 cm (1 ft) apart. The rate of germination is low, so it is best to raise seedlings first, and then transplant.					
Meadowsweet	seed, cuttings, transplant	10-13°	50-55°	14-21	◑	perennial
sow autumn to mid spring 180 cm	This plant naturally grows in boggy fields, near water and open woodland. Failing that, provide plenty of mulch and keep moist and fertile. It likes partial shade but will tolerate full sun if the ground is kept boggy.					
Mustard	seed	13-15°	55-60°	3	◑	ann./per.
sow early spring and early autumn 75-100 cm	Sow in rows about 6 mm (1/2 in) deep or scatter over a large area. Thin to 15 cm (6 in) spacing. Plant every 3 weeks throughout the year. Mustard likes sun, but benefits from shade in the summer.					
Onion	seed, transplant	8-30°	45-85°	14-21	◯	biennial
sow later summer or early winter 10 to 60 cm	Grow in seed trays and plant out after 4-6 weeks for best results. When transplanting, don't bury the bulb, only the roots. Transplant or thin seedlings to 15 cm (6 in) apart when about 7.5 cm (3 in) high.					
Oregano	seed, division, cuttings	18°	65°	15	◯	perennial
sow in spring 20 to 45 cm	Oregano grows well in poor soil. Don't cover seeds when sowing. Plant outdoors after the danger of frost has passed.					
Rhodiola Rosea	seed, division	5°	40°	10-40	◑	perennial
sow autumn to early spring 25 cm	Plant seeds in deep, moist and sandy soil, sheltered from sun and wind, when there is still cold weather. Condition seeds in cold weather (or the fridge) for a few weeks before sowing. Plant 12 to 25 mm (1/2 to 1 in) deep. It can take 3-5 years to mature for medicinal purposes.					
Rosemary	seed, division, cuttings	20°	70°	21	◯	perennial
sow mid spring 30 cm to 2 m	Sow seeds 3 mm (1/8 in) deep, and transplant 50 cm (2 ft) apart in the garden when 8 cm (3 in) tall. Rosemary is best propagated from cuttings if possible due to a low germination rate.					
Roses	seed, cuttings	20°	70°	~	◯	perennial
sow early spring or after the last frost up to 2m	Roses like fertile well drained soil. Plant the seeds in about 10 mm (1/2 in) of very light soil. Seeds do better if 'cold stratified' at around 4°C (40°F) for 4 months. Best started from cuttings about 15 cm (6 in) long, covered with a glass jar or plastic bottle. Water often but not too much.					
Sesame	seed, cuttings	27°	80°	7-14	◯	annual
sow in spring after the last frost up to 2m	Plant seeds about 10 cm (1/2 in) deep in slightly damp soil. Transplant seedlings about 1 m (3 ft) apart. Don't have too much nitrogen in the soil or you will not get much seed production.					
Spinach	seed, cuttings	10-25°	50-75°	7-14	◖◗	annual
sow early spring 30 cm	Sow at a depth about three times the diameter of the seed, at about 20 cm (8 in) apart. Best grown in cooler climates. Spinach tolerates full sun and shaded positions. Sow monthly in cool weather to stagger the supply.					
Thyme	seed, division, cuttings	15-18°	60-65°	12-28	◯	perennial
sow mid spring 40 to 45 cm	Thyme likes full sun and good drainage, such as a rock garden. Leaves can be picked any time of the year but is best when in full bloom. Sow seeds 2-3 weeks before last spring frost.					
Turmeric	division	18°+	-65°+		◯	perennial
plant early to mid spring 1 m	Turmeric does not produce seeds. Simply plant the root. A large root will have several 'fingers' that can be cut up. Bury under about 5 cm (2 in) of loose soil, with the buds turned up. Harvest after about 10 months.					
Yarrow	seed, division, cuttings	18-30°	65-85°	10-14	◯	perennial
sow late winter to early spring Up to 1 m	Yarrow will thrive in a hot sunny spot where few other plants will. It likes well drained soil, but do not overfeed or over-water. Soak the seeds overnight and plant about 3 mm (1/8 in) deep.					

◯ - Full sun – At least 6 hours direct sunlight a day – usually needs regular water
◑ - Partial sun – Between 3 to 6 hours sun a day – usually in the morning.
● - Full shade – Less than 3 hours direct sunlight, then with filtered sun. (not NO sun)

10.4 PROPAGATION FROM CUTTINGS

Plants propagated from cuttings are genetically identical to the original plant. If you discover a wild plant that is edible or otherwise useful, propagation in this way may be preferable to growing from seed. Note that not all plants can be propagated from cuttings, so experiment.

Cuttings should be taken from firm, current season growth. Hard, woody material and soft 'floppy' growth are likely to be unsuccessful. Bend the stem 60 – 90° and if it springs back to its original position it is suitable. Although there are exceptions to this rule and less than ideal specimens may take root.

10.4.1 PREPARING THE CUTTINGS

There are three general types of cutting that vary from the lower hardwood to the softwood tip. The most suitable cutting will depend on the plant being propagated so experimenting may be necessary. Generally, the tip will take root faster than the hardwood.

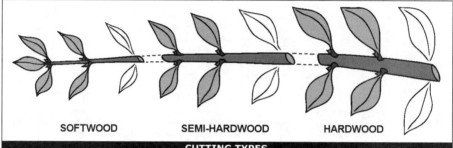

SOFTWOOD   SEMI-HARDWOOD   HARDWOOD

CUTTING TYPES

Collect cuttings in the early morning and ensure they are kept cool and moist. Wrap cuttings in moist paper or other material and keep shaded until planting. Cut at a length that leaves 3 to 4 nodes on the stem.

The diameter of a cutting should be from the size of a small finger to the size of a thumb.

Make the cut directly below a node and at an angle – this exposes more surface area for better absorption of nutrients and root formation. If you are not taking the tip, make a straight cut at the top to minimise water loss. Use a clean sharp blade or pruner to make the cut to ensure you don't crush the tissue. Strip to leave a maximum of two nodes with foliage (some plant cuttings can be stripped bare).

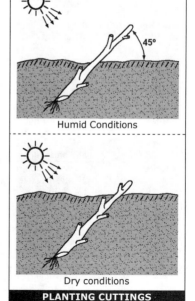

Humid Conditions

10.4.2 PLANTING THE CUTTINGS

Place the cutting at a 45° angle in the soil with at least one node facing the sunlight. In dry areas or seasons, cover all but one node with soil. Use a well drained medium, such as sand mixed with soil to aid in root growth.

The soil should be free from diseases and competing weeds. To sterilise soil it can be heated in a pot. Heat and stir it long enough to ensure the soil reaches at least 80°C (175°F). Do this before adding any nutrients such as compost, manure or worm water.

Cuttings should be kept moist until they start to take root. Misting with a spray bottle and keeping in part

Dry conditions

PLANTING CUTTINGS

shade will help this. Cuttings need to be watered at least twice daily. If propagation is successful, the cuttings will start to sprout in 3 to 4 weeks.

10.5 CROP ROTATION

Crop rotation is important for organic gardening and provides many benefits. Pests and diseases tend to attack specific plant families, so rotation breaks the life cycles and build-up is reduced. Some crops, such as potatoes and squashes, can suppress weeds and minimise problems for following crops.

By planting the same crop in the same soil every year, the soil becomes depleted of the particular nutrients the plant needs, while others go to waste. It can also allow the build up of pests and diseases to unmanageable levels.

Different crops have different soil requirements and benefits. Rotating each year allows the soil to replenish and minimises deficiencies. Alternating between deep-rooted and fibrous-rooted crops improves soil structure.

Family	Examples	Soil Requirements	Soil Benefits
Brassicas	broccoli, brussel sprouts, cabbage, cauliflower, kohlrabi, mustard seed, oilseed rape, radish, swede, turnips	Leafy crops need nitrogen-rich soil	
Legumes	beans, lentils, lupins, peanuts, peas	Well-drained but moisture-retentive. Not nitrogen rich	Fix atmospheric nitrogen in roots for future crops
Alliaceae (Onions)	chives, garlic, leek, onion, shallots	High organic matter	
Solanaceae (Potato family)	capsicum, chilli eggplant, paprika, potato tobacco, tomato	High organic matter and nitrogen	Suppresses weeds, breaks up soil structure
Umbellifers	beets, caraway, carrot, celery, coriander, cumin, dill, fennel, parsley, parsnip	Root crops need stone-free soil. Not freshly manured	Root crops break up soil structure

PLANT TYPES AND BENEFITS

Some plants have so few soil-dwelling pests or disease that they can be fitted in anywhere in the rotation, such as chicory, courgettes, cucumbers, eggplant, endive, fennel, french beans, lettuces, marrows, peppers, pumpkins, radish, runner beans, squashes and sweet corn.

10.5.1 ROTATION SCHEMES

There are many types of rotation schemes in use. Rotation should be on at least a four year cycle and thus is one of the most popular methods. Below is a 5 year rotation which is mirrored in **General Planting and Rotation Guide** (Page 10-2).

	Bed 1	Bed 2	Bed 3	Bed 4	Bed 5
Year 1	Legumes	Onions	Potato Family	Umbellifers	Brassicas
Year 2	Onions	Potato Family	Umbellifers	Brassicas	Legumes
Year 3	Potato Family	Umbellifers	Brassicas	Legumes	Onions
Year 4	Umbellifers	Brassicas	Legumes	Onions	Potato Family
Year 5	Brassicas	Legumes	Onions	Potato Family	Umbellifers

5 YEAR ROTATION SCHEME

10.5.2 COVER CROPS

Cover crops are grown to protect and rebuild the soil between crops. Bare soil is susceptible to erosion, and may develop weeds which are time consuming to remove and take nutrients from the soil.

A cover crop will prevent this and when destroyed and worked back into the soil, will provide for the next crop.

Types of Cover Crops

Legume crops fix atmospheric nitrogen into a form that plants and micro-organisms can use. Other species recycle existing soil nitrogen and can reduce leaching losses.

Legumes	Non-Legumes
Clovers	Rye
Hairy Vetch	Oats
Field Peas	Wheats
Annual Medic	Forage Turnips
Alfalfa	Oilseed Radish
Soybean	Buckwheat
TYPES OF COVER CROPS	

10.6 COMPANION PLANTING

Many problems associated with growing food, such as pest and vermin control, can be solved simply by growing the right plants together.

PLANT	FRIENDS	FUNCTION	FOES
Apple	Nasturtium	Climbs tree and repels codling moth	
Asparagus	Tomatoes, Parsley, Basil		
Balm	Tomatoes	Improves growth and flavour, attracts bees	
Basil	Tomatoes	Helps repel flies and mosquitoes	Rue
Beans	Potatoes, Carrots, Cucumber, Cauliflower, Summer savoury, most Vegetables and Herbs		Onions, Garlic, Gladiolus
Beetroot	Onions, Lettuce, Cabbage, Silver beet, Kohlrabi		
Birch		Dead leaves encourage compost fermentation	
Borage	Tomatoes, Squash and Strawberries	Deters tomato worm, improves growth and flavour	
Cabbage, Cauliflower, Broccoli	Sage, Dill, Camomile, Beets, Peppermint, Rosemary, Beans, Celery, Onions, Potatoes	Dill attracts a wasp to control cabbage moth. Zinnias attract lady bugs to protect plants	Strawberries, Tomatoes
Broad beans	Potatoes, Peas, Beans		
Caraway		Helps breakdown heavy soils	
Carrots	Lettuce, Peas, Leeks, Chives, Onions, Cucumbers, Beans, Tomatoes, Wormwood, Sage, Rosemary		Dill in flower, storage with apples
Catnip		Repels fleas, ants and rodents	
Cauliflower	Celery		
Celery & Celeriac	Chives, Leeks, Tomatoes, Dwarf Beans, Brassicas		
Chamomile	Cabbages, Onions	Deters flies and mosquitoes. Gives strength to any plant growing nearby	

PLANT	FRIENDS	FUNCTION	FOES
Chives	Carrots	Deters aphids. Spray will deter downy and powdery mildew	
Citrus	Bracken fern, Grape vines	Repels stink beetles	
Comfrey	Avocados and most Fruit trees	Compost activator, medicinal, foliage spray, nutrient miner. Useful to all gardens	
Cucumbers	Beans, Corn, Peas, Radish, Sunflowers		Potatoes, Aromatic herbs
Dill	Brassicas	Dill attracts predator wasp for cabbage moth	
Elderberry		General insecticide. The leaves help compost fermentation, the flowers and berries make lovely wine!	
Fennel		Repels flies, fleas and ants	Most plants dislike it
French Marigold	Tomatoes, Most vegetables	Root secretions kill nematodes in the soil. Will repel white fly	
Fruit trees	Nettles, Garlic, Chives, Tansy, Southernwood and Horseradish		
Garlic	Roses, Raspberry	Repels aphids from roses and raspberries. Repels cabbage butterfly and vampires	Peas, Beans
Geranium		Strong aroma - deters insects and encourages bees	
Grapes	Hyssop, Tansy and Sage		
Leek	Onion, Celery, Carrot		
Lettuce	Tall flowers, Carrots, Radish, Onion family	Flowers offer light shade for lettuce	
Marigolds	Tomatoes, Most vegetables	Kills couch and nematodes	
Melon	Radish		
Mint	Cabbage, Tomatoes	Deters white cabbage moth, ants, fleas and clothes moths	
Nasturtium	Radishes, Cabbages, Zucchini, Cucurbits (melons), Fruit trees	Secretes a mustard oil, which many insects find attractive. The flowers repel aphids and the cucumber beetle	
Nettle		Beneficial anywhere. Increases aroma of other herbs	
Onion and Garlic	Beets, Summer savoury, Tomatoes, Lettuce, Strawberries, Camomile		
Parsley	Tomato, Asparagus, Roses	Deters rose beetle, improves tomato and asparagus	
Peas	Carrots, Turnips, Corn, Beans, Radishes, Cucumbers, Most Vegetables and Herbs		Onions, Garlic Gladiolas, Potatoes

PLANT	FRIENDS	FUNCTION	FOES
Potato	Beans, Cabbage, Marigold, Horseradish, Eggplant, Sweet Alyssum.	Alyssum attracts beneficial wasps and acts as a living ground cover	Pumpkin, Squash, Cucumber, Sunflower, Tomato, Raspberry
Pumpkin	Corn		Potato
Pyrethrum		Will repel bugs if grown around the vegetable garden	
Radish	Peas, Nasturtium, Lettuce, Cucumbers, Spinach	Radish attracts leaf minor away from spinach	
Raspberry	Most vegetables		Blackberries, Tomatoes, Potato
Rosemary	Cabbage, Beans, Carrots, Sage	Deters cabbage moth, bean beetles and carrot fly	
Roses	Garlic, Chives, Parsley, Mignonette Lettuce		
Rue		Keeps animals off garden beds if planted round the borders	
Sage	Rosemary, Cabbage, Carrots	Deters cabbage moth and carrot fly	
Spinach	Strawberries		
Squash	Nasturtium Corn		
Strawberries	Bush bean, Spinach, Borage, Lettuce		Cabbage
Sunflower	Cucumbers		Potato
Sweet Corn	Potatoes, Peas, Beans, Cucumbers, Pumpkin, Squash	Corn acts as a trellis for beans which attract predators of corn pests.	
Tansy	Fruit trees, Roses and Raspberries	Repels moths, flies and ants. Tansy leaves assist compost fermentation.	
Thyme	Here and there in the garden	Protects Cabbages, improves growth of vegetables, general insect repellent	
Tomatoes	Asparagus, Parsley, Chives, onion, Broccoli, Sweet Basil, Marigold, Carrots, Parsley.		Kohlrabi, Potato, Fennel, Cabbage
Turnip	Peas, Nasturtium, Lettuce, Cucumbers		
Wormwood		Although it can inhibit the growth of plants near it, wormwood repels moths, flies and fleas and keeps animals off the garden.	
Yarrow	Near aromatic herbs and vegetables	Plant along borders and paths. Enhances essential oil production and flavour	

10.7 COMPOSTING

A balance of five essential ingredients – moisture, air, carbon, nitrogen and decomposing organisms such as insects, worms and bacteria – are the key to rapid composting. A well managed pile can produce compost in about 3 months.

Water	Water is required by all living organisms including decomposers. The pile should be moist but not too wet. A bad odour may indicate that excess moisture is inhibiting decomposition.
Oxygen	Oxygen is essential. The compost pile should not be too high, tight or wet.
Carbon	Carbon is abundant in most organic materials and is broken down by decomposers to create food energy. However, other ingredients are needed for carbon to be readily eaten. Wood and paper are examples that are high in carbon, but deficient in other nutrients and are slow to decompose.
Nitrogen	Nitrogen is required by decomposers in relatively large amounts. It is a major ingredient in protein. Without sufficient nitrogen, decomposition is slow.
Decomposing Organisms	These organisms produce heat by their activity. This heat speeds the process and also helps to kill disease organisms and weed seeds. The speed varies but at some point the centre of the heap should feel hot or very warm. More mass, water, air or nitrogen may be needed to get the process going.

10.7.1 COMPOST MATERIALS

DESIRABLE MATERIALS	UNDESIRABLE MATERIALS
Nitrogen-Rich Materials: • Grass Clippings • Green leaves and garden trimmings. • Seaweed and aquatic plants (wash to remove salt) • Food scraps like fruit and vegetable scraps, egg shells, leftover bread. **Carbon Sources:** • Woodchips and sawdust • Small branches/twigs from trees and shrubs (broken into pieces) • Stems of fibrous grasses	**May contribute weeds and plant diseases when inadequately composted:** • Weedy, persistent plants • Diseased plants **Human Health Hazard:** • Dog or cat feces • Other animal manure is OK to use **May Attract Flies, Rats, Animals:** • Oils • Dairy products • Meat or bones, poultry, fish

10.7.2 GETTING STARTED

The best location is a shady area protected from the wind to prevent it drying out. Place in an area that can't be flooded. The dimensions of a pile should be roughly 1 meter high, 1 meter wide. There is no limit to the length. Protect the pile from rain by covering with a tarp or build it under a roof.

Have a protected area to store the compost if you aren't going to use it immediately. Do not mix undecomposed materials with finished compost.

10.7.3 COMPOSTING METHODS

Basic Compost Heap

Simply pile and mix the compost materials on the ground. Cover when it rains to prevent it getting too wet or losing nutrients to leaching. Turn the heap every week or so. To aid in aeration, build the pile over scrap pipes drilled with holes. This reduces the need for turning.

Compost Pit

A pit is ideal for composting materials consisting of mostly food scraps. Dig a hole in the ground, add the materials and mix with soil. Refill the hole with at least 20 cm (8 in) of soil.

Holding Bins

Bins help to contain the pile, keep animals out and aid in turning. They can be made from concrete blocks, bricks, stones, wire mesh or wood. The bin should be made bottomless to allow organisms such as worms to come up through the soil and should have ample gaps in the sides to allow airflow. If the bin is moveable, the heap can be turned by removing the bin, placing next to the heap and simply shovel the heap back into the bin.

If several bins are lined in a row, the turning can be done by shovelling the compost into the next bin down the line. Usually by the third or fourth monthly turning, the compost is done.

10.7.4 COMPOST PROCESS

Accumulate enough material for a 1 x 1 x 1 meter heap. Shred or chop the materials to 5 cm or less to expose more surface area for decomposition. Start the pile with 10-15 cm of carbon-rich materials. Moisten and add 5-10 cm of nitrogen-rich materials and food scraps. Continue this layering and moistening process until about 1 meter high. Cover with a tarp.

Test the moisture content by feeling a handful and squeezing it. It should feel moist but not yield more than a few drops. If too wet, turn to allow air in and improve drainage. If too dry, water and turn it.

Periodically check the temperature in the piles centre. It should be very warm to the touch. When the temperature begins to drop, turn the pile and move material from the outside to the inside. The pile is being aerated in the process. Add water and mix it in well if the pile seems to be dry.

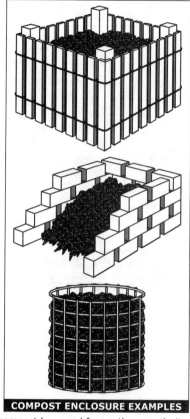

COMPOST ENCLOSURE EXAMPLES

The process is complete when the pile does not generate any more heat. When the pile is cool and the compost has aged for another month, it should be finished. The pile should be much smaller than the original pile. The compost should be dark, loose and without a strong or unpleasant odour.

Use the compost to mix into the soil or to make compost tea for watering crops and seedlings.

10.7.5 TROUBLESHOOTING

SYMPTOMS	LIKELY CAUSE	SOLUTIONS
Offensive odour	Insufficient aeration	Turn and loosen pile
Ammonia odour	Too much nitrogen	Add carbon-rich materials
Pile doesn't heap up	Insufficient nitrogen	Add nitrogen-rich materials
	Pile too wet	Turn, add carbon sources and protect from rain
	Pile too dry	Turn and sprinkle with water
	Pile too small	Add more materials
Pile attracts flies and animals	Inappropriate materials	Don't use meats or oils. Remove such materials or rotate them to the centre of the pile and cover with carbon-rich materials.

10.8 SAVING SEEDS

Proper seed saving practice is extremely important for a long term garden. The seeds you start with should be of the heirloom variety, sourced from nurseries, markets or backyard gardeners. Commercial produce is usually hybrid (designated by F1 or F2). Seeds from hybrids will only produce for a few generations, if at all.

10.8.1 GENERAL NOTES

Seeds should always be stored in cool, dry conditions. If cured seeds come in contact with moisture, they will become useless. Store most seeds in paper bags inside an airtight container if you can, with the exception of legumes which store best in breathable bags. Placing silica gel packets (or a cloth bag with some powdered milk or charcoal) in with your seeds will absorb any remaining moisture and help keep them dry between growing seasons.

Select the healthiest plants to harvest the seeds from. This will aid natural selection in developing strains that are suited to your climate and less likely to suffer failure or disease.

Avoid drying seeds in direct sunlight or ovens. The temperature inside the seeds can easily rise to destructive levels, especially with darker seeds.

When planting your seeds the following year, don't plant them all at once but save a few for later planting in case there is a crop failure.

Types of Pollination

Plants fall into two basic types when it comes to breeding, in-breeders (self-pollinators) and out-breeders (cross-pollinators). Most in-breeders can also be cross-pollinated however.

In-breeders can often self-pollinate forever without suffering problems. Seed from a single healthy plant or even a single pod can be enough to keep the variety going.

Out-breeders need to cross-pollinate with other plants and need a lot of genetic diversity. Without other plants around to provide the cross pollination, they will suffer in-breeding depression and start to lose health over a few generations. To prevent this you will need to save seeds from as many different plants as you can.

Out-breeders can cross pollinate with other compatible plants so if you want to keep a variety of plant true, you may need to keep them isolated from other similar plants, (some need over a km separation!). If physical isolation is not practical, a cage can be made with material such as flyscreen, or you can keep flower clusters covered individually in bags. You will then need to pollinate by hand. This is time consuming and you must decide if it is really worth it.

If you don't mind a bit of genetic diversity then isolation is unnecessary and may even help your plants adjust to a changing climate.

Brassicas

The seeds from brassicas can be difficult to save. Most are biennial and flower in the second season. The long thin pods crumble when they are ripe and are often raided by birds. Cut the flower stalks as soon as they reach maturity and hang them upside down indoors in a paper bag to catch the little seeds as they drop off.

Brassicas are strongly out-breeding and can't self-pollinate. Try to grow around 20 or more plants to ensure enough diversity to prevent inbreeding depression.

Wet Method (Fermenting)

Seed contained in fleshy fruits, or any seeds that are covered in a slimy gel, should be cleaned using the wet method. Tomatoes, melons, squash, cucumber and roses are prepared this way.

Scoop the seed masses out of the fruit or lightly crush fruits. Put the seed mass and a small amount of warm water in a bucket or jar. Let the mix ferment for 2-4 days, stirring daily.

The fermentation process kills viruses and separates the good seed from the bad seed and fruit pulp. A layer of fungus will begin to appear on the top of the mixture after a couple of days. This coat eats the germination-preventing coating that surrounds each seed and produces antibiotics to reduce seed-borne diseases. Expect it to be a little smelly.

After 2-4 days, the good viable seeds will sink to the bottom of the container while the pulp and bad seed float. Pour off the pulp, water, bad seed and mold. Spread the good seed on a screen or paper towel to dry. Allow to dry thoroughly for a few days before storing.

Life Cycles - Annuals, Biennials, Perennials

Annual plants will go from seed to flower in a single growing season, and then die. Biennials will flower in the second season's growth and then die.

Perennials will persist for many growing seasons (sometimes decades). The top of the plant will generally die back in winter and regrow the following spring.

10.8.2 SEED SAVING GUIDE

PLANT	ISOLATION	POLLINATION	SEED LIFE
Asparagus *Perennial*	90 m (300 ft)	Cross by insects	
		Cut the ferny plant top late in autumn when the berries are red. Hang inside to dry then soak the dried berries in water to soften the skins. Squeeze out the seeds and rinse off the pulp. Dry for a few days and store in a cool dry place.	
		Asparagus is a perennial and you must wait 3-4 years before harvesting, even if small shoots appear. A well-tended bed will last from 20-30 years.	
		Asparagus has both male and female plants. Grow at least 40 plants to ensure genetic diversity.	
Basil *Annual*	45 m (150 ft)	Cross by insects	5 years
		Ripe seed heads can be harvested and dried inside while the rest of the plant continues to grow. Each flower contains 4 seeds which can be difficult to extract from the dried seed pod.	
Beans, Peas, other legumes *Annual*	15 m (100 ft)	Self or cross by insects	2-3 years
		Leave the pods on the plant as long as possible until they are dry or start to change colour. Harvest them and further dry them indoors. Shell out the beans when the pods are dry and brittle (ie, when they rattle).	
		If frost threatens, pull entire plant by the roots and hang until pods are dry.	
		It takes about 5-7 weeks to produce mature pods and with peas It is sometimes possible to get two generations in a single growing season.	
Beetroot, Chard *Biennial*	800 m (0.5 mi)	Cross by wind	3-5 years
		These seeds grow on long straggly spikes and take a long time to mature. Pick individually as they turn brown or wait until all are nearly brown.	
		These are strongly out-breeding. Grow at least 16 plants to ensure diversity. Beetroot, chard and leaf beet will all cross-pollinate with each other.	
Cauliflower, Broccoli *Biennial-Annual*	800 m (0.5 mi)	Cross by insects	3-5 years
		As part of the mustard family, these seeds can be difficult to save. All varieties within each species will cross pollinate with each other. Broccoli and cauliflower seeds can rot even at low temperatures. Allow the central head of the broccoli to bloom before harvesting the seeds.	
		Individual plants are self-sterile and you will need to grow at least 6 plants to guarantee genetic diversity, preferably 20 or more.	
		See cabbage for harvesting notes.	
Brussels Sprouts, Cabbage *Biennial*	800 m (0.5 mi)	Cross by insects	3-5 years
		Subject to inbreeding depression and part of the mustard family. At least 6 plants should be grown to maintain genetic diversity. Flowering plants can reach over 1 m high (3 ft) and should be at least 60 cm (2 ft) apart for good seed production.	
		Broccoli, cauliflower, cabbage and kohlrabi heads grown for seed should not be trimmed for consumption. Brussels sprouts, collards and kale can be lightly trimmed for eating without affecting quality seed production.	
		Allow seed pods to dry before picking and opening by hand. Lower pods will dry before higher ones. For larger amounts of seed, pull the entire plant after most pods have dried. Green pods will rarely produce viable seed if allowed to dry after the plant is pulled.	

PLANT	ISOLATION	POLLINATION	SEED LIFE
Carrot	800 m (0.5 mi)	Cross by insects	3-5 years
Biennial	Flower heads develop over 30 days. Carrots require cold winter-like temperatures for several weeks before flowering occurs. They suffer from extreme inbreeding depression so save and mix seeds from at least 10 plants.		
	Carrots produce flowers in round, flat groups called umbels. Hand pick each umbel as it turns brown or cut the entire flowering top as it begins to dry. Allow to mature for a further 2-3 weeks in a cool dry location.		
Celery	1.6 km (1 mi)	Cross by insects	
Biennial	Leave some celery plants after harvest so they can produce seed. Wait until the plants send up flower stalks. Pick the flower stalks when the petals are withered and stalks begin to dry. Break open the seed heads and collect the dry seeds.		
	Celery is subject to inbreeding depression so grow 20 or more plants.		
Coriander, Dill	1.6 km (1 mi)	Cross by insects	
Annual	Pull and discard the earliest plants to go to seed. Harvest as soon as the seed is brown and dry as they tend to drop off the seed heads.		
	Save only from plants that flower late and produce plenty of leaf.		
Corn, Sweet Corn	800 m (0.5 mi)	Cross by wind	2-3 years
Annual	Corn suffers from extreme inbreeding depression. You will need about 200 plants (100 as a bare minimum) to be able to continue growing and saving seed generation after generation. Planting even a single generation of inbred plants can produce an inferior crop.		
	Leave the cob on the plant for as long as possible or harvest when it's mature and bring it indoors to dry. Remove the kernels by rubbing two cobs together.		
Cucumber	800 m (0.5 mi)	Cross by insects	
	Cucumbers will change colour after ripening and become mushy (cucumbers are usually eaten in the unripe green state). Cut in half and scrape out the seeds. Ferment the seeds in water for 2-4 days, and then rinse, dry and store.		
Eggplant	15 m (50 ft)	Self or cross by insects	5-7 years
Annual	Eggplants suffer little inbreeding. They are self-fertile but insects will visit. Grow at least 6 plants.		
	To save seed, let the fruits grow long past the edible stage, to a dull purple brown. Seeds from edible eggplants will not be viable. Cut the eggplant in half and pull the flesh away from the seeded area.		
Garlic	0	n/a	Bulbs keep 6-8 mo at 5°C (40°F)
Annual	Garlic is normally propagated by dividing and planting the cloves. Save the biggest and healthiest bulbs from regular harvest. Dig the whole plant out and let cure for 3-4 weeks in a cool dry place.		
	Once the roots and tops have dried, remove the bulbs and store until planting next autumn.		
Lettuce	9 m (30 ft)	Self or cross by insects	2-3 years
Annual	Lettuce is largely self-pollinating and suffers no inbreeding depression. Seeds ripen irregularly and are ready to harvest 12-24 days after flowering.		
	To get the most seeds, harvest the plant daily by shaking the seed heads into a container, or cut the entire head and store.		
Lentils		Self	5 years
Annual	Select a few plants for harvesting seeds and don't pick any pods from these plants. Don't water these plants unless it is very dry or it can encourage leafy growth rather than pod development. Pick the pods when they are brown and dry and extract the seeds, don't pick green pods as the seeds are immature.		

PLANT	ISOLATION	POLLINATION	SEED LIFE
Onion	1.6 km (1 mi)	Cross by insects	1 year (50% viable after 2 years)
Biennial	Plant at least 10 plants to prevent inbreeding depression. Onions cannot self-pollinate easily, nor cross-pollinate easily between different species. When most of the flowers have dried then clip the umbels (the pods that hang off long stalks on the flower head) and allow to dry for 2-3 weeks.		
Peppers	150 m (500 ft)	Self or cross by insects	2-3 years
Annual	Peppers suffer little inbreeding depression and are self-pollinated, but bees will also cause cross-pollination so two varieties (eg mild & hot) will cross if planted close together and not isolated by manual means.		
	The seeds are ready for harvest when the fruit is. Pick and dry the fruit for 2-3 weeks, then remove and store the seeds in a cool dry location.		
Potato	0	Self or cross by insects	Tubers keep 4-6 mo at 5°C (40°F)
Perennial	Potatoes are usually propagated by planting pieces of the tubers, cut to include one or two eyes. Store the potatoes in cool dry conditions over the winter.		
	Unless the temperature is about 5°C (40°F) or less, then the eyes will begin to sprout. Just knock the sprouts off as they appear until you are ready to plant in spring. Cut the potatoes to include at least one eye in each section and plant.		
	Some varieties of potato will produce small green fruit that contain up to 300 true seeds. Finely chop the fruit and soak in water. After about a day, the seeds will sink to the bottom, separated from the flesh floating on top. Let these dry and store. These fruit contain a strong toxin called Solanine which has fungicide and pesticide properties, be sure to wash your hands thoroughly afterwards.		
	Very important note – when growing potatoes for the long term you need to stick to a crop rotation plan to prevent diseases in the soil from affecting the potatoes. Otherwise you will only get 3-5 generations of viable crops.		
Pumpkin, Squash	450 m (1500 ft)	Self or cross by insects	4-6 years
Annual	Scrape out the seeds, wash and let dry. Store in a cool, dry location. You will need at least 6 plants, preferably 12-20 to prevent inbreeding depression.		
Spinach	800 m (0.5 mi)	Cross by wind	2-3 years
Annual	Little inbreeding depression. Seed is either prickly or smooth, which determine the plants leaf texture. Smoother seeds produce mores wrinkled leaves.		
	To ensure maximum pollination, try to maintain a ratio of 1 male to 2 females, with a minimum of 2:4. The sex of the plants is difficult to determine until flowering. The male plants have small yellowish flowers on long tendrils.		
	Harvest the seeds from the female plant once the plant has gone mostly brown.		
Sunflower	800 m (0.5 mi)	Cross by insects	7 years
Annual	Subject to inbreeding depression, you will need at least 40 good plants to maintain genetic diversity. Harvest the seeds and then simply dry and store.		
Tomato	0 -30 m (100 ft)	Self or cross by insects	4-10 years
Annual	Tomatoes suffer no inbreeding depression, and generally do not cross-pollinate, although some breeds can - separate these breeds by 30 m (100 ft) to prevent cross-pollination. Allow tomatoes to completely ripen before harvesting for seed production. If picked before ripe, fruits will ripen slowly if kept in a cool, dry location. Process seeds using the wet method then dry and store.		

11 RAISING ANIMALS

Due to evolution alongside man, domestic animals are symbiotic creatures. Many animals, such as the chicken, cannot survive without man as they exist today.

In return for your care, feeding, housing and doctoring your animals will eat your garden waste and other matter inedible to humans, produce high quality foods, and contribute fertiliser to your soil.

11.1 CHICKENS

Choose a schedule between a small egg flock that produces all year, or a large meat production for a few months of the year, or both. Good egg layers will eat a lot compared to the weight they put on. Good meat birds will put on more weight but are not good layers.

GENERAL GUIDELINES

- Always start with at least a pair of poultry (whether chickens or other domestic birds). A trio – one cock, two hens – is better. An average hen will lay 220 eggs per year. A typical group will need 2 hens per member to ensure enough eggs.
- Give a generous and diverse diet. This will ensure the quality of the eggs and meat.
- Make sure you provide plenty of ventilation, space, sunshine and gravel for their gizzards.
- Raise new chicks every year and periodically cull the flock. If you are raising egg-layers, eat any birds that aren't performing well unless you cannot spare them.
- Shovel the enclosure at least twice a year. Compost the manure and use it in your garden.

11.1.1 STARTING WITH ADULT BIRDS

If you start with adult birds, there are a few things to consider. Moving birds to a new home will send layers molting, and will end egg-laying for a while. To minimise disease, do not use ground that has had other birds on for at least 3 years without a **Lye Clean** (Page 11-6).

Be aware of people trying to see you their culls. Health can be determined by the following —

- Check for skin and feather parasites by checking along the underarm feathers with a magnifying glass.
- Combs and wattles should be shiny red (unless the hen is broody or mothering). Eyes should be alert and bright. Feathers should be smooth and shiny.
- Droppings should be well formed rather than loose, and without the pinkish tinge of blood.
- The birds should be busy eating, dusting or preening – generally active and curious. If they are quiet with their feathers fluffed out – they are not healthy.

When you bring new birds home (do this near sunset if possible) confine them within the chicken house until they begin to roost there. After a few night of forcing them to roost where you want them to, this will become habit and you can open the outside door.

Setters and Non-Setters

Most chicken breeds have been developed to be good producers, and have had their motherly instinct bred out completely. Reliable incubation is complicated and requires accurate temperature and humidity regulation and frequent turning. This is usually done by a machine.

If you plan to let the hens mother their own eggs, you should select a breed like Orpingtons, Turkens, Partridge Rocks, Buff Rocks, Speckled Sussex, Dark Cornish, Columbian Wyandottes, Buff Cochins, Partridge Cochins, and Light Brahmas, or any good bantam mothering breed.

Introducing New Birds to an Existing Flock

Birds can be cruel to strangers. The new birds should be about equal size of the existing flock. Pen new birds where others can see them for about 3 weeks then leave the cage open and observe from a distance. Alternatively, put the new birds in at night so they roost together before having a chance to fight. For a few days, evict the old birds from the pen in the morning, leaving the new ones with food and water.

The new birds get a chance to eat in peace and take possession of the new space. When the other birds are let back in, they are too busy eating and drinking to make trouble.

11.1.2 RAISING CHICKS (BROODING)

Chickens get along best when raised together, so it is best to start your intended flock all at once. Young birds need a setup that is warm, dry, draft-free, clean, cleanable, escape-proof, and safe from predators.

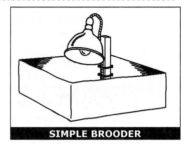

A typical homemade brooder is a cardboard box and a low wattage light bulb as a heat source. A box about 75 cm (30 in) square with high sides and an adequate heat source will handle around 50 chicks.

There should be adequate ventilation to remove moisture and gases without taking away too much heat. The brooder should not be too large or the chicks can wander too far from food, water or the source or heat.

SIMPLE BROODER

Wood Stove Brooding

If you have no electricity or fossil fuels, you can still keep chicks warm. Put the chicks in a cardboard box. Put that cardboard box inside another larger box that has a layer of hay or other insulating material along the bottom and sides. Cover most of the top with a cloth or board – remember to allow ventilation.

Place the box a suitable distance from a source of heat – a wood stove or fireplace. If this is not warm enough, or the nights are cold – place a large jar or tin of very hot water in the middle of the box. Wrap this with a cloth to prevent burns. Refill with hot water as needed.

If you are using a cardboard box and need to extend the area, you can fix extra boxes to the sides and cut a hole between them. Place a cloth flap between the partitions to keep in heat.

Open Area Brooding

Brooding in an open area will require fencing. Normal chicken wire is too large for baby chicks, but you can buy finer mesh. The walls need to be at 30 cm (1 ft) tall, baby chicks can fly over short obstacles by about 1 week old.

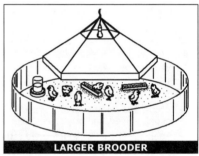

One method is to use sturdy cardboard to form a circle about 30 cm (1 ft) tall. This prevents chicks huddling in corners which can result in smothering. Start about 1.2 m (4 ft) diameter, and expand as necessary. Place the heat source in the centre.

LARGER BROODER

Heat and Light Sources

Bright sources of light should be avoided. Bright light will cause more pecking between the chicks. An infrared heat lamp or a red or green 'party' globe is preferred. Get them used to darkness gradually by switching to a dimmer globe at night, but maintain the temperature.

Chicks raised in constant lighting will associate light with warmth and safety and may become frightened when real darkness comes. They may pile up on, and suffocate one and other.

Temperature Control

Broiler chicks (raised for meat, not eggs) should start off at about 30°C (85°F) as they are more sensitive to heat than other breeds. Other breeds should start off at about 35°C (95°F). For the first week or two, it is a good idea to get up 2 or 3 times a night to check on them.

After week one, temperature is fairly easy to estimate by the chicks behaviour. If the chicks aren't warm enough, they'll huddle together directly under the heat source, or in a corner. If it's too hot in the heat circle, they will avoid it. They may also spread their wings and pant. Under ideal conditions they will form a circle around the edge of the heat source.

Weening Chicks from the External Heat Source

As the chicks grow older they need less external warmth. Decrease the temperature by 2.8°C (5°F) per week by raising the heat source, or moving the brooder away from the heat source.

When the birds are 6 weeks old, the temperature has been reduced by 14°C (25°F). When to ween them completely off the heat depends on the outside temperature, and wether your birds have 'feathered out' enough. You may start by turning the heat on only during the night.

Flooring

Slippery flooring such as hay or flat newspaper, or a wire mesh floor, will cause a condition in young chicks known as 'spraddle legs'. Use something with grip like a burlap sack or clean rags. Replace with clean flooring daily and remove loose threads that can snare the chicks.

Once the chicks have learnt what is and isn't food, and their legs have grown strong, you can change the flooring to a thick layer of newspapers. Remove the top few layers every day to remove feces and ensure a dry environment.

NOTE – Don't use newspapers for ducklings, gooselings or turkey poults.

Rather than newspaper you can use loose litter, absorbent organic material. Use something harmless like potting soil, or something that is too large to fit in their mouths, such as wood shavings. Don't use hay or sawdust. Hay is not absorbent and sawdust will be eaten.

Make sure you rotate the litter daily and remove any wet areas.

Health Hazard - Chick Dust

Chicks create a powdery dust caused by shed down from molting, chick feed and droppings turning to powder. Because this dust presents health hazards to humans it is best to isolate indoor chicks form main areas of a house, and use a dust mask when dealing with the chicks.

Sick and Dead Baby Chicks

Even with careful daily observation, expect a mortality rate of 2-3% or higher. If you find a sick one, isolate in its own box and give plenty of care. Remove dead birds as you find them.

Roosting Chicks

Chickens have the urge to start roosting at about 5 weeks old, and will hop on to a perch if available. Long poles about 15 cm (6 in) apart will suffice. Their first perch can be as high as 30 cm (1 ft). Slant the poles to ease the transition. Provide at least 10 cm (4 in) for each bird. Providing roosting perches maximise enclosure space and helps keep the chicks clean.

Moving into the Chicken House

It's best to wait until the birds are big enough to defend themselves before introducing them to an existing flock. This is usually around 10-12 weeks after hatching. Move them into the hen house before they start laying to prevent disruption.

Moving larger birds into a new house should be done at night. Place them on the roosts in their new quarters so they sleep once before going out in the morning. If they are not sure the next night, shoo them in again. If still reluctant, let them get hungry and feed them in there.

Chick Water

To make a home-made waterer, fill a large, heavy jar with water. Place a shallow bowl upside down over the mouth and turn it upside down quickly (and away from the chick pen).

Slip a matchstick under the mouth so keep the water flowing as the chicks need. You will need at least 4.5 litre (1 gallon) water per 50 chicks.

Give mail ordered chicks food and water immediately after they arrive. Water first, and then feed. If the chicks don't know what to do with the water teach them by gently and briefly dunking their heads in the water, one by one.

They will quickly catch on and others will imitate. If a few are slow learners, separate the rest and give them each another dunk.

If the chicks arrive cold, first warm them and then serve lukewarm water with a little sugar.

Chicks drink a lot of water so ensure the supply is clean and plentiful. Change water a few times a day and disinfect the containers once a week using hot and soapy water, or by boiling.

Place their water supply as far away as possible from their food to prevent it going soggy.

Chick Water Don'ts

- Don't give water in containers with edges over an inch high.
- Don't use containers deep enough so a chick could fall in and drown (they will if they can).
- Don't use a container that the chicks can tilt or tip over.
- Don't have a setup that allows chick droppings to fall into the water.
- Don't use icy-cold water. Serve lukewarm, baby bottle temperature.
- Don't let the water run out.
- Don't place the water (or food) directly under the heat source.

Chick Food

Hatched chicks won't be hungry straight away and should not be fed prematurely. Once they start pecking at their flooring, it's time to feed them (after you have watered them). If you are using organic material for flooring, cover in newspaper and cloth for the first 4 days – until they have learnt what is definitely food. For the first week, feed in shallow containers such as paper plates, jar lids, or the bottoms of egg cups. After that, use tuna-can sized containers.

A young chick will eat about a thimble of food a day, so that small amount must supply all the nutrients the young chicks need. If using home grown feed, mix up a feed that contains —

- 2 parts finely ground wheat, corn (not too much), and oats combined
- 1 part protein such as fish meal, meat meal, cat food, chopped hard-boiled or scrambled eggs, yoghurt, cottage cheese, or small worms, bugs or grubs.
- 1 part greens such as alfalfa meal or leaves, comfrey, chard, clover, lettuce, dandelion, cress, chives, grass, spinach, weeds (finely chopped).
- Other good diet components could be wheat germ, sunflower seeds, powdered seaweed, powdered milk, and linseed meal.

Their diet should be about 20% protein. To collect bugs, lay boards on the ground where bugs might gather and check under the boards every morning.

They will also need ground eggshells and/or oyster shell to provide calcium, fine grit or sand for their gizzards and a sprinkle of salt. As they grow they will need coarser grit and can handle coarser grain, being able to eat whole grain at the 4 weeks old.

On sunny days you can take them out to pasture on clean dry ground. Small chicks are vulnerable as prey and quick to tire so do this briefly at first and longer as they grow older.

11.1.3 HEALTH PROBLEMS

Chick Diarrhoea or Coccidiosis is a widespread problem for poultry that is caused by a parasite that birds pick up from feces. Some varieties won't make a bird sick and most varieties trouble only one type of bird and not others. Symptoms are blood in the droppings and a sick bird.

To prevent this, avoid overcrowding, feed a balanced diet and keep it available. Minimise the possibility of chicks eating feces, refill water containers at least twice daily and sterilise weekly. Coccidiosis is more likely to strike in damp, chilly weather so keep young birds dry and warm.

A home remedy is to add 1 tablespoon plain vinegar per litre (quart) drinking water for 3 days or until the droppings look normal again. Sick or weak chicks that are being bullied by siblings should be quarantined together in a separate 'hospital' box. Remove dead chicks immediately.

Worms

If you suspect worms, add some garlic – in any form – to the chickens diet or drinking water. It does not hurt to do this on a routine basis as a preventative measure.

Broken Leg

A chick's leg can be splinted with small sticks and tape. A larger bird's leg can be splinted in the same manner with heavier-duty materials.

Egg-Bound

The chicken squats, strains, maybe looking constipated. Pour warmed olive oil into her vent. Feed her castor oil. Then gently try to manoeuvre the jammed egg out.

11.1.4 HATCHING EGGS

When hatching eggs, there is a mortality rate between 50-90%. Look at the egg to see if one end is pointy or round. Pointy eggs make roosters – this is around 90% accurate.

Raise purebred chickens from a kind you like. If you collect eggs from hybrids or crosses, the offspring will not be like the parent. To raise crosses, there is a lot of crossing involved to find out which 2 chickens produces the kind you want. Raise eggs chosen from only the best birds.

If you are breeding from birds in their first laying season, wait several weeks before storing for incubation. The first eggs tend to be smaller and have lower fertility rates.

Getting Hatchable Eggs

Be sure to feed your birds a good diet high in protein and greens, with comparatively little grain. Laying mash is not suitable for birds you want to hatch chicks from. Both roosters and hens need to be well fed to minimise risk of sterility. The lighter the yolk, the less fertile it is.

Rooster

You need a rooster among your hens or the eggs won't hatch. The younger the rooster, the more potent he is. A young light-breed rooster can service 10-20 hens while an older one will manage about 5-10. A heavy-breed rooster, even a young one, should never be assigned to more than 8-12 hens. A bantam rooster is best with 2-5 hens.

Too many roosters will reduce fertility, as they spend more time fighting. Too much lovin' can affect the hens' health. Hens can be discriminating and may just say "No". A molting rooster will also not be interested. Roosters are more fertile in spring because more daylight increases his potency. Hens start producing fertile eggs 2 or 3 weeks after the days are long enough.

At 3-8 weeks old you can start to distinguish the young cockerels from their slightly larger combs (red decoration on their head) and wattles (the one that hangs off the chin). Roosters are usually larger than pullets (young hens). When they have grown, eat most of them and save the healthiest and strongest for breeding. You need something like 1 rooster per 15 hens.

Extra roosters will start to pick on the pullets after they get to about 20 weeks old.

Collecting and Storing Eggs

Gather them before night, if the nights are chilly, to prevent harm from low temperatures. Handle carefully and <u>always</u> keep them on the side or with the large end up (to prevent rupture to the air cell) Choose normal shaped, normal sized, uncracked eggs. Don't wash eggs in waiting – this can transmit bacteria through the eggs' pores.

Store the eggs for up to 14 days in a place with reasonable humidity at 7-25°C (45-60°F). A temperature too low will kill the embryo, too high and the embryo will start a slow growth that weakens and kills it. Eggs that are going to be incubated should be turned or tipped 3 times a day. This can easily be done by alternately raising each end of the carton.

Incubators

The proper brooding temperature is 37.64°C (99.75°F). Homemade incubators can be as simple as a bucket with eggs in it. The eggs are wrapped in cloth with a light bulb suspended overhead. This setup is least likely to work, though sometimes does. To incubate, maintain temperature and above-normal humidity and rotate the eggs a 1/4 turn, 3 to 5 times a day. The hen would naturally do this and is absolutely necessary for healthy growth.

Chickens that Hatch Their Own Eggs

When a hen decides to start her family, she will stop walking away after laying eggs, and instead stay to sit on them. You can recognise a broody hen when the manner of her clucking changes from an everyday song to more urgent 'come-here' clucking, such that she would use with her offspring. There's no known way to force a hen to become broody, a commercial breed layer will almost never brood, so you must manually incubate the eggs.

When brooding starts, a hen may make a nest away from the fleas and mites that may infest a chicken house, or she may sit where she usually lays her eggs. She begins laying eggs in her nest one per day until she has enough. She may pull feathers off to help insulate the nest.

The nest needs to be big enough so the hen can move and turn her eggs, and on the ground so falls aren't deadly. An ideal nest is a box about 40 cm (15 in) square at least 40 cm deep, directly on the ground, with the top roofed and the front side open. A section of turf is ideal for nesting material, pound down the middle to make a shallow bowl, and moisten with water.

Egg Adoption

You can give a setting hen other eggs to incubate, even eggs from other species such as ducks, turkeys and geese. Don't give the hen too many eggs, especially if they are large. The hen will rotate the outside ones to the inside and you may lose the lot. If the eggs are too large for the hen to turn, you will need to manually turn them 3 times a day.

After a hen has begun to set, on one of the first few nights, slip the eggs to be adopted under her late at night. It can take 3-5 weeks for eggs to hatch, depending on the species of poultry.

Human body warmth is just right to hatch eggs. Women of ample mammary endowment can incubate eggs between their breasts for the necessary number of days.

Once the hen is setting, she will be devoted to her clutch and will leave her nest at most once a day, for 15-30 minutes for food and water. Help her by placing food and water nearby. Don't handle her nest while she's gone, too much disruption and she will abandon her clutch.

Birth

As chicks hatch, take them away from the mother to allow her to concentrate on the rest of the eggs, and to protect the chicks from predators and bullying from other birds. Remove any abandoned eggshells from the nest. When all have been hatched, house the hen and her chicks in a separate environment until they are big and strong enough to fend for themselves.

11.1.5 CHICKEN HOUSING

Chickens need shelter from weather and protection from predators. If your chickens roam free in a pen during the day, they will only need a small amount of space each to sleep – enough to contain their nests. If they are totally confined, they will need a much larger space to avoid overcrowding – about 1.2 to 2.4 sq metre (4 to 8 sq ft) per bird.

Sunlight is important to the cycles and health of hens and roosters, so ensure there is enough. They will also need ventilation to bring in oxygen and remove moisture and ammonia gases.

A suitable shelter can be made using the techniques in **Shelters** (Page 8-1), as long as

CHICKEN YARD AND COOP

the chickens are safe from predators, have ample room and ventilation, and have a place to nest.

Nests

Nests can be individual boxes about 40 cm (15 in) square, with a top and sides. Leave one side half-open for entry. A simple nesting place can be made by leaning a sheet of tin or plywood against a wall. This gives the chickens a dark comfortable place to nest in. Put plenty of hay, chopped straw, woodchips or something similar to provide more insulation and comfort.

Roosts

Chickens like to roost and will fly to a rafter or tree branch if they can. Make roosts with a thick pole 5 to 10 cm (2 to 4 in) in diameter, at about 1 m (3 ft) or higher. Don't use smooth material and fix it so it can't rotate. Provide about 50 cm (20 in) per bird, and don't place too close to a wall. Don't place one roost above another or feces will drop on the lower birds.

Flooring

A stone or concrete floor is easier to clean than a dirt floor but not necessary. The chickens will have more bugs and worms to eat if directly on the ground. If possible, slope the floor away from the roosting area to allow water to drain. A wooden floor is also acceptable.

Lye Clean

If you are using an existing chicken house that has had other birds within the last 3 years, you should thoroughly clean the enclosure to remove any parasites and other health hazards. This should also be done once or twice a year regardless.

- Shovel all manure and litter from the floor. Scrape manure off the roosts and clean old litter out of nest boxes. Most chicken diseases are transmitted through feces.

- Give a soaking of dilute disinfectant or lye see **Making Lye** (Page 9-22). Lye is most effective if applied hot, but is not effective unless most of the manure has been removed.

- Let it dry and put fresh litter on the floor before moving in the tenants.

11.2 TURKEYS

You will need at least 2 turkeys. Turkeys don't like being alone and a single bird may refuse to eat, and die. However, turkeys are large birds and need a lot to eat, so don't keep more than you can feed. They are more vulnerable to diseases than other poultry, especially when kept in large numbers. Turkeys can be a little slow to learn to eat and drink.

11.2.1 EGGS

Provide nests for the turkey hens that are 60 cm (24 in) square, and 60 cm deep in a dimly lit part of the pen, 1 nest for every 4 or 5 hens. A 1 m x 2 m (4 ft x 8 ft) 'community' nest can accommodate about 20 hens. Gather eggs frequently to prevent turkeys breaking each others eggs. Heavy hens can lay 50 eggs a season, where light breeds can lay up to 100.

Turkey eggs are good to eat, but are often spared to raise more turkeys. As with chickens, egg production declines about 20% each year. Egg size increases in the second year, like chickens.

11.2.2 REPRODUCTION

Most commercial turkeys are one of two breeds – the broad breasted bronze and broad breasted white. Like commercial chickens, the motherly instinct is almost bred out of them so if you would like turkeys that breed without human assistance, you will need a breed such as Beltsville whites, bourbon reds, royal palms, wild or bush turkeys.

When hens begin to lay, the male begins courting and with luck, mating. Sperm stored inside the hen will fertilise eggs for between a few days to a few weeks. If your turkey hens aren't very motherly, you can let chickens, ducks or geese brood the eggs. A medium sized chicken can comfortably sit on 6 to 7 turkey eggs. The incubation period is 28 days.

If you have motherly turkeys, provide a nest for each hen with a reasonable sized A-frame lined with straw. Something about 40 x 60 cm (16 x 24 in) on the ground is a good size.

Artificial Insemination

The commercial heavy breeders are not very fertile, so AI is an option. First capture the tom and have the hen nearby because semen must be used within 30 minutes. Inseminate once, wait 4 days and do it again, then once every 2-3 weeks during the egg laying season.

You need at least two people for this seedy business. 'Milk' the tom by flipping him on his back and stroking the abdomen and pushing his tail up and towards his head. His organ enlarges and protrudes a little bit, and then someone must grab it high up and stroke it up and down. Have something ready to collect the semen – you get about 1 cubic centimetre.

Give the tom a cigarette and send him on his way.

To inseminate the hen, flip her on her back, flipping up her tail. For the best results, expose the opening of the oviduct and use a glass or plastic straw, or needle-less syringe to insert the semen about 4 cm (1.5 in) into that oviduct. If you can't find the oviduct then you may have a hen that is not in lay, in which case the whole sordid exercise is a waste of time.

Incubating and Brooding

Turkey eggs are incubated for 28 days at 39°C (102°F). Relative humidity for the first 25 days should be 62%, and 70% for the last 3 days. To brood the poults (newly hatched turkeys), follow the same principles as for brooding chicks. Clean the brooding area thoroughly and if the area has previously housed chickens, let it stand for a month to prevent coccidiosis.

Teach the poults to eat and drink in the same manner as chickens. Turkeys however don't scratch obsessively like chickens, and usually need something to catch their eye before pecking at it. It can help initially to put something bright and shiny in their feeders, like marbles or strips of shiny metal. A laser pointer can also be useful for this encouragement.

11.2.3 HOUSING

Until they are 8 weeks old, poults can do with 25 cm (1 ft) square each. Turkeys grow fast and this space requirement will increase. An all-tom flock will eventually need 1.5 m (5 ft) each, where hens will require only 90 cm (3 ft) each. Some breeds are smaller than others however.

Turkeys can be raised in complete confinement, but as with chickens, having a fenced yard for them to roam in and a shelter for them to sleep is a better option. Turkeys should get plenty of sunlight to help prevent a disease known as blackhead, but be sure to also provide shade.

The symptoms of blackhead are brownish foamy droppings and a droopy bird. The liver of a blackhead affected turkey may have ulcers, and inflammation of the intestine may be present.

Turkey Roosts

Turkeys will get along fine without roosts, they will just sleep on the litter floor. In that case, keep the floor clean and dry. Turkeys are prone to piling however, and will pile at the drop of a hat if something frightens them, like sudden light or a loud or unexpected noise. If you see them doing this, break up the pile as soon as possible to prevent suffocation and injury.

Roosts for turkeys should be about 5 cm (2 in) poles, or 2x4's laid flat. Put them about 50 cm (1.5 ft) from the ground and provide at least 30 cm (1 ft) along the roost for each bird.

Moving Turkeys to a Yard

Turkeys are not the sharpest birds around. If they have been previously kept in confinement and suddenly set loose in the open, they will not know how to use shade to protect them from sunlight or shelter to protect them from weather. They are likely to pile in a corner and smother one and other, or not know how to use their new feeding arrangement.

Make the move on the morning of a good day and watch them carefully. Move their feeder and water to as needed to prevent muddy spots that can harbour disease and organisms.

11.3 DUCKS AND GEESE

Many of the principles of waterfowl care are the same as for chickens. This section covers areas that differ. Waterfowl have better resistance to disease than chickens, especially when in small flocks. Duck and goose eggs contain about 50% more fat than chicken eggs.

For best health, waterfowl need to get at least their heads and feet wet. You don't need a pond, a small tub will do. If you make a pond, putting gravel around the edge will prevent it from getting muddy and help to keep the water clean. If using a tub, change the water often.

Ducks and geese are the healthiest of fowl (ducks being the hardiest), and rarely get diseases. They require little to no shelter, even in winter.

11.3.1 PONDS

Some waterfowl need water to mate in. This includes heavy duck and goose breeds, wild ducks and geese, and domesticated birds closely related to the wild. A tub won't be enough but a reasonable pond will. Waterfowl that are sitting on eggs don't need a pond, but will still need water to jump in and out of to provide the moisture required to incubate the eggs.

Large Ponds

If you have a pond, about 25 ducks and 6 geese per acre of water is the maximum population. A flock of ducks will clean filamentous algae from a pond, and provide food (droppings) for fish. However, Waterfowl will not effectively control tropical water plants such as water lettuce.

They will eat water weed roots, lilies, frogs and will clean up the banks. Be aware that too many ducks will muddy the water and erode the banks looking for worms and roots. Ducks thrive in salt-water too, but you will still need to provide fresh water for drinking.

If you are planning on raising waterfowl on a large body of water, wether it is a natural body or a dam, be aware of potential pollution problems that may exist.

Small Ponds

The water should be 20 cm (8 in) deep or more, but shallow enough to get in and out of – or provide a ramp or other means of access. They will drown if they are exhausted with no escape. Clean the water container at least once a week to remove sludge and prevent bacteria.

11.3.2 RAISING YOUNG WATERFOWL

It's best to start with about 6 birds or less to avoid overcrowding, and to get a feel for caring for these birds. You will need about 3.5 m (12 ft) square of housing and 12 m (40 ft) square of run area for 1 goose or 2 ducks. The care of goslings or ducklings is different from chicks, but the basic principles are the same – or you could let breeder birds raise the babies.

Incubating Eggs

Waterfowl keep their eggs very moist. High humidity is not good enough. You need to spray them with lukewarm water once a day. The incubating temperature is 39°C (102°F), and remember to turn the eggs, as with chickens. Stop turning the eggs after 25 days, but keep spraying water. The eggs will hatch after 28 days for most birds, though some will take longer.

Brooding

Ducklings and goslings need a warm, dry environment in their first month. They will need twice as much space as chicks. Waterfowl develop faster and grow warm feathers faster than other birds. Because of this you can get away with unheated boxes insulated with up 5 to 10 cm (2 to 4 in) of rags, straw, sawdust or grass covered with burlap. The younglings can stay warm in such a setup, but you must ensure they don't suffocate, or get tangled in loose fibres.

Ideally you should let a duck raise her own – they will learn faster how to fend for themselves. Ducks with broods should be separated from the flock until they are 6 to 8 weeks old.

Waterfowl Mothering Chicks

A duck sitting on chicken eggs will do a good job but care must be taken once they've hatched. A mother duck will lead her flock to water, where the chicks are likely to drown. Brood them separately. If you have chickens and turkeys sitting on ducks eggs, keep the number to around 8-9. Unless a hen has set and hatched ducklings, don't trust ducklings to her care.

11.3.3 FOOD AND WATER

Once they are started, ducks require little extra feed if they have enough ground to forage in. They will eat the same sort of diet as chickens – grain, green stuff, bugs and worms. Geese can live on grass. Both ducks and geese are efficient in turning food to meat and tend to get fat if overfed. If raised on a large body of water, waterfowl will find plenty to eat.

Water

Careful attention must be paid to young waterfowl as they have a tendency to get soaked and chill, or drown in their water. A suitable container would be a trough about 5 cm (2 in) deep and about 2.5 cm (1 in) wide. They can dunk their heads into it, but not jump into it. Ducks are messy with their water so it should always be kept away from their food supply

Starter Food

Commercial food meant for one species' babies should not be fed to another. Not only are the nutritional requirements different, but they often contain medicines which can be harmful to a species it was not intended for. Commercial chick feed that is *non-medicated* will do for ducklings and goslings in a pinch, but should not be relied upon permanently.

Suitable homemade foods include cooked or raw oatmeal, scrambled eggs, bread – cover all of these with a little water or milk.

Feed greens, but not grass or tough stems at first. They enjoy finely chopped onion greens, dandelion greens, watermint and cresses – anything fresh and tender. Increase the amount of greens week by week. Young waterfowl hungry for greens will pull each others feathers out.

When they are older and their beaks are stronger, you can switch from cooked and tender greens to grains and weeds. You can take young goslings out to pasture. Grass is an important part of a gosling's diet, as is protein. Feed about 20% protein – eggs are perfect for this.

Adult Food

A diet of mixed grains and greens is sufficient if you keep it varied. Ducks and geese will eat whole ears of corn – this will also prevent the more aggressive birds from hogging the whole food supply. Oats and wheat are good, as are firm fruits and vegetables - apples, beets, turnips, potatoes. Crush them up first – between two boards is ideal.

11.3.4 HOUSING

If you only have a few waterfowl you can keep them with your chickens. Ducks and geese don't roost and will sleep on the floor. Chickens like to peck at ducklings and goslings however, so a separate pen might be necessary for the little ones.

The sheltering options are fairly flexible. You can go for no shelter at all, except perhaps for a windbreak, a three-sided shelter or a complete shelter such as a barn.

No Shelter

Waterfowl will always need shade, but once past 6 weeks old they can do without other shelter as long as you are not having a long run of chilly rain or stormy weather. Adult waterfowl have a thick layer of feathers which are waterproof. Wild ducks build their nests near water on the ground, a wild flock can do just fine with what nature provides, but expect many casualties due to predators and weather.

Some breeds, especially commercial breeds are not so hardy as the wild ones, so at least a minimum shelter is recommended, especially since the weather will most likely be erratic. In a no-shelter environment there is a constant danger of younglings being taken by predators.

Partial Shelter

A 3-sided shelter is a fairly good compromise between shelter and freedom. Waterfowl like plenty of fresh flowing air and will not appreciate a poorly-ventilated structure, but they don't like wind. A 3-sided roofed, shelter only needs to be high enough for protection.

African and Chinese geese are prone to frostbite on their beaks in winter and will need at least minimal shelter.

Total Shelter

Waterfowl can be housed only at night, or permanently. Ducks adapt well to night-time housing only. If there are many predators in your area such as rats, racoons, skunks, weasels, you will probably want to shelter your birds at night to minimise losses.

Some birds are not as hardy as others and will need night-time shelter at least during winter. Ducks will start laying earlier if provided with warm shelter, geese don't care. If your flock is becoming spooked at night, it may help to provide some kind of night-time lighting. Birds that are allowed out to run during the day need about 120 cm (4 ft) square each.

If your shelter is totally confined, you will need to provide at least 180 to 240 cm (6 to 8 ft) per bird. Large but shallow nesting boxes – 40 cm (15 in) square, if located on the floor in a secluded corner – will attract egg-layers. Also ensure there is plenty of ventilation.

11.4 COMMON POULTRY ISSUES

11.4.1 WATER AND FOOD FOR ADULT POULTRY

Poultry need twice as much water as food so you must have clean drinking water available at all times. A water shortage even for a short time will affect growth and egg production.

Poultry have no teeth and swallow their food whole. They have two stomachs, an upper one for food and a lower one – the gizzard – which 'chews' the food by grinding it up with small rocks that the bird will swallow for that purpose.

Train poultry of any variety to come when called by rewarding them with food. Use a distinctive sound like a whistle or hand clap. This makes them easy to lure when necessary.

Food

Poultry will eat peelings, sour or sweet milk, pickles, meat scraps, rancid lard, overripe or damaged vegetables and fruit, pea pods and vines, garden trimmings, general table scraps. Avoid feeding onions, peppers, cabbage or citrus fruits, and don't feed them mouldy food.

Once over 20 weeks old, the birds' gizzards are ideal for grinding grain. A mixture of grain is better than a single grain if possible. Coarser grinds are better than flour or mash, which may get stuck. Some good grains are corn, buckwheat, sorghum heads, oats and barley.

Don't give too much fatty grains such as corn, fat birds don't perform as well. Chickens do not actually need grain at all to live, but will put on a protective layer of fat if fed grain in winter.

If you come across a maggot-ridden carcass (even if it is human), don't let it go to waste. Take your poultry for a walk (on a leash if you need to) and let them feast.

Poultry will need more food during the winter than warmer months to maintain enough fat to stay warm. In a below-freezing environment, the food requirements will be extremely high. A better use of your resources is to take the time to properly insulate their environment.

11.4.2 KILLING POULTRY

There are many ways of killing things. Whichever way you do it, bear in mind that these are living creatures and after a life of servitude, deserve a humane death.

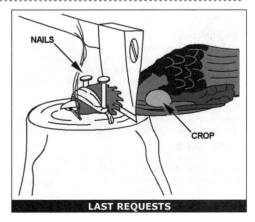

Blood

Be sure to let the bird bleed out properly once killed. Remove the head (if it still has it), and hold the neck over a container or hole in the ground. This will greatly improve eating and keeping quality.

Chopping Block

To hold a bird on a chopping block, drive two nails into the block, spaced so they fit the neck but do not allow the head to slip through. A cloth tied between the nails and across the head will help hold the bird. Gently pull the bird by its feet to stretch its neck enough to drive a sharp axe through. Be careful not to hit the nails (bad for the axe) or the crop (located at the base of the neck). Use a well-aimed, determined and fast blow to ensure you make a clean cut.

Stretching the Neck

This is done by grabbing the bird by its feet and head, and stretching it full length. With a hard, sharp pull, bend the neck backwards to dislocate it.

Wringing the Neck

Grasp the bird by the upper part of the neck or head. Get the body swinging rapidly, like you would a rope on the end of a string. Swing once, twice, thrice, then a sharp downward 'snap'.

Hanging

Tie the bird by its feet to a tree branch. Grasp the head firmly and sever the head with a sharp knife, just at the top of the head. This will allow the blood to drain away without much mess.

11.4.3 PICKING POULTRY

You can simply skin the bird to remove feathers, which is somewhat easier but you miss out on the delicious skin. You can also dry-pick a bird, but an easier method is to scald first, and then pluck. Some very anal people wanting feathers sometimes prefer dry-picked ones.

Scalding and Plucking

To scald and pluck, put a large amount of water on the boil before you kill the bird. The water needs to be 55-80°C (130-180°F). Too hot will loosen the feathers and cook the bird a little, too cold won't do anything. It's better to start too hot than tool cold, and top up as necessary.

Grasp the bird by the ankles and immerse it in the water. If you are using a flat container for the water, dip the breast in first then the back. Make sure the wing and tail feathers get a good scalding as these are the toughest to pull out. 30 seconds should do it, more for large birds, less for smaller ones. Older birds will also need more time.

If the first dip doesn't do it, give another. You need plenty of heat and motion to loosen the feathers. If you soak the dead birds with cold water first, the hot water penetrates easier.

Take the bird out and start plucking. Start with the breast while it is still hot, as the skin is tender and can tear. Then pluck the rest of the feathers, the biggest ones first. Pull the larger feathers in the direction of growing. The smaller ones can be pulled any way you can get them.

Singeing

After the pinfeathers have been removed, down and very fine long hairs will remain. Singe these off by passing quickly over a flame until all remaining down has been burned off.

11.4.4 CLEANING POULTRY

To clean a bird, the head, feet and innards are removed. First put the bird into very cold water to cool the body quickly.

Poultry Tuberculosis (TB)

A bird with TB will feel very light, wasted and the innards will look weird, possibly with abscesses on them (particularly the digestive tract and intestines). If you suspect TB, do not eat the bird.

Head, Feet and Oil Sac

Remove and discard the head if still attached. Carefully feel for the knee joint where the scaly leg meets the feathered knee. Bend the knee and cut across each joint. Cut off the small oil sack at the end of the birds back.

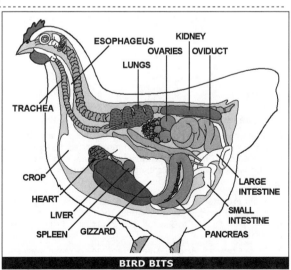

BIRD BITS

Removing the Innards

Place the bird on its back with its hind end closest to you. Cut across the abdomen from thigh to thigh – just above the anus, making sure you do not cut into any of the intestines in the cavity. Reach inside carefully between the intestines and breastbone until you reach heart level. Loosen the membranes between the innards and the body wall, and gently pull the entrails in one mass. The gizzard, heart and liver will come out with it.

Be careful of the gallbladder – a greenish sac embedded in the under-surface of the right lobe of the liver. If this breaks and spills its bile, it will render any part of the chicken it touches bitter and undesirable.

Carefully cut around the excretory vent allowing enough room so you don't cut into it or the attached intestine. This can now be removed with the intestines. The kidneys – a soft, brown tissue in the back cavity – adhere closely and should be at least partly removed. Scoop out what you can with your fingers. Don't worry about getting every last scrap out.

At the front of the bird is a thin-skinned pouch called the 'crop'. This is attached to the esophagus and is the first stomach. Cut the skin on the back of the neck and gently remove the crop from the skin. Carefully pull out the crop, windpipe and esophagus and discard.

Removing Giblets

Giblets mean heart, liver, gizzard, and sometimes the neck. To get the liver, cut the part of it that holds the gallbladder (leave plenty of margin) and discard the gallbladder. Cut the gizzard open along its narrow edge, rinse and discard the insides (rocks and food bits). Peel off the yellowish lining of the gizzard and discard. Cut the heart free from its attached arteries.

11.4.5 CLIPPING WINGS

If you have low fences for your poultry, or are constantly trying to coax birds down from tree limbs, then clipping is necessary. Clip only one wing because birds can learn to fly with two clipped wings. Using heavy scissors, cut the long feathers along one wing when they first develop, and then after each molt – if you keep the birds that long.

11.5 RABBITS

Rabbits are docile, quiet and small animals – perfect for raising for meat and pelts in a situation where you want to keep a low profile. Rabbits are famous for their breeding abilities so as long as you can feed them and keep them healthy, you can have rabbit for dinner every night.

11.5.1 GETTING STARTED

The minimal option is to start with a single pregnant female. It is better however to start with more, such as two pregnant females and the mature male that impregnated them. This will provide some insurance.

The rabbits you acquire will take the transition to their new home better if their diet does not change. Try to find out what they have been fed, how much, and the schedule, gradually changing over time if necessary.

Any new animals you bring into your farm should be quarantined from other animals of their kind for 2 weeks or so. Should a new animal get sick, this will prevent you from losing the lot.

Meat Breeds

Rabbits produce more meat for less feed than any other livestock, and rabbit is the leanest land grown meat. The only 2 commercially sold meat breeds are the New Zealand White and the California. They both produce good pelts and are recommended if you are raising rabbits for survival purposes. Basically though, rabbits are rabbits and you can choose what you like.

Angoras

Angoras are the wool breed of rabbits. This wool is fine for spinning or stuffing. You pull the wool off of them just as they would themselves – do not shear them like a sheep. Even if you do not plan to use the wool, you must still brush or pluck them to keep them clean and healthy.

The wool can be used in small amounts to make warm nests for baby animals, just as the angora rabbits do themselves for their young.

11.5.2 HOUSING

Rabbits cannot stand too much heat. Their shelter should protect against predators and excessive heat build-up. If very hot days are an issue in your climate, their shelter should be shaded by a tree, or a double roof. Make sure they have plenty of water on hot days.

Predators

Rabbits are defenceless and fairly low on the food chain. Predators include dogs and cats – wild or tame, large birds of prey, coyotes, wildcats and foxes. Even if a predator can't get through a well-built cage, the scare might be enough to cause the female to kill and/or eat her young.

Young children should be treated as predators as they may leave a cage door open, upset a new mother and cause cannibalism, or feed a poisonous plant.

House Rabbits

Rabbits can be litter-box trained. Do this by leaving a few papers down where you want the rabbit to potty. It helps to demonstrate by leaving some rabbit droppings and urine on the paper. The biggest problem with rabbits raised indoors is that you must be careful taking them outdoors – since they are used to indoors, they can get sick easier than an outside rabbit.

Rabbit Runs

A rabbit run is a large area where rabbits run free. Such an arrangement can house dozens of rabbits, even hundreds. The advantages are low stress, potentially less feeding, better meat because of exercise, better pelts because of cold air, and generally better immune systems.

Bear in mind they will be less likely to act like pets and will be harder to catch. To catch them easier – always feed them in one corner of the run, and when it's time to catch them, have someone hold a barrier across the corner while you catch them.

A rabbit run can take many forms —

Enclosed Garage	A garage with a dirt or wooden floor. If the floor is concrete it will prevent the rabbits burrowing to freedom. If you provide a thick layer of earth over the concrete it will provide comfort and warmth.
Open Area	An area with a wall of at least 1.2 m (4 ft) high can house rabbits quite happily. Rabbits in the open will be alert to birds in the area and develop places to hide, alternatively you can provide one.
	The wall should be dug deep enough into the ground to prevent the rabbits burrowing under.
Fenced Pit	A pit can be dug in the ground with loose hay inside to provide bedding. Care must be taken to ensure the pit does not fill with water in heavy rains – provide a plastic, tin or thatched roof and build up the sides.
Portable Pasture Run	An A-frame cage that can be moved around is an ideal enclosure for rabbits. It should have a solid wooden shelter at one end to protect from the weather, and wire on the other sides to let in fresh air and sunshine.
	There is no floor as it is moved around to green pasture as the rabbits feed.
	A similar setup is good for chickens as well, and the manure the animals drop will fertilize the ground, making it suitable for growing food later.
TYPES OF RABBIT RUNS	

Flooring for Rabbits

The rabbits will be happy in any building as long as you don't mind the floor being covered in manure. Concrete is fine for rabbits and easy to clean – shovel out and hose down. A wooden floor will eventually rot, but this can be delayed by laying down heavy plastic. Better flooring for rabbits is a dry dirt floor, or best of all, green pasture.

Cages and Hutches

Cages can be made of wood or wire. You can make them single or built as units in a row. A rule of thumb is 30 cm (1 ft) square floor space for every 0.5 kg (1 lb) of rabbits living there. A minimum size is roughly 60 x 90 cm (2 x 3 ft). When you build it, make sure you can reach every corner from the door, else a reluctant bunny may put themselves out of your reach.

Another option is a hutch that built out in the open. These cages are built solidly enough to stand outside and still keep the occupants warm. A good hutch is fairly large, airy and up on posts. To protect from draughts in colder weather, consider placing a skirting around the bottom, maybe a temporary one that can be removed in summer.

You can have a door on the side, or the roof may be hinged. A hinged roof is an easier building option and will make catching bunnies easier in a larger cage.

Make sure the roof includes overhanging eaves to protect against excessive sunshine and rain.

The sides can be wire all round, solid on three sides

OUTDOOR HUTCH

and only wire at the front, or anywhere in between. This depends on your climate. If you use poultry wire, check it regularly for tears – a determined rabbit may make holes in it with its teeth. Wire will weaken with age.

The flooring can be wood or wire. A wooden floor will be chewed on, soaked with urine, smell and generally are not considered as healthy as wire. However, the rabbits will be happy on them as long as they are in good condition.

There should be at least some solid flooring because rabbits need to eat their night time feces.

11.5.3 WATER

Rabbits must be supplied with plentiful clean water. Clean out the water dish often, because hair and feces will get into it. It is important to shelter the water dish from bird droppings which can cause coccidiosis.

In hot weather supply as much as 5 litres (1 gallon) per day for a doe plus her family. If you haven't got a large container, be sure to check it during the day, especially if it's hot.

If their water freezes in the winter, go out twice a day with warm water. Hanging water bottles are suitable for a single rabbit in a cage, but not for large groups. They are not suitable in freezing climates. A good container is about 9 cm (3.5 in) high and too heavy to be tipped over, or fixed to the cage.

11.5.4 FOOD

In the wild, rabbits have the experience to know the right foods from the wrong foods, but domesticated rabbits rely on their keepers to know the difference. You won't be able to feed your rabbits pellets forever so you must grow food and/or feed them scraps.

RABBIT FEEDING TIPS

- Rabbits need a regular feeding schedule, same time each day, same number of feedings, same order of various feeds. Most people feed them in the morning and afternoon.
- Rabbits are physically unable to eat fine foods such as powder or finely ground meal
- Cut hay-type feed into sections no longer than 8 cm (3 in)
- Rabbits don't like oily foods

- Rabbits are very vulnerable to insecticides
- Wash garden foods before feeding as an accumulation of dirt can make a rabbit sick.
- Slice root vegetables into sticks
- Don't feed soggy, rotten food
- Introduce new feed gradually
- Don't feed potato sprouts, eyes or peels
- Eating spoiled – yellowish or fermented – greens can make a rabbit very sick

- It is normal and necessary for rabbits to eat their own night time feces. They do this in the late night and early morning hours. The night droppings are loaded with B vitamins, and are essential for the rabbit's health.

How Much Feed?

Like many animals, rabbits vary in the amount of food they take. Some rabbits can eat themselves to illness if not limited. An overweight doe will have trouble getting pregnant and will have more risky birth. Obese bucks may lose interest in mating with the does.

One of the easiest ways to control their feed amounts is the feed them hay, all they want. Rabbits very seldom overeat on hay. Then just give small, measured amounts of richer food.

Pregnant and nursing does and young bunnies should generally be allowed to eat all they like, until they are about 6 months old.

SUITABLE RABBIT FOODS

- Acacia: has no food value, but twigs can be entertainment
- Alfalfa: fresh or hay
- Apples: all parts
- Barley
- Beans and bean vines (not soybean)
- Beets: both top and root of regular sugar, or mangel
- Bermuda grass
- Blackberry bush leaves
- Bluegrasses
- Bread: dry, or soaked in milk
- Buckwheat
- Cabbage: not too much
- Canadian bluegrass
- Carpet grass
- Carrot: root and tops.
- Cereals (if fat-free and fresh)
- Cheeseweed (malva)
- Chicories
- Clovers: any but sweet clover
- Coltsfoot
- Corn
- Cow parsnip
- Crabgrass
- Dandelion
- Dogwood
- Fescue: red, etc.
- Filaree (stork's bill)
- Grains: any, unless dirty, damp, or moldy
- Grapefruit: all parts (don't feed too much)
- Grass/lawn clippings, grass grains: as long as they bear no insecticides
- Hazelnut leaves
- Jerusalem artichokes: tops, stems, roots
- Kale
- Kentucky bluegrass
- Knotgrass Kohlrabi: all parts of plant okay to feed
- Lettuce: all kinds
- Malva (cheeseweed)
- Meadow fescue
- Milk: fresh or sour, as well as milk products
- Millet: foxtail and Japanese
- Milo
- Napier grass
- Oats
- Oranges: all parts (don't feed too much)
- Orchard grass
- Panicgrass
- Parsnips
- Peas and pea vines
- Plantain
- Poplar
- Potato: but not peelings, sprouts or leaves
- Prairie grass
- Redtop grass
- Rhodes grass
- Root vegetables
- Rye, rye grass, and Italian rye grass
- Sheep sorrel
- Sorghum grains
- Sprouted grains
- Sudan grass
- Sumac
- Sunflower leaves or seeds
- Sweet potatoes: vines or tubers
- Turnips: all parts of plant
- Vetch
- Wheat
- Willow

NOT GOOD FOR RABBITS!

- Amaranth
- Arrowgrass
- Bracken fern
- Bromweed
- Buckeye
- Burdock
- Castor beans
- Chinaberry
- Chokecherry leaves or pits
- Comfrey
- Fireweed
- Foxglove
- Goldenrod
- Hemlock, poison/water
- Horehound
- Jimson weed
- Johnson grass
- Larkspur
- Laurel
- Lima beans
- Lupine
- Mesquite
- Milkweed
- Miner's lettuce
- Moldy bread: or moldy anything
- Oak
- Oleander
- Pigweed
- Poppy
- Potato leaves, sprouts, or peelings
- Rhubarb leaves
- Soybeans or soybean vines
- Spinach
- Sweet clover
- Swiss chard
- Tarweed
- Tomato leaves

These range from having no nutritional value, to being deadly poisonous.

Hay and Grain Diet

A diet of mixed grains is more nutritious than any single grain. Feed mixed grains for 30% of the rabbit's diet by weight. Oats, soft wheats, and grain sorghums are rabbit favourites.

Protein is a small but extremely important necessity in a rabbit's diet. They can get some from grain and good legume hay, but none from non-legume hay. Any grains may be fed whole, although chopped is better, except for oats which should be rolled, mashed or ground.

Dry corn kernels should also be cracked, don't get them too small.

Feed good alfalfa hay for the remaining 70% of the diet. Good hay is very leafy, has thin stems and clean of mold or dirt. It will smell fresh. Good alfalfa hay has around 12 to 14% protein.

Home Grown Rabbit Food

Pea and bean vines can be cured down as a good substitute for hay. Stock beets and cabbage are suitable winter feed. In season, rabbits like anything green, but be careful not to feed them anything outrightly poisonous, such as chokecherry or rhubarb leaves, or potato peels with sprouts, or ones in the sun long enough to get even the slightest touch of green.

Some greens are only mildly poisonous when uncooked, such as pigweed, amaranth greens, spinach, comfrey, and swiss chard – but for the rabbit, these can be a problem.

Stick to feeding them human-type salad greens unless you are sure a wild food is safe. If cooking is advised for a green food (the amaranth family), do not feed it to the rabbit (who would be eating it raw). Plant extra rows of lettuce for the rabbits, and when weeding in the summer, collect the edible ones.

Salt

Rabbits enjoy a salt-and-mineral block in their hutch. They'll lick it for the food value, and are less likely to gnaw on their cage. Don't give them iodized table salt. Rabbits also like bones and toys to chew on. You can combine the two by soaking a lump of non-resinous wood in very salty water for about 3 days. Air-dry it and give it to your rabbit.

11.5.5 BREEDING

Simply put the doe (female) into the buck's (male) cage. **Don't put the buck in with the doe!** As the doe has motherly instinct to protect her hutch. If she has been in there a while, she may even attack after another doe is introduced.

If your doe is not pregnant, she will let the buck mount her. It takes about 1 minute to be over. The buck may tumble over on his side at the conclusion. This is normal. After about a minute to recover, he will be ready to mate again. If the doe is receptive, you can allow a second mating, but then get her out of there. Don't leave them in together.

For the best chance of conception, bring the doe back 6 hours after the first mating.

Maternity Cage

When does aren't bred, they can be housed together, but a doe who is expecting needs separate quarters in a pen that provides her with a nesting box and plenty of room for the litter – a couple of square metres at least. Make sure the door is big enough to get the nesting box in and out, and the cage is shaped so you can reach into the corners.

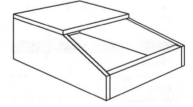

Nesting Box

The nesting box should be like a separate little room inside the larger cage she lives in. It should at least have sides and a top. This allows her to pretend she is in a burrow. Almost fully enclosed is best. You can improvise one from rabbit wire lined internally with cardboard.

Dimensions are about 30 cm x 45-60 cm (12 in x 18-24 in) and about 30 cm (12 in) tall.

Kindling Management

To test for pregnancy you can put the doe into the buck's cage when she's supposed to be 2 weeks pregnant. If she lets him mount her, she's probably not pregnant. But be prepared to get her out quick, because if she really is pregnant she'll fight him.

Another way to test is to feel her abdomen. Baby rabbits inside feel like marbles. The problem with this is that you usually have to press so hard to feel them, that it can harm them.

Check the doe for being overweight because an obese doe may die during kindling or deliver dead babies. Put her on a diet if needed, early in the pregnancy. A few days of short rations generally does it. Rabbit pregnancy lasts 28-35 days, but most rabbits kindle on day 31 or 32.

As her pregnancy progresses, gradually increase the amount of protein in their feed. Towards the end, let her eat all she can. If she doesn't get enough food at this stage, she may abort some of the babies. Get her moved into a maternity pen well before the due date.

5 Days Before Kindling (Giving Birth)
About 5 days before the due date, move a nest box into her private hutch. Provide her with ample straw, hay, maybe even some cotton rags if it is cold. She will use it to make a nest. She will pull out some of her own fur to line her nest – you can help her out if you collect pieces of rabbit fur you find when cleaning the cages. Save them in a dry spot until needed.

Kindling Day 1
First time mothers can be a worry. If she made a nest but didn't give birth inside it, they may die of exposure. If you find them alive, then wait till the mother is out of the nest and gently place the babies in there. It helps to smear a salve (e.g. vapo-rub) or something similar on the mother's nose to desensitise her sense of smell, and decrease the risk of her rejecting them.

If the mother gets upset at this stage – say from a dog, change in feed, water shortage, too much handling, or is just that way inclined – she may cannibalise the babies. If this happens then give her 1 or 2 more chances to raise a family, after that eat her or put her in a nunnery.

Day 2 / Day 3 / Day 6
If all babies appear to be in the nest, wait 24 hours and check them on day 2 for the sake of mum's nerves. Get the doe out of there, rub salve on her nose and check the nest. Rabbits may have up to 16 babies, but most won't successfully nurse more than 8 – more than that are best fostered out. Remove dead babies from the nest.

Day 10
The little bunnies will be opening their eyes and becoming active at this stage. You do not need to supply food as mothers milk is enough. Make sure the mother is well fed.

Day 21
The bunnies can start eating something besides mother's milk now. Milk soaked bread is a good first supplement. Very young rabbits have delicate digestive tracts, add new foods gradually. Avoid foods with a harsh texture. Home grown grain should be crushed and de-husked.

Day 56
It's at this stage that meat rabbits should be butchered and the mother re-bred. If you wait too long to re-breed the rabbit, she may become sterile. If you leave the rabbit brothers and sisters together, at this stage they will start breeding with each other like the royal family.

If you want to breed them rather than butcher them, then proceed as above with the cycle of reproduction. If you want them to continue eating then it's best to house the sexes in different accommodation. Any rabbit you don't want to keep for reproduction should be butchered at 13 weeks (91 days) because after that the feed conversion efficiency goes down.

11.5.6 RABBIT BUTCHERING

Rabbit meat is the leanest of all non-fish meats. Precise weight at butchering age varies between breeds. The meat you end up with will be about half the live weight. Young rabbits can be distinguished by their soft ears and paws – stiffness is a sign of age. An old rabbit can be stewed like a chicken. Rabbit meat is almost fat free.

Killing
Some recommend that you stun the rabbit first with a sharp blow to the head, right behind the ears, then chop the head off on the chopping block as close to the head as possible.

Some people find it difficult to get a well-placed effective blow and prefer to begin by snapping the neck. To do this, hold the rabbit's hind legs about chest-high – hanging down with the belly facing you, and hold the head firmly around the neck with your dominant hand.

Pull the body down by the neck, and bend the head up and back as far as possible at the same time as you pull down. Do this with a steady firm motion until you feel the neck snap.

With an axe and chopping block, or sharp knife, cut through the spinal column cartilage. Hold the rabbit upside down or hang it for a few minutes to bleed them out.

Hanging

You can hang a rabbit in the same manner as large animals: Cut the skin from the hock joint (ankle) toward the body and peel it back to expose the Achilles tendons.

Insert hooks or rope between the bone and Achilles tendons just above the hock. Alternatively, you can tie a couple of loops around each leg as illustrated.

Skinning

With the rabbit hung, cut off the front feet and tail. With a small sharp knife, slit the skin between the hock and crotch on the inside of each leg.

Cut the skin from each front leg to the neck. Do not cut down the belly centreline at this time. Then peel the skin down off the body, starting at the hind hocks, like taking off a banana peel or sock.

Cut around the anal opening and any place the skin is not coming off freely. Pull the skin off inside out, clear down to the front feet. Then it should be off completely.

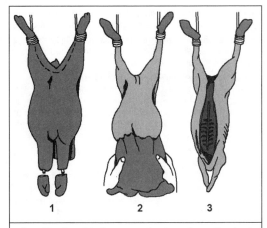

1) Slit the skin between the legs from the hock joints to root of tail (dotted line).

2) Peel off the skin like you are peeling off a sweater.

3) Cut around anal vent and down abdomen. Remove innards.

HANGING AND SKINNING A RABBIT

If you have taken the skin off cleanly, See **Tanning Animal Hides** (Page 9-8) to use it.

Easy Skinning

If you don't care about the skin, skinning is easy. Just hold the rabbit by a hind leg and with your other hand, pinch the hide at the hock joint and pull downward. The skin will tear at this point and you can peel it off without a knife. Alternatively, you can remove the head and feet, then pinch up the hide in the middle of the back and cut through it with a knife. Then grasp the hide on either side of the cut and pull away.

Cleaning (Dressing)

You can take the animal down from the hanging position, or work on it in place. Cut around the anal vent and then toward the breastbone along the middle of the abdomen, being careful not to sever any intestines. You may want to keep a finger inside to keep the intestines away from the knife. You may or may not cut through the breastbone (or "brisket") to the neck.

Pull out the intestines. If you didn't cut the breastbone, reach up into the chest and pull out the heart and lungs. You will have to help the lungs out because they will stick in the cavity.

Save the heart, and pause to take a careful look at the liver.

If the liver has white coccidiosis spots, dispose of the carcass. Do not eat the meat. The liver need not to be fully spotted, any slight discoloration is a sign of infection.

If the liver tissue has white streaks or there are small, white cysts attached to the stomach or intestinal membranes, that's tapeworm. Don't feed the uncooked intestines to other animals. You may eat the animal, but it must be thoroughly cooked – like pork or long pork.

Cutting It Up

First cut off both front legs at the shoulder joints and both hind legs at the hip joints. Cut through the ribs on both the left and right sides, parallel to the backbone, to cut free the breast piece of the rabbit carcass. The big meat pieces are found on the hind legs and the haunches (loins) where they are easy to cut from the body. The loin pieces are choicest on the rabbit, great for stews. It's a good idea to bone the thigh, leaving the shank intact. The forelegs of a rabbit have very little meat and are best used in the stock pot.

12 DESERT SURVIVAL

To survive and evade in arid or desert areas, you must understand and prepare for the environment you will face. You must determine your equipment needs, the tactics you will use, and how the environment will affect you and your tactics. Your survival will depend upon your knowledge of the terrain, basic climatic elements, your ability to cope with these elements, and your will to survive.

12.1 TERRAIN

Most arid areas have several types of terrain. The five basic desert terrain types are —

- Mountainous (High Altitude).
- Rocky plateau.
- Sand dunes.
- Salt marshes.
- Broken, dissected terrain ("gebel" or "wadi").

Desert terrain makes movement difficult and demanding. Land navigation will be extremely difficult as there may be very few landmarks.

Cover and concealment may be very limited; therefore, the threat of exposure to the enemy remains constant.

Mountain Deserts

Scattered ranges or areas of barren hills or mountains separated by dry, flat basins characterize mountain deserts. High ground may rise gradually or abruptly from flat areas to several thousand meters above sea level. Most of the infrequent rainfall occurs on high ground and runs off rapidly in the form of flash floods. These floodwaters erode deep gullies and ravines and deposit sand and gravel around the edges of the basins. Water rapidly evaporates, leaving the land as barren as before, although there may be short-lived vegetation. If enough water enters the basin to compensate for the rate of evaporation, shallow lakes may develop, such as the Great Salt Lake in Utah. Most of these lakes have a high salt content.

Rocky Plateau Deserts

Rocky plateau deserts have relatively slight relief interspersed with extensive flat areas with quantities of solid or broken rock at or near the surface. There may be steep-walled, eroded valleys, known as wadis in the Middle East and arroyos or canyons in the United States and Mexico. Although their flat bottoms may be superficially attractive as assembly areas, the narrower valleys can be extremely dangerous to men and material due to flash flooding after rains. The Golan Heights is an example of a rocky plateau desert.

Sandy or Dune Deserts

Sandy or dune deserts are extensive flat areas covered with sand or gravel. "Flat" is a relative term, as some areas may contain sand dunes that are over 300 meters high and 16 - 24 km long. Traffic ability in such terrain will depend on the windward slope of the dunes and the texture of the sand. Other areas, however, may be flat for 3 kilometres or more. Plant life may vary from none to scrub over 2 meters high. Examples of this type of desert include the edges of the Sahara, areas of California and New Mexico, and the Kalahari in South Africa.

Salt Marshes

Salt marshes are flat, desolate areas, sometimes studded with clumps of grass but devoid of other vegetation. They occur in arid areas where rainwater has collected, evaporated, and left large deposits of alkali salts and water with a high salt concentration. The water is so salty it is undrinkable. A crust that may be 2.5 - 30 cm thick forms over the saltwater.

In arid areas there are huge salt marshes. These areas usually support many biting insects. Avoid salt marshes. This type of terrain is highly corrosive to boots, clothing, and skin.

Broken Terrain

All arid areas contain broken terrain. Rainstorms that erode soft sand and carve out canyons form this terrain. A wadi may range from 3 meters wide and 2 meters deep to several hundred meters wide and deep. The direction it takes varies as much as its width and depth. It twists and turns and forms a mazelike pattern. A wadi will give you good cover and concealment, but do not try to move through it because it is very difficult terrain to negotiate.

12.2 ENVIRONMENTAL FACTORS

Surviving and evading the enemy in an arid area depends on what you know and how prepared you are for the environmental conditions you will face. Determine what equipment you will need, the tactics you will use, and the environment's impact on them and you.

In a desert area there are seven environmental factors that you must consider —

- Low rainfall
- Intense sunlight and heat
- Wide temperature range
- Sparse vegetation
- High mineral content near ground surface
- Sandstorms
- Mirages

Low Rainfall

Some areas receive less than 10 cm of rain annually, and this rain comes in brief torrents that quickly run off the ground. You cannot survive long without water in high desert temperatures. You must first consider "How much water do I have?" and "Where are other water sources?"

Intense Sunlight and Heat

Air temperature can rise as high as 60°C (140°F) during the day. Heat gain results from direct sunlight, hot blowing winds, reflective heat (the sun's rays bouncing off the sand), and conductive heat from direct contact with the desert sand and rock.

The temperature of desert sand and rock averages 16 - 22°C (30 - 40°F) more than the air.

Intense sunlight and heat increase the body's need for water. To conserve your body fluids and energy, you will need a shelter to reduce your exposure to the heat of the day. Travel at night to lessen your use of water.

Radios and sensitive items of equipment exposed to direct intense sunlight may malfunction.

Wide Temperature Range

Temperatures in arid areas may get as high as 55°C during the day and as low as -10°C during the night. The drop in temperature at night occurs rapidly and will chill a person who lacks warm clothing. The cool evenings and nights are the best times to work or travel. For the night you will find a wool sweater, long underwear, and a wool stocking cap extremely helpful.

Sparse Vegetation

Vegetation is sparse in arid areas. You will therefore have trouble finding shelter and camouflaging your movements. During daylight hours large areas of terrain are visible and easily controlled by a small opposing force.

If travelling in hostile territory, follow the principles of desert camouflage —

- Hide or seek shelter in dry washes (wadis) with thicker growths of vegetation and cover from oblique observation.
- Use the shadows cast from brush, rocks, or outcropping. The temperature in shaded areas will be 11 - 17°C cooler than the air temperature.
- Cover objects that will reflect the light from the sun.

Before moving, survey the area for sites that provide cover. You will have trouble estimating distance. The emptiness of desert terrain causes most people to underestimate distance by a factor of three: What appears to be 1 km away is really 3 km away.

High Mineral Content

All arid regions have areas where the surface soil has a high mineral content (borax, salt, alkali, and lime). Material in contact with this soil wears out quickly, and water in these areas is extremely hard and undrinkable. Wetting your uniform in such water to cool off may cause a skin rash. The Great Salt Lake area is an example of this type of mineral-laden water and soil. There is little or no plant life; there-fore, shelter is hard to find. Avoid these areas if possible.

Sandstorms

Sandstorms occur frequently in most deserts. The greatest danger is getting lost in a swirling wall of sand. Wear goggles and cover your mouth and nose with cloth. If natural shelter is unavailable, mark your direction of travel, lie down, and sit out the storm.

Mirages

Mirages occur in the interior of the desert about 10 km from the coast. They make objects that are 1.5 km or more away appear to move. This mirage effect makes it difficult for you to identify an object from a distance. It also blurs distant range contours so much that you feel surrounded by a sheet of water from which elevations stand out as "islands."

Light levels in desert areas are more intense than in other geographic areas. Moonlit nights are usually crystal clear, winds die down, haze and glare disappear, and visibility is excellent. You can see lights at great distances. Sound carries very far. Conversely, during nights with little moonlight, visibility is extremely poor. Travelling is extremely hazardous.

12.3 NEED FOR WATER

The subject of man and water in the desert has generated considerable interest and confusion since the early days of World War II when the U.S. Army was preparing to fight in North Africa. At one time the U.S. Army thought it could condition men to do with less water by progressively reducing their water supplies during training. They called it water discipline. It caused many deaths.

The body requires a certain amount of water for a certain level of activity at a certain temperature. For example, a person performing hard work in the sun at 43°C (104°F) can require 19 litres of water daily. Lack of the required amount of water causes a rapid decline in an individual's ability to make decisions and to perform tasks efficiently.

Your body's normal temperature is 36.9°C (98.6°F). Your body gets rid of excess heat (cools off) by sweating. The warmer your body becomes – whether caused by work, exercise, or air temperature — the more you sweat. The more you sweat, the more moisture you lose. Sweating is the principal cause of water loss. If a person stops sweating during periods of high air temperature and heavy work or exercise, they will quickly develop heat stroke. This is an emergency that requires immediate medical attention.

Understanding how the air temperature and your physical activity affect your water requirements allows you to take measures to get the most from your water supply. These measures are —

- **Find shade!** Get out of the sun!
- Place something between you and the hot ground.
- **Limit your movements!**
- **Conserve your sweat.** Wear your complete uniform to include T-shirt. Roll the sleeves down, cover your head, and protect your neck with a scarf or similar item. These steps will protect your body from hot-blowing winds and the direct rays of the sun. Your clothing will absorb your sweat, keeping it against your skin so that you gain its full cooling effect. By staying in the shade quietly, fully clothed, not talking, keeping your mouth closed, and breathing through your nose, your water requirement for survival drops dramatically.
- If water is scarce, **do not eat.** Food requires water for digestion; therefore, eating food will use water that you need for cooling.
- If you must eat, eat small morsels at a time. Eating a large meal requires a large amount of water to digest. Your body is more efficient with its water when eating small amounts.

Thirst is not a reliable guide for your need for water. A person who uses thirst as a guide will drink only two-thirds of their daily water requirement. To prevent this "voluntary" dehydration, use the following guide —

- At temperatures below 38°C (100°F), drink 0.5 litre of water every hour.
- At temperatures above 38°C, drink 1 litre of water every hour.

Drinking water at regular intervals helps your body remain cool and decreases sweating. Even when your water supply is low, sipping water constantly will keep your body cooler and reduce water loss through sweating. Conserve your fluids by reducing activity during the heat of day. Do not ration your water! If you try to ration water, you stand a good chance of becoming a heat casualty.

12.4 HEAT CASUALTIES

Your chances of becoming a heat casualty as a survivor are great, due to injury, stress, and lack of critical items of equipment. Following are the major types of heat casualties and their treatment when little water and no medical help are available.

Heat Cramps

The loss of salt due to excessive sweating causes heat cramps. Symptoms are moderate to severe muscle cramps in legs, arms, or abdomen. These symptoms may start as a mild muscular discomfort. You should then stop all activity, get in the shade, and drink water. If you fail to recognize the early symptoms and continue your physical activity, you will have severe muscle cramps and pain. Treat as for heat exhaustion, below.

Heat Exhaustion

A large loss of body water and salt causes heat exhaustion. Symptoms are headache, mental confusion, irritability, excessive sweating, weakness, dizziness, cramps, and pale, clammy skin. Immediately get the patient under shade. Make them lie on a stretcher or similar item about 45 cm off the ground. Loosen their clothing. Sprinkle them with water and fan them. Have them drink small amounts of water every 3 minutes. Ensure they stay quiet and rest.

Heat Stroke

Heat stroke is a severe injury caused by extreme loss of water and salt and the body's inability to cool itself. The patient may die if not cooled immediately. Symptoms are the lack of sweat, hot and dry skin, headache, dizziness, fast pulse, nausea and vomiting, and mental confusion leading to unconsciousness. Immediately get the person to shade. Lay them on a stretcher or similar item about 45 cm off the ground. Loosen their clothing. Pour water on them (it does not matter if the water is polluted or brackish) and fan them. Massage their arms, legs, and body. If they regain consciousness, let them drink small amounts of water every 3 minutes.

12.5 PRECAUTIONS

In a desert survival and evasion situation, it is unlikely that you will have a medic or medical supplies with you to treat heat injuries. Therefore, take extra care to avoid heat injuries. Rest during the day, work during the cool evenings and nights. Use a buddy system to watch for heat injury, and observe the following guidelines —

- Make sure you tell someone where you are going and when you will return.
- Watch for signs of heat injury. If someone complains of tiredness or wanders away from the group, they may be a heat casualty.
- Drink water at least once an hour.
- Get in the shade when resting; do not lie directly on the ground.
- Do not take off your shirt and work during the day.
- Check the colour of your urine. A light colour means you are drinking enough water, a dark colour means you need to drink more.

12.6 DESERT HAZARDS

There are several hazards unique to desert survival. These include insects, snakes, thorned plants and cacti, contaminated water, sunburn, eye irritation, and climatic stress.

Insects of almost every type abound in the desert. Man, as a source of water and food, attracts lice, mites, wasps, and flies. They are extremely unpleasant and may carry diseases. Old buildings, ruins, and caves are favourite habitats of spiders, scorpions, centipedes, lice, and mites. These areas provide protection from the elements and also attract other wild-life.

Wear gloves at all times in the desert. Do not place your hands anywhere without first looking to see what is there. Visually inspect an area before sitting or lying down. When you get up, shake out and inspect your boots and clothing. All desert areas have snakes.

They inhabit ruins, native villages, garbage dumps, caves, and natural rock outcroppings that offer shade. Never go barefoot or walk through these areas without carefully inspecting them for snakes. Pay attention to where you place your feet and hands. Most snakebites result from stepping on or handling snakes. Avoid them. Once you see a snake, give it a wide berth.

13 TROPICAL SURVIVAL

Knowledge of field skills, the ability to improvise, and the application of the principles of survival will increase the prospects of survival. Do not be afraid of being alone in the jungle; fear will lead to panic. Panic will lead to exhaustion and decrease your chance of survival.

Everything in the jungle thrives, including disease germs and parasites. Nature will provide water, food, and plenty of materials to build shelters.

Indigenous peoples have lived for millennia by hunting and gathering. However, it will take an outsider some time to get used to the conditions and the non-stop activity of tropical survival.

13.1 TROPICAL WEATHER

High temperatures, heavy rainfall, and oppressive humidity characterize equatorial and subtropical regions, except at high altitudes. At low altitudes, temperature variation is seldom less than 10°C and is often more than 35°C. At altitudes over 1,500 meters, ice often forms at night. The rain has a cooling effect, but when it stops, the temperature soars.

Rainfall is heavy, often with thunder and lightning. Sudden rain beats on the tree canopy, turning trickles into raging torrents and causing rivers to rise. Just as suddenly, the rain stops. Violent storms may occur, usually toward the end of the summer months.

Hurricanes, cyclones, and typhoons develop over the sea and rush inland, causing tidal waves and devastation ashore. In choosing campsites, make sure you are above any potential flooding. Prevailing winds vary between winter and summer. The dry season has rain once a day and the monsoon has continuous rain. In Southeast Asia, winds from the Indian Ocean bring the monsoon, but it is dry when the wind blows from the landmass of China.

Tropical day and night are of equal length. Darkness falls quickly and daybreak is just as sudden.

13.2 JUNGLE TYPES

There is no standard jungle. The tropical area may be any of the following —

- Rain forests.
- Secondary jungles.
- Semi-evergreen seasonal and monsoon forests.
- Scrub and thorn forests.
- Savannas.
- Saltwater swamps.
- Freshwater swamps.

Tropical Rain Forests

The climate varies little in rain forests. You find these forests across the equator in the Amazon and Congo basins, parts of Indonesia, and several Pacific islands. Up to 3.5 meters of rain fall evenly throughout the year. Temperatures range from about 35°C in the day to 20°C at night.

There are five layers of vegetation in this jungle. Where untouched by man, jungle trees rise from buttress roots to heights of 60 meters. Below them, smaller trees produce a canopy so thick that little light reaches the jungle floor. Seedlings struggle beneath them to reach light, and masses of vines and lianas twine up to the sun. Ferns, mosses, and herbaceous plants push through a thick carpet of leaves, and a great variety of fungi grow on leaves and fallen tree trunks.

Because of the lack of light on the jungle floor, there is little undergrowth to hamper movement, but dense growth limits visibility to about 50 meters. You can easily lose your sense of direction in this jungle. It is extremely hard for aircraft to see you, which can be an advantage.

Secondary Jungles

Secondary jungle is very similar to rain forest. Prolific growth, where sunlight penetrates to the jungle floor, typifies this type of forest.

Such growth happens mainly along river banks, on jungle fringes, and where man has cleared rain forest.

When abandoned, tangled masses of vegetation quickly reclaim these cultivated areas. You can often find cultivated food plants among this vegetation.

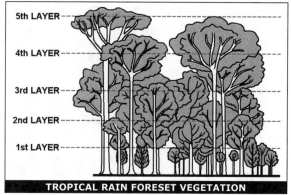

5th LAYER
4th LAYER
3rd LAYER
2nd LAYER
1st LAYER

TROPICAL RAIN FORESET VEGETATION

Semi-evergreen Seasonal and Monsoon Forests

The characteristics of the American and African semi-evergreen seasonal forests correspond with those of the Asian monsoon forests. These characteristics are —

- Their trees fall into two stories of tree strata. Those in the upper story average 18 to 24 meters; those in the lower story average 7 to 13 meters.
- The diameter of the trees averages 0.5 meter.
- Their leaves fall during a seasonal drought.

Except for the sago, nipa, and coconut palms, the same edible plants grow in these areas as in the tropical rain forests.

Tropical Scrub and Thorn Forests

The chief characteristics of tropical scrub and thorn forests are —

- There is a definite dry season.
- Trees are leafless during the dry season.
- The ground is bare except for a few tufted plants in bunches; grasses are uncommon.
- Plants with thorns predominate.
- Fires occur frequently.

Within the tropical scrub and thorn forest areas, you will find it hard to obtain food plants during the dry season. During the rainy season, plants are considerably more abundant.

Tropical Savannas

General characteristics of the savannah are —

- It is found within the tropical zones in South America and Africa.
- It looks like a broad, grassy meadow, with trees spaced at wide intervals.
- It frequently has red soil.
- It grows scattered trees that usually appear stunted and gnarled like apple trees. Palms also occur on savannas.

Saltwater Swamps

Saltwater swamps are common in coastal areas subject to tidal flooding. Mangrove trees thrive in these swamps. Mangrove trees can reach heights of 12 meters, and their tangled roots are an obstacle to movement. Visibility in this type of swamp is poor, and movement is extremely difficult. Sometimes, streams that you can raft form channels, but you usually must travel on foot through this swamp.

Everything in a saltwater swamp may appear hostile to you, from leeches and insects to crocodiles and caimans.

Avoid the dangerous animals in this swamp, avoid this swamp altogether if you can. If there are water channels through it, you may be able to use a raft to escape.

Freshwater Swamps

You find freshwater swamps in low-lying inland areas. Their characteristics are masses of thorny undergrowth, reeds, grasses, and occasional short palms that reduce visibility and make travel difficult. There are often islands that dot these swamps, allowing you to get out of the water. Wildlife is abundant in these swamps.

13.3 TRAVEL THROUGH JUNGLE AREAS

With practice, movement through thick undergrowth and jungle can be done efficiently. Always wear long sleeves to avoid cuts and scratches.

To move easily, you must develop "jungle eye," that is, you should not concentrate on the pattern of bushes and trees to your immediate front. Focus on the jungle further out and find natural breaks in the foliage. Look through the jungle, not at it. Stop and stoop down occasionally to look along the jungle floor. This may reveal game trails that you can follow.

Stay alert and move slowly and steadily through dense forest. Stop periodically to listen and take your bearings. Use a machete to cut through dense vegetation, but do not cut unnecessarily or you will quickly wear yourself out.

If using a machete, stroke upward when cutting vines to reduce noise because sound carries long distances in the jungle. Use a stick to part the vegetation. Using a stick will also help dislodge biting ants, spiders, or snakes. Do not grasp at brush or vines when climbing slopes; they may have irritating spines or sharp thorns.

Many jungle and forest animals follow game trails. These trails wind and cross, but frequently lead to water or clearings. Use these trails if they lead in your desired direction of travel.

In many countries, electric and telephone lines run for miles through sparsely inhabited areas. Usually, the right-of-way is clear enough to allow easy travel. When travelling along these lines, be careful as you approach transformer and relay stations. In enemy territory, they may be guarded.

Travel Tips

- Pinpoint your initial location as accurately as possible to determine a general line of travel to safety. If you do not have a compass, use a field-expedient direction finding method.
- Take stock of water supplies and equipment.
- Move in one direction, but not necessarily in a straight line. Avoid obstacles. In enemy territory, take advantage of natural cover and concealment.
- Move smoothly through the jungle. Do not blunder through it since you will get many cuts and scratches. Turn your shoulders, shift your hips, bend your body, and shorten or lengthen your stride as necessary to slide between the undergrowth.

Immediate Considerations

- Take shelter from tropical rain, sun, and insects. Malaria-carrying mosquitoes and other insects are immediate dangers, so protect yourself against bites.
- In the tropics, even the smallest scratch can quickly become dangerously infected. Promptly treat any wound, no matter how minor.

13.4 WATER PROCUREMENT

Even though water is abundant in most tropical environments, you may, as a survivor, have trouble finding it. If you do find water, it may not be safe to drink. Some of the many sources are vines, roots, palm trees, and condensation. You can sometimes follow animals to water.

Often you can get nearly clear water from muddy streams or lakes by digging a hole in sandy soil about 1 meter from the bank. Water will seep into the hole. You must purify any water obtained in this manner.

13.4.1 ANIMALS AS SIGNS OF WATER

Animals can often lead you to water. Most animals require water regularly. Grazing animals such as deer are usually never far from water and usually drink at dawn and dusk. Converging game trails often lead to water. Carnivores (meat eaters) are not reliable indicators of water. They get moisture from the animals they eat and can go without water for long periods.

Birds can sometimes also lead you to water. Grain eaters, such as finches and pigeons, are never far from water. They drink at dawn and dusk. When they fly straight and low, they are heading for water. When returning from water, they are full and will fly from tree to tree, resting frequently. Do not rely on water birds to lead you to water. They fly long distances without stopping. Hawks, eagles, and other birds of prey get liquids from their victims; you cannot use them as a water indicator.

Insects can be good indicators of water, especially bees. Bees seldom range more than 6 km from their nests or hives. They usually will have a water source in this range. Ants need water. A column of ants marching up a tree is going to a small reservoir of trapped water. You find such reservoirs even in arid areas. Most flies stay within 100 meters of water, especially the European mason fly, easily recognized by its iridescent green body.

Human tracks will usually lead to a well, bore hole, or soak. Scrub or rocks may cover it to reduce evaporation. Replace the cover after use.

13.4.2 WATER FROM PLANTS

Plants such as vines, roots, and palm trees are good sources of water.

Vines

Vines with rough bark and shoots about 5 cm thick can be a useful source of water. You must learn by experience which are the water-bearing vines, because not all have drinkable water. Some may even have a poisonous sap. The poisonous ones yield a sticky, milky sap when cut. Non-poisonous vines will give a clear fluid. Some vines cause a skin irritation on contact; therefore let the liquid drip into your mouth, rather than put your mouth to the vine. Preferably, use some type of container. See **Water from Vegetable Sources** (Page 3-2) to obtain water from a vine.

Roots

In Australia, the water tree, desert oak, and bloodwood have roots near the surface. Pry these roots out of the ground and cut them into 30-centimeter lengths. Remove the bark and suck out the moisture, or shave the root to a pulp and squeeze it over your mouth.

Palm Trees

The buri, coconut, and nipa palms all contain a sugary fluid that is very good to drink. To obtain the liquid, bend a flowering stalk of one of these palms downward, and cut off its tip. If you cut a thin slice off the stalk every 12 hours, the flow will renew, making it possible to collect up to a litre per day. Nipa palm shoots grow from the base, so that you can work at ground level. On trees of other species, you may have to climb them to reach a flowering stalk. Milk from coconuts has a large water content, but may contain a strong laxative in ripe nuts. Drinking too much of this milk may cause you to lose more fluid than you drink.

13.4.3 WATER FROM CONDENSATION

Often it requires too much effort to dig for roots containing water. It may be easier to let a plant produce water in the form of condensation. Tying a clear plastic bag around a green leafy branch will cause water in the leaves to evaporate and condense in the bag. Placing cut vegetation in a plastic bag will also produce condensation. See **Solar Still** (Page 3-4).

13.5 FOOD

Food is usually abundant in a tropical survival situation. To obtain animal food, use the procedures outlined in **Food Procurement** (Page 4-1).

In addition to animal food, you will have to supplement your diet with edible plants. The best places to forage are the banks of streams and rivers. Wherever the sun penetrates the jungle, there will be a mass of vegetation, but river banks may be the most accessible areas.

If you are weak, do not expend energy climbing a tree for food. There are easier sources of food nearer the ground. Do not pick more food than you need. Food spoils rapidly in tropical conditions. Leave food on the growing plant until you need it, and eat it fresh.

There are an almost unlimited number of edible plants from which to choose. Unless you can positively identify these plants, it may be safer at first to begin with palms, bamboos, and common fruits.

14 COLD WEATHER SURVIVAL

One of the most difficult survival situations is a cold weather scenario. Remember, cold weather is an adversary that can be as dangerous as an enemy soldier. Every time you venture into the cold, you are pitting yourself against the elements. With a little knowledge of the environment, proper plans, and appropriate equipment, you can overcome the elements. As you remove one or more of these factors, survival becomes increasingly difficult. Remember, winter weather is highly variable. Prepare yourself to adapt to blizzard conditions even during sunny and clear weather.

Cold is a far greater threat to survival than it appears. It decreases your ability to think and weakens your will to do anything except to get warm. Cold is an insidious enemy; as it numbs the mind and body, it subdues the will to survive.

Cold makes it very easy to forget your ultimate goal — to survive.

14.1 COLD REGIONS AND LOCATIONS

Cold regions include arctic and sub arctic areas and areas immediately adjoining them. You can classify about 48% of the northern hemisphere's total landmass as a cold region due to the influence and extent of air temperatures. Ocean currents affect cold weather and cause large areas normally included in the temperate zone to fall within the cold regions during winter periods. Elevation also has a marked effect on defining cold regions.

Within the cold weather regions, you may face two types of cold weather environments — wet or dry. Knowing in which environment your area of operations falls will affect planning and execution of a cold weather operation.

Wet Cold Weather Environments

Wet cold weather conditions exist when the average temperature in a 24-hour period is -10°C (14°F) or above. Characteristics of this condition are freezing during the colder night hours and thawing during the day. Even though the temperatures are warmer during this condition, the terrain is usually very sloppy due to slush and mud. You must concentrate on protecting yourself from the wet ground and from freezing rain or wet snow.

Dry Cold Weather Environments

Dry cold weather conditions exist when the average temperature in a 24-hour period remains below -10°C (14°F). Even though the temperatures in this condition are much lower than normal, you do not have to contend with the freezing and thawing.

In these conditions, you need more layers of inner clothing to protect you from temperatures as low as -60°C (-76°F). Extremely hazardous conditions exist when wind and low temperature combine.

14.2 BASIC PRINCIPLES

It is more difficult for you to satisfy your basic water, food, and shelter needs in a cold environment than in a warm environment. Even if you have the basic requirements, you must also have adequate protective clothing and the will to survive.

The will to survive is as important as the basic needs. There have been incidents when trained and well-equipped individuals have not survived cold weather situations because they lacked the will to live. Conversely, this will has sustained individuals less well-trained and equipped.

You must not only have enough clothing to protect you from the cold, you must also know how to maximize the warmth you get from it. For example, always keep your head covered. You can lose 40 - 45% of body heat from an unprotected head and even more from the unprotected neck, wrist, and ankles.

These areas of the body are good radiators of heat and have very little insulating fat. The brain is very susceptible to cold and can stand the least amount of cooling. Because there is much blood circulation in the head, most of which is on the surface, you can lose heat quickly if you do not cover your head.

There are four basic principles to follow to keep warm —

Keep Clothing Clean

This principle is always important for sanitation and comfort. In winter, it is also important from the standpoint of warmth. Clothes matted with dirt and grease lose much of their insulation value. Heat can escape more easily from the body through the clothing's crushed or filled up air pockets.

Avoid Overheating

When you get too hot, you sweat and your clothing absorbs the moisture. This affects you in two ways: dampness decreases the insulation quality of clothing, and as sweat evaporates, your body cools.

Adjust your clothing so that you do not sweat. Do this by partially opening your jacket, removing an inner layer of clothing, removing mittens, or by changing to lighter headgear. The head and hands act as efficient heat dissipaters when overheated.

Wear Your Clothing Loose and in Layers

Wearing tight clothing and footgear restricts blood circulation and invites cold injury. It also decreases the volume of air trapped between the layers, reducing its insulating value.

Several layers of lightweight clothing are better than one equally thick layer of clothing, because the layers have dead-air space between them which provides insulation. Also, layers of clothing allow you to take off or add clothing layers to prevent excessive sweating or to increase warmth.

Keep Clothing Dry

In cold temperatures, your inner layers of clothing can become wet from sweat and your outer layer, if not water repellent, can become wet from snow and frost melted by body heat. Wear water repellent outer clothing, if available. It will shed most of the water collected from melting snow and frost.

Before entering a heated shelter, brush off the snow and frost. Despite the precautions you take, there will be times when you cannot keep from getting wet. At such times, drying your clothing may become a major problem.

On the march, hang your damp mittens and socks on your rucksack. Sometimes in freezing temperatures, the wind and sun will dry this clothing. You can also place damp socks or mittens, unfolded, near your body so that your body heat can dry them. In a campsite, hang damp clothing inside the shelter near the top, using drying lines or improvised racks. You may even be able to dry each item by holding it before an open fire. Dry leather items slowly. If no other means are available for drying your boots, put them between your sleeping bag shell and liner. Your body heat will help to dry the leather.

14.2.1 WINDCHILL

Windchill increases the hazards in cold regions. Windchill is the effect of moving air on exposed flesh. For instance, with a 27.8-kph (15-knot) wind and a temperature of -10°C (14°F), the equivalent windchill temperature is -23°C (-9°F). Remember, even when there is no wind, you will create the equivalent wind by skiing, running, being towed on skis behind a vehicle, working around aircraft that produce wind blasts.

14.2.2 HYGIENE

Although washing yourself may be impractical and uncomfortable in a cold environment, you must do so. Washing helps prevent skin rashes that can develop into more serious problems.

In some situations, you may be able to take a snow bath. Take a handful of snow and wash your body where sweat and moisture accumulate, such as under the arms and between the legs, and then wipe yourself dry. If possible, wash your feet daily and put on clean, dry socks. Change your underwear at least twice a week. If you are unable to wash your underwear, take it off, shake it, and let it air out for an hour or two.

If your clothing has become infested with lice you can hang your clothes in the cold, then beat and brush them. This will help get rid of the lice, but not the eggs.

If you shave, try to do so before going to bed. This will give your skin a chance to recover before exposing it to the elements.

14.3 MEDICAL ASPECTS

When you are healthy, your inner core temperature (torso temperature) remains almost constant at 37°C (98.6°F). Since your limbs and head have less protective body tissue than your torso, their temperatures vary and may not reach core temperature.

Your body has a control system that lets it react to temperature extremes to maintain a temperature balance. There are three main factors that affect this temperature balance – heat production, heat loss, and evaporation.

The difference between the body's core temperature and the environment's temperature governs the heat production rate. Your body can get rid of heat better than it can produce it. Sweating helps to control the heat balance. Maximum sweating will get rid of heat about as fast as maximum exertion produces it.

Shivering causes the body to produce heat. It also causes fatigue that, in turn, leads to a drop in body temperature. Air movement around your body affects heat loss. It has been calculated that a naked man exposed to still air at or about 0°C (32°F) can maintain a heat balance if they shiver as hard as they can. However, you can't shiver forever.

It has also been calculated that a man at rest wearing the maximum arctic clothing in a cold environment can keep their internal heat balance during temperatures well below freezing. To withstand really cold conditions for any length of time, however, they will have to become active or shiver.

14.3.1 COLD INJURIES

The best way to deal with injuries and sicknesses is to take measures to prevent them from happening in the first place. Treat any injury or sickness that occurs as soon as possible to prevent it from worsening.

The knowledge of signs and symptoms and the use of the buddy system are critical in maintaining health. Following are cold injuries that can occur.

Hypothermia

Hypothermia is the lowering of the body temperature at a rate faster than the body can produce heat. Causes of hypothermia may be general exposure or the sudden wetting of the body by falling into a lake or spraying with fuel or other liquids.

The initial symptom is shivering. This shivering may progress to the point that it is uncontrollable. This begins when the body's core (rectal) temperature falls to about 35.5°C (96°F).

When the core temperature reaches 35 - 32°C (95 - 90°F), sluggish thinking, irrational reasoning, and a false feeling of warmth may occur.

Core temperatures of 32 - 30°C (90 - 86°F) and below will result in muscle rigidity, unconsciousness, and barely detectable signs of life. If the victim's core temperature falls below 25°C (77°F), death is almost certain.

To treat hypothermia, rewarm the entire body. If there are means available, rewarm the person by first immersing the trunk area only in warm water of 37.7 - 43.3°C (100 - 110°F). There is an increased risk of cardiac arrest with this method.

One of the quickest ways to get heat to the inner core is to give warm water enemas. Such an action, however, may not be possible in a survival situation. Another method is to wrap the victim in a warmed sleeping bag with another person who is already warm; both should be naked. Note the other individual in the sleeping bag could also get hypothermia if left too long.

If the person is conscious, give them hot, sweetened fluids. One of the best sources of calories is honey or dextrose; if unavailable, use sugar, cocoa, or a similar soluble sweetener.

There are two dangers in treating hypothermia – rewarming too rapidly and "after drop." Rewarming too rapidly can cause the victim to have circulatory problems, resulting in heart failure. After drop is the sharp body core temperature drop that occurs when taking the victim from the warm water. Its probable muse is the return of previously stagnant limb blood to the core (inner torso) area as recirculation occurs. Concentrating on warming the core area and stimulating peripheral circulation will lessen the effects of after drop. Immersing the torso in a warm bath, if possible, is the best treatment.

Frost Bite

This injury is the result of frozen tissues. Light frostbite involves only the skin that takes on a dull whitish pallor. Deep frostbite extends to a depth below the skin. The tissues become solid and immovable. Feet, hands, and exposed facial areas are particularly vulnerable to frostbite.

The best frostbite prevention, when you are with others, is to use the buddy system. Check your buddy's face often and make sure that they check yours. If you are alone, periodically cover your nose and lower part of your face with your mittened hand.

The following pointers will aid you in keeping warm and preventing frostbite when it is extremely cold or when you have less than adequate clothing —

Face	Maintain circulation by twitching and wrinkling the skin on your face making faces. Warm with your hands.
Ears	Wiggle and move your ears. Warm with your hands.
Hands	Move your hands inside your gloves. Warm by placing your hands close to your body.
Feet	Move your feet and wiggle your toes inside your boots.

A loss of feeling in your hands and feet is a sign of frostbite. If you have lost feeling for only a short time, the frostbite is probably light. Otherwise, assume the frostbite is deep. To rewarm a light frostbite, use your hands or mittens to warm your face and ears. Place your hands under your armpits. Place your feet next to your buddy's stomach. A deep frostbite injury, if thawed and refrozen, will cause more damage than a non-medically trained person can handle.

Do's —

- Periodically check for frostbite.
- Rewarm light frostbite.
- Keep injured areas from refreezing.

Do Not's —

- Rub injury with snow.
- Drink alcoholic beverages.
- Smoke.

Trench Foot and Immersion Foot

These conditions result from many hours or days of exposure to wet or damp conditions at a temperature just above freezing. The symptoms are a sensation of pins and needles, tingling, numbness, and then pain.

The skin will initially appear wet, soggy, white, and shrivelled. As it progresses and damage appears, the skin will take on a red and then a bluish or black discoloration. The feet become cold, swollen, and have a waxy appearance.

Walking becomes difficult and the feet feel heavy and numb. The nerves and muscles sustain the main damage, but gangrene can occur. In extreme cases, the flesh dies and it may become necessary to have the foot or leg amputated.

The best prevention is to keep your feet dry. Carry extra socks with you in a waterproof packet. You can dry wet socks against your torso (back or chest). Wash your feet and put on dry socks daily.

Dehydration

When bundled up in many layers of clothing during cold weather, you may be unaware that you are losing body moisture. Your heavy clothing absorbs the moisture that evaporates in the air. You must drink water to replace this loss of fluid.

Your need for water is as great in a cold environment as it is in a warm environment. One way to tell if you are becoming dehydrated is to check the colour of your urine on snow. If your urine makes the snow dark yellow, you are becoming dehydrated and need to replace body fluids. If it makes the snow light yellow to no colour, your body fluids have a more normal balance.

Cold Diuresis

Exposure to cold increases urine output. This decreases body fluids that you must replace.

Sunburn

Exposed skin can become sunburned even when the air temperature is below freezing. The sun's rays reflect at all angles from snow, ice, and water, hitting sensitive areas of skin - lips, nostrils, and eyelids. Exposure to the sun results in sunburn more quickly at high altitudes than at low altitudes. Apply sunburn cream or lip salve to your face when in the sun.

Snow Blindness

The reflection of the sun's ultraviolet rays off a snow-covered area causes this condition. The symptoms of snow blindness are a sensation of grit in the eyes, pain in and over the eyes that increases with eyeball movement, red and teary eyes, and a headache that intensifies with continued exposure to light. Prolonged exposure to these rays can result in permanent eye damage. To treat snow blindness, bandage your eyes until the symptoms disappear.

You can prevent snow blindness by wearing sunglasses. If you don't have sunglasses, improvise. Cut slits in a piece of cardboard, thin wood, tree bark, or other available material. Putting soot under your eyes will help reduce shine and glare.

Constipation

It is very important to relieve yourself when needed. Do not delay because of the cold condition. Delaying relieving yourself because of the cold, eating dehydrated foods, drinking too little liquid, and irregular eating habits can cause you to become constipated.

Although not disabling, constipation can cause some discomfort. Increase your fluid intake to at least 2 litres above your normal 2 - 3 litres daily intake and, if available, eat fruit and other foods that will loosen the stool.

14.4 SHELTERS

Your environment and the equipment you carry with you will determine the type of shelter you can build. You can build shelters in wooded areas, open country, and barren areas. Wooded areas usually provide the best location, while barren areas have only snow as building material. Wooded areas provide timber for shelter construction, wood for fire, concealment from observation, and protection from the wind.

 CAUTION – In extreme cold, do not use metal, such as an aircraft fuselage, for shelter. The metal will conduct away from the shelter what little heat you can generate.

Shelters made from ice or snow usually require tools such as ice axes or saws. You must also expend much time and energy to build such a shelter. Be sure to ventilate an enclosed shelter, especially if you intend to build a fire in it.

Always block a shelter's entrance, if possible, to keep the heat in and the wind out. Use a rucksack or snow block. Construct a shelter no larger than needed. This will reduce the amount of space to heat. A fatal error in cold weather shelter construction is making the shelter so large that it steals body heat rather than saving it. Keep shelter space small.

Never sleep directly on the ground. Lay down some pine boughs, grass, or other insulating material to keep the ground from absorbing your body heat.

Never fall asleep without turning out your stove or lamp. Carbon monoxide poisoning can result from a fire burning in an unventilated shelter. Carbon monoxide is colourless and odourless. Always check your ventilation. Even in a ventilated shelter, incomplete combustion can cause carbon monoxide poisoning.

Usually, there are no symptoms. Unconsciousness and death can occur without warning. Sometimes, however, pressure at the temples, burning of the eyes, headache, pounding pulse, drowsiness, or nausea may occur. The one characteristic, visible sign of carbon monoxide poisoning is a cherry red colouring in the tissues of the lips, mouth, and inside of the eyelids. Get into fresh air at once if you have any of these symptoms.

There are several types of field-expedient shelters you can quickly build or employ. Many use snow for insulation.

Snow Cave Shelter

The snow cave shelter is an effective shelter because of the insulating qualities of snow. Remember that it takes time and energy to build and that you will get wet while building it.

First, you need to find a drift about 3 m (10 ft) deep into which you can dig. While building this shelter, keep the roof arched for strength and to allow melted snow to drain down the sides.

Build the sleeping platform higher than the entrance. Separate the platform from the snow cave's walls or dig a small trench between the platform and the wall. This will prevent the melting snow from wetting you and your equipment.

This construction is especially important if you have a good source of heat in the snow cave. Ensure the roof is high enough so that you can sit up. Block the entrance with a snow block or other material and use the lower entrance area for cooking.

The walls and ceiling should be at least 30 cm (1 ft) thick. Install a ventilation shaft. If you do not have a drift large enough to build a snow cave, you can make a variation of it by piling snow into a mound large enough to dig out.

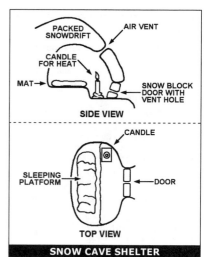

SNOW CAVE SHELTER

Snow Trench Shelter

The idea behind this shelter is to get you below the snow and wind level and use the snow's insulating qualities. If you are in an area of compacted snow, cut snow blocks and use them as overhead cover. If not, you can use a poncho or other material. Build only one entrance and use a snow block or rucksack as a door.

Snow Block and Parachute Shelter

Use snow blocks for the sides and heavy tarp or canvas for overhead cover. Make a double roof for insulation. If snowfall is heavy, make sure to clear the snow from the top occasionally to prevent collapse.

SNOW TRENCH SHELTER

Snow House or Igloo

In certain areas, the natives frequently use this type of shelter as hunting and fishing shelters. They are efficient shelters but require some practice to make them properly. Also, you must be in an area that is suitable for cutting snow blocks and have the equipment to cut them (snow saw or knife).

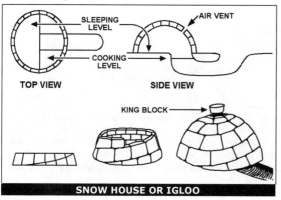

SNOW HOUSE OR IGLOO

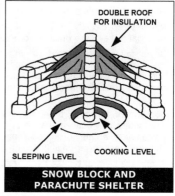

SNOW BLOCK AND PARACHUTE SHELTER

Lean-to Shelter

Construct this shelter in the same manner as for other environments; however, pile snow around the sides for insulation.

Fallen Tree Shelter

To build this shelter, find a fallen tree and dig out the snow underneath it. The snow will not be deep under the tree. If you must remove branches from the inside, use them to line the floor.

FALLEN TREE SHELTER

Tree Pit Shelter

Dig snow out from under a suitable large tree. It will not be as deep near the base of the tree. Use the cut branches to line the shelter. Use a ground sheet as overhead cover to prevent snow from falling off the tree into the shelter. If built properly, you can have 360-degree visibility. See **Tree Pit Snow Shelter** (Page 8-4).

14.5 FIRE

Fire is especially important in cold weather. It not only provides a means to prepare food, but also to get warm and to melt snow or ice for water.

All wood will burn, but some types of wood create more smoke than others. For instance, coniferous trees that contain resin and tar create more and darker smoke than deciduous trees.

There are few materials to use for fuel in the high mountainous regions of the arctic. You may find some grasses and moss, but very little. The lower the elevation, the more fuel available. You may find some scrub willow and small, stunted spruce trees above the tree line. On sea ice, fuels are seemingly nonexistent. Driftwood or fats may be the only fuels available to a survivor on the barren coastlines in the arctic and subarctic regions.

If fuel or oil is available from a wrecked vehicle or downed aircraft, use it for fuel. Leave the fuel in the tank for storage, drawing on the supply only as you need it. Oil congeals in extremely cold temperatures, therefore, drain it from the vehicle or aircraft while still warm if there is no danger of explosion or fire. If you have no container, let the oil drain onto the snow or ice. Scoop up the fuel as you need it.

CAUTION – Do not expose flesh to petroleum, oil, or lubricants in extremely cold temperatures. These products evaporate quickly from the skin and can cause frostbite.

WARNING!!!

Do not use petroleum as a fuel. Petrol explodes rather than burns when ignited and does so with extreme force. Petrol is OK to use in small amounts to help get a fire started but is not suitable as a sole fuel.

Some plastic products, such as drink bottles, plastic bags, and foam rubber will ignite quickly from a burning match. They will also burn long enough to help start a fire. For example, a plastic spoon will burn for about 5 minutes.

In cold weather regions, there are some hazards in using fires, whether to keep warm or to cook. For example –

• Fires have been known to burn underground, resurfacing nearby. Therefore, do not build a fire too close to a shelter. Inside your shelter use a candle or very small fire for heat.

• In snow shelters, excessive heat will melt the snow, destroying your shelter and exposing you to the cold, probably drenched in water.

• A fire inside a shelter without proper ventilation can result in carbon monoxide poisoning. You are not likely to have a smoke detector installed in your igloo.

- A person trying to get warm or to dry clothes may become careless and burn or scorch their clothing and equipment. You cannot afford to lose clothing in a cold environment.

- Melting overhead snow may get you wet, bury you and your equipment, and possibly extinguish your fire.

In general, a small fire and some type of stove is the best combination for cooking purposes.

A hobo stove is particularly suitable to the arctic. It is easy to make out of a tin can, and it conserves fuel.

If the fuel is available, a bed of hot coals provides the best cooking heat.

Coals from a crisscross fire will settle uniformly. Make this type of fire by crisscrossing the firewood.

For heating purposes, a single candle provides enough heat to warm an enclosed shelter, such as an igloo or snow cave. A small fire about the size of a man's hand is ideal for use in areas where you need to keep a low profile. It requires very little fuel, yet it generates considerable warmth and is hot enough to warm liquids.

Platform and Temple Fires

You cannot light a fire directly on deep snow for obvious reasons. Use any fireproof material you have at hand such as rocks, building rubble or metal from wrecked vehicles to build a fire. Build a fire directly on a vehicle if needed. See Page 6-3 for construction of platform fires if there are trees and logs in the area.

14.6 WATER

There are many sources of water in the arctic and sub-arctic. Your location, the apparent season and any recent disasters will determine where and how you obtain water.

Always purify the water before drinking it. During the warmer months, the best natural sources of water are freshwater lakes, streams, ponds, rivers, and springs. Water from ponds or lakes may be slightly stagnant, but still usable. Running water in streams, rivers, and bubbling springs is usually fresh and suitable for drinking.

The brownish surface water found in a tundra during the summer is a good source of water. However, you may have to filter the water before purifying it.

You can melt freshwater ice and snow for water. Completely melt before putting them in your mouth. Trying to melt ice or snow in your mouth takes away body heat and may cause internal cold injuries.

If you are on or near pack ice in the sea, you can use old sea ice to melt for water. In time, sea ice loses its salinity. You can identify this ice by its rounded corners and bluish colour.

You can use body heat to melt snow. Place the snow in a water bag and place the bag between your layers of clothing. This is a slow process, but you can use it on the move or when you have no fire.

 Do not waste fuel to melt ice or snow when drinkable water is available from other sources.

When ice is available, melt it, rather than snow. One cup of ice yields more water than one cup of snow. Ice also takes less time to melt. You can melt ice or snow in a water bag, MRE ration bag, tin can, or improvised container by placing the container near a fire. Begin with a small amount of ice or snow in the container and, as it turns to water, add more ice or snow.

Another way to melt ice or snow is by putting it in a bag made from porous material and suspending the bag near the fire. Place a container under the bag to catch the water.

During cold weather, avoid drinking a lot of liquid before going to bed. Crawling out of a warm sleeping bag at night to relieve yourself means less rest and more exposure to the cold.

Once you have water, keep it next to you to prevent refreezing. Also, do not fill your canteen completely. Allowing the water to slosh around will help keep it from freezing.

14.7 FOOD

There are several sources of food in the arctic and sub-arctic regions. The type of food – fish, animal, fowl, or plant – and the ease in obtaining it depend on the time of the year and your location.

14.7.1 FISH

During the summer months, you can easily get fish and other water life from coastal waters, streams, rivers, and lakes. Use the techniques described in Chapter 5 to catch fish.

The North Atlantic and North Pacific coastal waters are rich in seafood. You can easily find crawfish, snails, clams, oysters, and king crab. In areas where there is a great difference between the high and low tide water levels, you can easily find shellfish at low tide.

Dig in the sand on the tidal flats. Look in tidal pools and on offshore reefs. In areas where there is a small difference between the high and low tide water levels, storm waves often wash shellfish onto the beaches.

Most northern fish and fish eggs are edible. Exceptions are the meat of the arctic shark and the eggs of the sculpins.

The bivalves, such as clams and mussels, are usually more palatable than spiral-shelled seafood, such as snails.

WARNING!!!

The black mussel, a common mollusc of the far north, may be poisonous in any season. Toxins sometimes found in the mussel's tissue are as dangerous as strychnine.

The sea cucumber is another edible sea animal. Inside its body are five long white muscles that taste much like clam meat.

You can often find herring eggs on the seaweed in midsummer. Kelp – the long ribbon like seaweed – and other smaller seaweed that grow among offshore rocks are also edible.

14.7.2 SEA ICE ANIMALS

You find polar bears in practically all arctic coastal regions, but rarely inland. Avoid them if possible. They are the most dangerous of all bears. They are tireless, clever hunters with good sight and an extraordinary sense of smell. If you must kill one for food, approach it cautiously. Aim for the brain; a bullet elsewhere will rarely kill one. Always cook polar bear meat before eating it.

WARNING!!!

Do not eat polar bear liver! It contains a **toxic** concentration of vitamin A.

Skin and Butcher Game (Page 4-21) while it is still warm. If you do not have time to skin the game, at least remove its entrails, musk glands, and genitals before storing. If time allows, cut the meat into usable pieces and freeze each separately so that you can use the pieces as needed. Leave the fat on all animals except seals. During the winter, game freezes quickly if left in the open. During the summer, you can store it in underground ice holes.

14.8 TRAVEL

As a survivor in an arctic region, you will face many obstacles.

- Avoid travelling during a blizzard.
- Take care when crossing thin ice. Distribute your weight by lying flat and crawling.
- Cross streams when the water level is lowest. Normal freezing and thawing action may cause a stream level to vary as much as 2 - 2.5 meters per day. This variance may occur any time during the day, depending on the distance from a glacier, the temperature, and the terrain. Consider this variation in water level when selecting a campsite near a stream.
- Consider the clear arctic air. It makes estimating distance difficult. You more frequently underestimate than overestimate distances.

- Do not travel in "whiteout" conditions. The lack of contrasting colours makes it impossible to judge the nature of the terrain.
- Always cross a snow bridge at right angles to the obstacle it crosses. Find the strongest part of the bridge by poking ahead of you with a pole or ice axe. Distribute your weight by crawling or by wearing snowshoes or skis.
- Make camp early so that you have plenty of time to build a shelter.
- Consider frozen or unfrozen rivers as avenues of travel. However, some rivers that appear frozen may have soft, open areas that make travel very difficult or may not allow walking, skiing, or sledding.
- Use snowshoes if you are travelling over snow-covered terrain. Snow 30 or more cm deep makes travelling difficult. If you do not have snowshoes, make a pair using willow, strips of cloth, leather, or other suitable material.

It is almost impossible to travel in deep snow without snowshoes or skis. Travelling by foot leaves a well-marked trail for any pursuers to follow. If you must travel in deep snow, avoid snow-covered streams.

The snow, which acts as an insulator, may have prevented ice from forming over the water. In hilly terrain, avoid areas where avalanches appear possible. Travel in the early morning in areas where there is danger of avalanches. On ridges, snow gathers on the lee side in overhanging piles called cornices. These often extend far out from the ridge and may break loose if stepped on.

14.8.1 WEATHER SIGNS

There are several good indicators of climatic changes —

Wind

You can determine wind direction by dropping a few leaves or grass or by watching the treetops. Once you determine the wind direction, you can predict the type of weather that is imminent. Rapidly shifting winds indicate an unsettled atmosphere and a likely change in the weather.

Clouds

Clouds come in a variety of shapes and patterns. A general knowledge of clouds and the atmospheric conditions they indicate can help you predict the weather.

Smoke

Smoke rising in a thin vertical column indicates fair weather. Low rising or "flattened out" smoke indicates stormy weather.

Birds and Insects

Birds and insects fly lower to the ground than normal in heavy, moisture-laden air. Such flight indicates that rain is likely. Most insect activity increases before a storm, but bee activity increases before fair weather.

Low Pressure Front

Slow-moving or imperceptible winds and heavy, humid air often indicate a low-pressure front. Such a front promises bad weather that will probably linger for several days. You can "smell" and "hear" this front. The sluggish, humid air makes wilderness odours more pronounced than during high-pressure conditions. In addition, sounds are sharper and carry farther in low-pressure than high-pressure conditions.

15 SEA SURVIVAL

Perhaps the most difficult survival situation to be in is sea survival. Short or long-term survival depends upon rations and equipment available and your ingenuity.

You must be resourceful to survive.

Water covers about 75 percent of the earth's surface, with about 70 percent being oceans and seas. You can assume that you will sometime cross vast expanses of water. There is always the chance that the plane or ship you are on will become crippled by such hazards as storms, collision, fire, or a dumbass pilot.

15.1 THE OPEN SEA

As a survivor on the open sea, you will face waves and wind. You may also face extreme heat or cold. To keep these environmental hazards from becoming serious problems, take precautionary measures as soon as possible. Use the available resources to protect yourself from the elements and from heat or extreme cold and humidity.

Protecting yourself from the elements meets only one of your basic needs. You must also be able to obtain water and food. Satisfying these three basic needs will help prevent serious physical and psychological problems. However, you must know how to treat health problems that may result from your situation.

15.1.1 PRECAUTIONARY MEASURES

Your survival at sea depends upon —

- Your knowledge of and ability to use the available survival equipment.
- Your special skills and ability to apply them to cope with the hazards you face.
- Your will to live.

When you board a ship or aircraft, find out what survival equipment is on board, where it is stowed, and what it contains.

15.1.2 DOWN AT SEA

If you go down at sea, take the following actions once you clear the aircraft. Whether you are in the water or in a raft —

- Get clear and upwind of the aircraft as soon as possible, but stay in the vicinity until the aircraft sinks.
- Get clear of fuel-covered water in case the fuel ignites.
- Try to find other survivors.

The best technique for rescuing someone from the water is to throw them a life preserver attached to a line. Another is to send a rescuer from the raft with a line attached to a flotation device that will support the rescuer's weight. This device will help conserve a rescuer's energy while recovering the survivor.

The least acceptable technique is to send an attached swimmer without flotation devices to retrieve a survivor. In all cases, the rescuer wears a life preserver. A rescuer should not underestimate the strength of a panic-stricken person in the water. A careful approach can prevent injury to the rescuer.

RESCUE FROM WATER

If you are in the water, make your way to a raft, or a large piece of floating debris to cling to.

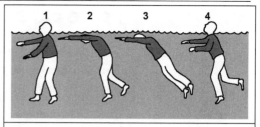

Relax; a person who knows how to relax in ocean water is in very little danger of drowning. The body's natural buoyancy will keep at least the top of the head above water, but some movement is needed to keep the face above water.

Floating on your back takes the least energy. Lie on your back in the water, spread your arms and legs, and arch your back. By controlling your breathing in and out, your face will always be out of the water and you may even sleep in this position for short periods.

1. Float upright in the water and take a deep breath

2. Lower your face into the water (keeping your mouth closed) and bring your arms forward to rest at water level

3. Relax in this position until you need to take in more air

4. Raise your head above the surface, treading water, and exhale. Take another breath and return to the relaxed position

Your head will be partially submerged, but your face will be above water. If you cannot float on your back or if the sea is too rough, float facedown in the water as shown.

FLOATING POSITION

The following are the best swimming strokes during a survival situation —

Dog paddle	This stroke is excellent when clothed or wearing a life jacket. Although slow in speed, it requires very little energy.
Breaststroke	Use this stroke to swim underwater, through oil or debris, or in rough seas. It is probably the best stroke for long-range swimming: it allows you to conserve your energy and maintain a reasonable speed.
Sidestroke	It is a good relief stroke because you use only one arm to maintain momentum and buoyancy.
Backstroke	This stroke is also an excellent relief stroke. It relieves the muscles that you use for other strokes. Use it if an underwater explosion is likely.

If you are in an area where surface oil is burning —

- Discard your shoes and buoyant life preserver. Note, if you have an uninflated life preserver, keep it.
- Cover your nose, mouth, and eyes and quickly go underwater.
- Swim underwater as far as possible before surfacing to breathe.
- Before surfacing to breathe and while still underwater, use your hands to push burning fluid away from the area where you wish to surface. Once an area is clear of burning liquid, you can surface and take a few breaths. Try to face downwind before inhaling.
- Submerge feet first and continue as above until clear of the flames.

If you are in oil-covered water that is free of fire, hold your head high to keep the oil out of your eyes. Attach your life preserver to your wrist and then use it as a raft.

15.1.3 INFLATABLE DINGHYS

Aircraft and many boats carry dinghy-type lifeboats. Many are self-inflating and some are even activated by salt-water immersion. If they do not self-inflate then there is probably a hand pump available. There will be several inflation points in a dinghy because they are built in sections so that if one punctures, the craft will remain afloat.

Ensure the dinghy is fully inflated. It should be firm – not rock – hard. If it is not, you will need to reinflate it using your own breath or a pump. The valves are one-way and will not let air out when the protective cap is removed.

Check for leaks. Escaping air will cause bubbles underwater and above water will make a hissing sound. Rub a wet hand over suspect points and bubbles will be present where there is a leak. There should be conical plugs in the dinghy kit for this purpose. They screw in and seal the leaks. There may also be a supply of rubber patches and adhesive.

Check for leaks regularly. If you suspect a leak on the underside, swim underneath and insert a plug. If you have no plugs, then whittle a piece of plastic or wood into a tapered shape and insert that carefully. Make sure the taper is a very shallow angle, and EXTREMELY smooth all round. Don't push in any more than necessary. Wood will swell when it is wet.

Boarding an Inflatable Dinghy

Get on board as soon as possible. If you are already in the water, move to the end (not the side) of the dinghy, place one leg over the edge and roll into the dinghy.

Do NOT jump into a dinghy from above as you may damage it.

To haul someone else aboard a dinghy, raft or lifeboat, hold their shoulders and lift one leg over the end and roll them in. Discourage them from putting their arms around your neck – they could pull you into the water.

Righting an Inflatable Dinghy

Most dinghies have righting straps on the bottom, and larger ones have righting straps attached to one side.

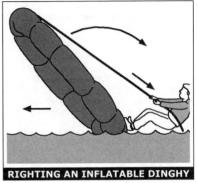

RIGHTING AN INFLATABLE DINGHY

Grab it from the opposite side, brace your feet against the craft and pull. The dinghy should rise up and over, pulling you out of the water momentarily. A hand-over hand motion may be necessary to pull it over. In heavy winds or high seas, this can be extremely difficult.

15.2 WATER PROCUREMENT

Water is your most important need. With it alone, you can live for ten days or longer, depending on your will to live. When drinking water, moisten your lips, tongue, and throat before swallowing.

Short Water Rations

When you have a limited water supply, use the water efficiently.

Protect freshwater supplies from seawater contamination. Keep your body well shaded, both from overhead sun and from reflection off the sea surface. Allow ventilation of air; dampen your clothes during the hottest part of the day.

Do not exert yourself. Relax and sleep when possible. Fix your daily water ration after considering the amount of water you have, the output of solar stills and desalting kit, and the number and physical condition of your party.

If you don't have water, don't eat. If your water ration is 2 litres or more per day, eat any part of your ration or any additional food that you may catch, such as birds, fish, shrimp. The life raft's motion and anxiety may cause nausea. If you eat when nauseated, you may lose your food immediately. If nauseated, rest and relax as much as you can, and take only water.

High protein foods, such fish and seaweed (or the meat cut from the ass of one of your dead companions) require more water to digest than carbohydrates (sugars and starches).

To reduce your loss of water through perspiration, soak your clothes in the sea and wring them out before putting them on again. Don't overdo this during hot days when no canopy or sun shield is available. This is a trade-off between cooling and saltwater boils and rashes that will result.

Watch the clouds and be ready for any chance of showers. Keep the tarpaulin handy for catching water. If it is encrusted with dried salt, wash it in seawater. Normally, a small amount of seawater mixed with rain will hardly be noticeable and will not cause any physical reaction. In rough seas you cannot get uncontaminated fresh water.

At night, secure the tarpaulin like a sunshade, and turn up its edges to collect dew. It is also possible to collect dew along the sides of the raft using a sponge or cloth. When it rains, drink as much as you can hold.

Solar Still

When solar stills are available, read the instructions and set them up immediately. Use as many stills as possible, depending on the number of people in the raft and the amount of sunlight available. Secure solar stills to the raft with care. This type of solar still only works on flat, calm seas.

Desalting Kits

When desalting kits are available in addition to solar stills, use them only for immediate water needs or during long overcast periods when you cannot use solar stills. In any event, keep desalting kits and emergency water stores for periods when you cannot use solar stills or catch rainwater.

Water from Fish

Drink the aqueous fluid found along the spine and in the eyes of large fish. Carefully cut the fish in half to get the fluid along the spine and suck the eye. If you are so short of water that you need to do this, then do not drink any of the other body fluids. These other fluids are rich in protein and fat and will use up more of your reserve water in digestion than they supply.

Do NOT –	• Drink seawater. • Drink urine. • Drink alcohol. • Smoke. • Eat, unless water is available.

Sea Ice

In arctic waters, use old sea ice for water. This ice is bluish, has rounded corners, and splinters easily. It is nearly free of salt. New ice is grey, milky, hard, and salty. Water from icebergs is fresh, but icebergs are dangerous to approach. Use them as a source of water only in emergencies.

Sleep and rest are the best ways of enduring periods of reduced water and food intake. However, make sure that you have enough shade when napping during the day. If the sea is rough, tie yourself to the raft, close any cover, and ride out the storm as best you can. Relax is the key word – at least try to relax.

Water Rationing

If you need to ration water, then limit water loss by limiting sweat producing activities and preserve the sweat that is produced by wearing clothes and headbands, and apply this regime.

Day 1	No water – the body is a reservoir and has a store.
Day 2-4	400ml (14oz) if available.
Day 5 onwards	55 to 225 ml (2 to 8 oz) daily, depending on the water available.

15.3 FOOD PROCUREMENT

In the open sea, fish will be the main food source. There are some poisonous and dangerous ocean fish, but, in general, when out of sight of land, fish are safe to eat. Nearer the shore there are fish that are both dangerous and poisonous to eat. There are some fish, such as the red snapper and barracuda that are normally edible but poisonous when taken from the waters of atolls and reefs.

15.3.1 FISH

In warm regions, gut and bleed fish immediately after catching. Cut fish that you do not eat immediately into thin, narrow strips and hang them to dry. A well-dried fish stays edible for several days. Fish not cleaned and dried may spoil in half a day. Fish with dark meat are very prone to decomposition. If you do not eat them all immediately, use the leftovers for bait.

Never eat fish that have pale, shiny gills, sunken eyes, flabby skin and flesh, or an unpleasant odour. Sea fish have a saltwater or clean fishy odour. The heart, blood, intestinal wall, and liver of most fish are edible. Cook the intestines. Also edible are the partly digested smaller fish that you may find in the stomachs of large fish. In addition, sea turtles are edible.

Shark meat is a good source of food whether raw, dried, or cooked. Shark meat spoils very rapidly due to the high concentration of urea in the blood, therefore, bleed it immediately and soak it in several changes of water.

Fishing Aids

You can use different materials to make fishing aids as described below —

Fish hooks	No survivor at sea should be without fishing equipment but if you are, improvise hooks as shown in **Fishing Devices** (Page 4-15).
Fish lures	You can fashion lures by attaching hooks to any shiny piece of metal. Shredded rags and plastic also work well.
Bait	You can use small fish as bait for larger ones. Scoop the small fish up with a net. If you don't have a net, make one from cloth of some type. Hold the net under the water and scoop upward. Use all the guts from birds and fish for bait. When using bait, try to keep it moving in the water to give it the appearance of being alive.

Fishing Hints

Your fishing should be successful if you remember the following important hints —

- Be extremely careful with fish that have teeth and spines.
- Cut a large fish loose rather than risk capsizing. Try to catch small rather than large fish.
- Do not fish when large sharks are in the area.
- Watch for schools of fish – try to move close to these schools.
- Fish at night using a light. The light attracts fish.
- Always take care of your fishing equipment. Dry your fishing lines, clean and sharpen the hooks, and do not allow the hooks to stick into the fishing lines.

15.3.2 THE UNFORTUNATE WHO DIDN'T SURVIVE

Don't be a pussy. Eat them. Trust me, they won't mind.

15.4 MEDICAL PROBLEMS FACED AT SEA

At sea, you may become seasick, get saltwater sores, or face some of the same medical problems that occur on land, such as dehydration or sunburn. These problems can become critical if left untreated.

Seasickness

Seasickness can result in —

- Extreme fluid loss and exhaustion.
- Others becoming seasick.
- Attraction of sharks to the raft.

To treat seasickness —

- Wash both the patient and the raft.
- Keep the patient from eating food until their nausea is gone.
- Have the patient lie down and rest.

 Some survivors have said that erecting a canopy or using the horizon as a focal point helped overcome seasickness. Others have said that swimming alongside the raft for short periods helped, but extreme care must be taken if swimming.

Saltwater Sores

These sores result from a break in skin exposed to saltwater for an extended period. The sores may form scabs and pus. Do not open or drain. Flush the sores with fresh water, if available, and allow to dry. Apply an antiseptic, if available.

Immersion Rot, Frostbite, and Hypothermia

These problems are similar to those encountered in cold weather environments. Symptoms and treatment are the same as covered in Chapter 14.

Blindness/Headache

If flame, smoke, or other contaminants get in the eyes, flush them immediately with salt water, then with fresh water, if available. Apply ointment, if available. Bandage both eyes 18 - 24 hours, or longer if damage is severe. If the glare from the sky and water causes your eyes to become bloodshot and inflamed, bandage them lightly. Try to prevent this problem by wearing sunglasses. Improvise sunglasses if necessary.

Constipation

This condition is a common problem on a raft. Do not take a laxative, as this will cause further dehydration. Exercise as much as possible and drink an adequate amount of water, if available.

Difficult Urination

This problem is not unusual and is due mainly to dehydration. It is best not to treat it, as it could cause further dehydration.

Whatever you do, don't drink it. The body will use more water to get rid of it than it gains.

Sunburn

Sunburn is a serious problem in sea survival. Try to prevent sunburn by staying in shade and keeping your head and skin covered. Use cream or Chap Stick from your first aid kit. Remember, reflection from the water also causes sunburn.

15.5 SHARKS

Whether you are in the water or in a boat or raft, you may see many types of sea life around you. Some may be more dangerous than others. Generally, sharks are the greatest danger to you. Other animals such as whales, porpoises, and stingrays may look dangerous, but really pose little threat in the open sea.

Consider any shark longer than 1 meter dangerous. Sharks in the tropical and subtropical seas are far more aggressive than those in temperate waters.

A shark will strike at injured or helpless animals. Sight, smell, or sound may guide them to their prey. Sharks have an acute sense of smell and the smell of blood in the water excites them. They are also very sensitive to any abnormal vibrations in the water. The struggles of a wounded animal or swimmer, underwater explosions, or even a fish struggling on a fish line will attract a shark.

Sharks can bite from almost any position; they do not have to turn on their side to bite. The jaws of some of the larger sharks are so far forward that they can bite floating objects easily without twisting to the side.

Sharks may hunt alone, but reports often cite more than one shark. The smaller sharks tend to travel in schools and attack in mass. Whenever one of the sharks finds a victim, the other sharks will quickly join it. Sharks will eat a wounded shark as quickly as their prey.

Some of the measures that you can take to protect yourself against sharks when you are in the water are —

- Stay with other swimmers. A group can maintain a 360-degree watch. A group can either frighten or fight off sharks better than one man.
- Always watch for sharks. Keep all your clothing on, to include your shoes. Historically, sharks have attacked the unclothed men in groups first, mainly in the feet. Clothing also protects against abrasions should the shark brush against you.
- Avoid urinating. If you must, only do so in small amounts. Let it dissipate between discharges.

If attacked, kick and strike the shark. Hit the shark on the gills or eyes if possible. If you hit the shark on the nose, you may injure your hand if it glances off and hits its teeth.

When you are in a raft and see sharks —

- Do not fish. If you have hooked a fish, let it go. Do not clean fish in the water.
- Do not throw garbage overboard.
- Do not let your arms, legs, or equipment hang in the water.
- Keep quiet and do not move around.
- Bury all dead as soon as possible. If there are many sharks in the area, conduct the burial at night.

When you are in a raft and a shark attack is imminent, hit the shark with anything you have, except your hands. You will do more damage to your hands than the shark. If you strike with an oar, be careful not to lose or break it.

15.6 DETECTING LAND

You should watch carefully for any signs of land. There are many indicators that land is near.

Clouds

Cumulus clouds in an otherwise clear sky are likely to be formed over land. In tropical waters, a greenish tint on the underside of clouds, known as lagoon glare, is produced by the reflection of sunlight from the shallow water over coral reefs.

In the arctic, light-coloured reflections on clouds often indicate ice fields or snow-covered land. These reflections are quite different from the dark grey ones caused by open water.

Birds

A lone bird is not a reliable indicator of land, and after rough weather birds can be blown a long way off course, but few seabirds sleep on the water of fly more than 100 miles from land.

Their direction of flight is usually outwards from land before noon and return in the late afternoon. During the day, birds are searching for food and the direction of flight has no significance.

The continuous sound of bird cries is usually an indicator that land is not far away.

Driftwood

Driftwood, coconuts and other drifting vegetation are often a sign that land is near (though they can be carried right across an ocean).

Sea Movement

The pattern of the swell may indicate land. A change in its direction may be caused by the tide pattern around an island.

Prevailing winds build up a swell pattern and the swell is less if the water is protected by land. If the wind is constant, but the swell and waves decreasing, you can be fairly certain that land lies in the direction from which the wind is coming (windward).

You may be able to detect land by the pattern of the waves (refracted) as they approach land. By travelling with the waves and parallel to the slightly

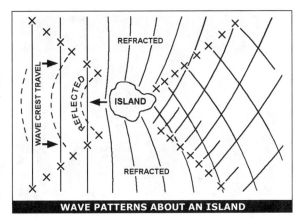

WAVE PATTERNS ABOUT AN ISLAND

turbulent area marked "X" on the illustration, you should reach land.

Mirages

Mirages occur at any latitude, but they are more likely in the tropics, especially during the middle of the day. Be careful not to mistake a mirage for nearby land. A mirage disappears or its appearance and elevation change when viewed from slightly different heights.

Odours

At night, or in fog, mist, or rain, you may detect land by odours and sounds. The musty odour of mangrove swamps and mud flats carry a long way. You hear the roar of surf long before you see the surf. The continued cries of seabirds coming from one direction indicate their roosting place on nearby land.

Sea Colour

Deep water is dark green or dark blue. Lighter colour indicates shallow water, which may mean land is near. Water that is muddy with silt is likely to come from the mouth of a large river.

Bodies

Large amounts of dead bodies in the water will indicate land is, or was, nearby. However, this will also indicate a major disaster. Be careful when approaching such land as survivors will likely be desperate, and resources will be limited. When making landfall, keep your head down.

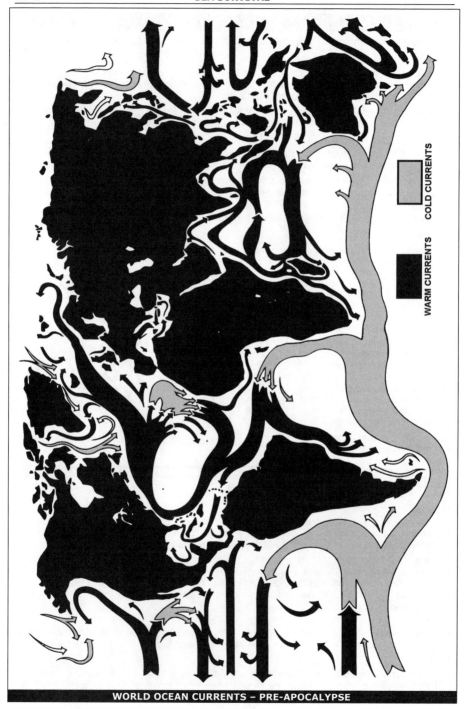

WARM CURRENTS

COLD CURRENTS

WORLD OCEAN CURRENTS – PRE-APOCALYPSE

16 DISASTER SURVIVAL

This chapter describes many different disasters that you may have to face.

It is likely in an apocalypse that you will be dealing with at least one of these scenarios, and probably several at once.

This includes both natural and unnatural catastrophes. As the world rumbles and shudders, people will get nervous and many will still be in positions of power before the apocalypse is complete.

The reactions of nervous humans may range from full blown warfare, to martial law, right down to kidnapping and looting. Be prepared for surprises.

16.1 THE NUCLEAR ENVIRONMENT

If you are in the vicinity of a nuclear blast, there will be no mistake as to the type of attack upon you.

16.1.1 EFFECTS OF NUCLEAR WEAPONS

The effects of nuclear weapons are classified as either initial or residual. Initial effects occur in the immediate area of the explosion and are hazardous in the first minute after the explosion. Residual effects can last for days or years. The principal initial effects are blast and radiation.

Blast

The initial blast is the brief and rapid movement of air away from the explosions centre and the pressure from this movement. Strong winds accompany the blast. The blast will hurl debris, collapse lungs, rupture eardrums, destroy structures, and cause immediate injury or death with its crushing effect.

Thermal Radiation

Thermal radiation is the heat and light that a nuclear explosions fireball emits. Light radiation consists of visible, ultraviolet and infrared light. This radiation produces extensive fires, skin burns, and flash blindness.

Nuclear Radiation

Initial nuclear radiation consists of intense gamma rays and neutrons produced during the first minute after the explosion. This causes extensive damage to body cells. Radiation damage may cause headaches, nausea, vomiting, diarrhoea, and death – depending on the dose received. The problem in protecting yourself against initial radiation is that you may have received a dangerous dose before taking protective action. Anyone exposed to lethal amounts of initial radiation may as well have been killed by the initial blast or thermal radiation.

Residual radiation consists of all radiation produced after one minute from the explosion. It has more effect on you than initial radiation. Residual radiation is discussed further in the chapter.

Electro-magnetic pulse (EMP)

Any electrical equipment in the vicinity of a nuclear blast will be subject to a massive magnetic pulse. Such a pulse will induce large currents in any conductive material. This has the effect of destroying almost all electrical and electronic equipment. Low voltage devices are more susceptible than high voltage devices. Valve equipment is virtually immune.

Despite some misconceptions, it does not matter wether the device is turned on or even connected to power. Anything with a chip, transistor or diode will be rendered useless.

Being **completely** surrounded by a conductive material can divert, or at least lessen, the effects of the pulse within the conductive container. Iron and aluminium are good shields against magnetic interference.

16.1.2 TYPES OF NUCLEAR BLASTS

There are three types of nuclear bursts – airburst, surface burst, and sub-surface burst. The type of burst directly affects your chances of survival. A sub-surface burst occurs completely underground or underwater. Its effects remain beneath the surface or in the immediate area where the surface collapses into a crater over the burst's location.

- **Sub-surface bursts** cause you little or no radioactive hazard unless you enter the immediate area of the crater. This type of deployment also produces the least danger of EMP damage to electrical equipment.

- **Airbursts** occur in the air above its intended target. The airburst provides the maximum radiation effect on the target and is, therefore, most dangerous to you in terms of immediate nuclear effects. An airburst also presents the greatest radius of EMP damage to electrical equipment.

- **Surface bursts** occur on the ground or water surface. Large amounts of fallout result, with serious long-term effects for you. This type of burst is your greatest nuclear hazard.

16.1.3 NUCLEAR INJURIES

Most injuries in the nuclear environment result from the initial effects of the detonation. These injuries are classed as blast, thermal, or radiation injuries. Further injuries may also occur if you do not take proper precautions against fallout.

Blast Injuries

Blast pressure can collapse lungs and rupture internal organs. Projectile wounds occur as the explosion's hurls debris at you. Blast pressure may throw you long distances, and you will suffer severe injury upon impact. Substantial cover and distance from the explosion are the best protection against blast injury. Cover blast injury wounds as soon as possible to prevent the entry of radioactive dust particles.

Thermal Injuries

The heat and light the nuclear fireball emits causes thermal injuries. Flash blindness can also occur. This blindness may be permanent or temporary depending on the degree of exposure. Substantial cover and distance from the explosion can prevent thermal injuries. First aid for thermal injuries is the same as first aid for burns. Cover open wounds to prevent the entry of radioactive particles. Wash all burns before covering.

Radiation Injuries

Neutrons, gamma radiation, alpha radiation, and beta radiation cause radiation injuries. Neutrons are high-speed, extremely penetrating particles that actually smash cells within your body. They will turn you into a pillar of salt. Gamma radiation is similar to X-rays and is also a highly penetrating radiation. During the initial fireball stage of a nuclear detonation, initial gamma radiation and neutrons are the most serious threat. Beta and alpha radiation are radioactive particles normally associated with radioactive dust from fallout. They are short-range particles and you can easily protect yourself against them if you take precautions. See **Bodily Reactions to Radiation** below, for the symptoms of radiation injuries.

16.1.4 RESIDUAL RADIATION

Residual radiation is all radiation emitted after 1 minute from the instant of the nuclear explosion. Residual radiation consists of induced radiation and fallout.

Induced Radiation

Induced radiation is a relatively small, intensely radioactive area directly underneath the nuclear weapon's fireball. The irradiated earth in this area will remain highly radioactive for an extremely long time. You should not travel into an area of induced radiation.

Fallout

Fallout consists of radioactive soil and water particles, as well as weapon fragments. During a surface detonation, large amounts of soil and water are vaporized along with the bomb's fragments, and forced to altitudes of 25 km or more. When these vaporized contents cool, they can form over 200 different radioactive products. The vaporized contents condense into tiny radioactive particles that the wind carries and they fall to earth as radioactive dust. Fallout emits alpha, beta, and gamma radiation. Alpha and beta radiation are relatively easy to counteract, and residual gamma radiation is much less intense than from the initial blast.

16.1.5 BODILY REACTIONS TO RADIATION

The effects of radiation can be classed as either chronic or acute. Chronic effects occur some years after exposure, such as cancer and genetic defects. Some acute effects occur within hours after exposure to radiation. Radiation sickness and beta burns are examples of acute effects. Symptoms include nausea, diarrhoea, vomiting, fatigue, weakness, and loss of hair. Penetrating beta rays cause radiation burns – the wounds are similar to fire burns.

Recovery Capability

The extent of damage depends on the part of the body exposed, the length of exposure, and its ability to recover. The brain and kidneys have little recovery capability. Other parts (skin and bone marrow) have a great ability to recover from damage. Usually, a dose of 600 centigrams to the entire body will result in almost certain death. If only your hands received this same dose, your overall health would not suffer much, although your hands would suffer severe damage.

External and Internal Hazards

Highly penetrating gamma radiation or the less penetrating beta radiation that causes burns can cause external damage. Alpha or beta radiation-emitting particles inside the body can cause internal damage. The external hazard produces overall irradiation and beta burns. The internal hazard results in irradiation of critical organs such as the gastrointestinal tract, thyroid gland, and bone.

A very small amount of radioactive material can cause extreme damage to internal organs. The internal hazard can enter the body through consumption of contaminated water or food or by absorption through cuts or abrasions. Material that enters the body through breathing presents only a minor hazard. You can greatly reduce the internal radiation hazard by using good personal hygiene and carefully decontaminating your food and water.

Symptoms

The symptoms of radiation include nausea, diarrhoea, and vomiting. This is due to the extreme sensitivity of the gastrointestinal tract to radiation. The severity and speed of onset after exposure are indicators of the degree of radiation damage. The gastrointestinal damage can come from either the external or the internal radiation hazard.

16.1.6 COUNTERMEASURES AGAINST EXTERNAL RADIATION

Knowledge of the radiation hazards is extremely important in surviving in a fallout area. It is also critical to know how to protect yourself from the most dangerous form of residual radiation – penetrating external radiation.

The means you can use to protect yourself from penetrating external radiation are time, distance, and shielding. You can reduce the level of radiation and help increase your chance of survival by controlling the duration of exposure. You can also get as far away from the radiation source as possible. Finally you can place some radiation-absorbing or shielding material between you and the radiation.

Time

Time is important in two ways. First, The longer you are exposed to a radioactive source, the greater the dose you will receive. Second, radioactivity decreases or decays over time.

Distance

Distance provides effective protection against penetrating gamma radiation because radiation intensity decreases significantly with every meter from the source.

Shielding

Shielding is the most important method of protection from penetrating radiation. Shielding provides the greatest protection and is the easiest to use under survival conditions. Shielding works by absorbing or weakening the penetrating radiation, thereby reducing the amount of radiation reaching your body. The denser the material, the better the shielding effect. Lead, iron, concrete, and water are good examples of shielding materials.

Special Medical Aspects

Fallout material in your area requires changes in first aid procedures. Cover all wounds to prevent contamination and the entry of radioactive particles. Wash burns of beta radiation, then treat them as ordinary burns. Take extra measures to prevent infection. Your body will be extremely sensitive to infections due to changes in your blood chemistry. Pay close attention to the prevention of colds or respiratory infections. Rigorously practice personal hygiene to prevent infections. Cover your eyes with improvised goggles to prevent the entry of particles.

16.1.7 SHELTER

The effectiveness of shielding material depends on its thickness and density. An ample thickness of shielding material will reduce the level of radiation to negligible amounts.

Speed in finding shelter is absolutely essential. Five minutes to locate the shelter is a good guide. Without shelter, the dosage received in the first few hours will exceed that received during the rest of a week in a contaminated area. The dosage received in this first week will exceed the dosage accumulated during the rest of a lifetime in the same contaminated area.

Shielding Materials

The thickness required to weaken gamma radiation from fallout is far less than that needed to shield against initial gamma radiation. Fallout has less energy than a nuclear detonation's initial radiation. For fallout radiation, a relatively small amount of shielding material can provide adequate protection. This table gives an idea of the

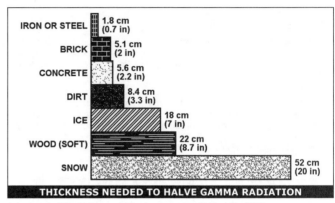

IRON OR STEEL	1.8 cm (0.7 in)
BRICK	5.1 cm (2 in)
CONCRETE	5.6 cm (2.2 in)
DIRT	8.4 cm (3.3 in)
ICE	18 cm (7 in)
WOOD (SOFT)	22 cm (8.7 in)
SNOW	52 cm (20 in)

THICKNESS NEEDED TO HALVE GAMMA RADIATION

thickness of various materials needed to reduce residual gamma radiation by 50%.

The principle is useful in understanding the absorption of radiation by various materials. If 5 cm of brick reduce the gamma radiation level by 50%, adding another 5 cm will reduce the intensity by another half – to 25%.

Natural Shelters

Terrain that provides natural shielding and easy shelter construction is the ideal location for an emergency shelter. Remember – speed is of the essence. Good examples are ditches, ravines, rocky outcropping, hills, and river banks. In level areas without natural protection, dig a fighting position or slit trench.

Trenches

When digging a trench, work from inside the trench as soon as it is large enough to cover part of your body thereby not exposing all your body to radiation. In open country, try to dig the trench from a prone (on your stomach) position, stacking the dirt evenly around the trench. On level ground, pile the dirt around your body for additional shielding. Depending upon soil conditions, shelter construction time will vary from a few minutes to a few hours. If you dig as quickly as possible, you will reduce the dosage you receive.

Other Shelters

While an underground shelter covered by 1 meter of earth provides the best protection against radiation, the following structures (in order listed) offer the next best protection —

- Caves and tunnels covered by more than 1 meter of earth.
- Storm or storage cellars.
- Culverts.
- Basements or cellars of abandoned buildings.
- Abandoned buildings made of stone or mud.

Roofs

A roof is not mandatory. Build one only if the materials are readily available with only a brief exposure to outside contamination. If building a roof would require extended exposure to penetrating radiation, it would be wiser to leave the shelter roofless. A roof's sole function is to reduce radiation from the fallout source to your body. Unless you use a thick roof, a roof provides very little shielding.

You can construct a simple roof from a poncho anchored down with dirt or rocks. You can remove debris from the top of the poncho by beating it from the inside. This cover will not offer shielding from the radioactive particles deposited on the surface, but it will increase the distance from the fallout source and keep the shelter area from further contamination.

Shelter Site Selection and Preparation

To reduce your exposure time and dosage received, follow these guidelines —

- Seek an existing shelter that you can improve. If none is available, dig a trench.

- Dig the shelter deep enough to get good protection, then enlarge it as required for comfort.

- Cover the top of trench with any readily available material and a thick layer of earth, if you can do so without leaving the shelter. While a roof is desirable, it is probably safer to do without them than to expose yourself to radiation outside your position.

- While building your shelter, keep your body covered to protect against beta burns.

- Clean the shelter of any surface deposit to remove contaminated materials from your area. The cleaned area should extend at least 2 meters beyond your shelter.

- Decontaminate anything you bring into the shelter. This includes clothing and footgear. If you have contaminated clothing, remove it and bury it under a foot of earth until the radioactivity decays. If the clothing is dry, decontaminate it by beating or shaking it outside the shelter to remove the radioactive dust. You may use any body of water, even if contaminated, to rid materials of excess particles. Dip the material into the water and shake it. Do not wring it out, this will trap the particles.

- If possible without leaving the shelter, wash your body thoroughly with soap and water, even if the water may be contaminated. This washing will remove most of the radioactive particles. If water is not available, wipe your face and any other exposed skin surface to remove contaminated dust and dirt. You may wipe your face with a clean piece of cloth or a handful of uncontaminated dirt. You get this uncontaminated dirt by scraping off the top few inches of soil and using the "clean" dirt.

- Upon completing the shelter, lie down, keep warm, and rest as much as possible.

- Don't panic if you experience nausea and symptoms of radiation sickness. Your main danger from radiation sickness is infection. There is no first aid for this sickness. Resting, drinking fluids, taking any medicine that prevents vomiting, maintaining your food intake, and preventing additional exposure will help avoid infection and aid recovery. Even small doses of radiation can cause these symptoms which may disappear in a short time.

Exposure Timetable

The following timetable provides you with the information needed to avoid receiving serious dosage and still let you cope with survival problems —

- Complete isolation from 4 to 6 days following delivery of the last weapon.

- A very brief exposure to procure water on the third day is permissible, but exposure should not exceed 30 minutes.

- One exposure of not more than 30 minutes on the seventh day.

- One exposure of not more than 1 hour on the eighth day.

- Exposure of 2 to 4 hours from the ninth day through the twelfth day.

- Normal operation, followed by rest in a protected shelter, from the thirteenth day on.

- In all instances, make your exposures as brief as possible. Consider only mandatory requirements as valid reasons for exposure. Decontaminate at every stop.

The times given above are conservative. If forced to move after the first or second day, you may do so, Make sure that the exposure is no longer than absolutely necessary.

16.1.8 WATER PROCUREMENT

In a fallout area, water sources will be contaminated. If you wait at least 48 hours before drinking any water to allow for radioactive decay and select the safest possible water source, you will greatly reduce the danger of ingesting harmful amounts of radioactivity.

Although many factors (wind direction, rainfall, and sediment) will influence your choice in selecting water sources, consider the following guidelines.

Safest Water Sources

Water from springs, wells, or other underground sources that undergo natural filtration will be your safest source. Water found in the pipes or containers of abandoned houses will also be free from radioactive particles. This water will be safe to drink, although you will have to take precautions against bacteria in the water. Snow taken from 15 cm or more below the surface is also a safe source of water.

Streams and Rivers

Water from streams and rivers will be relatively free from fallout within days after the nuclear explosion because of dilution. If possible, filter such water before drinking to get rid of radioactive particles. The best filtration method is to dig sediment holes or seepage basins along the side of a water source. The water will seep into the hole through the soil that will filter contaminated fallout that settled on the body of water. This method can remove up to 99 percent of the radioactivity in water. You must cover the hole in order to prevent further contamination. See **Water Filtration Devices** (Page 3-6) for an example of a filter.

Standing Water

Water from standing sources is likely to be contaminated, though most of the heavier, long-lived radioactive isotopes will settle to the bottom. Use this technique to purify the water —

- Fill a bucket 3/4 with contaminated water
- Take dirt from 10 cm or more below the ground and stir it into the water. Use about 2.5 cm of dirt for every 10 cm of water.
- Stir the water until most particles are suspended in the water.
- Let the water settle for at least 6 hours, then dip out the clear water.
- Purify this water using a filtration device.

The settling dirt will carry most of the fallout particles to the bottom and cover them. As a further precaution against disease, treat water with purification tablets, boil it or distil it.

16.1.9 FOOD PROCUREMENT

Although it is a problem to obtain food in a contaminated area, it is not impossible. There are special procedures in selecting and preparing foods for use. Securely packaged foods, such as canned foods are safe for use. Supplement these with any food you can find outside your shelter. Most processed foods you may are safe for use after decontaminating them. These include packaged foods after removing the containers or washing them free of fallout particles.

If little or no processed food is available in your area, you may have to supplement your diet with local food sources, such as animals and plants.

Animals as a Food Source

Most of the wild animals living in a fallout area are likely to become sick or die during the first month after a nuclear explosion. Even though animals may not be free from harmful radioactive materials, you can and must use them in survival conditions as a food source if other foods are not available. With careful preparation and by following several important principles, animals can be safe food sources.

Do not eat an animal that appears to be sick. It may have developed a bacterial infection as a result of radiation poisoning. Contaminated meat could cause severe illness or death if eaten.

Carefully skin all animals to prevent particles on the skin from entering the body. Do not eat meat close to the bones and joints as an animal's skeleton contains over 90 percent of the radioactivity. The remaining animal muscle tissue, however, will be safe to eat. Before cooking it, cut the meat away from the bone, leaving at least 3 mm of meat on the bone. Discard all internal organs since they tend to concentrate radioactivity. Cook all meat until it is very well done. To ensure this, cut it into pieces less than 15 mm thick before cooking.

The extent of contamination in fish and aquatic animals will be much greater than that of land animals. This is also true for water plants, especially in coastal areas. Use aquatic food sources only in conditions of extreme emergency.

All eggs, even if laid during the period of fallout, will be safe to eat. Completely avoid milk from any animals in a fallout area because animals absorb large amounts of radioactivity from the plants they eat.

Plants as a Food Source

Plant contamination occurs by the accumulation of fallout on their outer surfaces or by absorption of radioactive elements through their roots. Your first choice of plant food should be vegetables such as potatoes, turnips, carrots, and other plants whose edible portion grows underground. These are the safest to eat once you scrub them and remove their skins.

Second in order of preference are those plants with edible parts that you can decontaminate by washing and peeling their outer surfaces. Examples are bananas, apples, tomatoes and other such fruits and vegetables.

Any smooth-skinned vegetable, fruit, or plant that you cannot easily peel or effectively decontaminate by washing will be your third choice of emergency food. The rougher the surface of the food is, the more radioactive particles it will trap. Rough-surfaced plants (such as lettuce and dried fruits) should only be eaten as a last resort because they cannot be easily decontaminated by peeling or washing.

In general, you can use any plant food that is ready for harvest if you can effectively decontaminate it. Growing plants, however, can absorb some radioactive materials through their leaves as well as from the soil, especially if rains have occurred during or after the fallout period. Avoid using these plants for food except in an emergency.

16.2 BIOLOGICAL ENVIRONMENTS

16.2.1 BIOLOGICAL AGENTS AND EFFECTS

Biological agents can spread far and wide. Biological agents are micro-organisms that can cause disease among people, animals, or plants. They can also cause the deterioration of material. These agents fall into two broad categories – pathogens (germs) and toxins.

Pathogens are living micro-organisms that cause lethal or incapacitating diseases, such as bacteria, rickettsiae, fungi, and viruses. Toxins are poisons that plants, animals, or micro-organisms produce naturally. Possible biological warfare toxins include a variety of neurotoxic (affecting the central nervous system) and cytotoxic (causing cell death) compounds.

Germs

Only a few germs are needed to start an infection, especially if inhaled into the lungs. Germs are tiny and weigh so little that they can spread far and enter places that aren't airtight. Buildings can trap them and cause a higher concentration.

Germs must multiply inside the body and overcome the body's defences – a process called the incubation period. Incubation periods vary from several hours to months. Most germs must live within another host, such as you, to survive and grow. Outside a host most germs die rapidly.

Some germs can form protective shells called spores and survive outside the host. Spore-producing agents are a long-term hazard you must neutralize by decontaminating infected areas and people. Fortunately, most agents are not spore-producing. These agents must find a host within a day or so of their delivery or they die. Germs have three basic routes of entry into your body – through the respiratory tract, through a break in the skin, and through the digestive tract. Symptoms of infection vary according to the disease.

Toxins

Botulism is an example of a toxin that is produced by the botulin bacteria. Modern science can produce these toxins without the need for the bacteria. Yay for science. Toxins may produce effects similar to chemical agents, although victims may not respond to first aid measures in the same way as for a chemical agent. Toxins enter the body in the same manner as germs. However, some toxins, unlike germs, can penetrate unbroken skin. Symptoms appear almost immediately, since there is no incubation period. Many toxins are extremely lethal, even in very small doses. Symptoms may include any of the following —

- Dizziness.
- Mental confusion.
- Blurred or double vision.
- Numbness or tingling of skin.
- Paralysis.
- Convulsions.
- Rashes or blisters.
- Coughing.

- Fever.
- Aching muscles.
- Tiredness.
- Nausea, vomiting, and/or diarrhoea.
- Bleeding from body openings.
- Blood in urine, stool, or saliva.
- Shock.
- Death.

16.2.2 DETECTION OF BIOLOGICAL AGENTS

Biological agents are by nature difficult to detect. You cannot detect them by any of the five physical senses. Often, the first sign of a biological agent will be symptoms of the victims exposed to the agent. Your best chance of detecting biological agents before they can affect you is to recognize their means of delivery. The three main means of delivery are —

- Bursting-type munitions. These may be bombs or projectiles whose burst causes very little damage. The burst will produce a small cloud of liquid or powder in the immediate impact area. This cloud will disperse eventually – the rate of dispersion depends on terrain and weather conditions.
- Spray tanks or generators. Aircraft or vehicle spray tanks or ground-level aerosol generators produce an aerosol cloud of biological agents.
- Vectors. Insects such as mosquitoes, fleas, lice, and ticks deliver pathogens. Large infestations of these insects may indicate the use of biological agents.

Another sign of a possible biological attack is the presence of unusual substances on the ground or on vegetation, or sick-looking plants, crops, or animals.

16.2.3 INFLUENCE OF WEATHER AND TERRAIN

Knowledge of weather and terrain can help you avoid contamination. Major weather factors that affect biological agents are sunlight, wind, and rain. Sunlight rapidly kills most germs exposed. However, natural or man-made cover may protect some agents from sunlight.

High winds increase the dispersion of biological agents, dilute their concentration, and dehydrate them. The further downwind the agent travels, the less effective it becomes due to dilution and death of the pathogens. However, the downwind hazard area of the biological agent is significant and you cannot ignore it.

Rain tends to wash biological agents out of the air, reducing downwind hazard areas. However, the agents may still be very effective where they were deposited on the ground.

16.2.4 PROTECTION AGAINST BIOLOGICAL AGENTS

While you must maintain a respect for biological agents, there is no reason to panic. You can reduce your susceptibility to biological agents by maintaining current immunizations, avoiding contaminated areas, and controlling rodents and pests. You must also use proper first aid measures in the treatment of wounds and only properly treated sources of food and water.

If you don't have a protective mask, try to keep your face covered with cloth to protect yourself. Dust may contain biological agents so wear a mask when dust is in the air.

Clothes and gloves will protect you against bites from vectors (mosquitoes and ticks) that carry diseases. Tuck your trousers tightly into your boots. Wear a hazmat suit if available. Covering your skin will also reduce the chance of the agent entering your body through cuts or scratches. Practice high standards of personal hygiene to help prevent the spread of vectors.

Bathe with soap and water whenever possible. Use germicidal soap, if available. Wash your hair and body thoroughly, and clean under your fingernails. Clean teeth, gums, tongue, and the roof of your mouth frequently. Wash your clothing in hot, soapy water if you can. If you cannot wash your clothing, lay it out in an area of bright sunlight and allow the light to kill the micro-organisms.

16.2.5 SHELTER

You can build shelters under contamination conditions using the techniques in **Shelters** (Page 8-1). However, you must make slight changes to reduce the chance of biological contamination. Do not build your shelter in depressions in the ground. Aerosol sprays tend to concentrate in these depressions. Avoid building your shelter in areas of vegetation, as vegetation provides shade and some degree of protection to biological agents.

Avoid using vegetation in constructing your shelter. Place your shelter's entrance at a 90-degree angle to the prevailing winds. Such placement will limit the entry of airborne agents and prevent air stagnation in your shelter. Always keep your shelter clean.

16.2.6 WATER PROCUREMENT

Water procurement under biological conditions is difficult but not impossible. Whenever possible, try to use water that has been in a sealed container. You can assume that the water inside the sealed container is not contaminated. Wash the water container thoroughly with soap and water or boil it for at least 10 minutes before breaking the seal.

If water in sealed containers is not available, your next choice under emergency conditions is water from springs. Boil the water and keep it covered while boiling to prevent contamination by airborne pathogens. Your last choice is to use standing water. Vectors and germs survive easily in stagnant water. Boil this water and filter it to kill all organisms. Use purification tablets or a few drops of bleach if possible.

16.2.7 FOOD PROCUREMENT

Food procurement is not impossible, but you must take special precautions. You can assume that sealed containers of food are safe. To ensure safety, decontaminate all food containers by washing with soap and water or by boiling the container in water for 10 minutes.

Consider local plants or animals only in extreme emergencies. There is no guarantee that cooking will kill the biological agents. Use local food only in life or death situations. Remember, you can survive for a long time without food, especially if the food you eat may kill you!

If you must use local food, select only healthy looking plants and animals. Do not select known carriers of vectors such as rats or other vermin. Select and prepare plants as you would in radioactive areas. Prepare animals as you do plants. Always use gloves and protective clothing when handling animals or plants. Cook all plant and animal food by boiling only. Boil all food for at least 10 minutes to kill all pathogens. Do not try to fry, bake, or roast local food. There is no guarantee that all infected portions have reached the required temperature to kill all pathogens. Do not eat raw food.

16.3 CHEMICAL ENVIRONMENTS

Chemical warfare can create extreme problems in a survival situation, but you can overcome the problems with the proper equipment, knowledge, and training. As a survivor, your first line of defence is your proficiency in nuclear, biological, and chemical (NBC) training.

This training includes donning and wearing a protective mask, hazmat suit, personal decontamination, recognition of chemical agent symptoms, individual and specific first aid for chemical agent contamination, and many other things you don't have. If you are not proficient in these skills, you will have little chance of surviving a chemical environment.

The subject matter covered below is not a substitute for any of the individual tasks in which you must be proficient. Military documents, that you don't have, address the various chemical agents, their effects, and first aid for these agents. The following information is only useful providing you are proficient in the use of chemical protective equipment and the symptoms of various chemical agents. Which you aren't. Good luck.

16.3.1 DETECTION OF CHEMICAL AGENTS

The best method for detecting chemical agents is the use of a chemical agent detector. Since you don't have one, you will have to rely on your physical senses. You must be alert and able to detect any clues indicating the use of chemical warfare. General indicators of the presence of chemical agents are tears, difficult breathing, choking, itching, coughing, and dizziness. With agents that are very hard to detect, you must watch for symptoms in fellow survivors. Your surroundings will provide valuable clues to the presence of chemical agents – for example, dead animals, sick people, or zombies.

Your sense of smell may alert you to some chemical agents, but most will be odourless. The odour of newly cut grass or hay may indicate the presence of choking agents. A smell of almonds may indicate blood agents.

Sight will help you detect chemical agents. Most chemical agents in the solid or liquid state have some colour. In the vapour state, you can see some chemical agents as a mist or thin fog immediately after the bomb or shell bursts. By observing for symptoms in others and by observing delivery means, you may be able to have some warning of chemical agents. Mustard gas in the liquid state will appear as oily patches on leaves or on buildings.

The sound of enemy munitions will give some clue to the presence of chemical weapons. Muffled shell or bomb detonations are a good indicator.

Irritation in the nose or eyes or on the skin is an urgent warning to protect your body from chemical agents. Additionally, a strange taste in food, water, or cigarettes may serve as a warning that they have been contaminated.

16.3.2 PROTECTION AGAINST CHEMICAL AGENTS

As a survivor, use the following general steps, to protect yourself from a chemical attack —

- Use protective equipment.
- Give fast and correct self-aid when contaminated.
- Avoid areas where chemical agents exist.
- Decontaminate your equipment and body as soon as possible.

Your protective mask and hazmat suit, that you don't have, are your key to survival. Without these, you stand very little chance. You must take care of these items and protect them from damage. Practice correct self-aid procedures before exposure to chemical agents.

Detection of chemical agents and the avoidance of contaminated areas are extremely important to your survival. Use whatever detection kits that may be available. Since you are in a survival situation, avoid contaminated areas at all costs. You can expect no help should you become contaminated. If you do become contaminated, decontaminate yourself as soon as possible using proper procedures.

16.3.3 SHELTER

If you find yourself in a contaminated area, move out of the area as fast as possible. Travel crosswind or upwind to reduce the exposure to the hazard.

If you cannot leave immediately and have to build a shelter, use normal construction techniques, with a few changes. Build in a clearing, away from vegetation. Remove all topsoil in the area of the shelter to decontaminate the area. Keep the shelter's entrance closed and oriented at a 90-degree angle to the prevailing wind.

Do not build a fire using contaminated wood—the smoke will be toxic. Use extreme caution when entering your shelter so that you will not bring contamination inside.

16.3.4 WATER PROCUREMENT

As with biological and nuclear environments, getting water in a chemical environment is difficult. Obviously, water in sealed containers is your best and safest source. You must protect this water as much as possible. Be sure to decontaminate the containers before opening.

If you cannot get water in sealed containers, try to get it from a closed source such as underground water pipes. You may use rainwater or snow if there is no evidence of contamination. Use water from slow-moving streams, if necessary, but always check first for signs of contamination, and always filter the water as described under nuclear conditions.

Signs of water source contamination are foreign odours such as garlic, mustard, geranium, or bitter almonds. Oily spots on the surface of the water or nearby the water, or the presence of dead fish or animals are signs of contamination.

If these signs are present, do not use the water. Always boil or purify the water to prevent bacteriological infection.

16.3.5 FOOD PROCUREMENT

It is extremely difficult to eat while in a contaminated area. You will have to break the seal on your protective mask to eat so find an area where you can safely unmask. The safest source of food is sealed containers. Decontaminate all sealed food containers by boiling the container before opening, otherwise you will contaminate the food.

If you must eat local plants or animals, do not use plants from contaminated areas or animals that appear to be sick. When handling plants or animals, use protective gloves and clothing.

16.4 DROUGHT

Drought, caused by long periods of dry weather or insufficient rainfall, creates desert in areas where it is a permanent condition. The areas of desert in the world today are that way because of their position on the planet. If the rotational axis of the world changes during a pole shift, areas that are lush today may slowly become desert.

Where it is balanced by a wet season, water can be stored to last throughout the dry periods. The storage of large amounts of water is advisable in any case, if at all possible.

In temperate regions, if rainfall drops below far the normal, periodic drought may be produced with vegetation unable to obtain enough water to compensate for what it loses to that air.

Invisible Drought

In cases where the dry spell may not be so obvious, but there is still sufficient moisture to keep plants barely alive, a condition known as an invisible – or green – drought occurs.

The decreasing quality of vegetation causes deprivation throughout the food chains that are dependant upon it – including you. Learn to preserve food when supplies are plentiful and waste nothing. Dead and dying animals may even pollute the water supplies that still remain.

Dead Animal Disease Risk

The corpses of dead animals should be buried in deep graves. Dry ground can be very hard, but burying is the best way to remove sources of infection. They could be burned but because drought leaves everything tinder dry, a fire could easily get out of hand.

If it is impossible to simply avoid areas where the dead could be an infection risk, and digging deep graves is impractical, consider digging a shallow pit to incinerate the dead. Keep the fire small and do not leave the fire unguarded. Make sure it is extinguished with sand or soil.

Hygiene

Lack of water for washing and sanitation can bring the risk of infection. If you are in a house with a working toilet, lack of water in the S-bend will allow gasses and bacteria to rise up from the sewers. Do not use the toilet, but leave water in the bowl to form a seal. Make an outdoor latrine to use instead.

Sweating will help to keep pores open and free of dirt, but – even when you need all available water for drinking – try to wash hands after defecating and before preparing food.

Store and Conserve Water

If a monsoon does not start at an expected time, or a long hot dry season parches the earth, take precautions by storing as much water as possible and using it wisely. Keep it covered and shaded to prevent evaporation if you do not have water tight containers.

Consider digging a damn if resources and time permits. Dig a pit for storage in a shady spot, avoiding water-sapping tree roots. Line it with plastic sheeting or cement if available, or if there is clay in the area, line the bottom and sides with a thick layer.

NEVER waste water. Water used for cooking can later be used for washing or drinking. Boil all drinking water. If a well runs dry, you may be able to gain more by digging deeper. See **WATER SOURCES** (Page 3-1) for details on how to find water in arid environments.

16.5 FIRE

Fire requires heat, fuel and oxygen, and produces smoke, heat and toxic gases. The best protection from fire is prevention. Carelessness with cigarettes, matches and cooking is the cause of many fires. The sun shining through a discarded bottle or piece of broken glass can start a blaze in a dry season.

16.5.1 FOREST FIRES

If you are present when a fire starts (or when a camp fire accidentally spreads) in woodland, or on hearth or grassland, your first action should be to SMOTHER it.

The first sign of approaching fire will be smoke, then you will probably hear the fire before you see flames. You may notice unusual animal behaviour before you realise the cause.

Escape Route

If caught in an area where fire is raging, and when it is too late to put it out, do NOT immediately flee – unless the fire is so close that you have no choice. Although you may feel that clothing hampers your movement, remain clothed as this will shield you from the full force of the heat.

Smoke will indicate the direction of the wind, and the fire will be moving fastest in that direction. If the wind is blowing away from you, towards the fire, move INTO the wind. Try to head for any natural fire break – such as a clearing.

A river is the best fire break – even if the flames can leap you will be reasonably safe in the water. In forestry plantations look for the roadways and firebreaks. **Do not run wildly.**

Choose your escape route. Check the surrounding terrain and the wind direction to assess the possible spread of the fire.

If the wind is blowing towards you, the fire is likely to reach you more quickly – and the flames can leap a larger gap. Try to go around the fire if possible – but some fires can be several kilometres wide. If you can neither skirt or outdistance the blaze, take refuge in a large clearing, deep ravine, watercourse or gully.

Into the Fire

Sometimes the best escape route may be to run THROUGH the flames. This is impossible if they are very intense and the area covered by the actual fire is great. In a large clearing or on heathland however, it may be possible to run through less dense fire to refuge on the already burned out land.

Cover as much exposed skin as possible. If you have water available, tip some over you to damp down clothing, hair and any flesh you have not been able to cover. Dampen a piece of cloth to cover your nose and mouth.

Thick vegetation will burn fiercely and slow you down – so chose the spot for your breakthrough with care. Make your mind up then do not delay. Take a deep breath, cover your nose and mouth, and RUN.

Stay in a Vehicle

If caught in a forest fire in a vehicle, stay inside and keep the windows tightly shut. Close all vents in the ventilation system. The car will give you some protection from radiant heat and smoke inhalation. Drive away from the fire if possible, but if immobilised – stay put.

People have survived by staying in a vehicle until the glass began to melt, by which time the fire had moved beyond them. If they had panicked and ran into the fire they would have died.

There is a danger of a petrol tank exploding, but your chances of survival are much inside than out if the fire is intense around the vehicle. Diesel does not explode as petrol does.

Going to Earth

If there is no natural break or gully in which to shelter and the fire is too deep to think of running through it, you may have to seek the shelter of the earth itself.

People have survived fires by digging themselves in and covering themselves with earth, allowing the fire to burn over the top of them. The risk is considerable – not only from the heat, but from suffocation as the fire consumes the available oxygen.

Scrape as much of a hollow, throwing the earth onto a coat or sheet if you have one, then pull the sheet over you with its earth covering. Cup your hands over your mouth and breath through them. This will protect the respiratory system from the very hot air and sparks. Try to hold your breath as the fire passes over.

Fight Fire With Fire

It may be possible to use the fire itself as protection, if there is no way of getting out of the path of the fire – but it is still some distance away.

The technique is to burn a patch of ground before the main fire reaches it. With nothing left to ignite the fire cannot advance, providing a place of refuge. The main fire must be sufficiently far away for your fire to burn a large enough space before it arrives.

Light your own fire along as wide a line as possible – at least 10 m (30 ft) wide, but 100 m (300 ft) would be better. It will burn in the same direction as the main fire, creating a break in which to move into. Make sure you determine the direction of wind carefully.

WARNING!!!

Winds may be swirling and fires create their own draughts, so you may still have to make a dash through your own flames. The main fire must be far enough away for your own fire to burn and pass.

Do not underestimate the speed at which flames travel – they may be approaching faster than you can run. Do NOT light another fire unless you are desperate and fairly certain of the outcome.

16.5.2 BURNING BUILDINGS

Smoke will usually be the first indication of fire. If the fire is still small, attempt to extinguish it by covering with a blanket or thick curtain, or using sand, water or appropriate fire extinguisher.

Electrical Fires

If there is any possibility of a fire being caused by an electrical fault, do not use water until the power has been turned off, preferably at the mains. Turn off gas at the mains too. Be careful with CRT monitors – cold water can make them implode and they can carry a large charge, even after being disconnected. Try to smother them and approach them from behind.

Evacuation

If a fire is already too big to fight with the resources available, evacuate the building. Turn off power and gas at the mains if possible and close all reachable doors and windows. Fire travels faster upward than downward, though collapsing structure can bring flames to a lower level. Staircases, lift-wells and ventilation shafts are particularly dangerous.

NEVER use a lift during a fire. If you need to move down, use a smoke-free staircase.

Before opening any doors, looks for smoke around the edges and check for heat. Metal doorknobs are a good test. If they feel warm, do not open the door. Use the back of your hand for the test – grasping a knob can cause a burn. A strong door can keep flames out for 30 minutes or more, but do not rely on this – unless they are fire doors.

 If there is no alternative to going into a burning room and the door opens in your direction – brace your foot against the door and open it only a crack. This will help to stop it from being forced wide open by the pressure of hot air and gasses inside.

When moving into a burning room, crouch low to enter and open the door as little as possible. This will expose you to less smoke and heat and give less chance for the fire to pass through the gap. Close the door behind you to slow the fires spread.

To break a window, use a piece of furniture. You can kick it out, but do not pull your foot back quickly – you will have to negotiate broken glass. If you use your fist, wrap it first. Alternatively, an elbow protected by a thick jacket can be effective.

Preparing to Jump

Do NOT jump – drop. Tie sheets, blankets, curtains, or anything else you can find to make a rope. Even if it does not reach the ground, it will reduce the distance you have to fall. Tie them with reef knots and test they are strong by pulling.

Move a heavy piece of furniture to the window to tie the rope on to, or tie it to heating pipes, or smash out a window and tie to a thick part of the frame. If possible, drop cushions, pillows, a mattress or anything soft to reduce the impact. The first two people down may hold a sheet or blanket to catch subsequent people.

If there is no rope available, lower yourself out the window and hang from the sill. If there is no sill, hang from the bottom of the window frame. Try to remove any shards of broken glass.

Falling Onto a Slope

Face down the slope as you drop, with legs together and the knees slightly bent. As you drop, bring the head down onto the chest and elbows tightly into the sides, the hands protecting the head. Land on flat feet, allowing the knees to bend fully, rolling forward in a tight somersault.

This is the method that parachutists use.

Wait until the very last chance of rescue before risking a drop greater that 4 m (14 ft).

Escaping Through Fire

- If forced to travel through flames to reach safety, cover yourself (including your head) in a blanket, curtain, overcoat or whatever you can – wet if you can, take a deep breath and go.
- If your clothes catch alight – do not stay on your feet when out of the fire. The flames and smoke will travel up your body, over your face and into your lungs.
- Do NOT run – this will only fan the flames.
- Roll on the ground and try to wrap yourself in something that will smother the flames.
- If someone else comes running out of the fire with their clothes alight, push them to the ground and use the same methods of depriving the flames of oxygen. Do not hug them to you or your own clothes may catch on fire.

16.5.3 VEHICLE FIRES

The greatest danger of a vehicle fire is the risk of the fuel tank being ignited. A petrol tank may explode like a bomb – scattering burning petrol everywhere. Try to control the fire before it can reach the tank, or get the hell away from it.

In a Confined Space

If a car catches fire in a confined space, such as a garage, smoke and fumes will soon build up. If you cannot put the fire out, try to remove the car from the building. Do NOT get in the car – everything can be done from the outside including steering. If possible push or pull the car out, otherwise select low gear or reverse and start the car. Careful - it will probably jerk forward.

- **In a crashed car:** Doors may jam – If it catches fire then get through any window or kick the windscreen out.
- **If the fire is inside the car:** use the extinguisher or smother it with a rug, coat or car seat cover. Synthetic materials used in upholstery in many cars burn rapidly and give off thick smoke and toxic gases.
  These will persist even when the flames are out so get out as soon as possible.
- **If the fire is also outside the car:** amid spilt fuel for example – keep the windows shut and drive out of the danger zone, abandoning the car as soon as it is safe to do so.

16.6 FLOOD

Flooding may be caused by —

- The overflowing of rivers, lakes and reservoirs caused by heavy rains – not necessarily at the place where the rainfall occurs.
- The build-up of sea or lake water due to the effects of submarine earthquakes, hurricanes and freak high-tides and winds.
- The subduction of tectonic plates – ie, the land you are on may sink.
- The collapse of dams or dykes.

Heavy rain can produce torrents where there was once a dry riverbed, or build up in a narrow channel or behind a barrier which then gives way to a destructive rushing wall of water.

Persistent rainfall over a long period after a dry spell and heavy storms should alert you to keep clear of water channels and low-lying ground, but a flood can effect much wider areas.

Try to set up on high ground whenever possible. If water is rising, move to higher ground sooner rather than later. In hilly areas, stay away from valley bottoms which are particularly prone to flash floods.

Food and Water

If you are already hunting or trapping, food is not likely to be a problem, at least at first – animals will also head for high ground. Both predators and prey are likely to concentrate on getting to safety – but be aware of panic stricken animals in the water.

Drinking water may be difficult to obtain, for the water may be contaminated. Collect rainwater to drink and boil any other water before you use it.

Flash Floods

In times of heavy sudden rainfall, keep out of valley bottoms and stream beds both during and after rainfall. Remember that you don't have to be at the bottom of a hill to be swept away from water rushing down it – often carrying mud and deadly debris or trees and rocks.

Coastal Flooding

Is usually a combination of high tides and winds that make them even higher. Flood warnings may be given if communications are still active.

A very important indicator is an unusually high tide that keeps coming in – this indicates plate subduction. If you notice the tide creeping ever further inland, pack up and get ready to move out permanently. Take everything useful that you can and prepare to be on foot if necessary.

Main routes will be congested (they will look like parking lots) and may even be broken up from earthquake activity, or congested with large immovable debris. A 4 wheel drive vehicle – preferably diesel – is far more likely to be able to take alternate routes.

Flood Aftermath

As the waters recede (IF they recede) they leave behind a scene of devastation littered with debris and the bodies of flood victims. With decay and the pollution of the water comes the risk of disease and extra precautions are necessary.

Burn all animal corpses – do not risk eating them – and thoroughly boil all water before use. Some crops may still be viable after the waters recede and birds will be safe and good to eat.

16.6.1 FLOODED BUILDINGS

If you are in a solid building when the water begins to rise, stay where you are if it is rising rapidly. You will be less at risk than trying to escape on foot or in a vehicle. Turn off gas and electricity and prepare emergency food supplies, warm clothing, drinking water in water-tight containers. It is important to keep all containers well sealed to avoid accidental spillage or contamination.

> If you think the water may continue to rise, an evacuation may be a lesser risk than staying put. Remember – **rescue by helicopter is extremely unlikely – do NOT expect this**. Make your decision early and take everything you need. Make sure you know where you are going beforehand. If you have a boat and a rugged vehicle (ie a diesel engine with a snorkel) take it with you – if there is time. Make your decision early, get your shit together and GO.

If you have them prepared, take your survival kits with you. This should include a torch and batteries. A portable gas stove will also be handy. Don't forget something to light it with.

Move Upwards

Move to an upper floor, or on to the roof. If you are forced to occupy the roof, try to erect some type of shelter. If it is a sloping roof, tie everyone to a chimney stack or other solid point. Use bed sheets if you have no rope. Use reef knots as they are easy to untie if you need to, or make sure you carry a sharp knife. A serrated kitchen knife is perfect for cutting rope.

16.6.2 FLOOD READINESS

If you live in a river valley or in coastal area prone to flooding, find out how high you are above normal water levels. Learn the easiest route to high ground – not necessarily via main roads, or roads at all.

Even a few inches of floodwater can do a lot of damage and it's worth laying sandbags or plastic shopping bags full of earth along the bottom of doorways to keep out as much water as possible. The central heating flue, ventilation bricks and other spaces must all be sealed.

Basements

If a high flood is likely, there is little point in trying to keep water out of basements. In some houses, this may cause more damage do to uneven pressure on the basement walls. If you are bound to be flooded, you may consider letting the basement flood with the clean flood water, before the debris starts floating in.

16.6.3 EVACUATION

If you are abandoning your home, bring outdoor furniture and all the other crap you have in your yard inside. This will reduce the amount of debris floating or being swept along outside.

When walking or driving to a safer location, remember that a small drop in the level of the roadway can make a considerable difference to the water level.

Do NOT attempt to cross a pool or stream of water unless you are CERTAIN that the water level is not above the centre of the wheels, or higher than your knees (outside the vehicle).

Alternatively, if you have a diesel engine with a snorkel, you can drive the car while it is almost completely submerged – providing you can breathe of course. Bear in mind the power of moving water and in any case, more than 1 m (3 ft) of water is extremely risky to drive through. Remove your seatbelts and have your survival bags on your lap in case of accident.

Consider abandoning your car and using **Expedient Water Crossings** (Page 19-1) instead.

If crossing a bridge which is underwater, take special care – you may not be able to see that the flood has already washed parts of the bridge away. Consider walking across before attempting to drive. If you do this, take a walking stick to gauge the path ahead and tether yourself with a strong rope to avoid being washed away.

16.7 TSUNAMI

A tsunami is linked with an earthquake beneath the ocean – tectonic plates moving and displacing a large volume of ocean water. Since the Boxing Day 2004, and the Japan 2011 tsunami, most people are aware of the nature of a tsunami and the devastation it can cause.

The effect and scale of a tsunami is dependant on many factors – the position of the quake, the shape of the shoreline, the shape of the land under the ocean, and the movement of the earth herself. One that is quite small on one coastline may be monstrous on another.

Warnings may be issued but do not rely on this. To give you an example of the heart and minds of the powers that be, I will outline the strategy of the Australian government regarding tsunami warnings, once the threat is confirmed to be likely —

1	Emergency services are notified to fill their vehicles, generators and reserve tanks at any available fuel station – leaving little or no fuel for anyone else.
2	Bank managers are notified to clear out their vaults and transfer cash and valuables to undisclosed storage areas to prevent the chance of looting by civilians.
3	45 minutes after the threat is confirmed to be likely, the general public is informed.

This is a rather tame strategy, and does consider the wellbeing of the general public – sort of. Leaders and people in positions of power (both official and shadow) in other countries can and DO have more selfish intentions with the information channels they have access to.

It is easier for emergency services to evacuate dead bodies than living people

Not all earthquakes will cause a tsunami, but any could – the science of earthquakes is unfortunately not nearly accurate enough for reliable predictions. Keep away from shores and take to higher ground if there are tremors and you are near the coast – especially if you do not normally experience quakes in your area.

One dead giveaway that a tsunami is inevitable is seeing the ocean recede. If you see the ocean suddenly pulling back – or ANY unusual activity on the shore – EVACUATE IMMEDIATELY – you don't have much time. NOTE – The ocean receding is a warning only on one side of the water displacement, on the other side – there is NO warning. Coastlines are extremely dangerous places.

Do NOT go looking for a tsunami. Water moves quickly and if you see the wave approaching – you are almost certainly doomed. There is no defence against a wall of moving water. MOVE!

16.8 HURRICANE

A hurricane is a high speed wind. These can bring torrential rain and destroy flimsy structures. It is a tropical form of cyclone, which in more temperate latitudes would be prevented from developing in the upper levels of the air by the prevailing westerly winds.

Hurricanes are also known by various other names around the world —

- **Hurricane** – Caribbean and North Atlantic, eastern North Pacific, western South Pacific.
- **Cyclone** – Arabian Sea, Bay of Bengal, southern Indian Ocean.
- **Typhoon** – China Sea, west North Pacific.

Hurricanes develop over the ocean when sea temperatures are at their highest, especially in the late summer. Warm air creates a low pressure core around which winds may rotate at speeds of 200 kph (300 mph) or more. These winds circle anti-clockwise in the Northern hemisphere and clockwise in the southern.

The strongest winds are usually 16-19 km (10-12 mi) from the centre of the hurricane, but the centre (or 'eye') brings temporary calm.

They can occur at any time of the year, but in the northern hemisphere the main season is June to November, and November to April in the southern – especially January and February. Hurricanes are not currently a feature of the South Atlantic.

Pattern of the Hurricane

Out at sea hurricanes will build up force and veer toward the pole, the wind speed is usually greatest at the pole side of the eye. They can travel as fast as 50 kph (30 mph) bringing devastation on any islands and coastlines they pass over, but usually slowing down when they reach mainland to around 16 kph (10 mph).

Hurricane Warnings

With satellites, communications, media and infrastructure in place, you should be given plenty of warning about an approaching hurricane and the likely strength. Without this convenience, the growth of a swell can be an indication of a hurricane – when coupled with other conditions such as —

- Highly coloured sunsets or sunrises.
- Dense barriers of cirrus cloud converging towards the vertex of the approaching storm.
- Abnormal rise in barometric pressure following by an equally rapid drop.

Safety Precautions

Get out of the hurricanes path if possible and practical. If hurricane warnings are given, you will usually have 24 hours notice, which will give you plenty of time to evacuate.

- Keep away from the coast, where destruction will be worst, with flooding and a tidal wave. Stay away from river banks as well.
- Board up all windows and secure any objects outdoors that may be blown away. If you cannot board up the windows, place a cross (X) of Gaffa tape over the window pane to reduce the risk of shards of glass causing injuries.
- At sea, take down all canvas, batten down the hatches and stow all gear. Put on your life preservers if you have them – which you should.

If you are in a solid building and on high ground – STAY WHERE YOU ARE – travel in a hurricane is extremely dangerous. The safest place is usually in a basement or under stairs. Water and power supplies are likely to be cut off in a heavy storm so store drinking water and carry torches, a radio, and plenty of batteries.

Keep a first aid kit handy and a portable gas stove if you have one.

Seeking Shelter

Outdoors a cave will offer the best protection, next best is a ditch. If unable to escape lie flat on the ground where at least you will be less likely to be hit by flying debris. Crawl to the leeside of any really solid structure such as a stable rocky outcrop or a wide belt of large trees. Beware of small trees or fences which may be uprooted.

Stay where you are when the hurricane appears to have passed – there will usually be less than an hour of calm as the eye passes overhead, and then the winds will resume in the opposite direction.

If sheltering outdoors, move to the other side of your windbreak in preparation, or move to a shelter if nearby.

16.9 TORNADO

Tornadoes are violent storms associated with low atmospheric pressure and swirling winds. They develop when air on the surface has been warmed and a column of cool air descends from the base of cumulonimbus storm clouds above. Air rushing into the low pressure area begins to rotate fiercely.

Cloud layers moving in different directions indicate instability in the atmosphere, and different densities within the layers. This may be an indication that turbulence is approaching.

Tornadoes are the most violent of atmospheric phenomena and are extremely destructive over a narrow path. Wind speeds have been estimated at 620 kph (400 mph). The diameter of a 'twister' at ground level is usually only 25-50 m (80-160 ft) but within it, the destruction is immense. Everything in its path except the most solid structures is sucked up into the air.

The difference in air pressure between the inside and outside of a building is often the cause of collapse – or explosion. Tornadoes can sound like a spinning top or engine and have been heard up to 40 km (25 mi) away. They travel at 50-65 kph (30-40 mph).

At sea, tornadoes can form water spouts. Although they can occur elsewhere – and probably will – currently they are most prevalent over the prairies of the United States, in the Mississippi-Missouri valley and in Australia. They can develop in a hurricane.

Tornado Precautions

Take shelter in the most solid structure available – reinforced concrete or steel-framed if possible, or in a cave. In a cellar stay close to the outside wall, or in a specially reinforced section.

If there is no basement, go to the centre of the lowest floor or shelter under sturdy furniture – but not where there is heavy furniture on a floor above. Keep well away from windows.

Firmly close all doors and windows on the side facing the oncoming whirlwind and open the windows on the other side. This will prevent the wind getting in and taking your roof away as it approaches and equalise the pressure to reduce the risk of the house exploding.

Do not stay in a caravan or car – they could be drawn up by the storm.

Outdoors you are vulnerable to flying debris and to being lifted up. You CAN see a tornado approaching – so get out of the way. Travel at right angles to its apparent path. Take a shelter in a ditch or depression in the ground, lie flat and cover your head with your arms.

16.10 LIGHTNING

The release of electrical charges built up in clouds can be especially dangerous on high ground or when you are the tallest object. In a lightning storm, keep away from hill brows, from tall trees and lone boulders. Make for low, level ground and lie flat.

Stay away from anything conductive if possible, such as metal fences and structures. Stay away from anything tall.

Insulation

Air is normally an insulator, but every material has a 'punch-through' point when a significant charge is applied to it, therefore trying to insulate yourself from lightning strike is almost impossible – to the extent of being ridiculous. However, it is still advisable to insulate yourself from wet ground and other conductive surfaces, because a nearby strike will cause residual currents – of considerable energy – to flow for some distance around a strike.

Having a thick layer of insulation – over a wide area – under you can also prevent the lesser energy streamers which rise up from the ground – these positive streamers attract the main strike. Use any dry material you can find to sit on and do not touch the ground.

Path of Least Resistance

Sometimes the safest place to be is INSIDE a metal structure, such as a metal shed or vehicle. This is because an electric current will follow the path of least resistance, travelling through the easy path of the metal, rather than the difficult path of air, if given a chance.

If you shelter inside a conductive container, do not touch the sides or any metal surface. Try to insulate yourself from the bottom if possible. Be as far away from the walls as possible. Block your ears with your palms, put your head down and shield your eyes. Try not to take deep breaths as the shockwave can be damaging to lungs, the risk is minimised with less air inside.

> A thin tin shed without thick metal beams (ie garden shed) will not offer suitable protection as the metal will probably vaporize at the point of the strike. A shipping container is better.
>
> If the metal structure is the highest point around, do NOT shelter inside.

Sensing a Strike

You can sometimes sense that a lightning strike is imminent by a tingling in the skin and the sensation of hair standing on end – this is a positively charged streamer rising from the earth and there is a very good chance that a strike will meet at this point – within a second.

Drop to the ground IMMEDIATELY, first to your knees with your hands touching the ground – this may cause the strike to take the path of least resistance through your arms missing vital organs. Then quickly lie flat.

Shelter in Caves

One of the best places to shelter in a lightning storm is at least 3 m (10 ft) inside a cave with a minimum of 1 m (3 ft) space either side of you. Do not shelter in a cave mouth or under and overhanging rock in mountainous country – the lightning can spark across the gap.

Small openings in rocks are frequently the ends of fissures which are also drainage routes and automatic lightning channels.

16.11 EARTHQUAKE

Earthquakes are perhaps the most fearsome of all natures' violence – they come suddenly with little or no warning and the scope is not often known until after the event. Sometimes the first quake is only a pre-shock, with stronger quakes to follow.

Unlike other natural hazards, very little can be done to prepare for an earthquake. Urban areas and large cities are very dangerous during an earthquake. There large structures that may collapse around you as well as gas and water lines that may rupture, producing other hazards.

Quakes strike most often at the boundaries of tectonic plates, but these areas are not the only places in which a quake can strike. Expect *large* magnitude earthquakes worldwide, yes – in YOUR area. Do NOT take this warning lightly.

With constant monitoring by seismologists, major earthquakes can be predicted and evacuation is possible, but won't ever happen due to these reasons —

- The science of predicting earthquakes is not nearly accurate enough for a guarantee.
- Evacuations are costly and messy and if no earthquake comes, then civilians are less likely to heed consequent warnings.
- The powers that be couldn't care less about you.

Warning Signs

There are some warning signs that you can look out for. These are not guarantees, but if you see such indicators – especially when combined – then you should at least be on alert —

- **Animals** – Strange behaviour in animals is well documented to precede an earthquake. Animals become very alert, tense and ready to run at the slightest provocation.
- **Radio** – If you hear static or 'screeches' on the radio or through an amplified sound system this may indicate seismic activity. These will come in bursts. Rock under pressure produces both heat and electromagnetic signals – it is the electromagnetic signals that are detected.
- **Clouds** – Strange cloud formations are on historical record as being indicators of seismic activity. The water vapour that clouds are made of is susceptible to the many particle flows that are generated when rock is under pressure.
  Such clouds may precede an earthquake by hours, days or months.
- **Volcanoes** – Volcanoes often show signs of increased activity before a major eruption. Sulphurous smells from rivers, stinging acidic rain, loud rumblings or plumes of steam from a volcano are all warning signs.

Pictured right are some examples of clouds that have preceded earthquakes. Due to the nature of the many frequencies that may be involved, and the physics of the clouds themselves, it is impossible to give a definitive example of an earthquake-preceding cloud. Any strange cloud with a wave-like pattern may – or may not – be an indicator.

16.11.1 PRECAUTIONS

If you have had tremors which you believe may be foreshocks, or you are otherwise expecting an earthquake, there are some precautions to take.

- Stay tuned to local a radio station if possible for reports and advice.
- Turn off gas, electricity and water.
- Remove large and heavy objects from high shelves.
- Have on hand: fresh water, emergency food, flashlights, first aid materials and batteries.

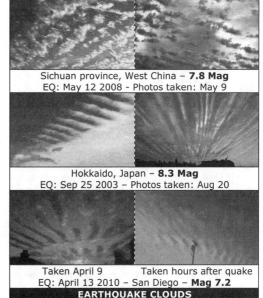

Sichuan province, West China – **7.8 Mag**
EQ: May 12 2008 - Photos taken: May 9

Hokkaido, Japan – **8.3 Mag**
EQ: Sep 25 2003 – Photos taken: Aug 20

Taken April 9   Taken hours after quake
EQ: April 13 2010 – San Diego – **Mag 7.2**
EARTHQUAKE CLOUDS

In a Building

Stay indoors unless the structure is in danger of collapsing completely. Douse fires. Stay away from glass such as mirrors and large windows. An inside corner of the house, or a well-supported interior doorway are good places to shelter. A lower floor or a cellar gives the best chance of survival.

Make sure there are plenty of exits. Get under a table or large, strong piece of furniture which will give both protection and an air space. In a shop, keep away from large displays of goods. In high-rise offices never get into an elevator. Staircases may attract panicking people. Get under a desk.

In a Car

Stop as quickly as you can, but stay in the car – it will offer some protection from falling objects. Crouch down below seat level and you will be further protection. When the tremors stop keep a watch for any obstructions and hazards such as broken cables and undermined roadways or bridges which could give way.

Outdoors

Lie flat on the ground. Do not try to run. You will be thrown about and could be swallowed by a fissure. Keep away from tall buildings and trees. Do not deliberately go underground or into a tunnel where you could be trapped by collapse. If you have managed to get to an open space, do not move back into buildings until you are sure that all tremors have ceased.

On a hillside, it is safer to get to the top. Slopes are prone to landslides and there would be little chance of survival. People have been known to survive by rolling into a tight ball.

Beaches – providing they are not below cliffs – are initially fairly safe but, since tidal waves often follow a quake you should move off the beach onto high ground as soon as the tremor has finished. Further tremors are unlikely to be as dangerous as a tsunami.

Be calm and think fast. Speed is essential if an earthquake strikes. There is little time to organise others. Use force if necessary to get them to safety or pull them to the ground.

16.11.2 AFTER THE EARTHQUAKE

Check yourself and others for injuries. Apply first aid if necessary.

Rupture of sewerage systems, contamination of water and the hazards of the bodies trapped in the wreckage can all make the risk of disease as deadly as the earthquake itself. If practical, bury all corpses – animal and human. Take special precautions over sanitation and hygiene. Filter and boil all water. Check that sewerage services are intact before using lavatories.

Do not shelter in damaged buildings or ruins. Build a shelter from debris. Be prepared for aftershocks. Open cupboards carefully as heavy objects may fall out. Clean up spilled chemicals and potentially harmful substances. Do not strike matches or lighters or use electrical appliances. There may be natural gas released from below the ground in the quake – natural gas has no odour. The odour in mains and bottled gas is added to allow detection.

16.12 VOLCANO

Active volcanoes are found in the areas of the world which are also most prone to earthquakes. Expect any volcano to become active, even if it has been dormant for thousands of years.

16.12.1 ERUPTION HAZARDS

Although it is possible to outrun most basalt lava flows they continue relentlessly until they reach a valley bottom or eventually cool off. They crush and bury everything in their path. Lava flows are the least hazardous to life as the able-bodied can escape them.

Missiles

Volcanic missiles, ranging from pebble-size fragments to huge lumps of rock and hot lava, can be scattered over vast distances. Volcanic ash can cover a massive area.

If escaping from close to a volcano, hard helmets will offer some protection. Over a wider area, evacuation may not be necessary, but protection should be worn against the ash and any rain.

Ash

Volcanic ash is pulverised rock forced out in a cloud of steam and gasses. Abrasive, irritant and heavy, its weight can cause roofs to collapse. It smothers crops, blocks transport routes and watercourses.

Combined with toxic gases ash can cause lung damage to the very young, the old, and people with respiratory problems. Only very close to eruptions are gases concentrated enough to poison healthy people.

When ash is combined with rain, sulphuric and other acids are produced in concentrations which can burn the skin, eyes and mucus membranes. Any water collected should be distilled before being consumed. Wear goggles that seal around the eyes (such as swimming goggles, not sunglasses). Use a damp cloth over the mouth and nose, or industrial dust masks.

On reaching shelter, remove clothing, wash exposed skin and flush eyes with clean water.

Gas Balls

A ball of red-hot gas and dust may roll down the side of a volcano at speeds of over 160 kph (100 mph). Unless there is an underground shelter nearby, the only chance of survival is to submerge under water and hold your breath for the 30 seconds or so it will take to pass.

16.12.2 MUD FLOWS

The volcano may melt ice and snow and cause a glacial floor or – combined with earth – create a mudflow. This can move up to 100 kph (60 mph) with devastating effect. In a narrow valley a mudflow can be as much as 30 m (100 ft) high. They are a danger long after the major eruption is over and are a risk even when the volcano is dormant if it generates enough heat to produce meltwater retained by ice barriers. Heavy rains may cause it to breach the ice.

16.13 AVALANCHE

There are several types of avalanche.

Soft-Slab Avalanche

Snow falling on lee slopes, often below a cornice, fails to settle and compact like the snow below. A gap forms behind. It may feel hard and safe but any disturbance or loud noise can set the whole slab in motion.

Airborne Avalanche

These are frequently the result of new snow falling on an already hard crust or in cold, dry conditions. This may begin as a slab avalanche, but gathers momentum and more powdered snow to reach very high speeds. Cover nose and mouth to stand a chance of survival – death is caused by drowning from inhaling snow.

Wet-Snow Avalanche

These are more common in times of thaw, often following a rapid temperature rise after snowfall. It moves more slowly than an airborne avalanche, picking up trees and rocks in its path. When it stops it freezes solid almost instantly, making rescue very difficult.

Lay flat and use crawl stroke to sit on top of slide (the debris can form a very deep layer). Get rid of pack and other encumbrances. Cover nose and mouth to avoid swallowing snow. When you come to rest, make as big a cavity around you as you can before the snow freezes, and try to reach the surface. Slip off any kit you have not been able to discard – it will hamper your extraction. Save your energy to shout when you hear people.

Surviving the Night

An avalanche in your area may not hit you directly, but it may change conditions in a way that isolates you, for at least a night, probably more. The most immediate need may be to get out of the weather. This will mean to build a snow cave or other appropriate shelter. After that water and food are priorities. See **Cold Weather Survival** (Chapter 14) for survival tips.

16.14 PLANET X

This section was compiled from the information provided by Nancy Lieder of ZetaTalk.

The Planet X prophecy describes a periodic disruption of our planet from an officially unknown object in our solar system. Far beyond Pluto resides a dead binary sun, similar in mass to our own. Planet X orbits between these two objects in a long thin path. This orbit takes approximately 3,600 years to complete – the duration of the Mayan calendar.

This peculiar planet also comes with many moons and other debris, which travel behind it like a string of pearls. This can give the appearance similar to that of a comet from one angle, or a 'winged' planet when viewed head on, due to the smaller moons that trail and snake behind it.

As well as moons, boulders, stones and gasses – attracted during past visits through our solar system – there is a fine iron ore dust surrounding the beast.

Planet X is a dying smouldering sun, and although it does emit light, it is extremely dim compared to our sun, and further diffused due to the massive dust cloud surrounding it.

Where is Planet X?

At the time of writing, Planet X is between the Earth and the Sun – approaching us. After a long journey along its orbit, Planet X moved through our inner solar system around the millennium. Since then it has swung around the sun, and is heading towards Earth.

The signs of its first approach were erratic weather, fine red dust falling from the sky in places, increased fireball sightings, an increase in earthquake activity – include Boxing Day 2004, and Japan 2011. Approaching it appeared as a star, but on its journey past earth and toward the sun, there were some sightings of a second sun.

16.14.1 THE EFFECTS OF THE PASSAGE

Planet X is approximately 4 times the size of the Earth, 12 times the mass, and a huge magnet. As it travels through our inner solar system, it can have dramatic effects on the planets it passes by.

Interaction between Planets

The prophecy in its simplest form states: As Planet X leaves our solar system, it grabs the Earths' South pole with its North pole, and drags us along with it. This results in a 180° shift for the core, and a 90° shift for the crust – after which normal rotation continues but with a changed axis of rotation, and a different geography.

As it approaches Earth, complex interactions occur between the two planets. The first effect is a wobble in the rotation of Earth. This is caused in part by a highly magnetised deposit of iron, located between fault boundaries in the Atlantic Ocean – The Atlantic Rift.

The wobble increases until Planet X is eventually close enough to grip earth by the Atlantic Rift and slow down rotation to a complete stop. This condition last for almost 6 days, leaving one side of the earth in darkness and the other with perpetual sunlight.

Rotation resumes when Planet X leaves and pulls us around. While it takes a whole day for Earth to slow to a stop, it only takes an hour to resume rotation. This is the hour of the shift.

Before the Shift

Leading up to the shift is a period of great turmoil. Weather will become unpredictable and erratic. Snow will fall where is hasn't before. Earthquakes and tsunamis will increase. Volcanoes will pop.

There will be major changes in geography as plates rattle.

LONG DAWN   LONG DAY   LONG DUSK   LONG NIGHT

6 DAYS OF ROTATION STOPPAGE

During the Rotation Stop

One of the signs that rotation is starting to slow is fine red dust falling from the sky, as Planet X's tail drifts towards us. Then, over a 24 hour period, Earth slows down to a complete stop, and stays locked for 5.9 days. During this time Planet X looks huge in the sky. The ancients recorded this as a fire dragon in the sky, due to the appearance of the trail of moons and debris.

During this slowing and rotation stoppage, there is an increasing and almost continuous moan coming from the earth, as the plates are stressed, but cannot relieve the pressure. Sensitive people will become ill from the energy that rock under pressure creates, increasingly so.

During the Shift

When the rotation finally starts after 5.9 days of being gripped by Planet X – it will do so with a jolt as Planet X moves past earth into the inky blackness. It is best to be sitting or lying down when the time is getting close – you will be thrown towards the (current) North.

At this point, a great wind will start as the earth is dragged under her atmosphere. This wind will come from what is now South, but due to the change in axis, this is the new East.

As the earth gets dragged, the oceans try to stay in place, this causes sloshing of the oceans on the coastlines, first the (currently) Southern coastlines, and then the Northern as the water sloshes back. Be at least 160 km (100 mi) from any coastline.

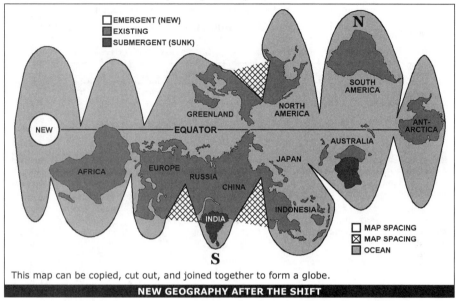

This map can be copied, cut out, and joined together to form a globe.

NEW GEOGRAPHY AFTER THE SHIFT

Many major events will take place before the actual shift. This includes the subduction of India and the Western 2/3 of Australia.

This new arrangement will place the existing poles at the equator, where they will melt before the new poles freeze. The above map shows the extent of the flooding due to this temporary rise in the ocean level.

16.14.2 TIMELINE OF THE LAST WEEKS

When you can see Planet x with the naked eye, undeniably in the sky, time is short. This is the indication that the final seven weeks have arrived. A timeline of events is provided.

At this point, emergency management teams are exhausted from the constant calls for help. By now you should have a plan and be determined to implement it.

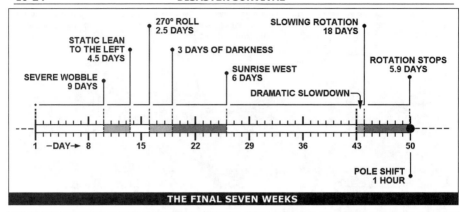

THE FINAL SEVEN WEEKS

These images show Earth. Planet X and the sun, as viewed from the side. The centre-line represents the ecliptic – the ecliptic is the flat plane that the planets orbit along.

As Planet X approaches our Earth, it lies horizontally below the ecliptic. At this point, earth is aligned to the N and S poles of the sun.

This is the position for some time before the final weeks. It is when Planet X pushes up through the ecliptic that the situation begins to change rapidly and a **SEVERE WOBBLE** develops in Earths obit. The sun and moon will often be in erratic positions during this time.

At this point, Planet X starts to turn in a clockwise manner.

As Planet X swings its N pole to the right, Earth moves her N pole away, falling on her side in a **LEAN TO THE LEFT**. Keep an eye on Polaris or the Southern Cross to determine this event. This will also bring the tail of Planet X towards the Earth. Expect increased fireballs in the sky and red dust.

This slow **270° ROLL** continues and Earth must avoid the N Pole of Planet X. It does so by pushing her N Pole away, lying down on her side. This produces **3 DAYS OF DARKNESS** for the Northern Hemisphere.

Earth continues to roll in sync with Planet X and is eventually turned upside down. This creates a condition of **SUNRISE WEST** which lasts for 6 days.

Following this, the roll of Earth continues until she returns to align side-by-side with the Sun and Planet X. It is in this position that the daily grab of the Atlantic Rift begins **SLOWING ROTATION** increasingly as Planet X approaches. The most **DRAMATIC SLOWDOWN** occurs in the last 24 hours, after which **ROTATION STOPS** for 5.9 days – 141 hours, 36 minutes.

Rising up above the ecliptic, Planet X aligns itself with the magnetic flow lines coming from the sun.

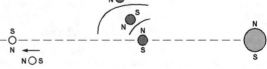

The upwards roll forces the gripped earth to move up with it. The crust wants to stay inline with Planet X as a magnet, and the core wants to stay inline with the sun. The crust then tears away from the core, finally relieving the pressure, and they move independently. This is the hour of the **POLE SHIFT**, the most dangerous time for all.

16.14.3 DETERMINING A SAFE LOCATION

This short guide, copied verbatim with permission from ZetaTalk, will give you general guidelines for safety in your area. The ZetaTalk website has a comprehensive document entitled "safe locations" which you should consult for information regarding your location.

1) The first to consider is whether the area will be viable at all for a ride through the pole shift. India will go under the waves, as will Western Australia. Indonesia, except for the high mountains in Borneo, will be iffy for survival at all, as will be true in Central America and the Caribbean and Florida. But it is theoretically possible for someone to survive the rough water and disappearing land, to stay afloat or be on a high peak that remains above the waves.

2) Next is to consider where the new poles will be located, and the distance of the safe location from a new pole. Considering northern Siberia, northern Canada, Iceland and the northern reaches of Norway, Sweden and Finland as representative lands near a pole, consider whether a survival community could sustain itself in such a place. But it would be possible to survive in Tibet and then migrate toward Alaska after the pole shift, for instance, or survive the pole shift in the Bulge of Brazil and migrate toward the new Equator off the Andes.

3) Next is whether the area is a mountain building zone. The Andes, the West Coast of the US and Canada, the Aleutian Islands, Kamchatka in Russia and Japan - all will sustain subduction with consequent mountain building. But in such areas there are hard rock plateaus that have withstood pressure in the past that could be considered safe for a ride through the pole shift. We have also stated that the mountains in the eastern US, the Alps, and in eastern Russia and Mongolia and China are not in a mountain building state, but in a stretch zone. These are safe zones.

4) Then there is the issue of volcanic zones, which most often are located in mountain building areas. Volcanoes edge the Ring of Fire, and for the same reason that mountain building can be expected in these areas, volcanic eruptions from any volcano which has erupted in the past 10,000 years should be expected. But not all volcanoes expected to erupt will do so violently. Yellowstone or the Hawaii volcanoes where rock layers are folding under them will be less explosive than assumed.

5) Then there is the issue of tidal waves, which will roll inland in some areas for hundreds of miles and at great height. Texas will be scoured to the Escarpment, and the southern coast of Brazil flooded over the coastal mountains. The general guide is to be 100 miles inland and 200 feet high. But survival along coastlines is possible if above 600 feet and tidal bore or special circumstances are taken into consideration.

6) Then there is the issue of hot or melting Earth, where subduction in river valleys is so rapid and aggressive that the heat melts the ground, as has been recorded by the West Coast Indians in the past. The eastern Mediterranean coastline also recorded this during the Exodus. But being on high ground is a guard against hot or melting Earth, as the rock only melts when it is close to the point of friction between rock layers.

7) Then there is the matter of hot springs or places where the Earth is so thin that magma is near the surface. These have the potential during the pole shift of releasing gasses and ash, in the worst case being the equivalent of a volcanic eruption. This is more likely in a subduction zone such as the West Coast of the US. But hot springs will only be a danger in areas where violent subduction or violent stretching occurs, such as in the Rift Valley in Africa. Danger in the Alps or in Mongolia is virtually nil.

8) Next is proximity to flooding rivers, which will all top their banks. Such floods can spread in the interior of a continent for vast areas, melting the soil under buildings and toppling them and leaving survivors floating in an inland sea. But interior flooding from rivers overtopping their banks can be survived if one is in high ground well above the flood level of nearby rivers. Double the worst flood on record as a guide and be on rock, not soil that can melt.

16.14.4 SHELTER IN THE FINAL WEEK

In the final week before the shift – when rotation has halted – be in your shelter. This is a very dangerous time where the debris raining down from the tail of planet X will be at its worst. Emerge only to relieve yourself, occasionally to stretch and for a breath of fresh air, and at times when it is absolutely necessary.

Suitable Shelter

Building a totally underground shelter is NOT recommended. Depending on the location and composition of the underlying ground, it may shatter, crumble or sink – entombing you in darkness. A small steel-reinforced concrete dome is ideal as the dome shape itself is quite strong, and resistant to high winds, but of course most won't afford such a luxury.

Viable shelter may be constructed out of something like a shipping container, an old train carriage or bus. Reinforce such cabin like structures internally as best you can – for example by welding strong metal beams or bolting solid wood. Something like this should be buried about a meter (3 ft) in the ground to help stability, but no deeper. Mound dirt over the sides and compact it down to increase wind resistance, add stability, and to hide it to some degree.

If you have nothing else, dig a shallow trench, deep enough to be able to crouch in comfortably, but not so deep as to be able to stand. Cover this trench with metal or solid wood, and dirt on top. If your trench happens to collapse, you should still be able to claw your way out of it. Take special care to ensure rain cannot enter and drown you by mounding and packing dirt around your trench and covering the entrance.

Earth Moans

During this week there are very strong forces at play. The Earth is gripped magnetically by Planet X. The core wants to move but the crust wants to stay in place. Huge slabs of rock grind against each other in this battle, causing loud and constant groaning, as the Earth herself is in distress. This will make sleep difficult and add to the stress you are already experiencing.

During the Final Hour

In the final hour when rotation finally resumes, it will do so with a jolt. This strong jolt will throw objects towards the (current) North (the new West). Try to brace yourself against something solid (such as the northern wall of your shelter).

If you have lost track of time, the final hour can be determined by the development of an EXTREMELY strong wind. If you happen to be outside you may experience a heavy red dusting shortly before the wind develops. Get inside NOW.

16.14.5 AFTER THE SHIFT

After the pole shift, Planet X finally makes its journey out of our solar system. Rotation resumes and the worst of the earth-shaking events are over. Planet X exits quickly, leaving the residents of Earth to pick up the shattered pieces. It is now time to leave your shelter.

Society Falls

The time leading up to the shift will be devastating enough – infrastructure and the power structure damaged and weakened, emergency groups exhausted, and the general population weary of hardship, but the final earth-wrenching middle finger from Planet X will shatter the status quo beyond repair. **All** will be at the same level – in a struggle for survival.

People will be starving, sick, injured and confused, unable to be reined in and forced to go to their jobs. Police, military and 'authority' in general will turn rogue. Avoid authorities at all costs. The rules and consequences no longer apply to them, and they will be scared, confused and angry and armed.

Off the Grid

Forget about grid power. If you can't generate your own, get ready to live without it. Don't expect telephone systems, internet servers, radio, or television stations to be functional either.

Satellites will not be functioning – due to the debris hammering poor mother Earth they will be torn from the sky. This means no GPS or satellite communications. If you are resourceful enough, CB or shortwave radio will be your best avenue for communication.

Solar power will only be so effective as there will be extensive ash and cloud cover for some years after the shift, the sun only poking its head through occasionally. Solar power however may be sufficient to charge small batteries for such things as flashlights or handheld radios. Wind power is a good option, but care is needed to protect the wind generators before and during the shift. Store them and reassemble only after things have calmed down.

Prepare to be with minimal power or no power at all. Hand tools and the skills to use them will be a most valuable asset.

17 PROJECTS & REFERENCES

17.1 SOLAR DEHYDRATOR

A solar dehydrator can be made very cheaply with two cardboard boxes, some clear plastic wrap, and a little tape. Set it on a stool or chair and face it's solar collector towards the sun, and you have a functional food preservation machine for little work and even less money.

Use a long thin cardboard box for the hot-air collector and a taller, nearly square, cardboard box for the drying box.

Boxes could be made to size by cutting and taping together small cardboard pieces.

Line the bottom of the collector box with a black plastic garbage bag or paint the bottom with black paint - lamp black or soot mixed with a little vegetable oil would work as well.

If you use spray paint or other toxic paints, let the collector bake in the sun for a day or two before use.

Cover the top of the collector with clear plastic wrap or window glass. Tape it together as shown.

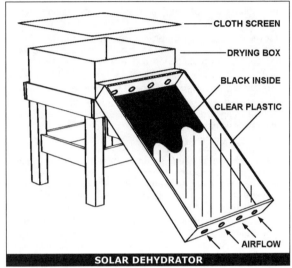

CLOTH SCREEN

DRYING BOX

BLACK INSIDE

CLEAR PLASTIC

AIRFLOW

SOLAR DEHYDRATOR

To increase the efficiency, you may want to cover the sides and bottom of both boxes with fibreglass or styrofoam insulation.

Tests for Dryness
- Rely on appearance and feel to judge dryness.
- Cool a test handful a few minutes before deciding whether the food is done.
- Consider fruit dry when no wetness can be squeezed from a piece which has been cut - it should be rather tough and pliable.
- Consider vegetables dry when brittle.

Pre and Post-Drying Treatments for Fruits & Vegetables
Steam blanching is safe pre-treatment which can prevent spoilage - especially of low acid foods such as vegetables. Important post-drying treatments are –
- Conditioning - i.e. leaving in open air for long periods to equalize moisture content.
- Pasteurizing - i.e. exposing the dried foods to high heat to eliminate harmful organisms.

Storage
- Ensure food is thoroughly cool before storing.
- Store in small quantities in glass or food-grade plastic.
- Check supplies frequently for contamination or dampness.
- Keep in a dry, cool place – between 4 – 21°C (40 – 70°F).

Preparing for Eating
- Fruits - cover with boiling water in saucepan and simmer the fruit covered for 10-15 min.
- Sweeten to taste at the very end of cooking.
- Remove from heat and cool still covered Vegetables.
- Soak all vegetables except greens in cold water until they are nearly restored to their original texture. Some take longer than others.
- Use only enough water to cover and always cook in the soaking water.
- Cover greens with enough boiling water to cover and simmer until tender.

17.2 ABS WATER FILTER

17.2.1 INTRODUCTION

Micro-organisms in a water supply can cause dysentery, which can lead to diarrhoea and fatal dehydration. If you're faced with the need of potable water – in the absence of a municipal water supply – you and your family could be faced with this problem as well.

Fortunately, we can purify water with bleach, and/or build inexpensive solar-powered distillation units, or stills, and pasteurization ponds which provide people with all the fresh water they need.

But the water coming from the pasteurization pond or from storage after it's been purified with bleach can taste bad. Even though pasteurization or purification has killed most of the pathogens, you could be left with a chlorine- or metallic-tasting drink.

That's where a good filter comes in: it will remove many remaining pathogens, as well as particulates, dissolved metals, and chlorine to make your water taste good.

This article shows you how to build a filter that uses activated charcoal available at aquarium stores to improve the taste of your water. The filter allows you to easily change the charcoal when necessary, as well.

17.2.2 CONSTRUCTION

There are two plastics commonly used in making pipes: poly-vinyl-chloride (PVC); and acrylonitrile-butadiene-styrene (ABS). Both of these formulations are completely safe when used to carry or store water. PVC is the (usually) thin-walled white plastic used in water delivery systems; ABS is the usually thick-walled black plastic used a lot in sewage connections.

The reason we're using ABS is that it's easier to get a threaded end-cap (in this case, a three-inch drain plug). Since we want to be able to take the filter apart to clean or replace the activated charcoal, we need these screw caps on both ends. You can make the filter as large as you want, but our size is based on three-inch ABS pipes. The end-cap, pipe adapter, and pipe itself can commonly be found in the three-inch size.

PARTS NEEDED TO BUILD THE FILTER			
qty	item	qty	item
1	ABS pipe, 3 inch outside diameter, between 12 and 18 inches long	1	4-lb bag fine activated charcoal
		1	Paper coffee filter
2	3 inch ABS drain plugs (used for the end caps)	1	PVC cement
		1	ABS cement
2	3 inch ABS adapters (used to connect the drain plug to the pipe)	1	Drill with 1/2 in bit
		1	Fine sandpaper
2	1/2 inch outside diameter PVC schedule 40 tubing, 4 inches long	2	3 inch diameter fine mesh brass or stainless steel screening

End-Cap Assemblies

Notice that the bottom of the drain plug has a hollow square protuberance or "knob" – this allows you to use a wrench to tighten the drain plug. Drill a half inch hole through the bottom of the knob.

The hole should be just big enough for the 4 inch long, 1/2 inch diameter PVC tube to fit in. Using the sandpaper, bevel the inside of one end of the PVC pipe, then lightly sand the outside of the pipe.

Carefully wipe out the hole you just drilled, then coat the outside of the bevelled end of the PVC pipe with a thin coat of PVC cement. Insert the pipe in the hole about a half-inch, give it a quarter-twist to spread the PVC cement, then set aside. Do the same with the other drain plug and PVC pipe.

Now take one of the brass or stainless steel screens and place it in the inside of the drain plug. If necessary, trim it so it will fit. Using a few drops of the ABS cement, glue the rim of the screen in place. Do the same with the other screen and end cap assembly.

Adapters and ABS Tube Assembly

Carefully clean and dry the inside and outside of the two adapters and the 3 inch ABS tube.

Spread a small amount of ABS cement around the outside of one end of the tube. Insert the tube into one of the adapters and give it a quarter-twist to spread the ABS cement, and then do the same with the other end of the ABS tube and the other adapter.

Final Assembly

Now screw in the two end-cap assemblies into the ends of the tube and adapters, checking for a secure fit. Mark one of the end caps "TOP" and the other "BOTTOM". Take off the top end cap and fill the filter with the activated charcoal to the top of the tube. Screw the top end-cap assembly on and, holding the filter upright, slowly run several gallons of clean water through the filter. This will remove the charcoal dust that was mixed in with the charcoal granules.

When the charcoal dust has been removed and the outflow is running clear, remove the top end cap and place a coffee paper filter on top of the charcoal granules. If necessary, trim it so to fit. Replace the upper end cap.

Filter Assembly is now complete and ready for use.

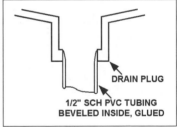

3" ABS PIPE
(12 - 18" LONG)

LOWER
ASSEMBLY
SHOWN

UPPER
ASSEMBLY
IDENTICAL

3" ABS
ADAPTER

3" ABS
DRAIN PLUG

1/2" SCH 40
PVC TUBING

1/2"
HOLE

DRAIN PLUG

1/2" SCH PVC TUBING
BEVELED INSIDE, GLUED

17.2.3 OPERATIONS AND MAINTENANCE

Operations

Using whatever adapters are required for your own water system, run the water to be filtered through the filter from top to bottom, keeping the filter upright. We have found that a flow rate is about one gallon per minute gives the best results.

Bear in mind that this filter is not designed to remove all pathogens and contaminants, although it will remove most of them. Our team designed and uses this filter to be the final step in water delivery for water that has already been chemically purified by sodium hypochlorate 5.5% solution (unscented chlorine bleach). We found that the filter, when used in this way, removed almost all of the solids and bleach taste. In addition to removing the bleach taste, the filter also aerated the water to some extent. For most of us, the result tasted like bottled water.

Maintenance

How often you change the activated charcoal depends on the level of bleach, particulates, and other chemicals/metals in the water. Four of these filters have treated one hundred gallons, and one of them has treated over three hundred gallons, with no apparent degradation in the way the filter aerates and removes the chemical taste from the treated water.

The coffee filter placed at the top is used as a 'pre-filter' to trap any large particulates, and it also helps to keep the charcoal granules in place. You can probably go through five or six paper filter changes before you need to change the charcoal.

There are some studies that claim backwashing the charcoal, and then heating it at a low (~65°C, ~150°F) temperature will allow you to recycle the charcoal and extend its life. We have not tested that.

17.3 SOLAR STILL

17.3.1 INTRODUCTION

Most illnesses from water come from bacteria and other micro-organisms that can be killed by pasteurization. Pasteurization is heating the fluid (water, in this case) to a temperature of about 80°C (175°F) and holding it for a half-hour. If your health problems can be solved by this method, you can build a pasteurization pond that will provide safe water for a large group.

Distillation is different. Distilling water turns it into a vapour by heating it, and the water vapour is condensed and collected. Distilled water is more pure and safer than pasteurized water, and no longer contains any dissolved solids like calcium carbonate. Also, distilled water should be used in batteries, electric irons, and anyplace else where you don't want dissolved solids to clog up the appliance.

17.3.2 HOW THE SOLAR STILL WORKS

The still is a flat box, hinged so that the top and the bottom are the same size. The box is tilted about five degrees from horizontal; this is the "high end". The top of the box is made of tempered glass, and the bottom is lined with black plastic. At the high end of the box is a PVC pipe with holes drilled in it. This pipe is connected to a hose that brings in the impure water. When the hose is turned on, the water pressure is set so that the water dribbles slowly out of the holes in the PVC pipe and down the bottom of the still (the part covered with black plastic). Gravity pulls the water down to the low end of the still, and covers the black plastic.

When the still is in the sun, the inside temperature rises quickly, and the thin film of water running down the inside begins to evaporate. It rises and condenses on the underside of the glass plate, and runs down to the low side. At the low edge of the glass plate is a trough made of PVC pipe. The distilled water drips into the trough and runs out a hole in the side of the still, through a small tube, and into the container that you are using to store the water.

17.3.3 BUILDING THE SOLAR STILL

There is no absolute dimensional requirement for the still; the larger you make it the more it will produce (and cost). The still we built was 4 x 4 ft, and 6 inches deep.

Step 1	**Build the lower half.** The base is a piece of 1/2" CDX plywood, four feet on a side. With the C side up, screw four 4" X 2-1/2" sides, also of 1/2" CDX, to the perimeter of the 4 X 4 plywood and to each other. Using a single piece of 2-mil black poly sheeting, line the inside of the box up to about an inch above the bottom. Secure the edges of the poly to the sides of the box with brads. Do not puncture the poly sheeting; if you do, water could leak through and damage the plywood. Set the lined box aside.
Step 2	**Build the upper half.** The base is a wooden frame, four feet on a side, into which the glass is placed and secured as convenient. Screw four 4" X 2-1/2" sides, also of 1/2" CDX, to the perimeter of the frame and to each other. Set aside.
Step 3	**Prepare and install the inflow tube.** Cut a piece of Schedule 40 3/4" ID PVC pipe 50 inches long. Starting about 4 inches from the end, drill a series of 1/8" holes about 3 inches apart until you get to within 4 inches of the other end. Drill a 3/4-inch hole through the side of the lower half of the still as shown in the cross-section view. Carefully cut a hole in the black poly lining and slide in the inflow tube.
	With the inflow tube partly in, cap the end with a PVC end cap. Slide the tube in the rest of the way until the capped end is resting snugly against the side of the box away from the hole. Secure that end. Now twist the tube until the row of holes is facing downward and almost touching the black poly lining, (These are the holes from which the water will come out and flow down the lining.)
	The other end of the inflow tube should be sticking out about an inch and a half from the hole. Using a non-toxic silicone sealant, carefully caulk the inside and outside of the hole, so that there will not be any leakage around the pipe and underneath the black poly lining. Glue the appropriate fitting to the protruding end of the inflow tube to attach the garden hose, or whatever tubing you will use to deliver the untreated water.

Step 4   **Prepare and install the collection trough.** Cut a piece of Schedule 40 1-1/2″ PVC pipe as long as the inside width of the upper half (about 47 inches). Then cut the pipe lengthwise, ending up with two troughs. (You will only use one; save the other one for a second still if you choose to build it.)

Place the trough as shown in the cross section view. Attach it, using small brass screws, to the end of the upper half. The trough should be butting against both sides of the upper half.

Using a non-toxic silicone sealant, carefully caulk the ends of the trough, so that no water can leak back down into the lower half after its condensed. Drill a 3/4″ hole in the side of the upper end so that it exactly matches the bottom of the trough, and insert a two-inch-long piece of 3/4″ Schedule 40 PVC pipe. (This is how the distilled water in the trough will flow out of the still.)

Step 5   **Assemble the still.** Carefully invert the upper half and place it over the lower half. At the inflow end, mark for two hinges and install them. a rubber strip along the rim of the lower half where it meets the upper half. This makes the still watertight, which avoids contamination and increases its thermal efficiency.

At the outflow end, mark for several spring latches (similar to those on a musical instrument case) and install them. (This will keep the still tightly closed unless you want to clean it.)

Step 6   **Set up the still.** Choose an unshaded outside location, and place the still about five degrees from horizontal facing south (if you're north of the equator). Attach the hose from the untreated water container to the inflow tube. Attach the tube from the collecting trough to the container you're using to collect your distilled water. Start the water flow.

Adjust the inflow water volume so that the water dribbles down the black poly lining. Once the still reaches stagnation temperature, adjust the volume so that the water never quite reaches the lower end of the still.

As the water evaporates away from the hot black poly lining, you will see droplets form on the underside of the glass surface. As gravity pulls these drops down to the trough, check to make sure the distilled water can flow unimpeded out of the trough, through the discharge tube, and into the collecting and storage container.

You may have to tilt the still about one degree to the discharge side so that the trough doesn't overflow.

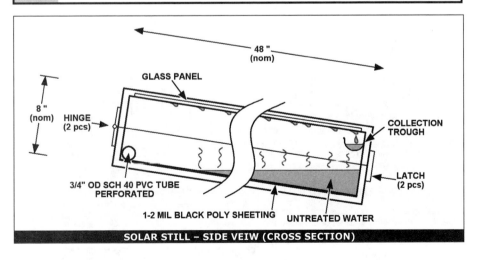

SOLAR STILL – SIDE VEIW (CROSS SECTION)

17.4 EVAPORATIVE COOLING

The natural phenomenon of evaporation can be used to make a cooler to help extend the life of your precious food. In some cases the life of food can be extended 10 times.

17.4.1 ZEER POT

The zeer pot is a pot within a pot. The smaller inner pot holds the food and the larger outer pot holds saturated sand.

The outer pot is unglazed and porous, such as terracotta.

The inner pot may be glazed if you wish. This will

Fill the space in between the two pots with sand and water. Top up as the water evaporates.

ZEER POT COOLER

keep water out of the food, but will reduce the cooling effect. Cover with cloth to keep flies away. Keep in a shaded position with lots of airflow.

Variations

A larger, more permanent version of the zeer pot can be constructed from bricks and sand. First lay a single layer of bricks for the ground, and then build a cavity wall. Fill this cavity with sand, and then saturate the sand with water.

Don't use mortar between the bricks but simply pack them tight. This will create a more porus wall and further aid evaporation.

Once the sand is saturated it will require topping up with water two or three times during the day. This can be accomplished with a raised water tank and a drip hose system running along the perimeter over the sand as illustrated.

Food should be stored in trays on long legs that keep the trays off the floor. Cover the cooler with a loose frame mesh made from sticks or bamboo, and place a cloth over this. Keep the cloth moist by sprinkling water periodically.

You may have to regulate the flow of water as the outside temperature changes to ensure the sand is always moist and the conditions inside remain constant.

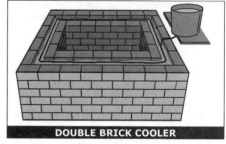

DOUBLE BRICK COOLER

17.4.2 OPEN FRAME COOLER

This simple cooler is made with a large diameter dish filled with water. Bricks or flat rocks are placed in this dish, above the waterline, and an open frame is placed on top of the bricks.

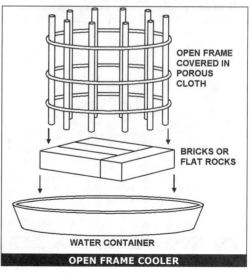

OPEN FRAME COVERED IN POROUS CLOTH

BRICKS OR FLAT ROCKS

WATER CONTAINER

OPEN FRAME COOLER

Wrap a Hessian cloth around the frame, making sure the cloth dips in the water all the way around.

The cloth will draw moisture up the sides, keeping the inside cool. Place a lid on top to keep the cool air in and insects out.

Make sure the water dish does not run dry during the day, and keep in a shaded spot with good airflow.

Variations

More sophisticated versions of the open frame cooler can be made, such as a square cabinet style with a hinged door and shelves.

17.4.3 CHARCOAL COOLER

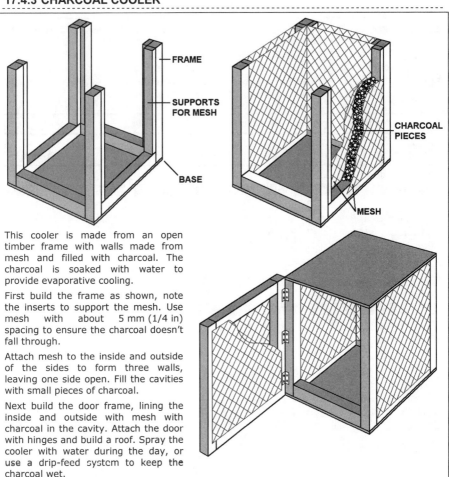

FRAME

SUPPORTS
FOR MESH

CHARCOAL
PIECES

BASE

MESH

This cooler is made from an open timber frame with walls made from mesh and filled with charcoal. The charcoal is soaked with water to provide evaporative cooling.

First build the frame as shown, note the inserts to support the mesh. Use mesh with about 5 mm (1/4 in) spacing to ensure the charcoal doesn't fall through.

Attach mesh to the inside and outside of the sides to form three walls, leaving one side open. Fill the cavities with small pieces of charcoal.

Next build the door frame, lining the inside and outside with mesh with charcoal in the cavity. Attach the door with hinges and build a roof. Spray the cooler with water during the day, or use a drip-feed system to keep the charcoal wet.

Protection

These simple coolers can be protected by mounting them on a pole with an inverted metal cone half way up to prevent rats climbing up. A good coating of grease around the pole will stop ants and other small critters.

17.5 RED CABBAGE pH INDICATOR

Red cabbage juice contains a natural pH indicator that changes colours according to the acidity of the solution. Being able to test acidity has important applications in farming, testing water, testing the strength of vinegar, lye, soap and other substances.

You can use the solution in its liquid form, or you use it to make litmus paper if you have coffee filters or similar paper.

Step 1	Chop the cabbage into small pieces until you have about 2 cups of chopped cabbage.
Step 2	Place the cabbage in a large container and add boiling water to cover the cabbage.
Step 3	Allow at least 10 minutes for the colour to leach out of the cabbage. If you have a blender, you can blend the cabbage and boiling water to speed up the process.
Step 4	Filter out the vegetable material and collect the liquid. This liquid should be somewhere from purple-blue, depending on the pH of the water. Distilled water has a pH of 6.8 to 7.0.
Step 5	Concentrate the liquid by boiling it to reduce the water content. Store or use.
Step 6	If you want to make litmus paper, soak some filter paper in the concentrated solution for a few hours. Remove it and allow it to dry by hanging. Cut the filter paper into strips if you like.

Red Cabbage Solution pH Indicator Colours

pH	2	-	4	-	6	7	8	-	10	-	12
Colour	Red		Purple		Violet		Blue		Blue-Green		Greenish-Yellow

pH of Common Products

PRODUCT	pH	PRODUCT	pH	PRODUCT	pH
Battery acid	0	Black coffee	5	Soapy water	12
HCl in stomach acid	1	Urine, salvia	6	Bleach	13
Lemon juice, vinegar	2 - 3	Pure water	7	Oven cleaner	13 - 14
Orange juice	3 - 4	Sea water	8	Drain cleaner	14
Acid rain	4	Baking soda	9	Paris Hilton	37
Beer	4 - 5	Ammonia solution	10 - 11		

Preferred Soil pH of Various Plants

PLANT	pH	PLANT	pH	PLANT	pH
Artichoke	6.5 - 7.5	Horseradish	6.0 - 7.0	Pepper	5.5 - 7.0
Asparagus	6.0 - 8.0	Kale	6.0 - 7.5	Pistachio	5.0 - 6.0
Basil	5.5 - 6.5	Kohlrabi	6.0 - 7.5	Potato	4.5 - 6.0
Bean	6.0 - 7.5	Leek	6.0 - 8.0	Potato – Sweet	5.5 - 6.0
Beetroot	6.0 - 7.5	Lentil	5.5 - 7.0	Pumpkin	5.5 - 7.5
Broccoli	6.0 - 7.5	Lettuce	6.0 – 7.0	Radish	6.0 - 7.0
Brussels Sprouts	6.0 - 7.5	Marjoram	6.0 - 8.0	Rice	5.0 - 6.5
Cabbage	6.0 - 7.5	Mint	7.0 - 8.0	Rosemary	5.0 - 6.0
Carrot	5.5 - 7.0	Mushroom	6.5 - 7.5	Sage	5.5 - 6.5
Cauliflower	5.5 - 7.5	Mustard	6.0 - 7.5	Shallot	5.5 - 7.0
Celery	6.0 - 7.0	Olive	5.5 - 6.5	Sorghum	5.5 - 7.5
Chives	6.0 - 7.0	Onion	6.0 - 7.0	Soya bean	5.5 - 6.5
Corn – Sweet	5.5 - 7.5	Paprika	7.0 - 8.5	Spinach	6.0 - 7.5
Cucumber	5.5 - 7.5	Parsley	5.0 - 7.0	Swede	5.5 - 7.0
Fennel	5.0 - 6.0	Parsnip	5.5 - 7.5	Thyme	5.5 - 7.0
Garlic	5.5 - 7.5	Pea	6.0 - 7.5	Tomato	5.5 - 7.5
Ginger	6.0 - 8.0	Peanut	5.0 - 6.5	Turnip	5.5 - 7.0

17.6 MATHS

17.6.1 BASIC MATHS – ADDITION AND SUBTRACTION

Basic Addition: 23 + 14

To add two numbers together, lay out the problem as shown. Starting with the column on the right, add the single digits together (3+4) and write the result (7) below. Move on to the next column to the left and repeat. This yields the result of 23 + 14 = 37.

```
  2 3      2 3      2 3
+ 1 4    + 1 4    + 1 4
-----    -----    -----
           7        3 7
```

Addition with Carry: 4 + 58

Lay the problem out as shown, note how the numbers are aligned to the right. Begin as before by adding the rightmost column first, and working to the left.

This column adds up to more than 10 (4+8=12). In this case, the extra 1 is 'carried' over to the next column.

```
    4        4          4
+ 5 8    + 5 8      + 5 8
-----    -----        1
           2         6 2
```

Write the last digit (2) below the column, and place a small (1) in the column to the left, forming the number (12). Move to the next column to the left, and include the carried (1) when adding. (5+**1**=6). This yields the result of 4 + 58 = 62.

Addition of Multiple Numbers: 13 + 245 + 77 + 115

To add a list of numbers, the principle is the same. Lay the problem out with the numbers aligned to the right, and start with the right column and work your way left.

In this example you can see that (3+5+7+5 = 20), and thus the (2) is carried to the left and the (0) is placed in the column, forming the number (20). In the next column this (2) is included in the addition, (1+4+7+1+**2** = 15). The last column is (2+1+**1** = 4). The result is 450.

```
    1 3
    2 4 5
    7 7
+ 1 1 5
---------
  1 2
  4 5 0
```

Basic Subtraction: 56 – 24

Similar to addition, lay out the problem as shown and work right to left. This time subtract the lower digit from the upper one, instead of adding them.

The first column (6-4) results in (2) and the next column (5-2) results in (3), yielding a final result of 32.

```
  5 6      5 6      5 6
- 2 4    - 2 4    - 2 4
-----    -----    -----
           2        3 2
```

Subtraction with Borrow: 74 – 28

Often the top digit is less than the one underneath it. In this example, the first column is (4-8).

For this, we need to 'borrow' a 1 from the digit to the left. Cross out the digit to the left (7) and decrease it by 1 to make it (6), and transfer this borrowed 1 over.

```
  7 4      6          6
- 2 8      7 4        7 4 1
-----    - 2 8      - 2 8
           -----      -----
             6          4 6
```

The (4) now becomes (14) because of the borrowed 1, and now you can subtract the (8) from (14), to yield (6). Move on to the column on the left, which is now (6-2) resulting in (4). The answer is 46.

Subtraction with Borrow from Zero

In these two examples, there are zeroes to borrow from. When you need to borrow from a zero, you also need to borrow from the next column over. Cross out the (0) and change it to (9), and then decrease the next digit to the left, in this case (3) changes to (2).

```
  2 9 1            9 9 1
  3 0 5          1 0 0 0
-   6 7        -     6 7
-------        ---------
  2 3 8          0 9 3 3
```

In the second example, there are multiple zeroes. In this case you keep borrowing from the left, changing zeroes to 9 until you reach a non-zero digit, which you then decrease it by 1.

Addition and Subtraction with Decimal Points

Simply line up the decimal points and proceed as normal. As was implied in the other examples, a blank space is mathematically the same as a zero.

Note in the subtraction example there is 0 minus 0 in the second column, therefore no need to borrow.

$$\begin{array}{r} 0.6\,5 \\ +\,2\,8.7 \\ \hline 2\,9.3\,5 \end{array} \qquad \begin{array}{r} {}^{2}\,{}^{1}\\ \cancel{3}\,6.0\,5 \\ -\quad 8. \\ \hline 2\,8.0\,5 \end{array}$$

Addition and Subtraction involving Negative Numbers

If you need to subtract a larger number from a smaller one, for example (15-90), swap the numbers around and treat the problem as (90-15), and then place a minus (-) sign in front of the result. For example, calculate (90-15 = 75) and then you know (15-90 = -75). Easy.

To add a negative number to a positive number, for example (12 + -8), or (-8 + 12), treat this problem as (12 – 8), i.e. subtract the smallest number from the largest (ignoring the negative (–) sign) i.e. (12 – 8 = 4). If the largest number is positive, the result is positive. If the largest number is negative, then the result is negative, i.e. (12 + -8 = 4) whereas (-12 + 8 = -4).

To subtract a negative number, i.e. (10 - -5), treat this as addition, (10+5).

To add a list of negative and positive numbers, for example (47 + -56 + -24 + 43 + 67 + -63), add the positive numbers together first (47+43+67 = 157), then add the negative numbers together, ignoring the –sign (56+24+63 = 143), and then subtract the negative result from the positive one, (157 – 143 = 14).

To add two or more negative numbers together, for example (-15 + -80), treat this as (15 + 80) and place a minus (-) in front of the result, i.e. (-95)

17.6.2 BASIC MATHS – MULTIPLICATION

Basic Multiplication: 35 x 4

Lay this problem out as shown, with the shortest number on the bottom and aligned to the right.

Starting with the bottom right digit (4), multiply by the digit above (5). Write in the result (20), carrying the (2) to the left.

$$\begin{array}{r} 3\,5 \\ \times\quad 4 \\ \hline \end{array} \quad \begin{array}{r} 3\,5 \\ \times\quad 4 \\ \hline {}_{2}\\ 0 \end{array} \quad \begin{array}{r} 3\,5 \\ \times\quad 4 \\ \hline {}_{1}\,{}_{2}\\ 2\,0 \end{array} \quad \begin{array}{r} 3\,5 \\ \times\quad 4 \\ \hline {}_{1}\,{}_{2}\\ 2\,0 \\ \hline 1\,4\,0 \end{array}$$

Now staying with the bottom right digit (4), multiply it by the next digit to the left (3) in the top number. Write the result (12) below, carrying the (1) to the left.

After multiplying, the result is added to the carries to produce the final result of 140.

Multiplying by a Two-Digit Number: 278 x 13

Again, lay the problem out with the shortest number on the bottom.

Start with the bottom right digit (3) and multiply this with the digits above, working right to left. Write the results of the multiplication below, carrying as needed. As you can see, we multiplied (3x8 = 24) then (3x7 = 21) then (3x2 = 6).

Now we move on digit left to the (1) in the lower number (13). For each digit in this number there is another row added below which is moved one space to the left. This space is marked with an arrow, but can of course be blank or a 0.

We multiply this (1) by all the digits in the top number and write the result in this new row. (1x8) (1x7) then (1x2). When all digits have been multiplied, add the rows to produce the final result. Don't forget to add all the carries.

$$\begin{array}{r} 2\,7\,8 \\ \times\quad 1\,3 \\ \hline \end{array} \quad \begin{array}{r} 2\,7\,8 \\ \times\quad 1\,3 \\ \hline {}_{2}\\ 4 \end{array} \quad \begin{array}{r} 2\,7\,8 \\ \times\quad 1\,3 \\ \hline {}_{2}\,{}_{2}\\ 1\,4 \end{array} \quad \begin{array}{r} 2\,7\,8 \\ \times\quad 1\,3 \\ \hline {}_{2}\,{}_{2}\\ 6\,1\,4 \end{array}$$

$$\begin{array}{r} 2\,7\,8 \\ \times\quad 1\,3 \\ \hline {}_{2}\,{}_{2}\\ 6\,1\,4 \end{array} \quad \begin{array}{r} 2\,7\,8 \\ \times\quad 1\,3 \\ \hline {}_{2}\,{}_{2}\\ 6\,1\,4 \\ 2\,7\,8\,\downarrow \end{array} \quad \begin{array}{r} 2\,7\,8 \\ \times\quad 1\,3 \\ \hline {}_{2}\,{}_{2}\\ 6\,1\,4 \\ 2\,7\,8\,\downarrow \\ \hline {}_{1}\,{}_{1}\\ 3\,6\,1\,4 \end{array}$$

Multiplication with Decimals: 37.5 x 2.98

When multiplying numbers with decimals, ignore the decimal places at first, and just line the numbers up to the right.

Proceed as normal as if you were multiplying 375 by 298, yielding the result 111750.

To correctly place the decimal point, count the positions in the original numbers. In 37.5 the decimal place is 1 place to the left, in 2.98 the decimal place is 2 places to left.

1 place + 2 places = 3, so the decimal point is 3 places to the left in the final result.

```
   3 7.5          3 7.5
 × 2.9 8        × 2.9 8
 2 5 4         2 5 4
   4 6 0          4 6 0
 2 6 4         2 6 4
   7 3 5 ↓        7 3 5 ↓
 1 1           1 1
 6 4 0 ↓ ↓     6 4 0 ↓ ↓
 1 2 1 1       1 2 1 1
 1 1 1 7 5 0   1 1 1.7 5 0
```

17.6.3 BASIC MATHS – LONG DIVISION

Long division is by far the most complicated of the basic math skills, but when you break it down into simple steps, complex problems can always be solved.

Basic Long division – 74 ÷ 2

Here, we are dividing 74 by 2. In division, we work left to right. Starting with (7), we divide this by (2) which gives an answer of (3.5) but we are only interested in whole numbers, so write (3) above. Next, we multiply this result (3) by (2) and write the answer (6) below.

We subtract this (6) from the (7) above to produce (1) – this is the remainder from 7 ÷ 2.

Moving to the right, bring down the (4) next to the previous remainder (1) and we have the number (14). We now divide the (14) by (2) to produce (7). Because there is no remainder from 14 ÷ 2 and no more numbers to divide, we finish with the answer 74 ÷ 2 = 37.

Basic Long Division – 584 ÷ 4

Again a basic example is shown so you can follow the steps through.

The mini-sums in order are (5÷4) (1x4) (5-4), then the next digit (8) is transferred down to produce (18) and we continue. (18÷4) (4x4) (18-16), then the (4) is transferred down to produce (24), we divide this by (4) to produce the last digit (6) and the result is 584 ÷ 4 = 146.

Long Division with a Remainder – 736 ÷ 25

$$
\begin{array}{r}
2 \\
25\,\overline{)\,[7]\,3\,6}
\end{array}
\qquad
\begin{array}{r}
2 \\
25\,\overline{)\,[7\ 3]\,6}
\end{array}
\qquad
\begin{array}{r}
[2] \\
[2\ 5]\,\overline{)\,7\ 3\ 6} \\
[5\ 0]
\end{array}
\qquad
\begin{array}{r}
2 \\
25\,\overline{)\,7\ 3\ 6} \\
-5\ 0 \\
\hline
[2\ 3]
\end{array}
$$

$$
\begin{array}{r}
2 \\
25\,\overline{)\,7\ 3\ 6} \\
-5\ 0\ \downarrow \\
\hline
2\ 3\ 6
\end{array}
\qquad
\begin{array}{r}
2\,[9] \\
[2\ 5]\,\overline{)\,7\ 3\ 6} \\
-5\ 0\ \downarrow \\
\hline
[2\ 3\ 6]
\end{array}
\qquad
\begin{array}{r}
2\,[9] \\
[2\ 5]\,\overline{)\,7\ 3\ 0} \\
-5\ 0\ \downarrow \\
\hline
2\ 3\ 6 \\
[2\ 2\ 5]
\end{array}
\qquad
\begin{array}{r}
2\ 9\,[r\ 11] \\
25\,\overline{)\,7\ 3\ 0} \\
-5\ 0\ \downarrow \\
\hline
2\ 3\ 6 \\
-2\ 2\ 5 \\
\hline
[1\ 1]
\end{array}
$$

This example gets a tad more complicated. We start trying to divide the first digit (7) by 25. 7 ÷ 25 doesn't work out to a whole number, so in this case, we need to expand the (7) one digit to the right and divide into (73) instead. (25) goes into (73) only (2) times, so we write (2), aligned to the right above the (73). We multiply this result (2) by (25) to produce (50), and subtract from (73) and yield the result of (23).

Moving to the right, transfer the next digit (6) down to produce the number (236). Now we have to divide 236 by 25. There is no step by step way to do this, you just have to do it in your head. How I did this was that I know (25 x 10 = 250), so (25 x 9 = 225). Sometimes you just have to estimate, and then do the multiplication problem separately to check.

Which ever way you do it, we now know that 25 goes into 236 only 9 times. Multiply the result (9) by (25) to yield (225). Subtract this from the previous result to yield (11).

This is the end of the calculation so (11) is the final remainder. Therefore, 763 ÷ 25 = 29 with a remainder of 11. In a complex calculation like this, sometimes it pays to check. Multiply 29 by 25. The result should be 725. Then calculate 736 – 725 to come up with 11, the remainder.

Long Division to Decimal Places – 84 ÷ 5

Instead of being content to have a remainder after a division, it is easy to continue the process to resolve the digits after the decimal place.

Here we calculate (84 ÷ 5 = 16) with a remainder of (4). The next step is to place the decimal point and start to bring down zeroes after the remainders.

$$
\begin{array}{r}
1\ 6 \\
5\,\overline{)\,8\ 4} \\
-5\ \downarrow \\
\hline
3\ 4 \\
3\ 0 \\
\hline
[4]
\end{array}
\qquad
\begin{array}{r}
1\ 6. \\
5\,\overline{)\,8\ 4.[0]} \\
-5\ \downarrow \\
\hline
3\ 4 \\
3\ 0 \\
\hline
4\,[0]
\end{array}
\qquad
\begin{array}{r}
1\ 6.8 \\
5\,\overline{)\,8\ 4.0} \\
-5\ \downarrow \\
\hline
3\ 4 \\
3\ 0\ \downarrow \\
\hline
4\ 0
\end{array}
$$

Now (4) becomes (40), divided by (5) this becomes (8). There is no remainder here, but if there was, then zeros can be bought down until resolved, or you get bored.

Short Division – 230 ÷ 8

Short division is exactly the same process, except less is written and more calculations are done in your mind. Only write the remainders.

Here we start off by dividing 23 by 8, returning 2. We know that 3 x 8 is 24, and 23 is one less, so the remainder must be one less than 8, thus 7. Write this remainder to the left of the next digit (0), forming (70), then divide into that.

8 x 8 is 64, so 70 ÷ 8 is (8), with a remainder of (6). Stop here, or continue on to resolve the decimal places. 230 ÷ 8 = 28.75

$$
8\,\overline{)\,2\ 3\ 0}
\qquad
\begin{array}{r}
2 \\
8\,\overline{)\,2\ 3\,{}^{7}0}
\end{array}
$$

$$
\begin{array}{r}
2\ 8 \\
8\,\overline{)\,2\ 3\,{}^{7}0\,{}^{6}}
\end{array}
\qquad
\begin{array}{r}
2\ 8. \\
8\,\overline{)\,2\ 3\,{}^{7}0.\,{}^{6}}
\end{array}
$$

$$
\begin{array}{r}
2\ 8.7\ 5 \\
8\,\overline{)\,2\ 3\,{}^{7}0.\,{}^{6}0\,{}^{4}0}
\end{array}
$$

Dividing by a Decimal Number

When the number you are dividing by has a decimal place in it, ignore it at first. For example, to work out (130 ÷ 2.5), treat it as (130 ÷ 25). This yields a result of (5.2). When finished, count the number of decimal places in the divisor. For every digit to the right of the decimal place in the divisor (2.5), shift the decimal place in the answer 1 place to the right, therefore (5.2) becomes (52).

130 ÷ 250 = 0.52
130 ÷ 25 = 5.2
130 ÷ 2.5 = 52.
130 ÷ 0.25 = 520.

Multiplication and Division with Negative Numbers

For both multiplication and division, the rules are simple. If both numbers are positive, the answer is positive. If both numbers are negative, the result is also positive. But if one number is positive, and one is negative, the result is negative.

10 x 5 = 50	50 ÷ 10 = 5
10 x -5 = -50	50 ÷ -10 = -5
-10 x 5 = -50	-50 ÷ 10 = -5
-10 x -5 = 50	-50 ÷ -10 = 5

17.6.4 MULTIPLICATION TABLE

This table is provided as a quick reference for multiplication and division problems. It is generally taught in schools to memorize up to 12 x 12.

x	2	3	4	5	6	7	8	9	10	11	12	13	14	15	16	17	18	19
2	4	6	8	10	12	14	16	18	20	22	24	26	28	30	32	34	36	38
3	6	9	12	15	18	21	24	27	30	33	36	39	42	45	48	51	54	57
4	8	12	16	20	24	28	32	36	40	44	48	52	56	60	64	68	72	76
5	10	15	20	25	30	35	40	45	50	55	60	65	70	75	80	85	90	95
6	12	18	24	30	36	42	48	54	60	66	72	78	84	90	96	102	108	114
7	14	21	28	35	42	49	56	63	70	77	84	91	98	105	112	119	126	133
8	16	24	32	40	48	56	64	72	80	88	96	104	112	120	128	136	144	152
9	18	27	36	45	54	63	72	81	90	99	108	117	126	135	144	153	162	171
10	20	30	40	50	60	70	80	90	100	110	120	130	140	150	160	170	180	190
11	22	33	44	55	66	77	88	99	110	121	132	143	154	165	176	187	198	209
12	24	36	48	60	72	84	96	108	120	132	144	156	168	180	192	204	216	228
13	26	39	52	65	78	91	104	117	130	143	156	169	182	195	208	221	234	247
14	28	42	56	70	84	98	112	126	140	154	168	182	196	210	224	238	252	266
15	30	45	60	75	90	105	120	135	150	165	180	195	210	225	240	255	270	285
16	32	48	64	80	96	112	128	144	160	176	192	208	224	240	256	272	288	304
17	34	51	68	85	102	119	136	153	170	187	204	221	238	255	272	289	306	323
18	36	54	72	90	108	126	144	162	180	198	216	234	252	270	288	306	324	342
19	38	57	76	95	114	133	152	171	190	209	228	247	266	285	304	323	342	361

17.7 CONVERSION TABLES

The metric system is relatively new. It has only been officially in use since 1799. Because of this, some countries still conveniently enforce arcane and disjointed systems of measurement.

The imperial system is based on scientifically exacting standards such as the weight of an average rock, the width of some dudes hand, the temperature of his armpit on a hot day, and how much fermented goats urine he can drink before vomiting.

This grants us the exciting task of unit conversion and makes an otherwise dull and mundane chore a fun and whimsical adventure.

As an example of such awesomeness, in 1999 a NASA spacecraft in orbit around Mars was due to gently enter Mars' atmosphere – yawn – but instead, because of confusion between imperial and metric units during engineering, it exploded and reined fiery debris down on the dead planet. High fives were enjoyed all round.

17.7.1 LENGTH AND DISTANCE

inches	cm	mm
1	2.54	25.4
2	5.08	50.8
5	12.70	127.0
0.39	1	10
0.79	2	20
1.97	5	50

1	metre=
100	centimetres (cm)=
1'000	millimetres (mm)

feet	metres	inches	yards
1	0.305	12	1/3
2	0.610	24	2/3
5	1.524	60	5/3
3.28	1	39.36	1.09
6.56	2	78.72	2.19
16.40	5	196.80	5.47
3	0.91	36	1
6	1.83	72	2
15	4.57	180	5

mile	km	feet	metres
1	1.61	5'282	1'610
2	3.22	10'564	3'221
5	8.06	26'409	8'062
0.62	1	3'280	1'000
1.24	2	6'560	2'000
3.11	5	16'400	5'000

1	kilometre (km)=
1'000	metres

17.7.2 WEIGHT

ounces (oz)	grams (g)
1	28.35
2	56.70
5	141.75
35.3	**1'000**
70.5	**2'000**
176.4	**5'000**

pounds (lb)	kg	ounces
1	0.453	16
2	0.906	32
5	2.265	80
2.21	1	35.36
4.42	2	70.72
11.04	5	176.64

stones	kg	pounds
1	6.35	14
2	12.70	28
5	31.75	70
0.158	1	2.212
0.315	2	4.410
0.788	5	11.032

1 imperial ton = 2'000 lb = 0.907 metric ton
1 metric ton = 1'000 kg = 1.102 imperial ton

1 kilogram (kg) = 1'000 grams (g)
1 gram (g) = 1'000 milligrams (mg)

17.7.3 AREA

sq. ft	sq. m	sq. yards
1	0.0929	1/9
2	0.1858	2/9
5	0.4645	5/9
10.764	1	1.196
21.529	2	2.392
53.821	5	5.980
9	0.836	1
18	1.672	2
45	4.181	5

sq. mi	sq. km
1	2.59
2	5.18
5	12.95
0.386	1
0.772	2
1.931	5

sq. in	sq. cm
1	6.452
2	12.90
5	32.26
0.155	1
0.310	2
0.775	5

acre	sq. metre
1	4'047
2	8'093
5	20'234
0.247	1'000

sq. km	acres
1	247.1
2	494.2
5	1'235.5

1 sq. mile = 640 acres
1 acre = 4840 sq yard
1 km^2 = 100 hectares

17.7.4 VOLUME

cubic in	cubic cm		quart (qt)	litre (l)		gallon (gal)	litre		fluid oz	ml
1	16.39		1	0.946		1	3.785		1	29.57
2	32.78		2	1.893		2	7.570		2	59.15
5	81.95		5	4.732		5	18.93		5	147.9
0.061	1		1.057	1		0.264	1		3.381	1
0.122	2		2.114	2		0.528	2		6.763	2
0.305	5		5.285	5		1.321	5		16.91	5

cup*	litre		pint	litre		imperial			metric	
1	0.237		1	0.473		1 cup	8 oz		1 cubic cm (cc)	1 millilitre (ml)
2	0.474		2	0.946		1 pint	16 oz		1000 ml	1 litre
5	1.185		5	2.366		1 quart	32 oz		1000 cc	1 litre
4.221	1		2.113	1		1 gallon	128 oz		1 metric cup	250 ml (1/4 l)
8.224	2		4.227	2		1 gallon	4 quarts		1000 l	1 kilolitre (kl)
21.11	5		10.57	5		*imperial cup				

17.7.5 TEMPERATURE

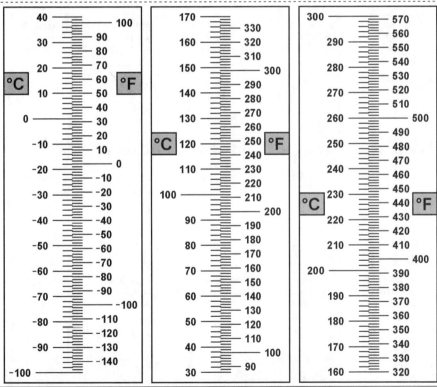

Celsius to Fahrenheit	$(\frac{9}{5} \times C) + 32$	Fahrenheit to Celsius	$\frac{5}{9} \times (F - 32)$
	$(1.8 \times C) + 32$		$0.556 \times (F - 32)$

17.8 RUNES

Runes can easily be made by cutting a thin branch into small discs and carving, painting or burning the symbols into them. They can also be cast from clay. As a tool for divination, runes can help your guides communicate with you and help you through hard times.

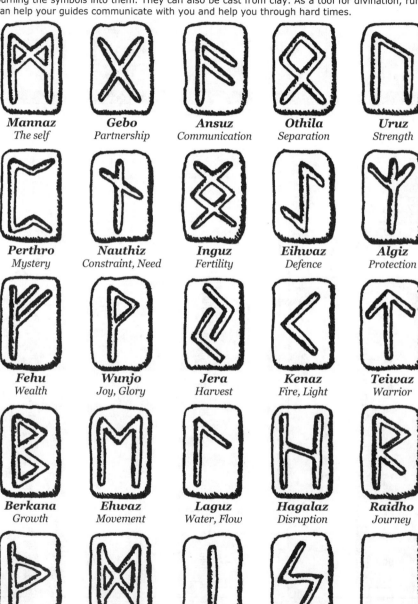

Mannaz *The self*	**Gebo** *Partnership*	**Ansuz** *Communication*	**Othila** *Separation*	**Uruz** *Strength*
Perthro *Mystery*	**Nauthiz** *Constraint, Need*	**Inguz** *Fertility*	**Eihwaz** *Defence*	**Algiz** *Protection*
Fehu *Wealth*	**Wunjo** *Joy, Glory*	**Jera** *Harvest*	**Kenaz** *Fire, Light*	**Teiwaz** *Warrior*
Berkana *Growth*	**Ehwaz** *Movement*	**Laguz** *Water, Flow*	**Hagalaz** *Disruption*	**Raidho** *Journey*
Thurisaz *Gateway*	**Dagaz** *Transformation*	**Isa** *Standstill*	**Sowilo** *Sun, Wholeness*	**Odin** *Unknowable*

17.8.1 RUNE CASTING LAYOUTS

Often drawing a single rune will provide the most concise and focused answer to the question at hand. Drawing a single rune every few days can help guide you through the difficult times. Other more complicated castings are done for times when the circumstances are complex and need clarification. This should only be done for oneself once or twice a year.

These layouts are only an example. You can devise your own as long as you understand the significance of each rune laid out.

Warning: Once you start pulling runes and see how specific and accurate they can be to your situation and thinking, it can become addictive. If you start seeking higher wisdom for every little thing that may pop up in your life, the runes pulled will become increasingly erratic and random – especially if the answer you seek is something you can work out for yourself, or a trivial matter. Use them wisely and only as needed, whether casting for your self or for others.

1	Past – Previous factors affecting the present.
2	Present – The current situation and state of mind.
3	Future – The final outcome.

1	Earth – Represents physical lessons.
2	Water – Represents emotional lessons.
3	Fire – Represents spiritual lessons linked to the unfolding future.
4	Air – Represents the place where you should seek future wisdom.

1	Present – Represents the current situation and state of mind.
2	Past – The previous events affecting the present.
3	Help you can expect to receive. If this is negative it may indicate an unwillingness to accept help, or that no help will come.
4	Aspects that cannot be altered and must be accepted.
5	Future – The final outcome.

1+2	The problem at hand.
3+4	Past factors affecting the present.
5+6	Guidance for the problem at hand, or an unrelated but more important issue.
7	The resulting outcome.

1	What mask do I show the world?
2	What fears are within me?
3	What am I seeking?
4	How should I best approach this?
5	What do I hope to become?
6	What is stopping me?
7	What is my destiny?
8	What do I need to learn to find my true self?
9	What is my true self?

17.8.2 RUNE MEANINGS

Fehu
F
Wealth

Abundance, harvest, financial strength in the present or near future. Possessions gained and good fortune. A rune of hope, success and happiness.

Reversed – Loss of property, self esteem, or something that you worked hard to gain. Possible failure or loss of income.

Uruz
U/V
Strength

Physical strength, power and great personal energy. Freedom, courage and tenacity. Unexpected changes, usually of a positive nature.

Reversed – Physical illness and weakness are a possibility. Could be dominated by others. Violence and brutality or ones own strength against oneself.

Thurisaz
Th
Gateway

Indicates the presence of new options. However, you should stop at the gate before crossing it to look at the road that led you here.

This is not the time for action. Review your past, bless it, and then cross the gate.

Reversed – Personal relationships could be in jeopardy. Expectations and desired outcomes could elude you. Full contemplation of choices is needed.

Ansuz
A
Communication

Expect the unexpected. You are called toward change and renovation. It is recommended that you keep your eyes open for new relationships and contacts. A revealing message of insight and communication.

Reversed – A sense of futility and wasted motion. Failed communication and lack of clarity. Inability to grasp a current situation.

Raidho
R
Journey

Journeys are at hand, both in physical and spiritual matters.

Reversed – Loss of relationships, a crisis, stasis. Disruption, dislocation and a possible death.

Kenaz
K
Fire, Light

The rune of opening, vision and relationships. This indicates the opening of knowledge and creativity, of relationships and understanding between people. The power to create your own reality. Passion and sex.

Reversed – The loss of light and vision, break-ups due to self closing. A loss or lack of creativity and imagination.

Gebo
G
Gift, Partnership

Fortune smiles and nice surprised will arrive unexpectedly. Gifts both in the sense of sacrifice and generosity, indicating balance.

Pay careful attention to the surrounding runes.

Wunjo
W
Joy, Glory

Joy, comfort and pleasure. A journey's happy end is here. Trouble has passed and tiresome tasks are complete. Success and recognition.

Reversed – Exactly the opposite. Sorrow, strife and alienation. Failure and feelings of worthlessness are upon you. Trouble is your rider.

Hagalaz
H
Disruption

This rune represents all things out of your control – elemental destruction, uncontrolled forces, limitations and delays.

A great awakening is at hand – either gradual, or a tearing away of the very fabric of ones reality.

Nauthiz N Need, Constraint	Obstacles and delays, restrictions and pain imposed by others or ourselves. Restraint leading to strength and innovation. Distress, confusion and conflict are yours – plus the strength to overcome them. A rune of major self-initiated change. **Reversed** – Constraint and suffering. A time of need, deprivation and poverty.
Isa I Standstill	A time of non-movement and a need for patience. Physical, mental and emotional blocks to thought or activity. Goals and desires are at a standstill. Now is a time to turn inward, wait for what is to come, and to seek clarity. This rune reinforces those around it.
Jera J Harvest	A rune of beneficial outcomes, it can break through the stasis. The results or earlier efforts are now realised. A time of peace and prosperity. The promise of success to come.
Eihwaz Ei Defense	The power to avert defeat, the strength to endure all. The driving force to achieve despite possible obstacles, providing motivation and a sense of purpose. This rune indicates you have sights on a goal and can achieve it. Even in a negative rune case, Eihwaz indicates things will work for the better.
Perthro P Mystery	A mystery rune. Uncertainty of meaning, a secret matter. A change out of your control, but not one that is easily seen. Often thought of as a death of some kind, you must let go of everything. A complex rune to understand and often ties to Odin – the unknowable. Watch carefully the surrounding runes. **Reversed** – Loneliness and unease, an inability to see one's direction.
Algiz Z Protection	A rune of protection and a shield against harm. New opportunities and influences are a characteristic of this rune. A rune of warding against evil, connection with gods. A reminder to follow your instincts to hold on to a position won or earned. **Reversed** – A warning of hidden dangers, vulnerability, a loss of your divine link.
Sowilo S Sun , Wholeness	A time when a great power will be available to you for positive changes. Guidance, hope, success and goals achieved. A wholeness, finding power, a cleansing fire.
Teiwaz T Warrior	Honour, justice, leadership and authority are characteristic of this rune. Shows victory and success over opposing or competing forces. Extreme motivation. Can also indicate an increase in money or power. **Reversed** – Blocking of energy or creative flow. Defeat in conflict, failure in competition. A loosening of passion, failure or loss at relationships.
Berkana B Growth	A fertility rune, a rebirth and growth – mentally, physically or spirituality. Re-generative power and the promise of new beginnings. An arousal of desire, the goddess is represented by Berkana. **Reversed** – A warning of domestic troubles. A loss of desire, of love. Possible miscarriage. Stagnation of the spirit. Impotence and lack of fertility.

Ehwaz
E

Movement

A rune of transit, transportation and movement. Indicates changes in dwellings, lifestyles or attitudes. Shows transition and change for the better. Whatever problem you are facing, you are on the correct path.

Reversed – A blockage of movement, a denial of desires, though not necessarily negative. What is truly yours will come to you.

Mannaz
M

The self

Represents humankind. Can show interdependence, assistance from another in matters. Seek out advice and help rather than taking on a burden.

Reversed – Expect no help from others. Look to yourself for the blockages and enemies of your progress.

Laguz
L

Water, Flow

Water, fluid, the ebb and flow of emotions, careers and relationships. Plus the healing powers of renewal. It signals a time for cleansing and re-aligning.

Reversed – A warning of a period of confusion, of failure to draw upon the wisdom of instinct. You may be making poor decisions, judgements and trying to exceed your own strength.

Inguz
Ng

Fertility

The need to be desired, to share. Male fertility, the home and family are also part of this rune. A rune of great powers, marking new life, or joyful deliverance.

A time when loose strings are tied and you are free to move in a new direction.

Dagaz
D

Day, Transformation

A major shift or breakthrough. Daylight clarity as opposed to night time uncertainty. A time to plan or embark on a new enterprise.

The power of change directed by your own will.

Othilo
O

Separation

This is a time of separated paths, a time to cast away the old. You can expect aid in physical and spiritual journeys. May indicate a source of safety, increase and abundance.

Reversed – Negligence and a refusal to see clearly. Pain and suffering caused to others by oneself.

Odin

The unknowable

This rune tells you that all is meant to happen based on karmic rules. You are not meant to know the outcome of your question right now, just know that what will happen is meant to.

This rune can be used as a significator for the great mysteries. The answer it gives is an important one.

17.8.3 RUNIC ALPHABET

This is only one variation on the runic alphabet, as the language has evolved over the centuries. Not sure what you will use it for. Note the lack of a C, Q, X and Y. Improvise.

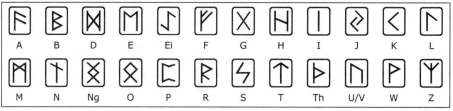

18 WEATHER PREDICTION

Being able to predict the weather is a valuable tool. Knowing that bad weather is coming can give you warning to batten down, move to higher ground or cancel travel plans, or perhaps to use it as cover for whatever you have in mind.

Knowing that good weather is on its way or continuing can give you the confidence to work on projects that may require a few days of clear skies.

18.1 CLOUD FORMATIONS

Clouds can be grouped into three categories, based on their appearance from the ground —

Cirrus	Thin, wispy streaks
Cumulus	Clumped globular forms
Stratus	Uniform 'blanket'

There are many variations and being able to recognise them is the first step in determining the coming weather.

18.1.1 HIGH CLOUDS

High clouds indicate a high pressure system which generally indicates good weather.

Cirrocumulus (above 6 km / 20,000 ft)

These clouds are globe shaped and can form wave-like patterns. These indicate a high-pressure system which generally means fine, clear weather.

Cirrus (above 7 km / 23,000 ft)

Cirrus clouds are formed when water vapour freezes into ice crystals at high altitudes. Cirrus clouds are characterized by thin, wisplike strands. They indicate a high-pressure system which usually means fine weather, though may indicate rain within 36 hours.

Sometimes these clouds are so extensive that they are virtually indistinguishable from each other. This forms a layer of cloud referred to as cirrostratus.

If these clouds are not so extensive as to blur into one another (i.e., cirrostratus), then they will not be rain producing clouds.

Cirrostratus (above 6 km / 20,000 ft)

These clouds often form a white semi-transparent veil across the sky. You can still see the sun or moon, although diffused, through these clouds. Again these indicate a high-pressure system and good weather.

Sometimes cirrostratus clouds are so thin that they are barely visible. This may indicate a large amount of moisture in the atmosphere.

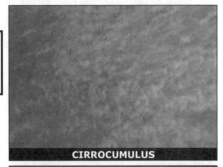
CIRROCUMULUS

CIRRUS

CIRROSTRATUS

These clouds may indicate the beginning of a warm front and may signal rain in the next 12-24 hours.

18.1.2 MIDDLE CLOUDS

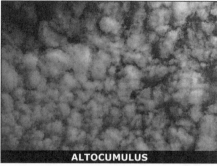

ALTOSTRATUS   ALTOCUMULUS

Altostratus (2-6 km / 8,000-20,000 ft)

Altostratus clouds are characterized by a generally uniform grey sheet or layer, lighter in colour than nimbostratus and darker than cirrostratus. The sun can be seen shining through them, and they frequently cover the sky. They are similar to lower altitude stratus clouds. On the coast they can bring rain but inland, especially in winter, they are uncertain.

Altocumulus (2-6 km / 8,000-20,000 ft)

Altocumulus clouds are characterized by globular masses or rolls in layers or patches, the individual elements being larger and darker than those of cirrocumulus and smaller than those of stratocumulus. These clouds often precede a cold front, and their presence on a warm, humid, summer morning frequently signals the development of thunderstorms later in the day.

18.1.3 LOW CLOUDS

CUMULUS   STRATOCUMULUS

Cumulus (base below 2 km / 6,500 ft – tops vary)

Cumulus clouds are fluffy, white, heaped-up clouds. These clouds, which are much lower than cirrus clouds, are often fair weather clouds. They usually appear around midday on a sunny day, looking like large cotton balls with flat bottoms. As the day advances, they may become bigger and push higher into the atmosphere. Piling up to appear like a mountain of clouds. These can turn into storm clouds.

Cumulus clouds are often precursors of other types of clouds, such as cumulonimbus, when influenced by weather factors such as instability, moisture, and temperature gradient.

Stratocumulus (usually below 2.4 km / 8,000 ft)

A dense grey cloud with darker shadings in patches, sheets or layers. Generally it is a fine weather cloud but can bring some light drizzle.

'Dull weather' commonly describes overcast stratocumulus days. If the air over land is moist and hot enough they may develop to various cumulus clouds, or more commonly, the sheets of thick stratocumuli may have a nimbostratus look to them. The distinction here is the amount of rain produced. On drier areas they quickly dissipate over land.

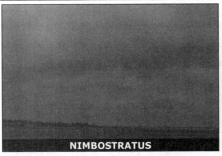
NIMBOSTRATUS

STRATUS

Nimbostratus (below 2.4 km / 8,000 ft)

A Nimbostratus cloud is characterized by a formless cloud layer that is almost uniformly dark grey. The prefix 'nimbo' is derived from the Latin 'nimbus', meaning rain.

Usually, nimbostratus is a sign of steady moderate to heavy rain, as opposed to the shorter period of typically heavier rain released by a cumulonimbus cloud. However, the rain may evaporate before it reaches the ground. Precipitation may last for several days.

Stratus (below 2 km / 6,000 ft)

Stratus is Latin for 'blanket' and used to describe flat, featureless clouds of low altitude varying in colour from dark grey to nearly white. When stratus clouds reach the ground, it is called fog.

These clouds are essentially above-ground fog formed either through the lifting of morning fog or when cold air moves at low altitudes over a region. These clouds do not usually bring heavy precipitation, although drizzle and snow may occur.

18.1.4 VERTICAL CLOUDS

These clouds can have strong up-currents, rise far above their bases and form at many heights. The most well known form is the cumulonimbus.

Cumulonimbus (2-16 km / 6,500-60,000 ft)

Cumulonimbus is a type of cloud that is tall, dense, and involved in thunderstorms and other intense weather. It is a result of atmospheric instability. These clouds can form alone, in clusters, or along a cold front.

Well-developed cumulonimbus clouds are also characterized by a flat, anvil-like top. This anvil shape can precede the main cloud structure for many miles, causing anvil lightning. This is the tallest of the clouds. Lightning and gale-force winds often accompany the cloud mass. The storms can be extremely dangerous, doing great damage to the area.

CUMULONIMBUS

CUMULUS CASTELLANUS

Castellanus (2-6 km / 6,500-20,000 ft)

These towering clouds (cumulus castellanus and altocumulus castellanus) indicate mid-atmospheric instability. In the summer time expect the possibility of showers in the afternoon. These clouds can develop into cumulonimbus which will usually bring a thunderstorm.

18.2 BAROMETERS

Perhaps the most useful of weather instruments is the barometer. Air pressure plays a significant role in weather and, unlike wind speed/direction, temperature or humidity, cannot usually be sensed directly by the human body.

There are many types of barometers commercially available and I suggest you buy one that doesn't require power. To take an accurate reading from a liquid barometer will require a simultaneous temperature reading due to the density of the fluid changing with temperature.

However, a liquid barometer is often quicker to react than a mechanical (aneroid) thermometer due to play and 'stickiness' in the mechanisms. It is also not necessary to know the exact reading on any particular scale, as it is the overall trend that is important.

Read the instructions for your type of barometer and consult with your local weather reports to calibrate the device, although this is not strictly necessary.

Improvised Air-Filled Barometer

A simple barometer can be made using a large jar or other container with a flexible membrane stretched tightly over the top.

If you use a balloon or rubber glove for the membrane, inflate it first to pre-stretch it, and then cut to fit.

The seal needs to be air-tight. This can be done with rubber bands or a few wraps of cordage.

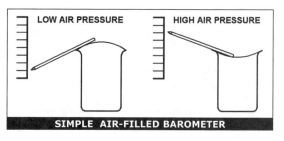

SIMPLE AIR-FILLED BAROMETER

Future readings will be relative to the air pressure at the time it was sealed. The membrane will bulge out when the pressure drops, and will bulge in when the pressure rises.

You can simply watch the membrane to determine changes in air pressure, or you can attach a long stick as shown to act as a lever and expand the scale.

Eventually the rubber will fatigue but this will be slowed if you keep it out of the sun.

Improvised Liquid-Filled Barometer

A more complicated barometer can be constructed if you have the time and the resources. If constructed properly, last longer than Yoda this instrument will.

The vertical tube needs to be about 2 metres (6 feet) tall to accommodate the range of likely pressures. It will be difficult to find a glass tube that long, but transparent beverage hose is inexpensive.

Beverage hose also has the advantage that it will not crack easily if the water freezes, and it is flexible which will simplify construction.

The top container is sealed airtight, while the bottom container is open to the air. It can be completely open, but if there is only a small air gap then evaporation is reduced.

When you have sealed the tube in the top container, create a partial vacuum by sucking the air out. Cap the end of the hose with your finger, and immerse in

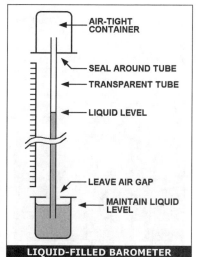

LIQUID-FILLED BAROMETER

the bottom container before letting go. The liquid will then rise up the tube.

When taking a reading, make sure the liquid in the bottom container is always at the same level. The level in the tube will rise with high pressure, and fall with low pressure.

Bear in mind that temperature will affect the density of the liquid, so try to take a reading at the same temperature each time.

18.3 GENERAL PREDICTION TIPS

These are no hard and fast rules for weather prediction, especially when looking at the local system from the ground, but these tips can give you a general idea of what is going on.

Check for Dew at Sunrise

If the grass is dry this can indicate clouds or strong breezes which can mean rain. If there's dew then it probably won't rain that day. This method is not reliable if it has rained overnight.

Red Sky at Night, Sailor's Delight, Red Sky at Morning, Sailor's Warning

Look for any sign of red in the sky (not a red sun). Depending on where you live, it will probably not be a bold orange or red most of the time.

If you see a red sky during sunset (when you're looking West), this can indicate a high pressure system with dry air that is stirring up dust particles. Since prevailing front movements and jet streams usually move from west to East (due to the rotation of the Earth below the atmosphere) the dry air is moving toward you.

A red sky in the morning (in the East) means that dry air has already moved past you and what follows behind it is a low pressure system that carries moisture.

Rainbow in the Morning, Heralds a Warning

A rainbow in the West at sunrise is the result of the rays of the sun striking moisture in the West. Most major storm fronts travel from West to East, and a rainbow in the west means moisture, which can mean rain is on its way.

A rainbow in the East at sunset means that the rain has passed and a sunny day is ahead.

Note the Wind Direction

Use a wind sock, weather vane, wet finger or simply drop a light piece of grass to determine the direction of the wind. Easterly winds can indicate an approaching storm front, westerly winds the opposite.

Strong winds indicate high pressure differences which can be a sign of advancing storm fronts.

Smell the Air

In a low pressure atmosphere, plants release their 'waste' which generates a smell like compost. A low pressure system can indicate bad weather approaching.

Swamps will release gasses just before a storm because of falling pressure.

According to a proverb, "flowers smell best before a rain". This is due to moist air. Humidity in the air can also usually be smelt, or felt directly. This usually means rain, but if you are in a tropical region, the humidity can build up and dissipate daily for a long time before raining.

Clouds on a Winter Night

This will bring warmer weather in the morning because the cloud cover prevents heat radiation that would lower the temperature on a clear night.

18.3.1 DROPPING PRESSURE

If the pressure is dropping, there can be many reasons why this is so —

- A low pressure system is approaching, such as a front or trough of low pressure
- An area of low pressure is not approaching, but deepening
- Both of the above conditions are present, in which case the pressure will drop rapidly, usually bringing heavier rains or snow. The greater the drop, the greater the winds will blow (usually from the direction of the equator)
- In this case, the weather will rapidly deteriorate and the pressure will continue to drop until the weather hits, and then rise rapidly because cold air is heavy.
- Warm air movements (usually from the direction of the equator) will bring warm air, which is lighter, causing a pressure drop.
- Pressure also changes due to daily air temperature changes. From a slight high in the morning, to a slight minimum in the late afternoon, with a slight increase as the sun sets into the night. These changes will be less if there is cloud cover and therefore less heating from the sun.

18.3.2 OBSERVATION OF ANIMALS

- If birds are flying high in the sky there will probably be fair weather. Falling air pressure will cause discomfort in birds ears, so they fly low to alleviate it. Large numbers of birds roosting in trees or on power lines indicate rapidly falling pressure.
- Seagulls tend to stop flying and take refuge at the coast if a storm is coming.
- Animals, especially birds get quiet immediately before it rains.
- Cows will typically lie down before a thunderstorm. They also tend to stay close together if bad weather is on the way.
- Ants build their hills with very steep sides just before a rain.

18.3.3 OTHER EMPIRICAL WEATHER RULES

Stand with Your Back to the Wind

The low pressure system will be to your left and the high pressure system will be to your right.

If low clouds move in from the left the weather will deteriorate, if they come from the right the weather will improve. If the clouds move in the same direction as the surface wind, expect no change for at least 12 hours.

Observe the Moon at Night

If it is reddish or pale, dust is in the air. But if the moon is bright and sharply focused, it's probably because low pressure has cleared out the dust, and low pressure can mean rain.

A ring around the moon (caused by light shining through cirrostratus clouds associated with warm fronts and moisture) can indicate that rain will probably fall within the next three days.

Remember: Circle around the moon, rain or snow soon.

Green Hue in Thunderstorm (Cumulonimbus) Clouds

This indicates extreme vertical height and is often linked to hail and extreme downburst winds.

Observe the edges of Cumulus Clouds

Cumulus clouds that have dark, raggedy edges are dissipating (usually with sunset). Cumulus that is white with rounded edges is building and may develop into storm clouds in the afternoon.

Wind Direction

If the wind is blowing from the equator, this will cause a temperature increase. If they are moving toward the equator, the temperature will fall.

Make a Campfire

Smoke that rises steadily indicates high pressure. If the smoke swirls and descends, there is low pressure and rain could be on the way.

18.3.4 PERSISTENCE AND TRENDS

The rule of persistence means if the weather was good yesterday and the wind sky and pressure haven't appreciably changed, then the weather will probably be good for the next 12-24 hours. Don't forecast a change without a good reason.

Observe the Long-Term Local Trends

The skill of weather forecasting is about pattern recognition in the local area. Consider all the evidence and trends (clouds, pressure, winds, time of year etc). If no records are available, then keeping your own will aid you greatly.

And remember, forecasting is difficult beyond 24 to 48 hours, even for the experts.

19 WATER CROSSINGS

In a survival situation, you may have to cross a water obstacle. It may be in the form of a river, a stream, a lake, a bog, quicksand, quagmire, or muskeg. Even in the desert, flash floods occur, making streams an obstacle. Whatever it is, you need to know how to cross it safely.

19.1 RIVERS AND STREAMS

You can apply almost every description to rivers and streams. They may be shallow or deep, slow or fast moving, narrow or wide. Before you try to cross a river or stream, develop a good plan.

Your first step is to look for a high place from which you can get a good view of the river or stream. From this place, you can look for a place to cross. If there is no high place, climb a tree. Good crossing locations include —

- A level stretch where it breaks into several channels. Two or three narrow channels are usually easier to cross than a wide river.

- A shallow bank or sandbar. If possible, select a point upstream from the bank or sandbar so that the current will carry you to it if you lose your footing.

- A course across the river that leads downstream so that you will cross the current at about a 45-degree angle.

The following areas possess potential hazards; avoid them, if possible —

- Obstacles on the opposite side of the river that might hinder your travel. Try to select the spot from which travel will be the safest and easiest.

- A ledge of rocks that crosses the river. This often indicates dangerous rapids or canyons.

- A deep or rapid waterfall or a deep channel. Never try to ford a stream directly above or even close to such hazards.

- Rocky places. You may sustain serious injuries from slipping or falling on rocks. Usually, submerged rocks are very slick, making balance extremely difficult. An occasional rock that breaks the current, however, may help you.

- An estuary of a river. An estuary is normally wide, has strong currents, and is subject to tides. These tides can influence some rivers many kilometres from their mouths. Go back upstream to an easier crossing site.

- Eddies. An eddy can produce a powerful backward pull downstream of the obstruction causing the eddy and pull you under the surface.

The depth of a fordable river or stream is no deterrent if you can keep your footing. In fact, deep water sometimes runs more slowly and is therefore safer than fast-moving shallow water. You can always dry your clothes later, or if necessary, you can make a raft to carry your clothing and equipment across the river.

You must not try to swim or wade across a stream or river when the water is at very low temperatures. This swim could be fatal. Try to make a raft of some type. Wade across if you can get only your feet wet. Dry them vigorously as soon as you reach the other bank.

19.2 RAPIDS

If necessary, you can safely cross a deep, swift river or rapids. To swim across a deep, swift river, swim with the current, never fight it. Try to keep your body horizontal to the water. This will reduce the danger of being pulled under.

In fast, shallow rapids, lie on your back, feet pointing downstream, finning your hands alongside your hips. This action will increase buoyancy and help you steer away from obstacles. Keep your feet up to avoid getting them bruised or caught by rocks.

In deep rapids, lie on your stomach, head downstream, angling toward the shore whenever you can. Watch for obstacles and be careful of backwater eddies and converging currents, as they often contain dangerous swirls. Converging currents occur where new watercourses enter the river or where water has been diverted around large obstacles such as small islands.

To cross a rapid or dangerous stream, use the following techniques —

- Remove your pants and shirt to lessen the water's pull on you. Keep your footgear on to protect your feet and ankles from rocks. It will also provide you with firmer footing.

- Tie your pants and other articles to the top of your rucksack or in a bundle, if you have no pack. This way, if you have to release your equipment, all your articles will be together.

- Carry your pack well up on your shoulders and be sure you can remove it if necessary. Not being able to get a pack off quickly enough can drag even the strongest swimmers under.

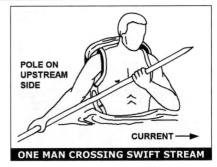

ONE MAN CROSSING SWIFT STREAM

- Find a strong pole about 2 - 3 meters long to help you ford the stream. Grasp the pole and plant it firmly on your upstream side to break the current. Plant your feet firmly with each step, and move the pole forward a little downstream from its previous position, but still upstream from you. With your next step, place your foot below the pole. Keep the pole well slanted so that the force of the current keeps the pole against your shoulder.

- Cross the stream so that you will cross the downstream current at a 45° angle.

Using this method, you can safely cross currents usually too strong for one person to stand against. Do not concern yourself about your pack's weight, as the weight will help rather than hinder you in fording the stream.

If there are other people with you, then cross the stream together. Ensure that everyone has prepared their pack and clothing as outlined above. Position the heaviest person on the downstream end of the pole and the lightest on the upstream end. In using this method, the upstream person breaks the current, and those below can move with relative ease in the eddy formed by the upstream person. If the upstream person gets temporarily swept off their feet, the others can hold steady while they regain their footing.

SEVERAL MEN CROSSING SWIFT STREAM

If you have three or more people and a rope available, you can use the technique shown to cross the stream. The length of the rope must be three times the width of the stream.

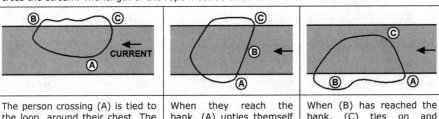

The person crossing (A) is tied to the loop, around their chest. The strongest person crosses first. The other two are not tied on - they pay out the rope as needed and can stop the person crossing from being washed away.	When they reach the bank, (A) unties themself and (B) ties on. (B) crosses, controlled by the others. Any number of people can be sent across this way.	When (B) has reached the bank, (C) ties on and crosses. (A) takes most of the strain, but (B) helps and is ready in case anything goes wrong.

INDIVIDUALS TIED TOGETHER TO CROSS STREAM

19.3 RAFTS

If you have a poncho or tarp you can construct simple rafts. These rafts can be used as flotation devices to aid you in crossing a passage of water safely. You may not be able to board these small rafts, but you will be able to use them to carry your gear, and as a flotation aid.

19.3.1 BRUSH RAFT

The brush raft, if properly constructed, will support about 120 kilograms. Use ponchos, fresh green brush, two small saplings, and rope or vine as follows —

- Push the hood of each poncho to the inner side and tie off the necks using the drawstrings.
- Attach the ropes or vines at the corner and side grommets of each poncho. Make sure they are long enough to cross to and tie with the others attached at the opposite corner or side.
- Spread one poncho on the ground with the inner side up. Pile fresh, green brush (no thick branches) on the poncho until the brush stack is about 50 cm high. Pull the drawstring up through the centre of the brush stack.

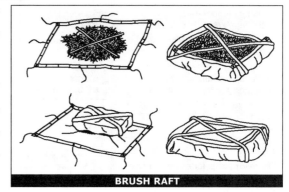

- Make an X-frame from two small saplings and place it on top of the brush stack. Tie the X-frame securely in place with the poncho drawstring.
- Pile another 50 cm of brush on top of the frame, then compress the brush slightly.
- Pull the poncho sides up around the brush and, using the ropes or vines attached to the comer or side grommets, tie diagonally from comer to corner and from side to side.
- Spread the second poncho, inner side up, next to the brush bundle.

BRUSH RAFT

- Roll the bundle onto the second poncho with the tied side down. Tie the second poncho around the bundle in the same manner as you tied the first poncho around the brush.
- Place it in the water with the tied side of the second poncho facing up.

19.3.2 PONCHO DONUT RAFT

Another type of raft is the poncho donut raft. It takes more time to construct than the brush raft, but it is effective. To construct it, use one poncho, small saplings, and rope or other material as follows —

- Make a framework for the circle by placing several stakes in the ground that roughly outline an inner and outer circle.

PONCHO DONUT RAFT

- Using young saplings, willow, or vines, construct a donut ring within the circles of stakes.
- Wrap several pieces of cordage around the ring about 30 cm apart and tie them securely.
- Push the poncho's hood to the inner side and tightly tie off the neck using the drawstring.
- Place the poncho on the ground, inner side up. Place the donut ring on the centre of the poncho. Wrap the poncho up and over the donut ring and tie off each grommet on the poncho to the ring.
- Tie an empty canteen to the raft with a length of rope. This will help you tow the raft.

When launching any of the above rafts, take care not to puncture or tear it by dragging it on the ground. Before you start to cross the river or stream, let the raft lay on the water a few minutes to ensure that it floats.

If the river is too deep to ford, push the raft in front of you while you are swimming. The designs of the above rafts do not allow them to carry a person's full body weight. Use them as a float to get you and your equipment safely across the river or stream.

Be sure to check the water temperature before trying to cross a river or water obstacle. If the water is extremely cold and you are unable to find a shallow fording place in the river, do not try to ford it. Devise other means for crossing. For instance, you might improvise a bridge by felling a tree over the river. Or you might build a raft large enough to carry you and your equipment. For this, however, you will need an axe, a knife, a rope or vines, and time.

19.3.3 LOG RAFTS

When choosing logs for a raft, the best ones are the lightest you can find. They will provide the most buoyancy and also be easier to work and carry.

Softwoods like pine and fir are good. Poplar, balsa and spruce trees make the best rafts. Standing timber that is dead is preferable to logs on the ground as they contain less water. Avoid hardwoods like maple, oak, jarrah etc.

Classic rafts are usually lashed together using two or more cross-beams, depending on the size of the raft. See **LASHINGS** Page 7-11).

If you have the time and materials, a raft can be made large enough to have a tent or even a small cabin. Sails can be made, but don't give much control. Steering poles are recommended. Rafts are generally stable in rough water, but can also break up if not made strong.

If you are short on cordage, another method is to use pressure bars lashed securely at each end to hold the logs together.

To ensure the logs are clamped tight, line them up from thickest to thinnest, with the largest log on one side, and the smallest on the other.

Alternatively, place the largest log in the centre and place smaller and smaller logs towards the edges. You may need to pack in some wedges in places.

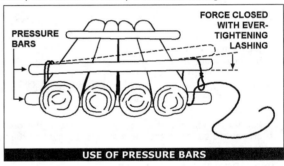

19.3.4 OTHER FLOTATION DEVICES

If the water is warm enough for swimming and you do not have the time or materials to construct one of the poncho-type rafts, you can use various flotation devices to negotiate the water obstacle. Some items you can use for flotation devices are —

Trousers	Knot each leg at the bottom and close the fly. With both hands, grasp the waistband and scoop air into the trousers. Quickly hold the top closed and hold it underwater so that the air will not escape. You now have water wings to keep you afloat as you cross the body of water.
	Wet the trousers before inflating to trap the air better. You may have to reinflate the trousers several times when crossing a large body of water.
Empty containers	Lash together her empty gas cans, water jugs, or other items that will hold air. Use them as water wings. Use only in a slow-moving river or stream.
Plastic bags and ponchos	Fill some plastic bags with air and secure them together at the opening, or use a poncho and roll green vegetation tightly inside it so that you have a roll at least 20 cm in diameter. Tie the ends of the roll securely.

Logs	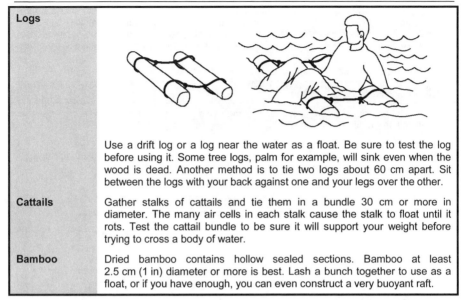
	Use a drift log or a log near the water as a float. Be sure to test the log before using it. Some tree logs, palm for example, will sink even when the wood is dead. Another method is to tie two logs about 60 cm apart. Sit between the logs with your back against one and your legs over the other.
Cattails	Gather stalks of cattails and tie them in a bundle 30 cm or more in diameter. The many air cells in each stalk cause the stalk to float until it rots. Test the cattail bundle to be sure it will support your weight before trying to cross a body of water.
Bamboo	Dried bamboo contains hollow sealed sections. Bamboo at least 2.5 cm (1 in) diameter or more is best. Lash a bunch together to use as a float, or if you have enough, you can even construct a very buoyant raft.

There are many other flotation devices that you can devise by using some imagination. Just make sure to test the device before trying to use it.

19.4 OTHER WATER OBSTACLES

Other water obstacles that you may face are bogs, quagmire, muskeg, or quicksand. Do not try to walk across these. Trying to lift your feet while standing upright will make you sink deeper. Try to bypass these obstacles. If you are unable to bypass them, you may be able to bridge them using logs, branches, or foliage.

A way to cross a bog is to lie face down, with your arms and legs spread. Use a flotation device or form pockets of air in your clothing. Swim or pull your way across moving slowly and trying to keep your body horizontal.

In swamps, the areas that have vegetation are usually firm enough to support your weight. However, vegetation will usually not be present in open mud or water areas. If you are an average swimmer, however, you should have no problem swimming, crawling, or pulling your way through miles of bog or swamp.

Quicksand is a mixture of sand and water that forms a shifting mass. It yields easily to pressure and sucks down and engulfs objects resting on its surface. It varies in depth and is usually localized. Quicksand commonly occurs on flat shores, in silt-choked rivers with shifting watercourses, and near the mouths of large rivers. If you are uncertain whether a sandy area is quicksand, toss a small stone on it. The stone will sink in quicksand. Although quicksand has more suction than mud or muck, you can cross it just as you would cross a bog. Lie face down, spread your arms and legs, and move slowly across.

19.4.1 VEGETATION OBSTACLES

Some water areas you must cross may have underwater and floating plants that will make swimming difficult. However, you can swim through relatively dense vegetation if you remain calm and do not thrash about. Stay as near the surface as possible and use the breaststroke with shallow leg and arm motion. Remove the plants around you as swim. When you get tired, float or swim on your back until you have rested enough to continue with the breaststroke.

The mangrove swamp is another type of obstacle that occurs along tropical coastlines. Mangrove trees or shrubs throw out many prop roots that form dense masses. To get through a mangrove swamp, wait for low tide. If you are on the inland side, look for a narrow grove of trees and work your way seaward through these. You can also try to find the bed of a waterway or creek through the trees and follow it to the sea. If you are on the seaward side, work inland along streams or channels. Be on the lookout for crocodiles that you find along channels and in shallow water. If there are any near you, leave the water and scramble over the mangrove roots. While crossing a mangrove swamp, it is possible to gather food from tidal pools or tree roots.

To cross a large swamp area, construct some type of raft.

19.5 ROPE BRIDGES

Building a rope bridge is no easy undertaking. This should be done only if the situation requires and allows, if you are crossing at this point often for example.

To build a rope bridge —

- Stretch two ropes taught across a river. Where possible trees should be used as the main support, but a **1-2-3 Anchor** (Page 8-3) can be used if made strong.
- Make a number of light 'V' frames, depending on the length of the crossing.
- The first V-frame is hooked onto the ropes and pushed forward with a long pole.
- The footing, a strong, straight sapling, is dropped into the crotch of the frame.
- The builder walks out along this and hooks on the next V-frame and pushes it out the required distance.
- These steps are repeated until the far bank is reached.

During building, bridges must not be overloaded – one worker at a time is the rule.

- Once the base poles have been extended to the far bank, crossbars should be lashed to the V-frames above the base pole.
- Short lengths of flat-split timber can then be lashed to these poles to provide secure decking.

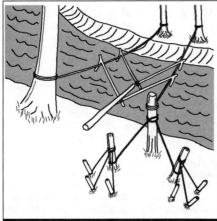

BEGINNING OF A ROPE BRIDGE

BRIDGE WITH AND WITHOUT DECK

If the situation is only semi-permanent, the single pole may be all that is needed.

Be sure to lash it securely.

The bottom frame lashings should be especially strong.

To provide extra stability and to stop violent swaying under heavy loads, the rope bridge can be 'anchored' by attaching a heavy stone to a rope and suspending it from the middle of the bridge span.

You should keep this anchor well above the flooding level of the river –

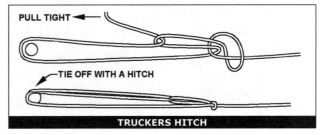

PULL TIGHT ◀—

TIE OFF WITH A HITCH

TRUCKERS HITCH

otherwise strong currents could drag the stone and rip the bridge in two.

To make the main lines tight, use the pulley action of a truckers hitch to increase the tension.

The ropes will probably stretch over time, so be sure to re-tension it periodically.

19.6 MEASURING CROSSING DISTANCE

To determine the width of a crossing without going to the other side, pick a visual marker on the other side – such as a tree or rock - and use the following technique —

- Select a visual site across the river to use as marker **A** and then drive a stake on the near bank **B** to match this site.
- Walk at 90° for a known number of paces and put another marker stake **C**.
- Continue an equal number of paces and put in a third marker **D**.
- Turn away from the river and keep moving back until the centre marker stake **C** lines up with visual marker **A**. Mark this spot **E**.
- The distance between **E** and **D** equals the distance of the river crossing.

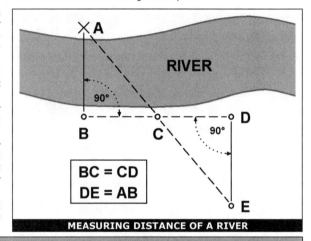

BC = CD
DE = AB

MEASURING DISTANCE OF A RIVER

19.7 CALCULATING CONTAINER BUOYANCY

If you use containers such as old oil drums, jerry cans or even many empty soda bottles to add buoyancy to a raft, you can calculate how much water is displaced. The weight in water that a container holds is how much weight that the empty container will carry above water.

1 litre of water weighs 1 Kg, so an empty 1 litre container of water will support 1 Kg of weight.

1 gallon will carry 8.35 pounds	A 44 gallon drum will carry 367 pounds
1 pint will carry 1.04 pounds	1 litre will carry 1 kilogram

To calculate how much weight an empty container will carry, work out the volume —

- Volume of a cylinder = $\pi \times R \times R \times H$
- Volume of a cube = $W \times H \times D$

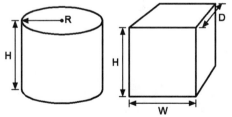

The dimensions are measured in cm, and the volume is given in cubic centimetres (cc). 1 cc = 1 millilitre (1/1000 of a litre).

For example, a 10 by 10 by 10 cm cube will hold 1000 millilitres, or 1 litre, and therefore the empty container will displace 1 kg of water, and so will support 1 kg of weight.

π = 3.14159 or roughly 22/7

20 DIRECTION FINDING

In most end-of-the-world scenarios it is likely that satellites, and with that – GPS, will be not be functioning. It is also likely that in the event of a pole shift, the earth's magnetic field will be weak and erratic – rendering compasses useless.

There are several other methods by which you can determine direction by using the sun and the stars. These methods, however, will give you only a general direction.

Bear in mind also that the order in the heavens will be completely different after a shift so you will need to take note of the earth's new movement in relation to the sun moon and stars.

20.1 USING THE SUN

The earth's relationship to the sun can help you to determine direction on earth. For now, the sun rises in the east and sets in the west, but not exactly due east or west. There is also some seasonal variation. In the northern hemisphere, the sun will be due south when at its highest point in the sky, or when an object casts it's smallest shadow. In the southern hemisphere, this same noon sun will mark due north.

Shadows move clockwise in the northern hemisphere and counter clockwise in the southern hemisphere. With practice, you can use shadows to determine both direction and time of day. The shadow methods used for direction finding are the shadow-tip and watch methods.

20.1.1 SHADOW-TIP METHODS

In the first shadow-tip method, find a straight stick 1 meter long and a level clear patch of dirt where the stick will cast a clear shadow. This method is simple and reasonably accurate.

Step 1	Place the stick or branch into the ground at a level spot where it will cast a distinctive shadow. Mark the shadow's tip with a stone, twig, or other means.
Step 2	Wait 15 to 30 minutes until the shadow tip moves a few cm. Mark the shadow tip's new position in the same way as the first.
Step 3	Draw a straight line through the two marks to obtain an approximate east-west line.

An alternate method is more accurate but requires more time.

Step 1	Set up your shadow stick and mark the first shadow in the morning. Use a piece of string to draw a clean arc through the tip of the shadow and around the stick.
Step 2	At midday, the shadow will shrink and almost disappear. In the afternoon, it will lengthen again and at the point where it touches the arc, make a second mark.
Step 3	Draw a line through the two marks to get an accurate east-west line.

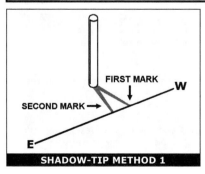

SHADOW-TIP METHOD 1

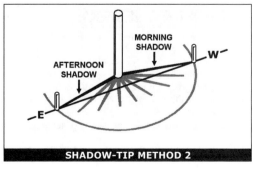

SHADOW-TIP METHOD 2

20.1.2 DETERMINING TIME

Once you have found the East-West line, you can create a sundial to approximate the local time. Place a vertical stick in the centre of the East-West line.

When the shadow is cast on the West line, the time is approximately 06:00 AM. When the shadow is cast on the East line, the time is approximately 06:00 PM.

The North-South line is 90° to the East-West. When the shadow is cast along this line, and at its shortest, the time is 12 noon.

This is as close to local time as you are likely to need. Unless you work for NASA and need to coordinate space shuttle launches, in which case – good luck with that.

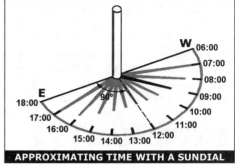

APPROXIMATING TIME WITH A SUNDIAL

20.1.3 USING A WATCH TO DETERMINE DIRECTION

You can determine direction using a common analogue watch. The direction will only be accurate if you are using true local time.

The further you are from the equator, the more accurate this method will be.

If you only have a digital watch, draw a watch on paper or the ground with the correct time.

In the northern hemisphere, hold the watch horizontal and point the hour hand at the sun. Find the middle point between the hour hand and the 12 o'clock mark to get the north-south line.

In the southern hemisphere, point the 12 o'clock mark at the sun and find the midpoint between the 12 o'clock mark and the hour hand.

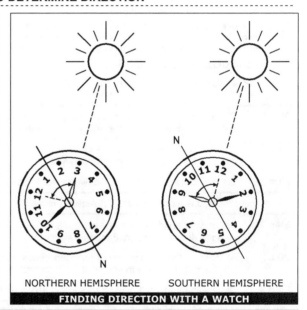

NORTHERN HEMISPHERE   SOUTHERN HEMISPHERE

FINDING DIRECTION WITH A WATCH

20.2 USING THE MOON

Because the moon has no light of its own, we can only see it when it reflects the sun's light. As it orbits the earth on its 28-day circuit, the shape of the reflected light varies according to its position and our position in relation to the sun.

When the moon moves closer to the sun than the earth, the reflected light diminishes until the unlit side of the moon faces us. As the moon moves to the opposite side of the earth, we see the lit hemisphere straight on. This is the full moon. We can use this information to identify direction.

If the moon rises before the sun has set, the illuminated side will be the West. If the moon rises after midnight, the illuminated side will be the East. This discovery provides us with a rough East-West reference during the night.

Using the Moon When You Know the Time

If you know the local time, you can use the moon to determine the approximate direction based on the adjacent table —

Local Time	18:00	21:00	00:00	03:00	06:00
First Quarter	S	SW	W	-	-
Full Moon	E	SE	S	SW	W
Last Quarter	-	-	E	SE	S
USING MOON AND TIME TO DETERMINE DIRECTION					

20.3 USING THE STARS

Your location in the Northern or Southern Hemisphere determines which constellation you use to determine your north or south direction.

20.3.1 THE NORTHERN SKY

The main constellations to learn are the Ursa Major, also known as the Big Dipper, and Cassiopeia. These constellations never set and are always visible on a clear night.

Use them to locate Polaris, also known as the North Star. The North Star forms part of the Little Dipper handle and can be confused with the Big Dipper. Prevent confusion by using both the Big Dipper and Cassiopeia together.

The Big Dipper and Cassiopeia are always directly opposite each other and rotate counter clockwise around Polaris. The Big Dipper is a seven star constellation in the shape of a 'dipper' or ladle.

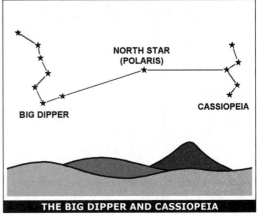

THE BIG DIPPER AND CASSIOPEIA

The two stars forming the outer lip of this dipper are the "pointer stars" because they point to the North Star. Mentally draw a line through these two stars and extend it by about five times to find the North Star.

20.3.2 THE SOUTHERN SKY

There is no star bright enough to be easily recognized near the South celestial pole, so a constellation known as the Southern Cross, or Crux, is used as a guide.

Crux has five stars. Its four brightest stars form a cross that rotates throughout the night. The two stars that make up the long axis are named Gacrux and Acrux.

To determine south, extend a line through these stars for about five times the distance between the two stars.

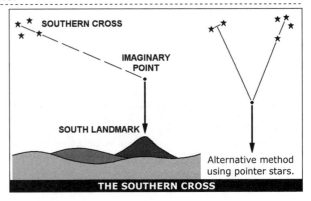

Alternative method using pointer stars.

THE SOUTHERN CROSS

The point where this imaginary line ends is in the general direction of South. Trace this point down to the horizon to select a landmark.

Alternative Method in the Southern Hemisphere

Another method to finding South in the Southern hemisphere is to use the pointer stars east of Crux. Take an imaginary line from between the pointer stars, at a 90° angle. Where this line intersects another imaginary line running from the long axis of the cross, is South.

20.3.3 USING ANY STAR TO DETERMINE DIRECTION

If you cannot find a directional star, pick any star and watch for 10-20 minutes.

If the star —

- Appears to be **falling**, it is approximately **West**
- Appears to be **rising**, it is approximately **East**
- Is travelling to the **right**, it is approximately **South**
- Is travelling to the **left**, it is approximately **North**

20.4 MAKING AN IMPROVISED COMPASS

You can construct an improvised compass using a piece of ferrous (containing iron) metal that is needle shaped or a flat double-edged razor blade and a piece of non-metallic string or long hair from which to suspend it, or you can place it on a light piece of material floating in liquid.

You can magnetize or polarize the metal by slowly stroking it in one direction on another magnet or even a piece of silk. Always rub in one direction only.

Magnetising Electrically

If you have a battery and some electric wire, you can polarize the metal electrically. The wire should be insulated. If not insulated, wrap the metal object in a single thin strip of paper to prevent contact. Form a coil with the electric wire and touch its ends to the battery's terminals.

Repeatedly insert one end of the metal object in and out of the coil. Don't be tempted to shortcut this procedure by simply tapping one end of the coil to the battery while leaving the material to be magnetised inside the coil. Due to the principles of induction, this will create an alternating magnetic field and is actually a good way to de-magnetise an object.

If the wire coil or battery is getting excessively hot, too much current is being drawn. In this case, use more turns of wire, or thinner wire to increase the resistance.

Magnetising By Heat

Another way to magnetise a piece of metal is to heat it red hot and let it cool while inside or next to a magnetic field. The magnetic field of the Earth itself can be used for this purpose, but of course, you need to determine first where north and south lie.

20.5 OTHER MEANS

The old saying about using moss on a tree to indicate North (in the Northern Hemisphere) is not accurate because moss grows completely around some trees. Actually, sometimes growth is more lush on the side of the tree facing the South in the Northern Hemisphere and vice versa in the Southern Hemisphere.

If there are several felled trees around for comparison, look at the stumps. Growth is more vigorous on the side toward the equator and the tree growth rings will be more widely spaced. This means fatter rings on the Southern side in the Northern Hemisphere and the Northern side in the Southern Hemisphere.

Wind direction may be helpful in some instances where there are prevailing directions. In all places on earth, the prevailing winds come from the East (due to the earth's rotation) this is mostly evident near or on the West coast.

21 STEALTH

In a survival situation, especially in an environment where discovery could be disastrous, you may find it necessary to camouflage yourself, your equipment, and your movement. It may mean the difference between survival and being rumbled. Camouflage and movement techniques, such as stalking, can help you move through undesirable areas to a safer location, it will also help you get animals or game for food using primitive weapons and skills.

21.1 PERSONAL CAMOUFLAGE

When camouflaging yourself, consider that certain shapes are particular to humans. The enemy will look for these shapes. The shape of a hat, helmet, or boots can give you away. Even animals know and run from the shape of a human silhouette. Break up your outline by placing small amounts of vegetation from the surrounding area in your clothes and equipment. Try to reduce any shine from skin or equipment. Blend in with the surrounding colours and simulate the texture of your surroundings.

21.1.1 SHAPE AND OUTLINE

Change your outline by tying vegetation or strips of cloth onto them. When hiding, cover yourself and your equipment with leaves, grass, or other local debris.

21.1.2 COLOUR AND TEXTURE

Each area of the world and climate condition has colour patterns and textures that are natural for that area. Surface textures may be smooth, rough, rocky, leafy, or many other possible combinations. Use colour and texture together to camouflage yourself effectively. It makes little sense to camouflage yourself with green grass in the middle of a desert or rocky area.

To hide movement, take on the colour and texture of the immediate surroundings. Use natural or man-made materials to camouflage yourself. Camouflage paint, charcoal, mud, grass, leaves, strips of cloth, vegetation, and camouflaged uniforms are a few examples.

Cover all areas of exposed skin, including face, hands, neck, and ears. Areas that stand out more and catch more light (forehead, nose, cheekbones, chin and ears) should be covered with darker colours. Recessed areas (around the eyes, under the chin) should be covered with lighter colours. Be sure to use irregular patterns.

Use large blotches for deciduous forests, vertical slashes for coniferous forests, broad slashes in jungle, thin slashes in desert, a wide blotch in barren snow and very thin slashes in grasslands.

Attach vegetation from the area or strips of cloth of the proper colour to clothing and equipment. If you use vegetation, replace it as it wilts. If you discard old wilted vegetation, do not leave it where it may be found, indicating your presence. As you move through an area, be alert to the colour changes and modify your camouflage colours as necessary.

21.1.3 SHINE

As skin gets oily it becomes shiny. Equipment with worn off paint is also shiny. Even painted objects may shine. Glass objects such as mirrors, glasses, binoculars, and telescopes shine. Cover these glass objects when not in use. Anything that shines attracts attention. When observing people through binoculars, be aware of the position of the sun or moon.

When possible, wash skin and reapply camouflage. Skin oil will wash off camouflage, so reapply it frequently. If you must wear glasses, apply a thin layer of dust to lenses to diffuse the reflected light. Cover shiny spots on equipment by painting, covering with mud, or wrapping with cloth. Pay attention to covering buckles, watches, jewellery, and zippers.

21.1.4 SHADOW

When hiding or travelling, stay in the deepest part of the shadows. If you are in an area where there is plenty of vegetation, keep as much vegetation between you and others as possible. This will make it very hard for the enemy to see you as the vegetation will mask you from his view. Forcing an enemy to look through many layers of masking vegetation will fatigue their eyes very quickly. Try not to disturb the vegetation as you move through it.

When travelling, especially in urban areas at night, be aware of where you cast your shadow. It may extend out around the comer of a building and give away your position. Also, if you are in a dark shadow and there is a light source to one side, an enemy on the other side can see your silhouette against the light.

21.1.5 MOVEMENT

Movement attracts attention. If possible avoid movement in the presence of an enemy. If capture appears imminent and you must move, move away slowly making as little noise as possible. By moving slowly, you decrease the chance of detection and conserve energy that you may need later.

When moving past obstacles, avoid going over them. If you must climb over an obstacle, keep your body level with its top to avoid silhouetting yourself. Do not silhouette yourself against the skyline when crossing hills or ridges. When you are moving, you will have difficulty detecting the movement of others. Stop frequently, listen, and look around slowly to detect signs of hostile movement.

21.1.6 NOISE

Noise attracts attention, especially a sequence of loud noises such as several snapping twigs. If possible, avoid making any noise at all. Slow down your pace as much as necessary to avoid making noise when moving around or away from possible threats.

Use background noises to cover the noise of your movement. Sounds of aircraft, trucks, generators, strong winds, and people talking will cover some or all the sounds produced by your movement. Rain will mask a lot of movement noise, but it also reduces your ability to detect potential enemy noise.

21.1.7 SCENT

Whether hunting animals or avoiding the enemy, it is always wise to camouflage the scent associated with humans. Start by washing yourself and your clothes without using soap. This will remove soap and body odours. Avoiding strong smelling foods such as garlic will help reduce body odours. Do not use tobacco products, candy, gum, or cosmetics.

You can use aromatic herbs or plants to wash yourself and your clothing, to rub on your body and clothing, or to chew on to camouflage your breath. Pine needles, mint, or any similar aromatic plant will help camouflage your scent from both animals and humans. Standing in smoke from a fire can help mask your scent from animals. While animals are afraid of fresh smoke, old smoke scents are normal after forest fires and do not scare them.

While travelling, use your sense of smell to help you find or avoid humans. Pay attention to smells associated with humans, such as fire, cigarettes, gasoline, oil, soap, and food. Such smells may alert you to their presence long before you can see or hear them, depending on wind speed and direction. Note the wind's direction and, when possible, approach from or skirt around on the downwind side when nearing humans or animals.

21.2 METHODS OF STALKING

If you need to get close to an enemy without being detected, for surveillance or an attack, you will need more than just camouflage to be successful. The ability to stalk or move without making any sudden quick movement or loud noise is essential to avoiding detection. Be especially careful to not produce any unnatural noises, such as metal on metal.

You must practice stalking if it is to be effective. Use the following techniques —

21.2.1 UPRIGHT STALKING

Take steps about half your normal stride when stalking in the upright position. Such strides help you to maintain your balance. You should be able to stop at any point in that movement and hold that position as long as necessary. Curl the toes up out of the way when stepping down so the outside edge of the ball of the foot touches the ground.

Feel for sticks and twigs that may snap when you place your weight on them. If you start to step on one, lift your foot and move it. After making contact with the outside edge of the ball of your foot, roll to the inside ball of your foot, place your heel down, followed by your toes. Then gradually shift your weight forward to the front foot. Lift the back foot to about knee height and start the process over again.

Keep your hands and arms close to your body and avoid waving them about or hitting vegetation. When moving in a crouch, you gain extra support by placing your hands on your knees. One step usually takes 1 minute to complete, but the time it takes will depend on the situation and your level of practice.

21.2.2 STEALTHY WALKING

This method is not as quiet as stalking, but is quicker. It is useful in situations where you need to move stealthily to avoid detection and drawing attention toward you, not to stalk prey.

Again, one foot is moved at a time, your weight is shifted to your rear leg. Push twigs and stones out of the way with the toes of your lead foot and place your heel down, gradually rolling the weight along the outside of the foot and lowering the sole to the ground. Then, shift your weight onto your lead foot and begin again.

21.2.3 CRAWLING

Crawl on your hands and knees when the vegetation is too low to allow you to walk upright unseen. Move one limb at a time and be sure to set it down softly, feeling for anything that may snap and make noise. Be careful that your toes and heels do not catch on vegetation.

21.2.4 PRONE STALKING

To stalk in the prone position, you do a low, modified push-up on your hands and toes, moving yourself forward slightly, and then lowering yourself again slowly. Avoid dragging and scraping along the ground as this makes excessive noise and leaves large trails for trackers to follow.

21.2.5 ANIMAL STALKING

Before stalking an animal, select the best route. If the animal is moving, you will need an intercepting route. Pick a route that puts objects between you and the animal to conceal your movement from it. By positioning yourself in this way, you will be able to move faster, until you pass that object. Some objects, such as large rocks and trees, may totally conceal you, and others, such as small bushes and grass, may only partially conceal you. Pick the route that offers the best concealment and requires the least amount of effort.

Keep your eyes on the animal and stop when it looks your way or turns its ears your way, especially if it suspects your presence. As you get close, squint your eyes slightly to conceal both the light-dark contrast of the whites of the eyes and any shine from your eyes. Keep your mouth closed so that the animal does not see the whiteness or shine of your teeth.

21.3 TRAVELLING UNDETECTED

If you or your group need to travel for a long distance, it is best to do it undetected. There will be many individuals that will take advantage of a lawless situation for their own gain. Spotting a single traveller or group out in the open may be all the encouragement they need to attack.

You may think that you are prepared for any attack, but some groups will be military units turned rogue. They will be well trained, and well armed. You may even find yourself up against a fully functioning military, in which case you will probably be dragged off to a camp.

Threats like this will be around – make no mistake. It is better for you to see them first, then the decision is yours wether to attack, avoid, or approach others. If you decide to avoid or attack, consider watching their movements for a day or more to better understand the threat.

Before undertaking a journey, consider —

- Where you are going. Do you have a destination or do you just need to move?
- If everyone in the group is fit enough for a long trek.
- If what you are seeking may have been destroyed or looted.
- If it will be any better or safer than where you are now.
- If you have enough supplies to last the journey or if you will need to hunt along the way.
- If others have had the same idea. Will you end up in a shitfight over a few scraps after travelling for days?

If you are determined to travel a large distance, your group should gather your resources and prepare. This won't be an easy undertaking and you may face many unexpected dangers along the way. Children especially must be protected so you need to be alert at all times.

21.3.1 GENERAL GUIDELINES FOR STEALTHY TRAVEL

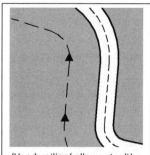

'Hand-railing' allows stealthy travel along main routes

HAND-RAILING

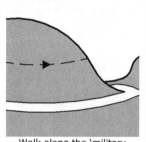

Walk along the 'military crest' of a hill to avoid creating silhouettes against the sky

TRAVEL ALONG HILLS

To minimise your risk of unwanted exposure to others, stay off beaten paths and main routes as much as possible. If you need to use a major road for direction, you can travel parallel to the road at some distance. This is known as 'hand-railing'. This way you can follow the road, but keep in cover.

Move at a slow but steady pace and keep your eyes and ears open for the presence of others. If time is not a factor, stop every now and then to rest and *listen*.

Distant noises such as vehicles or gunshots will alert you to a possible need to change your route. If you hear indications of a close human presence then quickly and quietly find cover. From cover you can decide if there is a threat and if so, wether you engage or remain hidden until they pass.

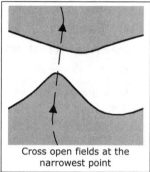

Cross open fields at the narrowest point

CROSSING OPEN FIELDS

You may need to cross an open field, in this case speed may be necessary.

Use any shadows and depressions in the ground for cover, crouch or crawl if you need to and consider waiting for nightfall.

Cross the area quickly, quietly and at the narrowest point possible.

If you need to travel through hilly areas, do not walk on the crest of the hill as your silhouette will be visible. Travel on what is known as the 'military crest', which is low enough to hide your silhouette, yet far enough from a main route.

Night Travel

When travelling at night, be careful of the use of torchlight – it can often be seen for great distances. Instead, let your eyes adjust to the darkness.

Even though travelling at night is generally safer, darkness brings its own dangers. Movement is slower and navigation more difficult. Shape, colour and distance are distorted. Light coloured objects appear closer and dark objects appear further away.

The moon may provide some light, but you must take care to ensure your form is not silhouetted against the sky, or casting long, moving shadows.

Sounds also travel further at night. This is not just because things are generally quieter, there is also a natural phenomenon that usually occurs around dusk and again before dawn.

A component of the atmosphere known as an inversion layer sinks almost to the ground at these times and sound travels along this dense layer of air very effectively. Many animals instinctively use this time to communicate to each other, so this may be an indication that the phenomenon is in effect.

Camping

If you need to camp during your trip, make sure your camp is well hidden and keep noise and fires to a minimum. Eat food cold if you have to. If a fire is essential then use a pit fire, ideally a **Dakota Fire Hole** (Page 6-1) to minimise the light radiation. While setting up the camp, have someone keep watch. If you are in a high risk area, someone may need to take one for the team and keep watch while everyone else sleeps.

Have a contingency plan in the case of discovery, either an escape route or choose a site with a narrow entrance so you are in a good position to defend yourself.

When leaving, bury any rubbish and evidence of fire. If you have cleared ground, then try to spread natural debris throughout to make it look like an old campsite should it be discovered.

21.4 TRACKING

There probably won't be much need for tracking but the situation may arise where you need to track down a thief who has invaded your camp, or to determine who else may be in your area. Having knowledge of tracking will also help you in your own stealthy travel practices.

21.4.1 SIGN

For a tracker, slight man-made disturbances in the environment are the first clue to the presence of others. These clues are known as 'sign'. Spotting them is like being presented with two nearly identical pictures, and trying to spot the differences.

There are two classifications of sign – top sign (above knee height) and ground sign (below knee height). These are further divided into permanent and temporary sign.

	Temporary sign	Permanent sign
Ground sign	Foot prints.	Animal traps and snares.
	Food cans, cigarette butts, scraps of paper, cloth.	Holes dug for latrines.
		Pegs driven into the ground.
	Old wilted camouflage.	Trenches.
	Rocks pushed into ground when stepped on.	Evidence of a cleared area.
		Well used vehicle tracks.
	Grass flattened in direction of travel.	Concrete slabs with aircraft hangers built on top.
	Piles of leaves disturbed so their rotting black undersides are showing.	
Top sign	Broken tree branches in the direction of travel.	Shelters.
		Scuff marks and wounds on tree trunks from equipment.
	Climbers and vines pulled free as a party moves through.	Obvious man made changes to trees, such as sawn off limbs.

EXAMPLES OF DIFFERENT CLASSIFICATIONS OF SIGN

Temporary sign is destroyed quickly by wind, rain, sunlight, frost and snow but is useful to indicate the age of the track. An old campsite will show many types of ground sign, Human waste eventually decays but the degree of decomposition and the number of flies and bugs will approximately indicate the age from hours to days.

Evidence such as food cans, cigarette butts, paper, cloth, and old fireplaces will eventually wither and age, but will persist for much longer. Rust can form on metal within 12 hours, paper exposed to the sun will at first turn yellow in about three days, then white. Cloth is flattened by rain and eventually covered in dirt and debris.

The type of sign may also give an indication of the type of group you are dealing with. MRE's and spent ammunition may indicate a military unit, while old baked bean cans and muesli-bar wrappers can indicate a civilian presence. Though this not a hard and fast rule, as many civilians carry MRE's and military equipment in their survival kits, and military groups may acquire civilian goods. Use your judgement.

21.4.2 FOOTPRINTS

Tracks or footprints are the best type of ground sign. These are often incomplete but provide positive evidence for the presence of other people. The prints will erode with time so can give you an estimate of the age. They will erode quicker in times of high wind or rainfall.

Tracks are most visible when a shadow is cast across them, therefore the best time to track is when the sun is low in the sky. However, tracking while moving toward the sun makes it difficult to see, so the tracks need to be followed from the side where they are more obvious.

If tracking at night, shine a torch low and across the print. If possible use a dim red light to prevent being spotted and preserve your night vision.

Calculating the Number of Travellers

If the group you are tracking are all wearing different shoes, then simply count the number of different tread patterns. If they are all barefoot, then note the different feet size and styles of walking. Some people are biased to one side of their feet, or have risen or fallen arches.

If the group are all wearing the same types of shoes, this is a good indication that they are part of the military. Wether they have turned rogue or still answer to the man, a frontal confrontation is not in your best interests, but it is useful to know their movements.

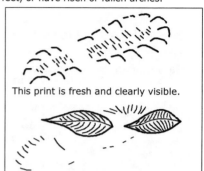

This print is fresh and clearly visible.

In this case there is another way to determine the size of the group based on the assumption that the stride length of most adults is similar.

First, seek out the clearest set of footprints, known as 'key prints', these are usually left by the last person in the group. Choose two successive prints and place a marker in line with the back of the heel of the rear key print. Place a second marker at the instep of the front print.

This print has been eroded over time. The leaves are not crushed into the print and so have been blown onto it later.

An imaginary box can now be drawn containing both markers. On average, each person within the group will have made one print inside, or partially inside the box. This estimate is good for groups of 18 or less people.

FRESH VS OLD PRINTS

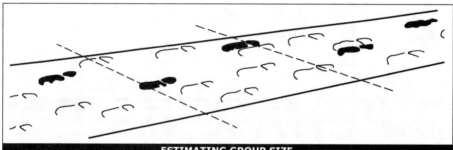

ESTIMATING GROUP SIZE

If you cannot find clear key prints, an estimate can be made by counting the prints in an area of 92 cm (36 in). To increase the accuracy of your count, take three readings at different points along the trail, then divide the total by three.

What can be Determined by Footprints

Carefully read footprints can reveal many facts about the party you are tracking. A runner will leave prints emphasizing the ball of the foot. Someone carrying a heavy load will leave deep prints that are again deepest at the front of the foot. The stride may be shorter and there may be top sign where a pack has snagged on foliage – of course, it may also be a fatty.

An injured person may leave blood drops, or favour one leg constantly. Wounded or exhausted travellers may fall behind and occasionally have to run to keep up.

Age of Prints

Heavy rain will erode footprints. If you know when the last rain was, you can determine if the party travelled through the area before or after the rain, giving a general idea of distance.

Animal prints may be over human footprints, or under them. Knowledge of local wildlife movements may help to determine the time of day when the humans passed through.

21.5 COUNTER-TRACKING

Even if you don't think you are being followed, it is good practice to limit the amount of evidence you leave. Other parties travelling through the area may spot signs of your recent or current presence. This may mean they will come looking for you, and if they are adept at tracking it will not take long. Another reaction is that they may begin or increase their own efforts at stealth, which will mean they might spot you before you spot them.

21.5.1 PASSIVE COUNTER-TRACKING

Passive counter-tracking is the efforts of the group to leave as little disturbances as possible.

Never drop any wrappings, empty containers or other man-made items. Carry them with you and when you stop to camp, burn or bury them.

Man-made objects stand out distinctly against nature and it is easy to tell the difference between a freshly dropped item and one that has been exposed to the weather over time.

Hiding Footprints

There are measures you can take to hide your footprints. Wrap your footwear in cloth or tape a piece of cardboard to the soles to remove the tread pattern.

Moving along a river and leaving your footprints below the waterline will hide your prints while the water is covering them, however mud can be suspended in still water for hours. If the river is tidal, your footprints may be revealed when the waterline recedes, however the movement of the water will destroy your footprints quicker than on dry land.

Beware of the danger of river banks, such as crocodiles or alligators.

Travelling Single File

If you are travelling through an area of soft ground where you can't help but leave footprints, you may be tempted to travel single file and step in the leaders' footprints to disguise your numbers. This may be useful in a military situation but in a lawless environment, a roaming gang is less likely to confront a large group, as such people are opportunistic and cowardly by nature. However, it is recommended that children step in the footprints of adults to hide their presence, and then have another adult step on those tracks to further confuse the print.

Vegetation

Try not to break branches or flatten vegetation as you pass through. It is easy to determine the direction of travel from flattened grass, or a tree limb that has been repeatedly bent back by members of your group passing through.

When walking through crops, it is easy to see a path made if care is not taken. At least when entering and exiting the crop, carefully move the stalks aside, one by one, and let them enclose you as you move through. You may need to do this through the entire crop.

Long grass will lie after being trodden on and will indicate the direction of travel. Man is one of very few animals that will break a stick in two places.

21.5.2 ACTIVE COUNTER TRACKING

Active counter-tracking is the deliberate attempt to confuse and mislead the tracker.

When moving through ground with little cover, travelling into the setting or rising sun forces the tracker to follow the sign from the side and track diagonally into the sun. As the sun rises or dusk falls, the tracks become increasingly difficult to follow.

Laying multiple trails will slow the tracker as they are forced to study each track, and determine your intentions.

Walking Backwards

Walking backwards for a long distance is not recommended. It is tiring and requires constant looking over your shoulder to navigate, reducing your awareness of potential threats. Walking backwards also results in a smaller and wider stride – easily spotted by a tracker. An experienced tracker will also notice that the age of the prints increases with apparent direction of travel, and dirt and stones kicked in the real direction.

Walking backwards for a short distance at a strategic point (such as crossing between two fields) may be sufficient to confuse the tracker and buy you some time.

In this time of chaos, one of the most important aspects to your survival is your ability to —

KEEP YOUR BLOODY HEAD DOWN!

22 Sources

BOOKS REFERENCED

SAS Survival Manual
US Army publication
FM 21-76

The Encyclopaedia of Country Living
Carla Emery
ISBN 1-57061-377-X

Australia Traditional Bushcraft
Ron Edwards
ISBN 0-7018-0681-0

Fighting Skills of the SAS
Terry White
ISBN 1-86309-581-0

Survival and Austere Medicine
The Remote, Austere, Wilderness and Third
World Medicine Discussion Board Moderators

Australian Bushcraft
Richard Graves
ISBN 0-909824-35-5

Where There is No Doctor
David Werner, Carol Thuman, Jane Maxwell
ISBN 0333516524

Basic Wilderness Survival Skills
Bradford Angier
ISBN 1-58574-226-0

Geoff Wilson's Fishing Knots & Rigs
Geoff Wilson

SAS Survival Handbook
John "Lofty" Wiseman
ISBN: 9780007158997

MAIN WEB SITES REFERENCED

Lunatic Outpost
www.lunaticoutpost.com

Acid Pulse
www.acidpulse.us

Pole Shift Ning
ning.poleshift.com

Native Tech
www.nativetech.org

Gardening with The Helpful Gardener
www.helpfulgardener.com

Ulrich Bretscher's Homepage
www.musketeer.ch

Alien Earth
www.alien-earth.org

The Survivalist Blog
www.thesurvivalistblog.net

Primitive Ways
www.primitiveways.com

Wildwood Survival
www.wildwoodsurvival.com

Canberra Organic Growers Society
www.cogs.asn.au

Jons Bushcraft
www.jonsbushcraft.com

22.1.1 CONTRIBUTORS

Thanks to Duncan Kunz for the following articles:

17.2	ABS WATER FILTER
17.3	SOLAR STILL

Thanks to Geogal of www.lunaticoutpost.com for the initial research and inspiration for:

5.3	MEDICINAL PLANT GUIDE

Thanks to User 619774 of www.linkremovedbecausetheysuck.now for help with the following:

2.8.2	FIELD AMPUTATION

Thanks to Nancy Lieder for permission to use her images and text in the following section:

16.14	PLANET X

Thanks to Julie Tylor for kindly drawing the images on the following pages:

4-2	EDIBLE MOLLUSCS
4-5	FISH WITH POISONOUS FLESH

Thank you to all those with your kind words, support, helpful suggestions and friendship over the years.

This book is much better because of you and much of it would not even be possible without you.

Thank you also to my publisher for being so patient and understanding, and for taking a chance on my crazy book.

May your apocalypse be pleasant and full of naked ladies and/or men as per your preference.

And last but not least,

THANK YOU MY SWEETHEART

For your love, for being there for me, and for bearing with me during my many obsessive hours to bring this thing to life.

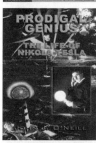

ROSWELL AND THE REICH
The Nazi Connection
By Joseph P. Farrell
Farrell has meticulously reviewed the best-known Roswell research from UFO-ET advocates and skeptics alike, as well as some little-known source material, and comes to a radically different scenario of what happened in Roswell, New Mexico in July 1947, and why the US military has continued to cover it up to this day. Farrell presents a fascinating case sure to disturb both ET believers and disbelievers, namely, that what crashed may have been representative of an independent postwar Nazi power—an extraterritorial Reich monitoring its old enemy, America, and the continuing development of the very technologies confiscated from Germany at the end of the War.
540 pages. 6x9 Paperback. Illustrated. $19.95. Code: RWR

SECRETS OF THE UNIFIED FIELD
The Philadelphia Experiment, the Nazi Bell, and the Discarded Theory
by Joseph P. Farrell
Farrell examines the now discarded Unified Field Theory. American and German wartime scientists and engineers determined that, while the theory was incomplete, it could nevertheless be engineered. Chapters include: The Meanings of "Torsion"; Wringing an Aluminum Can; The Mistake in Unified Field Theories and Their Discarding by Contemporary Physics; Three Routes to the Doomsday Weapon: Quantum Potential, Torsion, and Vortices; Tesla's Meeting with FDR; Arnold Sommerfeld and Electromagnetic Radar Stealth; Electromagnetic Phase Conjugations, Phase Conjugate Mirrors, and Templates; The Unified Field Theory, the Torsion Tensor, and Igor Witkowski's Idea of the Plasma Focus; tons more.
340 pages. 6x9 Paperback. Illustrated. $18.95. Code: SOUF

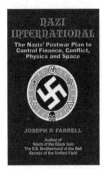

NAZI INTERNATIONAL
The Nazi's Postwar Plan to Control Finance, Conflict, Physics and Space
by Joseph P. Farrell
Beginning with prewar corporate partnerships in the USA, including some with the Bush family, he moves on to the surrender of Nazi Germany, and evacuation plans of the Germans. He then covers the vast, and still-little-known recreation of Nazi Germany in South America with help of Juan Peron, I.G. Farben and Martin Bormann. Farrell then covers Nazi Germany's penetration of the Muslim world including Wilhelm Voss and Otto Skorzeny in Gamel Abdul Nasser's Egypt before moving on to the development and control of new energy technologies including the Bariloche Fusion Project, Dr. Philo Farnsworth's Plasmator, and the work of Dr. Nikolai Kozyrev. Finally, Farrell discusses the Nazi desire to control space, and examines their connection with NASA, the esoteric meaning of NASA Mission Patches.
412 pages. 6x9 Paperback. Illustrated. $19.95. Code: NZIN

ARKTOS
The Polar Myth in Science, Symbolism & Nazi Survival
by Joscelyn Godwin
Explored are the many tales of an ancient race said to have lived in the Arctic regions, such as Thule and Hyperborea. Progressing onward, he looks at modern polar legends: including the survival of Hitler, German bases in Antarctica, UFOs, the hollow earth, and the hidden kingdoms of Agartha and Shambala. Chapters include: Prologue in Hyperborea; The Golden Age; The Northern Lights; The Arctic Homeland; The Aryan Myth; The Thule Society; The Black Order; The Hidden Lands; Agartha and the Polaires; Shambhala; The Hole at the Pole; Antarctica; more.
220 Pages. 6x9 Paperback. Illustrated. Bib. Index. $16.95. Code: ARK

REICH OF THE BLACK SUN
Nazi Secret Weapons & the Cold War Allied Legend
by Joseph P. Farrell
Why were the Allies worried about an atom bomb attack by the Germans in 1944? Why did the Soviets threaten to use poison gas against the Germans? Why did Hitler in 1945 insist that holding Prague could win the war for the Third Reich? Why did US General George Patton's Third Army race for the Skoda works at Pilsen in Czechoslovakia instead of Berlin? Why did the US Army not test the uranium atom bomb it dropped on Hiroshima? Why did the Luftwaffe fly a non-stop round trip mission to within twenty miles of New York City in 1944? *Reich of the Black Sun* takes the reader on a scientific-historical journey in order to answer these questions. Arguing that Nazi Germany actually won the race for the atom bomb in late 1944,

352 PAGES. 6x9 PAPERBACK. ILLUSTRATED. BIBLIOGRAPHY. $16.95. CODE: ROBS

THE GIZA DEATH STAR
The Paleophysics of the Great Pyramid & the Military Complex at Giza
by Joseph P. Farrell
Was the Giza complex part of a military installation over 10,000 years ago? Chapters include: An Archaeology of Mass Destruction, Thoth and Theories; The Machine Hypothesis; Pythagoras, Plato, Planck, and the Pyramid; The Weapon Hypothesis; Encoded Harmonics of the Planck Units in the Great Pyramid; High Fregquency Direct Current "Impulse" Technology; The Grand Gallery and its Crystals: Gravito-acoustic Resonators; The Other Two Large Pyramids; the "Causeways," and the "Temples"; A Phase Conjugate Howitzer; Evidence of the Use of Weapons of Mass Destruction in Ancient Times; more.

290 PAGES. 6x9 PAPERBACK. ILLUSTRATED. $16.95. CODE: GDS

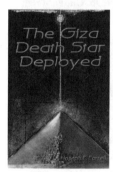

THE GIZA DEATH STAR DEPLOYED
The Physics & Engineering of the Great Pyramid
by Joseph P. Farrell
Farrell expands on his thesis that the Great Pyramid was a maser, designed as a weapon and eventually deployed—with disastrous results to the solar system. Includes: Exploding Planets: A Brief History of the Exoteric and Esoteric Investigations of the Great Pyramid; No Machines, Please!; The Stargate Conspiracy; The Scalar Weapons; Message or Machine?; A Tesla Analysis of the Putative Physics and Engineering of the Giza Death Star; Cohering the Zero Point, Vacuum Energy, Flux: Feedback Loops and Tetrahedral Physics; and more.

290 PAGES. 6x9 PAPERBACK. ILLUSTRATED. $16.95. CODE: GDSD

THE GIZA DEATH STAR DESTROYED
The Ancient War For Future Science
by Joseph P. Farrell
Farrell moves on to events of the final days of the Giza Death Star and its awesome power. These final events, eventually leading up to the destruction of this giant machine, are dissected one by one, leading us to the eventual abandonment of the Giza Military Complex—an event that hurled civilization back into the Stone Age. Chapters include: The Mars-Earth Connection; The Lost "Root Races" and the Moral Reasons for the Flood; The Destruction of Krypton: The Electrodynamic Solar System, Exploding Planets and Ancient Wars; Turning the Stream of the Flood: the Origin of Secret Societies and Esoteric Traditions; The Quest to Recover Ancient Mega-Technology; Non-Equilibrium Paleophysics; Monatomic Paleophysics; Frequencies, Vortices and Mass Particles; "Acoustic" Intensity of Fields; The Pyramid of Crystals; tons more.

292 pages. 6x9 paperback. Illustrated. $16.95. Code: GDES

ATLANTIS & THE POWER SYSTEM OF THE GODS
by David Hatcher Childress and Bill Clendenon
Childress' fascinating analysis of Nikola Tesla's broadcast system in light of Edgar Cayce's "Terrible Crystal" and the obelisks of ancient Egypt and Ethiopia. Includes: Atlantis and its crystal power towers that broadcast energy; how these incredible power stations may still exist today; inventor Nikola Tesla's nearly identical system of power transmission; Mercury Proton Gyros and mercury vortex propulsion; more. Richly illustrated, and packed with evidence that Atlantis not only existed—it had a world-wide energy system more sophisticated than ours today.
246 PAGES. 6x9 PAPERBACK. ILLUSTRATED. $15.95. CODE: APSG

THE ANTI-GRAVITY HANDBOOK
edited by David Hatcher Childress

The new expanded compilation of material on Anti-Gravity, Free Energy, Flying Saucer Propulsion, UFOs, Suppressed Technology, NASA Cover-ups and more. Highly illustrated with patents, technical illustrations and photos. This revised and expanded edition has more material, including photos of Area 51, Nevada, the government's secret testing facility. This classic on weird science is back in a new format!
230 PAGES. 7x10 PAPERBACK. ILLUSTRATED. $16.95. CODE: AGH

ANTI-GRAVITY & THE WORLD GRID
Is the earth surrounded by an intricate electromagnetic grid network offering free energy? This compilation of material on ley lines and world power points contains chapters on the geography, mathematics, and light harmonics of the earth grid. Learn the purpose of ley lines and ancient megalithic structures located on the grid. Discover how the grid made the Philadelphia Experiment possible. Explore the Coral Castle and many other mysteries, including acoustic levitation, Tesla Shields and scalar wave weaponry. Browse through the section on anti-gravity patents, and research resources.
274 PAGES. 7x10 PAPERBACK. ILLUSTRATED. $14.95. CODE: AGW

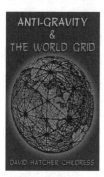

ANTI-GRAVITY & THE UNIFIED FIELD
edited by David Hatcher Childress
Is Einstein's Unified Field Theory the answer to all of our energy problems? Explored in this compilation of material is how gravity, electricity and magnetism manifest from a unified field around us. Why artificial gravity is possible; secrets of UFO propulsion; free energy; Nikola Tesla and anti-gravity airships of the 20s and 30s; flying saucers as superconducting whirls of plasma; anti-mass generators; vortex propulsion; suppressed technology; government cover-ups; gravitational pulse drive; spacecraft & more.
240 PAGES. 7x10 PAPERBACK. ILLUSTRATED. $14.95. CODE: AGU

THE TIME TRAVEL HANDBOOK
A Manual of Practical Teleportation & Time Travel
edited by David Hatcher Childress
The Time Travel Handbook takes the reader beyond the government experiments and deep into the uncharted territory of early time travellers such as Nikola Tesla and Guglielmo Marconi and their alleged time travel experiments, as well as the Wilson Brothers of EMI and their connection to the Philadelphia Experiment—the U.S. Navy's forays into invisibility, time travel, and teleportation. Childress looks into the claims of time travelling individuals, and investigates the unusual claim that the pyramids on Mars were built in the future and sent back in time. A highly visual, large format book, with patents, photos and schematics. Be the first on your block to build your own time travel device!
316 PAGES. 7x10 PAPERBACK. ILLUSTRATED. $16.95. CODE: TTH

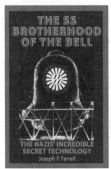

THE SS BROTHERHOOD OF THE BELL
The Nazis' Incredible Secret Technology
by Joseph P. Farrell

In 1945, a mysterious Nazi secret weapons project code-named "The Bell" left its underground bunker in lower Silesia, along with all its project documentation, and a four-star SS general named Hans Kammler. Taken aboard a massive six engine Junkers 390 ultra-long range aircraft, "The Bell," Kammler, and all project records disappeared completely, along with the gigantic aircraft. It is thought to have flown to America or Argentina. What was "The Bell"? What new physics might the Nazis have discovered with it? How far did the Nazis go after the war to protect the advanced energy technology that it represented?

456 pages. 6x9 Paperback. Illustrated.References. $16.95.

Code: SSBB

SECRETS OF THE HOLY LANCE
The Spear of Destiny in History & Legend
by Jerry E. Smith

Secrets of the Holy Lance traces the Spear from its possession by Constantine, Rome's first Christian Caesar, to Charlemagne's claim that with it he ruled the Holy Roman Empire by Divine Right, and on through two thousand years of kings and emperors, until it came within Hitler's grasp—and beyond! Did it rest for a while in Antarctic ice? Is it now hidden in Europe, awaiting the next person to claim its awesome power? Neither debunking nor worshiping, *Secrets of the Holy Lance* seeks to pierce the veil of myth and mystery around the Spear. Mere belief that it was infused with magic by virtue of its shedding the Savior's blood has made men kings. But what if it's more? What are "the powers it serves"?

312 PAGES. 6x9 PAPERBACK. ILLUSTRATED. BIBLIOGRAPHY. $16.95.
CODE: SOHL

THE FREE-ENERGY DEVICE HANDBOOK
A Compilation of Patents and Reports
by David Hatcher Childress

A large-format compilation of various patents, papers, descriptions and diagrams concerning free-energy devices and systems. *The Free-Energy Device Handbook* is a visual tool for experimenters and researchers into magnetic motors and other "over-unity" devices. With chapters on the Adams Motor, the Hans Coler Generator, cold fusion, superconductors, "N" machines, space-energy generators, Nikola Tesla, T. Townsend Brown, and the latest in free-energy devices. Packed with photos, technical diagrams, patents and fascinating information, this book belongs on every science shelf.

292 PAGES. 8x10 PAPERBACK. ILLUSTRATED. $16.95. CODE: FEH

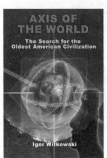

AXIS OF THE WORLD
The Search for the Oldest American Civilization
by Igor Witkowski

Witkowski's research reveals remnants of a high civilization that was able to exert its influence on almost the entire planet, and did so with full consciousness. Sites around South America show that this was not just one of the places influenced by this culture, but a place where they built their crowning achievements. Easter Island, in the southeastern Pacific, constitutes one of them. The Rongo-Rongo language that developed there points westward to the Indus Valley. Taken together, the facts presented by Witkowski provide a fresh, new proof that an antediluvian, great civilization flourished several millennia ago.

220 pages. 6x9 Paperback. Illustrated. References. $18.95.
Code: AXOW

GRAVITATIONAL MANIPULATION OF DOMED CRAFT
UFO Propulsion Dynamics
by Paul E. Potter

Potter's precise and lavish illustrations allow the reader to enter directly into the realm of the advanced technological engineer and to understand, quite straightforwardly, the aliens' methods of energy manipulation: their methods of electrical power generation; how they purposely designed their craft to employ the kinds of energy dynamics that are exclusive to space (discoverable in our astrophysics) in order that their craft may generate both attractive and repulsive gravitational forces; their control over the mass-density matrix surrounding their craft enabling them to alter their physical dimensions and even manufacture their own frame of reference in respect to time. Includes a 16-page color insert.

624 pages. 7x10 Paperback. Illustrated. References. $24.00. Code: GMDC

TAPPING THE ZERO POINT ENERGY
Free Energy & Anti-Gravity in Today's Physics
by Moray B. King

King explains how free energy and anti-gravity are possible. The theories of the zero point energy maintain there are tremendous fluctuations of electrical field energy imbedded within the fabric of space. This book tells how, in the 1930s, inventor T. Henry Moray could produce a fifty kilowatt "free energy" machine; how an electrified plasma vortex creates anti-gravity; how the Pons/Fleischmann "cold fusion" experiment could produce tremendous heat without fusion; and how certain experiments might produce a gravitational anomaly.

180 PAGES. 5x8 PAPERBACK. ILLUSTRATED. $12.95. CODE: TAP

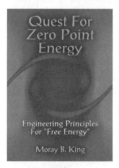

QUEST FOR ZERO-POINT ENERGY
Engineering Principles for "Free Energy"
by Moray B. King

King expands, with diagrams, on how free energy and anti-gravity are possible. The theories of zero point energy maintain there are tremendous fluctuations of electrical field energy embedded within the fabric of space. King explains the following topics: TFundamentals of a Zero-Point Energy Technology; Vacuum Energy Vortices; The Super Tube; Charge Clusters: The Basis of Zero-Point Energy Inventions; Vortex Filaments, Torsion Fields and the Zero-Point Energy; Transforming the Planet with a Zero-Point Energy Experiment; Dual Vortex Forms: The Key to a Large Zero-Point Energy Coherence. Packed with diagrams, patents and photos.

224 PAGES. 6x9 PAPERBACK. ILLUSTRATED. $14.95. CODE: QZPE

THE TESLA PAPERS
Nikola Tesla on Free Energy &
Wireless Transmission of Power
by Nikola Tesla, edited by David Hatcher Childress

David Hatcher Childress takes us into the incredible world of Nikola Tesla and his amazing inventions. Tesla's fantastic vision of the future, including wireless power, anti-gravity, free energy and highly advanced solar power. Also included are some of the papers, patents and material collected on Tesla at the Colorado Springs Tesla Symposiums, including papers on: •The Secret History of Wireless Transmission •Tesla and the Magnifying Transmitter •Design and Construction of a Half-Wave Tesla Coil •Electrostatics: A Key to Free Energy •Progress in Zero-Point Energy Research •Electromagnetic Energy from Antennas to Atoms •Tesla's Particle Beam Technology •Fundamental Excitatory Modes of the Earth-Ionosphere Cavity

325 PAGES. 8x10 PAPERBACK. ILLUSTRATED. $16.95. CODE: TTP

ORDER FORM

10% Discount When You Order 3 or More Items!

One Adventure Place
P.O. Box 74
Kempton, Illinois 60946
United States of America
Tel.: 815-253-6390 • Fax: 815-253-6300
Email: auphq@frontiernet.net
http://www.adventuresunlimitedpress.com

ORDERING INSTRUCTIONS

✓ Remit by USD$ Check, Money Order or Credit Card
✓ Visa, Master Card, Discover & AmEx Accepted
✓ Paypal Payments Can Be Made To:
    info@wexclub.com
✓ Prices May Change Without Notice
✓ 10% Discount for 3 or more Items

SHIPPING CHARGES

United States

✓ Postal Book Rate { $4.00 First Item / 50¢ Each Additional Item
✓ POSTAL BOOK RATE Cannot Be Tracked!
✓ Priority Mail { $5.00 First Item / $2.00 Each Additional Item
✓ UPS { $6.00 First Item / $1.50 Each Additional Item
    NOTE: UPS Delivery Available to Mainland USA Only

Canada

✓ Postal Air Mail { $10.00 First Item / $2.50 Each Additional Item
✓ Personal Checks or Bank Drafts MUST BE US$ and Drawn on a US Bank
✓ Canadian Postal Money Orders OK
✓ Payment MUST BE US$

All Other Countries

✓ Sorry, No Surface Delivery!
✓ Postal Air Mail { $16.00 First Item / $6.00 Each Additional Item
✓ Checks and Money Orders MUST BE US$ and Drawn on a US Bank or branch.
✓ Paypal Payments Can Be Made in US$ To:
    info@wexclub.com

SPECIAL NOTES

✓ RETAILERS: Standard Discounts Available
✓ BACKORDERS: We Backorder all Out-of-Stock Items Unless Otherwise Requested
✓ PRO FORMA INVOICES: Available on Request

ORDER ONLINE AT: www.adventuresunlimitedpress.com

Please check: ✓

☐ This is my first order   ☐ I have ordered before

Name				
Address				
City				
State/Province			Postal Code	
Country				
Phone day		Evening		
Fax		Email		

Item Code	Item Description	Qty	Total

Please check: ✓

	Subtotal ▶	
	Less Discount-10% for 3 or more items ▶	
☐ Postal-Surface	Balance ▶	
☐ Postal-Air Mail (Priority in USA)	Illinois Residents 6.25% Sales Tax ▶	
	Previous Credit ▶	
☐ UPS	Shipping ▶	
(Mainland USA only)	Total (check/MO in USD$ only) ▶	
☐ Visa/MasterCard/Discover/American Express		

Card Number

Expiration Date

10% Discount When You Order 3 or More Items!